Enlightenment

Kim Cormack

Mythomedia Press 2754 10th Ave,
V9Y2N9 Port Alberni B.C Canada

Acknowledgements

I am sending love and appreciation to my family and friends for being the light at the end of the tunnel during this journey.

To my incredible children. You are my reason for everything.

Haley and Leanne. My amazing editing crew. Thank you for coming on this wild adventure. XO

A Letter To My Readers

You keep me going when life becomes difficult. It's easy to feel overwhelmed by challenges. Your motivation and love made me see the purpose of this series. Stand back up when you fall. Always.

Happy Reading
Kim Cormack

Children Of Ankh Series Universe

Kayn's Series

Sweet Sleep
Enlightenment
Let There Be Dragons
Handlers Of Dragons
Tragic Fools

Lexy's Series

Wild Thing
Wicked Thing
Deplorable Me
Sacrificial Lamb Club

Novella Series

Bring Out Your Dead

New York Hive

Prologue

Kayn Of Ankh

The silken texture of the grass beneath her with warmth of the sunlight caressing the length of her bare legs felt magical. She lay next to him in the meadow as they quietly observed the sky above. *His hand always seemed to be just out of reach. She wanted to hold his hand so badly, it was torturous.* His fingers brushed a path across her fingertips as if to say in the exquisite beauty of the moment, "I will always be right here."

Opening her eyes long enough to know it was not reality, she'd close them again, willing herself to live in the moment with him… Forever. She'd attempt to slip back into the dream, even though in her heart, she knew it was hopeless.

Kevin's loss to Triad had been unbearable. She'd never been without his constant companionship. Her best friend had been lost to her just as their feelings evolved into something more. They hadn't had time to bask in the glorious joy of first love before being pulled in opposite directions by fate's twisted and, as she'd discovered, sick sense of humour. The weight of the devastation was too much for her mind to carry as her heart fought to accept the loss of her remaining family members and that of the one person on this Earth, she'd always assumed she could never lose... Kevin.

The days that passed had begun to melt together into weeks and months, creating a twisted mosaic of memories in her mind. As her dreams continued to travel a tortuous path between what happened and what could have been, Frost remained close by. She'd catch him staring at her, searching for a hint of Chloe.

Kayn had become part of a trio of newcomers. Melody had been taken from Trinity. Zach had been left behind by Triad. They were to become the sails on her ship of salvation. The three would need to carry each other through the impending storm of the Testing, towards Enlightenment.

During his Sweet Sleep there was an angelic creature, and in her eyes a look of joyous elation that filled Kevin's mind with anticipation for her existence in the real world. This freckle-faced vision with a wild mane of untamed blonde curls left an unexplainable ache in his soul. In his dreams, she would appear to him as a mirage of hope. He could feel the love in her heart, for it seeped through her essence into the air between them. She lay next to him in the grass as they quietly observed the sky above. Her hand was always just out of his reach. Kevin wanted to hold it so badly it was torturous. They were just about touching but not quite. Her fingers brushed a path across his fingertips as if to say in the exquisite beauty of the moment, "I will always be right here." This mystery girl haunted Kevin with her laughter during his countless restless nights. *Was this girl simply a figment of his imagination? He could never seem to remember her name during the daylight hours.* It was as though her memory would fade upon arrival of the sun. In those first moments after he opened his eyes each morning, the girl that haunted his dreams was all he could think about. Then, she would fade into a place in his mind where she would remain hidden until the next time he dreamt of her.

His memory had been erased. He knew this because he didn't remember anything before Triad. Maybe, she was someone he used to know? All Kevin of Triad knew was that he looked forward to sleep because when he went to sleep, he could see her. He would wake up knowing that as long as he was capable of having such beautiful dreams, a part of him must still be good.

Chapter 1

Beautiful Goodbyes And Warm Welcomes

With their unspoken words of love still echoing in her ears and aching in her heart, Kayn knew she had to be brave. *He was gone. This was where their roads separated. Right at the beginning. It wasn't fair.* She'd said goodbye to Kevin only moments earlier. *One last kiss, a final embrace and he was gone.* Concerned faces hovered around the tomb, she'd healed in. She noticed a few unfamiliar ones. *There was a dark-featured boy and a girl. She knew her. It was that girl from Trinity who'd joined her energy with Kevin's, so they could find each other in the In-between. She'd given them the opportunity for one last goodbye.* Kayn sat up in the tomb. Looking at the girl with shoulder-length, wavy chestnut hair, she sweetly said, "Thank you."

The girl replied, "My name's Melody."

She felt an immediate connection as the girl extended her hand and helped her up. Kayn looked around. *What in the hell?* The tombs were in a line in the back of what appeared to be an empty storage container. *Where was she?* Being embraced by both Lily and Lexy as they apologised for the loss of Kevin, her eyes met Frost's and he walked away. *He felt empathy. She'd seen it flash across his face.* She followed everyone down a ramp into a large dusty parking lot and looked back. *They'd been in the back of a big rig.* A light breeze danced across her skin. *He was really gone.*

Markus walked around the corner and startled her. Pulling her into a fatherly embrace, he whispered, "I'm sorry Kayn. There was nothing we could do. They knew about him. Triad has Kevin, his mother and brother from what I hear."

She understood why Kevin had to go with Triad. She wasn't sure if it was a choice or if he'd been taken. It made no difference. He was gone. Triad took his family. He wanted a say in what happened to them. She could comprehend his logic if it had been a choice. Her heart just couldn't fathom doing this without him. Kayn closed her eyes, allowing the embrace to carry on. *She needed it.* After a few moments, Kayn pulled away from Markus. *She needed to know everything, the whole sordid tale. She had to yank the band-aid off her heart while it was still raw.* Kayn met Markus' solemn eyes and probed, "I know my brother and Jenkins are dead. I need to know how they died."

Melody was the first to speak, "Your brother was higher than a kite and covered with toothpaste. Right?"

Calmly, Kayn responded, "He was grazed by a drugged arrow. He got out of the room. Jenkins convinced me to stay. Matt would've wanted me to."

"He was a funny guy and incredibly brave. He died trying to save my friend from Triad," the new girl replied.

Kayn smiled as she thought of Matt attacking a Triad to save a stranger. *He'd given his life in a final heroic act. She was proud of him.* Her eyes glazed over with tears as she asked the question her heart needed to know, "Did he suffer?"

Melody's eyes softened as she answered, "He jumped on one of the Triad's backs to stop him from strangling my friend and he was thrown against the wall. His neck was broken on impact. His death was instant. He didn't feel a thing. Your brother was brave."

Kayn nodded as she smiled through tears glistening in her eyes. Looking at the group, she asked, "What about Jenkins? Does anyone know what happened to him?"

Markus stepped forward, disclosing, "I did it myself. I had to. They would have sent a Correction. I know you thought you were helping him by telling him to hide in the attic, but if I hadn't found him, he would have died as violently as the rest of your family. I explained the situation. When I told Jenkins his daughter was there with him, his demeanour changed. I told him she was waiting for him and they'd be able to leave together. He agreed to go with her without hesitation. She was wrapped in his arms as they left. It was a beautiful goodbye."

Kayn's tears weren't prompted by sadness. *It was joy. She'd seen Jenkins' daughter at the hospital but Katy vanished when they returned home. She'd been able to hear Jenkins' thoughts, and even after a decade, most were of the daughter he lost. He'd never moved past it in his heart. They'd been together in his final moments. It was the most beautiful goodbye. A perfect release from life.* She whispered, "Thank you." Relieved, Markus smiled. Kayn understood so many things now. *Her mind felt like it had expanded to ten times its size over the last couple of months. She'd see her brother and Jenkins again someday and prayed their next life would be a happy one.* Her eyes were drawn to the only person she didn't know. A dark-featured boy, her age was standing solemnly beside Lily.

Grinning, Markus announced, "Ladies, meet Zach. He used to be Triad. We have our three new Ankh for Testing and one year to train you. Ideally, it would be three or four years but that's not how it worked out. We have to run with you three until you are eighteen. There's going to be many tedious days of driving ahead. You'll have to be trained while we're on the move. We can't risk running into other Clans and losing one of you. It's important you attach to each other. We must leave. The other Clans won't be far behind us. Everybody wants Miss Brighton."

With a handful of rose quartz stones as she exited the now empty big rig, Lexy chucked one at Frost and another at Lily. They caught them in midair. Lexy said, "I'll hold onto Grey's until he's back with the RV."

They were going to be travelling in an RV? That was strange. Kayn asked, "Are we just leaving this rig in the parking lot?"

Lily squeezed her shoulder, and whispered, "Let's just say I borrowed it from a friend. We had to heal and escape at the same time. We needed somewhere to house the tombs. Don't worry. The owner will find it here in perfect condition." Just as she finished the sentence, a huge RV approached, crackling through the parking lot with a cloud of dust trailing behind it. Lily beamed, announcing, "There's our ride."

The door opened. Grey hollered, "Let's put some miles between us and them!"

Kayn went into the enormous RV. Grey directed her to the table. She shimmied into the corner on the bench to make room. Melody sat beside her and then Zach slid in.

Opening the cupboard above their heads, Grey pointed like an immortal tour guide, "Board games and drawing materials are up here. Video games are in the drawer over there. Bunks are in the back. We take turns sleeping and driving. That black dual-cab truck outside is also ours. We have laptops and a TV in the room with pillows on the floor at the back. We took the bed out. We fought over it. We all sleep in bunks or pass out on the floor in the backroom. There are snacks in the fridge and in cupboards by the stove. No need to freak out over sleeping arrangements. The bunks are super comfy, and we stay at motels every third or fourth day while on the road. Be quick in the bathroom. There's only one." Everyone found a place to sit or stand as the RV began to move.

Markus cleared his throat. Everyone's eyes gravitated to him as he spoke, "I only have a few minutes with you guys. I'm leaving with the other group. If you have anything to say, now is the time."

Looking at Markus, Melody stated, "Thorne will come after me."

Markus replied, "Healers are a precious commodity. Does Trinity have more than three new recruits left, excluding you?"

Melody knit her brow as she responded, "They do."

Meeting her eyes, Markus replied, "I've known Thorne a long time. We may not have to worry. He knows there's only a year before the next scheduled Testing. He may opt to keep his people out of sight."

Zach was upset. What would he have to be upset about? Wasn't leaving Triad for Ankh supposed to be a good thing.

The new boy disclosed, "Triad has six. Well, five now. Why would Tiberius leave me behind?"

With a fatherly smile Markus reached across the table. He placed his hand on Zach's, explaining, "Son, he's running low on tombs if he has six recruits. Once Kevin's mother and brother have been placed in a tomb for the purpose of storage, it's taken out of commission. They can't be removed until after the next Testing. If they're removed before that time, they must go into the Testing with the group Triad is already preparing. Tiberius would never risk having a weak link. It sounds like he has a large group. It's important everyone attaches on a spiritual level. If you weren't compatible, his group wouldn't make it out of Testing. If he purposely left you with us, it was so you'd have a chance."

Addressing Kayn, Zach probed, "Was Kevin dark enough to be in Triad?"

They had to stop saying his name. The mere mention of his name made her heart ache. Kayn took a deep breath and replied, "No. He wasn't." Having a difficult time keeping it together, she stared at the wooden table beneath her fingertips.

"Tiberius will wipe Kevin's memory. He has an entire year to brainwash his grandson. That makes his odds of survival much higher than yours," Markus explained.

He was really gone. Kayn listened to the conversation numbly. *This wasn't happening.*

Zach questioned, "Why didn't he just wipe my memory?"

Smiling, Markus answered, "You liked him. He must have liked you. Tiberius doesn't have a lot of people that like him. He did you a favour. Aren't you happy to be here?"

Meeting their leader's eyes, Zach replied, "I never felt like I was supposed to be there. I can't explain why. I just knew I was with the wrong people."

"How about you?" Markus probed, looking at Melody.

"I made a choice. I never wanted to leave you guys in the first place, but they grew on me," Melody disclosed.

Markus grinned as he verbalized his thoughts, "If Triad has five, they may not risk coming after Kayn again. She wouldn't be compatible with his group and his grandson is too close to her. It would mess with his memory wipe."

Catching Zach's attention, Grey added, "Anytime more than three people are in a tomb, it's a strain on the Healer's. It takes an experienced one to create the energy to transport more than three people. This next year is going to be a shitty one for Triad's Healers."

The RV moved off the smooth road, there was a crackling sound under the tires again. *They were parking.*

Markus announced, "I won't be seeing you kids for a while. Become fast friends and learn to love each other. You three are going to be spending an insane amount of time together. I have faith in you." With that, he turned and walked out of the door.

That was rather abrupt. With a rumbling motor, they were moving again. Grey strolled over to the fridge. He poured peach cider into pink plastic wine glasses. Kayn wasn't sure she wanted to drink but didn't want to be rude. *Kevin was gone. She felt exposed without him.* Grey handed an overfull glass to each of them, poured one for himself and sat at the table.

Grey grinned as he raised his glass and gave a toast, "To the newest of the Ankh. May you kick ass and take no names."

She had no idea what that meant. They all raised their glasses and awkwardly clinked the exceptionally classy, pink flamingo plastic wine glasses. Kayn took a big gulp of the peach cider. *It was delicious.* She glanced at Grey and questioned, "May I ask who picked out these delightful pink flamingo wine glasses? They are absolutely amazing."

Grey chuckled, "That would be me. Do not mock my flamingo wine glasses."

Kayn casually replied, "How can one mock these flamingo wine glasses when they are so obviously awesome?"

Grey's face exploded into a contagious grin as he decreed, "And that is why Miss Brighton and I are going to be best friends."

Kayn smiled as her eyes darted to the two new Ankh and back to Grey as she conquered, "Miss Brighton is a way better nickname than frog sticker girl."

Grey took a drink from his pink flamingo glass and replied, "There's a cute story behind the frog sticker girl nickname but it's not mine to tell."

The RV rode over something with a thud. They all skillfully manoeuvred to avoid spilling their cider.

Frost hollered from the driver's seat, "Sorry about that! Roadkill! Already dead roadkill!"

Grey shook his head while taking a sip of his cider.

Melody took a sip of her own. Glaring at Grey, she quietly accused, "You could have mentioned you were Ankh."

"I'm sorry, my thoughts and lips were preoccupied," Grey flirtatiously sparred.

Glancing at the new guy, Kayn whispered, "I'm obviously missing something?"

Zach grinned and filled her in, "You have to read between the lines, Miss Brighton."

She clicked into what they were talking about. *Oh, they had a sexy moment.* She glanced at Melody and raised her eyebrows.

Zach nudged her and said, "Miss Brighton. That nickname makes you sound like a naughty librarian."

"Exactly," Grey chuckled. He finished his drink and jumped up to grab another.

Kevin used to call her Brighton. She called him Smith and he called her Brighton. She wasn't going to cry. She was not going to cry. She would see him again. It was only a matter of time. Grey held up a cider in front of her. She nodded and he refilled her flamingo glass. *If there was ever a time to have a drink, it was now.*

Grey sat back down, reached for her hand, leaned across the table, tenderly kissed it and apologised, "I'm sorry we lost him. Kevin was a great guy. I liked him."

Kayn gave him an unmotivated half smile as she stared at her plastic flamingo wine glass, tracing the rim with a finger. *It still didn't feel real. Here she was sitting in a motorhome drinking cider out of flamingo wine glasses, while he was having his memory wiped and lord knows what else.*

Zach enquired, "This Kevin guy was your boyfriend?"

She glanced up and realised he was waiting for a reply. Kayn explained, "He wasn't just my boyfriend. We'd been best friends since kindergarten. It's a long story but his grandmother was a psychic. He heard my dead twin Chloe screaming for me to run on the night of my Correction, it triggered his abilities. Then these guys helped him along. They took both of us into Ankh. It was too good to be true."

With empathy, Melody replied, "Isn't that a karmic kick in the ass?"

Kayn nodded and almost smiled. *It was a seriously messed-up karmic kick in the ass.* Grey was still holding her hand. *He reminded her of Matty. There was death, loss and two new additions to the Clan. It was a lot to absorb. Too much.* Kayn snatched Grey's pink flamingo glass and chugged his cider. He concealed the smile with a hand, but she saw his cheeks rise.

Melody looked at Kayn and said, "Trinity came for you. We didn't know about Kevin. Your gifts are supposed to be a big deal. What can you do?"

"That's what they keep telling me. I can't do anything yet," Kayn answered. "What if I can't ever do anything special?"

Grey squeezed her hand and affirmed, "I have faith in you Brighton."

In solidarity, Zach added, "I can't do anything either. I know how you feel."

Grey stood up, poured himself another drink and placed it on the table. As Kayn attempted to grab for it, he smacked her hand and scolded, "Simmer down Brighton! Getting hammered tonight will only postpone the inevitable. You must feel the pain in order to get past it. I also don't want to spend all night holding your hair while you ralph in the toilet. You three, go choose a bunk. Not the top bunk on the right, that's Lexy's. The one directly underneath it is Frost's. The rest of us are flexible. Most of the time, I just sleep wherever I happen to pass out. Lily usually sleeps in that backroom. Go relax. I'm making chili dogs for dinner."

The trio wandered through the spacious RV. The hallway narrowed around the bunks. The bathroom was tiny with a stand-up shower. *It would be difficult to puke in that toilet when they were moving.* She followed the others past the bathroom. The back room was kind of cool. There were large pillows on the floor and shelving with a TV on one side. They sprawled on the pillows.

Grinning as he stretched, Zach announced, "If this is where Lily sleeps, I'll just sleep back here. I'd hate for her to have to go looking for me in the middle of the night."

Melody smoked him in the face with a pillow. He chuckled as she teased, "Like that would ever happen."

Their comfortable comradery reminded her of Kevin. She closed her eyes to stop the tears that kept threatening to start. *She was without him for the first time in her life. What was she going to do? She couldn't do this without him. Her heart felt so empty.* She rested her back against the wall and covered her face with her hands.

Zach shuffled over to sit beside her, saying, "You haven't even had the chance to cry for him, have you?" He took her in his arms and the river of tears surged forth in an uncontrollable stream down her face.

Melody moved over, joined in and they embraced. Strangers bound together in a new life. Each one crying for different reasons. *They'd all lost something that mattered today.* Emotionally exhausted, they fell asleep in each other's arms.

Kayn stirred to Grey's voice, "Wake up you guys, dinner's waiting." She rubbed her puffy eyes, emotionally spent. Grey's eyes were glistening with tears. *Why was he upset?*

Zach looked up and asked, "What's wrong?"

Leaning against the door's frame, Grey replied, "You three remind me of Lexy, Arrianna and I. Nothing's wrong. It's just the opposite. For the first time in forty years, everything is right.

Chapter 2

The Moments We Take for Granted

They drove for days without any explanation of where they were going. On the fourth day, they awoke knowing they had parked. The scent of the ocean drifted in through an open window. Kayn was personally excited for a day that held the promise of more than just open road and Scrabble. She quickly brushed her teeth and got dressed. The three newest Ankh shoved past each other as they raced down the hall towards the welcoming scent of bacon.

Lily happily announced, "Breakfast will be ready in a few minutes. Eat quickly; we're going to spend the day at the beach. It's time for a break."

Lily was breathtakingly beautiful as always, even without a stitch of makeup on her face and glossy raven hair up in a messy bun. *It should be illegal to look that good in the morning.* Kayn shoved the door open and wandered outside. She inhaled the potent fragrance of trees mixed with salty ocean air. They were parked in a campground and in front of the RV was a rickety weathered looking picnic table.

Grey poured and passed them each a steaming mug of coffee. He proudly stood in front of them and said, "Settle an argument. This coffee is made with a french press. Tell me it's not the best coffee you've ever had?"

Lexy was sitting at the picnic table. She sighed, "I can't taste the difference."

Frost was sitting next to her. He winked and exclaimed, "Neither can I… Sorry buddy."

They were purposely messing with Grey. They all took a sip of their coffee.

Melody nodded and affirmed, "It's good Grey."

Kayn smiled sweetly, saying, "Yes, it's absolutely amazing."

Zach sat down across from Lexy, winked and said, "It's alright," trying to make up for their murderous introduction.

Frost kept a straight face as he sighed, "Well, that's three against two. The coffee tastes normal. It's all in your head."

Grey started huffing around having a hissy fit. He blurted, "You people wouldn't know class if it hit you in the face!" He stormed into the RV and dramatically slammed the door.

Kayn took another sip and thought, *Says the guy who picked out the plastic pink flamingo wine glasses.* Everyone chuckled and she remembered her thoughts were not always her own.

Lexy grinned and said, "Brighton, I like you." She smiled at Melody, then grimaced at Zach like he smelled funny. She got up and went inside after Grey.

Lily stuck her head out the door and scolded, "Frost! Was that really necessary?"

"A little bit," Frost chuckled. He winked at Lily. She shook her head as she closed the door.

Kayn got a kick out of the sibling relationship Frost and Grey had. She glanced up and caught Frost watching her and he immediately looked away.

After an enormous breakfast, they piled into the truck with plans to spend the day at the beach. Grey rolled the windows down, presumably to smell the scent of the ocean. *He was all about the little things. She felt bad about wrecking one of his little things this morning.* Grey often spoke about embracing the blissful moments in life. He'd been one of her emotional life rafts during her first days without Kevin by her side. He told her if she tried to find one moment of beauty in each day, she would always have something to look forward to and he'd been right. Some days it was difficult to find but not today. This was one of those moments. She felt the blissful sensation of her hair moving in the salty ocean breeze flowing through the open window and it occurred to her that there were so many small things you disregard as an adult. Adults rarely took pleasure in the rainbows found in bubbles or in allowing their imagination to run amuck. She recalled her mom asking her to try to keep her feet firmly planted on the ground and she grinned because if she'd listened to those particular words of wisdom, she'd sure be having a difficult time with all of this madness.

They pulled over and she stepped out of the vehicle to a gorgeous, deserted beach. Kayn stretched and smiled. They appeared to have the entire beach to themselves. She heard a kafuffle and noticed the four surf boards in the back of the truck. Grey, Zach and Lexy each grabbed one and sprinted away from the truck towards the water. They were stripping off clothes and tossing them aside without losing momentum until they were only in bathing suits. She wanted to go but there was only one surfboard left. *Frost probably wanted to go.*

She glanced at Frost as he said, "What are you waiting for? Grab a board."

Kayn smiled at him as she grabbed the last board and dashed after the others, while awkwardly struggling out of her clothes. She put the board down, to rid herself of them without making even more of an uncoordinated spectacle of herself. They'd made that look much easier than it was. Kayn glanced back to see if anyone witnessed her geeky moment, but they'd all found a spot on a towel with their books on the beach. Kayn sprinted into the water and caught up with the others. *How difficult could learning to surf be?* An hour and a dozen lungs full of salty water later she decided that it was impossible.

Grey found Kayn's comical exploits into the realm of the coordinated people hilarious. He chuckled, "Small children learn how to surf."

Kayn choked on the saltwater in her airway for the eight millionth time and sparred, "Small children that are secretly ninjas."

He patiently reassured, "You have to be willing to fall off the board and get back on a hundred times if that's what it takes." It was a surprisingly deep comment. He added, "Just relax and have fun. You'll figure it out."

By the end of the day Kayn was able to admit that surfing was clearly not going to be one of her gifts. Surfing was one of Grey's and Lexy's favourite pastimes. Zach learned how to s quickly. He was having the time of his life. Kayn walked back to the shore alone. *There was nobody left on the beach. They must have gone for a walk.* Kayn spread a towel on the sand. Then, grabbed a juice out of the cooler and drank it. Exhausted, she sprawled on the towel in the warmth of the afternoon sun and took a nap.

When she awoke, the sun was hovering low in the sky. Kayn sat up on her towel and shimmied her butt down so her feet would be in the sand. She wiggled her toes back and forth. She'd always enjoyed the warm, calming feeling of sand as it slipped like a silken scarf of liquid sunshine across her skin. Running a hand over the surface of the sand, it shifted like it was moved by a breeze without her making contact. *Her life now had no room for feet being firmly planted on the ground. She had to allow her mind to take off in flight and accept the impossible. She had to embrace life as a toddler. In a child's world, every breath of life is a mystery. Everything had the possibility of being magic.* Kayn smiled, imagining the sun's last rays were flames from a distant dragon. *She understood she was an immortal toddler of sorts.* A tiny crab strolled across her hand. She grinned because it tickled. The shade of the sky changed ever so slightly in her peripheral vision. She raised her eyes from her toes to the horizon, to witness the sun's last dance in the daylight as it began to descend slowly, magically into the distant sea. Exotic pastel hues of orange and fuchsia were now painted across the fading expression of the day. It was a calm yet isolating vision to take into her heart, for it made her feel exceedingly small in the grand scheme of things.

A shadow signalled a presence beside her. She raised her eyes. It was Grey. He held out his hand and she took it without question.

He tugged her to her feet, saying, "I have something incredible to show you."

They walked together into a tidal pool. The scenery was even more breathtaking than only a moment before. The sun had set the sky ablaze with glorious hues of orange. She squinted to focus in its brilliance as thoughts of distant fire breathing dragons lit up her imagination once again. Grey had become her makeshift replacement for the brother she'd lost. He seemed to see her the same way. She was a younger sister to him. He towed her through the surf so fast with shifting grains underfoot she barely kept her footing. It felt like the ocean floor was attempting to elude them as they abruptly stopped thigh-deep in the surf.

Grey whispered, "Do you trust me?" He covered her eyes with damp hands.

"You seem reasonably sane today." Kayn laughed nervously, trying to pry his hands off.

"I said... Trust me," he teased.

This time, it wasn't a question. Dramatically exhaling, she stopped squirming.

"What can you feel right now?" Grey questioned. "I want you to take it all in, the water lapping against your legs, the caress of sand between your toes. There are places where you won't be able to rely on what you see. You will have to trust in what you know."

"I know you'd never hurt me," Kayn said, sputtering out laughter as a crab's tickly legs scurried across her submerged feet.

"That's good," Grey chuckled as she squirmed in the surf.

Laughing, she blurted out, "I think I have crabs."

With his accent that always made her smile and hands covering her eyes, he teased, "Indeed you do." He brushed off her thigh as a crab scaled her leg. After a pause, Grey questioned, "What do you smell? What do you taste?"

Playing along, she declared, "I smell the ocean and a fishy scent." She licked her lips, "I can taste salt." The salt from the surf was tangy on her tongue. She felt something sticky slapping against her thighs. Squeamishly, she disclosed, "For the record, I hate seaweed. It's disgustingly slimy. It creeps me out."

Grey chuckled, "Suck it up, princess. Keep your eyes closed or you'll wreck the surprise."

She sighed and didn't attempt to peek as kelp wrapped around her legs as the water shifted between her thighs. *So gross. This is so gross.*

"What dangers could you encounter standing in the surf?" Grey questioned.

Kayn crinkled her nose. Her nerves were practically twitching from the seaweed clinging to her legs. *Come on, Guru Grey. Get to the bloody point.* She answered, "I don't know, jellyfish, sharks... A giant rogue wave?"

Grey's voice replied, "Right... What could you do about any of them right now?"

"Get the hell out of the water," Kayn laughed nervously. She swayed as a random wave almost caused her to lose her footing. The sand rapidly slid away underfoot as the ocean floor continued to shift.

He chuckled, almost falling himself. Keeping his hands over her eyes, Grey asked, "Do you remember which direction you need to go to get out of the water?"

This isn't a relaxing game anymore. All consumed by the disgusting seaweed entangling her submerged limbs, she squirmed uncomfortably.

Serious this time, Grey questioned, "Is the tide coming in or going out? Try to feel the direction of the current as it moves against your legs."

"I wasn't paying attention," she replied honestly. Grey shifted his hands, keeping her eyes covered with one he gave her wet hair a pet with the other. It felt condescending. *It has been a bloody long day, Grey. I'm too exhausted for deep thought.*

He spoke again, "The point is... While you are busy enjoying the beauty of a moment your mind needs to take in the other details."

"I'll pay attention next time," Kayn promised. She broke into a smile under his fingers and forced them up with her grin.

Grey took his hands off her eyes as the sun disappeared in the horizon. There was an explosion of glowing orange, followed by a pale sliver of colour as it sunk under the water's surface. *The last reminiscence of the sun. It was incredible.* Kayn gasped as she watched the sliver of light ripple across the water like it was reaching across the span of the ocean towards her. *She would have missed this experience had Grey's hands not been covering her eyes until that precise second.* "That was amazing. Thank you." It disappeared as she blinked her eyes, and the sea became an endless void.

Grey splashed her face and repeated her thought aloud, "Guru Grey. What in the hell, Brighton?"

Kayn sputtered as she inhaled a face full of ocean. *She kept forgetting to sensor her thoughts. She always had a comical internal dialogue going on.* Grey swam away from her, chuckling aloud. *He played the pesky older brother role to a tee. Almost as well as Matty had…* Her mind darted into the past but she'd trained herself to shut it off at the first twinge of pain. She chased Grey through the surf with legs weighted by the water trying to get close enough to give him a decent splash back. She mocked, "Feel the water Kayn. Embrace the seaweed Kayn. Be one with the ocean. What do you smell?" She jumped on his back. He dove underwater to get rid of her. *She had an older brother. It was going to take a hell of a lot more than that to get rid of her.*

Grey came to the surface sputtering, "You have a grip like a bloody koala, Brighton!"

She laughed and hung on as Grey trudged his way to shore giving her a piggyback ride.

"Let me go, Brighton. You're going to force me to embarrass you, "Grey teased. The rest of the Ankh were standing on the shore.

Lily hollered, "Quit messing around you two! We're all tired. It's time to go!"

Zach and Melody were standing by Lily waiting for the stragglers to make their way to shore. Kayn grinned at the trio as she tightened her grip on Grey's neck. He started to chuckle and she knew he was about to do something.

Grey teased, "You asked for it, Brighton."

He tugged on the string of her bikini top, she had to let Grey out of the chokehold and grab for it before she lost it. Grey dropped her into the water and took off running ahead of her laughing. She landed with a not so elegant splash in the surf. "You douche!" Kayn called after him. He was already running away from her, belly laughing. She had to stop to retie her bikini top.

By the time she made it to shore, Grey had already shaken the sand off a towel. He grinned and said, "Peace offering?" He chucked it right at her face.

In awe of Grey's bikini top removal skills, Zach declared, "That was amazing. You have to teach me how to do that."

Grey glanced at Melody and innocently enquired, "Want to volunteer for bikini top removal training?" Mel shook her head and walked away without answering. Grey had been mercilessly flirting with her since that first day.

Grey pointed at Melody as she walked away from him and announced, "She wants me."

Smiling, Kayn pulled on her jeans and her wet clinging t-shirt over her still damp bikini. She took a second to breathe. It was easy to appreciate the solitude of the beach at night. The soothing repetitive waves mixed with the faintest light from the slivered moon. Kayn searched her line of sight for Frost. *She'd found herself doing that a lot lately. Perhaps the part of her that was Chloe needed to see him. The sight of him felt like wrapping herself up in a security blanket. He'd been doing his best to avoid having any form of conversation with her.* There he was, carrying the cooler from the beach to the back of the truck. He unlocked the door, climbed into the passenger seat up front and shut it.

Kayn took the elastic from her wrist and put her damp hair in a ponytail as she ran to catch up with the others and scooted into the backseat beside Melody, who was already fast asleep, with her head resting peacefully on Zach's shoulder.

"Poor girl, she's tuckered out," Grey observed. He started the vehicle and they drove back to the campsite.

Kayn glanced out the window at the wide-open spans of the darkened shoreline as it dissolved into the endless sea of black.

"What shall we do tomorrow?" Grey asked the group.

The knowledge that death had been taken off the table made the possibilities endless. Kayn looked at the back of Frost's head. *He couldn't ignore her forever… Could he? Maybe it hurt him to talk to her because she wasn't Chloe.* He glanced back at her and she knew he'd heard her thoughts. Taking a page out of the Frost avoidance manoeuvre handbook, she quickly turned away from him. She sensed he was watching her as she continued to watch the sea of blackened night whirl by her window as a hypnotic mobile of sorts until her eyelids grew heavy. She succumbed to mental exhaustion and slipped off to join Mel in restful slumber.

She awoke the next morning in her bunk with the faint recollection of being carried by Frost. *He'd kissed her forehead. She must have been dreaming.*

In the days that followed, they ventured down this crazy unbucket list the new Ankh complied. She'd managed to add cool memories like jumping off a cliff as a group and swimming out to an empty dock in the middle of a lake, where they danced beneath the stars to music echoing from someone's house party across the water. As the opportunities presented themselves, they were each given a chance to do what they'd only dared fantasize about as mortals.

Melody and Lexy played the unbucket list games with no fear at all. The Healing ability was the coolest gift to have. Kayn could only manage to move a fork in the real world. She'd moved larger objects while training in the In-between, but if she was frightened, even that ability didn't work. She could whip objects around like a damn superhero when she was furious. *Power was an addictive feeling. It was the only time she felt any control over this crazy rollercoaster ride she'd made the choice to board. The In-between was her favourite immortal destination.*

They spent time together learning new skills and solidifying their bond throughout the summer into fall until winter descended, bringing an end to eating outdoors and it was time for heavy coats versus bare skin. During the daylight hours, she fought her growing fascination with Frost and on most nights, she dreamt of the boy she'd lost. Kayn Brighton was finally eighteen. She was old enough to go on her first job with Ankh.

Chapter 3

The Simplest Of Things

Moments… There are always moments where a decision must be made. In mortal life, there is always a choice. One road or another. The ultimate, choose your own adventure story. In Tri-Clan there is only one option and that is to do whatever your Oracle tells you to do.

Kayn's steps crunched through the icy landscape. Smiling, she watched her breath escape into the crisp evening air. She sat on the cold wooden bench outside of the clinic as white powdery snowflakes began floating from the heavens above. *She loved watching Grey's face as it lit up while experiencing something glorious, for he was the one who never forgot to enjoy the simplest of things. His euphoria was contagious, it made everyone want to join in.* Grey smiled, keeping his eyes open as the flakes caught in his eyelashes. He cupped his hands over his mouth, released a gust of warm air, directing the heat of his breath to the delicate flakes caught in his lashes, they melted instantly. *She'd never thought of doing that.* Kayn found herself trying to emulate him. She went one step further and stuck out her tongue. Flakes landed on it and melted. She'd now been to places where bubble gum froze inside of her mouth as she tried to chew it. Places where if her nose ran, it froze solid on her skin in seconds. It was a place like that where Zach learned peeing in the snow was an incredibly inept idea. She smiled at the memory. Kayn stuck her tongue out as far as it could go while attempting to see the flakes resting on its tip. Realising she was cross-eyed as she viewed the tip of her tongue, Kayn slipped it back in between her lips. *She must look hilarious.*

An instant of happiness was worth so much more to her now than it ever had been in the eighteen years prior to this new life. Last week was her eighteenth birthday. She'd been sealed to the Ankh forever on that day. She wasn't sure what she'd expected. Over the last couple of months, a million scenarios passed through her imagination. It would always be something big like the sky opening and shooting her with a brilliant laser beam, instantly changing her into a superhero. That wasn't how it played out. She was given a chocolate bar from Melody when they stopped at a convenience store, and Zach bought her a Ding Dong. They stuck a candle in it and sang happy birthday while the others stared at them like they were from another planet. She hadn't even received a happy you are stuck with us forever speech from Markus. Her eighteenth birthday had passed by rather uneventfully, until today. *It was her first time coming along on a job.* She honestly didn't know what to expect because nobody ever spoke about what they did when they came back from one. She stuck out her tongue again. This time the snowflakes remained on it long enough for her to cross her eyes like a weirdo and get a good look. When her eyes uncrossed, Frost was grinning at her from the other side of the chain link fence. *She was behaving like a child. He was openly amused by her behaviour.* She had a strange flash of his face through the rungs of a fence and shook it off as his gaze was drawn to Grey. If she wasn't mistaken, that was a genuine smile on Frost's face and a touch of longing in his eyes. It looked like he wanted to join in as they reenacted joyous moments from their childhood. *Did he even remember how it felt to be young and enraptured by every little thing the world had to offer?*

Frost's expression altered and he scolded, "Enough horsing around you two, it's time to be serious."

This was her first official duty as Ankh. *How many of these jobs would she do before she stopped attempting to catch snowflakes on her tongue?*

Frost began to speak, "This job is a basic one. They don't test the blood here in this clinic. They test in the next town over at the hospital's lab. The transporter of this blood is going to hit a deer and get into an accident. He'll roll the vehicle down an embankment. We need to intercept the wreck, make sure he is dead and burn the vehicle. I was only told some of the details. All you need to know is that he must not reach his destination. He was supposed to die six months ago, someone intervened. Melody and Zach, I know you've done this kind of disposal job before. Kayn, do what you're told. Don't worry about anything else. Just watch and learn."

Kayn wanted to know more about this stranger whose minutes were numbered. *Did he have a family? Was he a nice person? Why did he have to die today? What wasn't Frost telling them? Why were they expected to go along with the orders with little to no explanation?*

Lexy whispered in her ear, "He is a man whose life needs to come to an end to maintain the balance of things."

Lexy heard her thoughts. Panic surged within her. *She didn't want to do this. She needed to get away to clear her head. This was a human being. He was a normal guy; he wasn't an immortal, or a demon.* Kayn whispered, "I need to go to the bathroom." She slipped through the sliding doors before anyone could stop her.

Both Melody and Zach knew the drill because they'd been in other Clans before becoming Ankh. Melody attempted to follow Kayn. Frost grabbed her arm gently, "Let her go. There's no easy road to acceptance."

Kayn walked by the nurses' station and dove into the bathroom. There were two stalls. She got into one and closed the door. Nurses came in and started to chat in front of the sink.

"Tell me he's single," one voice whispered.

"He's the biggest sweetheart, isn't he?" The other one laughed and then answered, "No, his wife is pregnant, due next month. He has the cutest little boy on the planet."

"Of course, he does," the other one chuckled.

Kayn heard the stall next to her open and close.

A female voice teased from the stall beside her, "If he were an asshole, he'd still be single."

"If he were an asshole, I would have already had a perfectly unsatisfying and totally pointless relationship with him," the other voice sparred.

With her luck they were talking about the man with only a short time to live. She flushed, so it would sound like she was going through the motions. She turned on the tap just as the nurse came out of the stall and smiled at her. They washed their hands together in silence. Kayn looked at her reflection. *This isn't a choice. It is not a choice.* She left the bathroom and smiled at the man as she passed. He warmly smiled back and it tugged at her heart. She returned to the Ankh feeling defeated.

"Are you okay?" Melody mouthed to Kayn.

She smiled in response, opting out of a reply. *Anything she chose to say would reveal her inability to deal with this situation. Nobody with an inch of humanity left could be okay with this.* A cloud of guilt hovered around her repeating, *if you know someone is in trouble you should warn them. You're supposed to stop terrible things from happening, not create them. You are a good person.* Grey was avoiding her gaze, so she tried to make eye contact with Lily.

Lily walked right past her, opened the truck and announced, "Come on. We need to go."

They all got in and sat there for a minute. Kayn searched for Frost's eyes again. With a glare he warned, *don't you dare.* She knew he'd have no problem muzzling her with his hand. With the hum of the sliding door, the man walked out carrying a box and got into a small white van. Everything inside of her was screaming at her to stop him from leaving. As he backed out, the crunching of snow under his tires made her grab the handle of the door. After clenching it for a second, she relaxed her grip, knowing there was no point in trying to stop the inevitable. *This was a Correction. If they didn't do it, one of the other Clans would.* They trailed him for a while and pulled over as they hit the wooded area.

"This feels wrong," Kayn whispered to Melody.

Melody turned away from her, looked out the window at the darkened trees covered in snow and solemnly replied, "It always does." Melody kept staring out of the window as she quietly added, "It will all make sense later."

The tension was broken as Frost abruptly blurted, "Alright. Let's go."

They pulled out and drove until they saw a trail of smoke on the side of the road. Kayn got out of the truck on autopilot and wandered over to stand next to Zach.

Frost announced, "Listen up, this job needs to happen quickly before anyone else drives by and sees the smoke from the accident."

"I'll stay with the truck," Lily offered. "You know, in case any complications arise."

Without another word, Frost manoeuvered his way down the steep embankment. They followed, grabbing branches of trees and ferns to keep themselves from sliding down the icy hill. She could see the smoking crushed vehicle. You couldn't even tell what he'd started out driving. *Maybe he was already gone? Maybe they won't have to kill him?*

Frost looked at her and ordered, "Don't touch anything. Trust me. If you do, what happens next will not be pleasant."

"What are you going to do to him if he's still alive?" Kayn whispered.

He didn't even take a breath before answering, "I'll have to break his neck. It's always been the most efficient way to kill someone quickly. It will look like it happened in the accident."

I'm just going to break his neck. No big deal. It seemed absolutely absurd to talk casually about ending someone's life.

Frost addressed the entire group, "The car needs to be completely engulfed in flames long before any first responders show up because if that happens, this Correction will include more than just one man. Take your glove off and put it in your pocket. We have to make our point quickly."

Kayn watched as everyone pulled off their gloves without hesitation. She reluctantly tugged her white fingerless glove off and gazed at the symbol branded on her palm as her heart pounded a panicked rhythm in her chest. When she looked up, Lexy had an expression on her face that almost read as concern.

Lexy gave her a few words of assurance, "Just breathe hun. This isn't on you."

Zach protectively placed his arm around her, pulled her close and whispered in her ear, "Just watch and try to pay attention."

This felt so wrong. Kayn swallowed the lump of guilt in her throat and took a deep shuddering breath. She wanted to look elsewhere and pretend this wasn't happening. *She didn't want to be a part of this.* Kayn turned and used his shoulder to conceal her eyes.

"I promise it will all make sense, but only if you're watching," Zach whispered.

Grey strolled past her as he announced, "I've got the fire handled, if you have him handled."

The guilt felt like a weight on her heart. It was like life meant nothing to most of them. Unable to hold her tongue, she whispered to Zach, "Isn't brains before brawn our Clan's moto? We're not even looking for another way?"

Frost whipped his head around to meet her accusing eyes and said, "I'll tell you what sweetheart; let's just ask him what he wants to do? We'll give him a choice."

Kayn hated it when Frost used that condescending tone. She wasn't stupid. She just had this affliction that was apparently foreign to him called empathy.

Frost took those final strides towards the wreckage alone, leaned into the window and shook the man a little, "Hey buddy, you okay?"

The man came to and moaned," I'm stuck in here. I can't move. I thought it would be a long time before help found me down here."

"It depends on how you define help," Frost replied calmly.

The man grew silent, his instinct for self-preservation triggered by Frost's odd response.

"I'm terribly sorry. We don't have a lot of time. I'm going to have to skip the pleasantries and get right to business. Let me show you something." Frost took the blade out of his pocket and to the mortal's horror, he sliced his hand. The symbol of Ankh on Frost's palm exploded with light, triggering the rest of their hands to light up the landscape like fallen stars.

The man's eyes widened. With moments left, he flailed and thrashed around but his legs were crushed beneath the dash. He stammered, "What in the hell are you people? Are you aliens or something?"

"Or something," was Frost's reply.

Lexy reached out and touched Frost. He touched the wounded man's shoulder, sending some of Lexy's healing energy throughout his body to take away his pain.

Frost held up his healed hand. Kayn watched the wounded man struggle to accept his impossible situation.

A look of peace travelled through the wounded man's eyes as he whispered, "I'm going to die, aren't I?"

Frost's voice softened, "I am going to give you a choice. I know you're scared. I understand how crazy this must sound but it's important you absorb the gravity of what I'm about to tell you."

With his pain gone, the man's panicked breathing calmed.

"You've been exposed to a virus. It's mutated within you. Everyone you encounter tonight will get sick. Most will die. Your family will come to see you while you're recovering from surgery. Your son dies within twenty-four hours. Your pregnant wife will die the following day, taking your unborn daughter with her. The child in your wife's womb is tremendously valuable, more than you can possibly fathom. She has an important role to play in future events. Your unborn child will go on to do extraordinary things. If you choose life, nobody will ever know it was you who started this epidemic. You are only a carrier. You will have no symptoms. The choice is your life, or your family's. Everyone you love and many more will die, or you can make the choice to change the future and die right now. There is only a minute to make up your mind. We will abide by whatever you decide."

The man looked into Frost's eyes and nodded. Kayn's were clouded with tears for she knew what this man was about to say.

Without hesitation, he whispered, "Me, I choose it to be me."

"You won't feel a thing. To your family, this will look like a random accident. Your next life might be better than this one."

"No, it couldn't possibly be better," the man whispered with the strength of his love flowing from every pore. "This time was perfect. I would do it all again, even if I knew this was how it would end."

"That's what I like to hear. You were blessed. Be at peace," Frost softly replied. He touched the man's brow with his palm, lighting up his symbol. The man's eyes closed and when they opened, they were vacant of his being. His soul had been delivered to the in-between, leaving only what was left of his broken, empty mortal shell behind. Frost snapped his neck without ceremony. The man slumped in the driver's seat. Kayn was sobbing, the man's final loving words about his family had touched her heart. She made her way to the window wanting to grab the picture of his family off the visor before they burned the vehicle.

Grey blocked her path and scolded, "Everything in this car burns and anyone who touches anything in it."

Kayn turned to look at Frost. *Wait a minute. Was Grey going to burn Frost because he'd touched the driver?*

Frost held out his hands and solemnly stated, "Just do it."

Panicked, Kayn looked at Grey and then at Frost. *He wasn't going to actually do it?*

Grey winced as he asked, "This is going to suck. You ready buddy?"

"Never for this," Frost responded. He made eye contact with her as he said, "But it's not exactly a choice, is it?"

"Sorry man," Grey whispered. His hands hovered a few inches above Frost's skin. Brilliant flames of orange engulfed his muscular arms. Frost's flesh bubbled and melted away from the meat. Pitchy anguish spilled from his parted lips and his eyes rolled back in agony as he collapsed to his knees on the frozen forest floor.

Kayn staggered backwards in shock. Grey casually strolled over and lit the car on fire. The interior was instantly engulfed in flames. *They were sacrificial lambs.*

Lexy knelt before Frost, cupped his face and the raw exposed skin on his arms started to heal. She embraced him, consoling, "Shhh. It's okay." His wounds scabbed and closed. Looking a little faint, Lexy whispered, "If I keep going, you'll have to carry me up that hill."

There was quite an ominous slant to it. Kayn hadn't noticed how steep it was on the way down. Her mind had been elsewhere.

Melody reached for Frost and volunteered, "I'll finish healing you."

Frost politely refused, "We have to go, Hun. I'm okay, see." He showed her his now perfectly healed skin.

Once she knew Frost was healed, Kayn's eyes were drawn back towards the smouldering wreckage. She watched as his mortal shell floated away in the pungent billowing smoke and disappeared into the sky above. *She'd never forget the scent of burning flesh or how selfless that man had been today and dare she think his name… Frost. He'd sacrificed himself. Someone had to fix things that fell through the cracks. A kind, decent man had died tonight but his demise had a clear purpose. His Correction had saved his family and who knows how many others from being touched by a glitch in fate's design.*

Kayn followed the others silently, climbing the slippery slope by grabbing ahold of branches and ferns. Struggling, she pulled herself upwards. She pictured Lily sitting there with the engine idling as she heard the vehicle's engine purring. *She was trying to think of anything else.* Kayn's hand clasped a fern and the exposed root from a tree. Strangely enough they created almost perfect handles. She dug her heels into the icy trickery beneath her feet, actively ignoring the scent of burning human flesh. *This night had marked her soul. It would stay with her always.*

Chapter 4

Stand Back Up

A large part of training for Testing revolved around understanding they could not die. This was a surprisingly difficult thing to wrap your mind around. They met up with Markus, Arrianna and a girl named Flora at a storage unit that Lily borrowed. *Code for using her potent Siren pheromones to get it free.* Arrianna was going to run the tombs so they could take a training trip to the In-between. After they walked inside, Frost pulled the rope on the door to close it behind them. Grey created a flame in the palm of his hand and lit up the space. Grey, Lily, Lexy and Frost nonchalantly tossed their Ankh stones. Their rose quartz stones landed with oddly timed tings on cement, and in the dimly lit storage unit, four Ankh tombs appeared as a hologram, solidifying to stone.

"This is always so cool," Zach chuckled as he tapped the solid top of one.

Smiling, Kayn agreed, "Ditto."

Grey climbed into his and glanced at Arrianna. She chucked his tunes. He caught it mid-air and sweetly said, "Thanks, babe."

Everyone got into their tombs, leaving the three of them standing there waiting for an invitation. *Which Ankh would she be sharing a tomb with?*

Noticing their awkward moment, Grey teased, "Mel, come hop in mine. There's plenty of room."

Arrianna shook her head and sighed, "Oh… Just lay off the poor girl, Romeo." She directed Melody to Lily's tomb, assuring, "This one doesn't bite."

Grinning, Grey explained, "Just in case you three haven't figured it out I'm being mocked and ridiculed because Arrianna is my ex. I'll have you know that I haven't bitten anyone in a long time."

"Is that true Lily?" Arrianna teased.

From within her tomb, Lily laughed, "Don't drag me into this. He's still mad at me." Lily welcomed Melody into her tomb, and they laid side by side.

"Kayn, you go with Lexy. Zach can go with Grey," Arrianna instructed.

They climbed into the tombs. Kayn glanced at Lexy as the tomb closed above them with the unforgettable grinding of stone on stone. Grey's music started. Zach and Grey were cat calling and hooting, before the tombs were even pushed together. Kayn wondered if Lexy would be appalled if she began to hoot with the boys. *She wanted to.* Lexy cupped her lips and hooted at Grey. They hooted back. Laughter was coming from the other tombs as Kayn and Lexy hooted in unison. The tombs jerked sideways. *She was so excited.* They waited for a response. The boys were laughing. Kayn closed her eyes as the tombs began strobing with blinding light. Her stomach lurched as they were catapulted into oblivion encased within the tomb. There were shrieks of excitement as their tombs spun until they slowed and momentarily stopped. With only a second to catch her breath, the tombs began their stomach-churning descent, spinning as they plummeted until the wind was whipping against their bare skin. Their tombs were gone. They burst through the clouds, rapidly descending towards the desert floor. Slowing before impact, they landed, crouching in the warm sand of the In-between. They rose in unison. Kayn did what she always did. She stood in awe of the visual miracle of the place she was permitted to visit only because she was part of a Clan. The sky of vibrant blue stretched across the span of the desert. Kayn wiggled her toes in the warm, silky sand. This was the clean palate the Clans entered in. A sight familiar to each one. They could paint whatever picture they desired once they were alone. Her eyes travelled from one gorgeous thing to another. Kayn looked at Frost. *How long was he going to ignore her?* Frost had walked away from where they'd landed with Lily and Grey. *She couldn't hear what they were saying but imagined that was the point. They were probably planning their training.* She'd gapped out appreciating Frost's barely there attire. Zach walked up and playfully shoved her over in the sand. She tossed a handful back at him, scowling.

Bending over, he provoked, "You're being a little obvious."

She yanked his leg out from under him. They wrestled until she had Zach pinned. Straddling him, Kayn sparred, "I gapped out. I was staring at nothing."

"Hey, I get it. I catch myself staring at Lily all of the time," Zach teased.

Kayn jousted back, "And Melody," as she squeezed him with her thighs.

Melody kicked sand at the pair, scolding, "I'm right here you two. Stand up. They're coming back."

Looking into her eyes, Zach said, "All right, Brighton. Get off me."

Kayn provoked, "Is little Zachy wacky afraid Lily won't think he's all manly if he gets beaten up by a girl?" She tussled his hair like he was a kid.

Zach began to laugh, "Actually, I'm not even trying to get away. When a girl pins me down and straddles me like this, it totally turns me on."

Kayn leapt to her feet and groaned, "Gross Zach." *He was like her brother. She didn't think about him that way.* He stayed there in the sand, howling. Kayn kicked sand at him and walked over to stand beside Melody.

"You walked right into that one," Melody chuckled.

Frost marched over and scolded, "Enough horsing around you three."

Smiling, flat on his back in the sand, Zach said, "Like you'd try to stop a hot girl from pinning you down." He leapt to his feet.

Frost enquired, "Are you saying a girl couldn't pin you down, unless you let her?"

Lexy strolled towards Zach. He stammered, "Nope. No. That is totally not what I'm saying."

Motioning for Ankh's breathtakingly beautiful Siren, Frost chuckled, "What about Lily? Can she pin you down?"

"Anytime she wants," Zach dreamily sighed.

Lily rolled her eyes at him and shook her head.

"Go get him Lex," Frost chuckled.

Casually strolling over, Lexy swept Zach's leg and took him down with little to no effort. Straddling his chest, she declared, "That was pathetic. It took me all of two seconds. You're going to have to do better than that." She put pressure on his shoulders with her knees.

It looked excruciatingly painful.

Lexy looked directly at Kayn and instructed, "Do you see what I'm doing here, Brighton? You need just a little more pressure to inflict pain."

Zach had found himself in quite the predicament. Kayn managed to stop herself from smiling as she replied, "I see." *They'd only been messing around.* She decided to keep her mouth shut and just go with it.

Lexy scowled down at Zach's expression of agony and said, "I bet you're not turned on right now?"

Kayn looked at Melody as they both thought in unison, o*h, Zach. Don't say it. This was not the time for his dirty mind. Angry Lexy was not the audience for his shenanigans.* Kayn glanced at Grey as he moved his head slowly from side to side, hinting for Zach to say no.

Lexy interrogated, "Well?"

Biting his lip, Zach whispered, "I'm afraid to say."

Waving his hands behind Lexy, Grey mouthed, "Don't you say it."

Enraged by his refusal, Lexy pushed down on his shoulders, glaring.

While in excruciating pain, Zach was still a teenage boy. He looked up at Lexy, confessing, "I'm sorry. I don't know what's wrong with me."

"You pervert," Lexy hissed. She socked him in the stomach but smiled as she walked away.

It took giant balls to flirt with Lexy. She openly despised Zach because he'd killed her on the day Ankh took him from Triad. Zach had grown on her. She secretly liked him.

Lily addressed the group, "Let's break off into pairs and try out what Lexy just showed us. Melody, you take down Grey. Zach. You're with me. You really shouldn't be pushing your luck with Lexy. She's going to be training you for the next three weeks. Kayn, you can try to take down Frost."

Why in the hell did Lily pair her with Frost? He rarely acknowledged her existence. Wandering over, Frost smirked. *Clearly, he didn't think she had a hope in hell of taking him down. Oh, it's on. You superficial, cocky douche.*

Frost opened his mouth and pretended to be mortified at what floated through Kayn's mind.

She had to gain control over her inner dialogue.

He summoned her to him and teased, "Well… Come on then, Froggy. Show this superficial, cocky douche what you're made of."

Good, the condescending nickname. Kayn provoked, "Was that your best attempt at smack talk Frost?" Kayn noticed out of the corner of her eye that Melody had already pinned Grey down. *After a year with Trinity, she'd better be able to pin Grey down.*

"This is a battle you can't possibly win Princess," he jeered.

"Watch me," Kayn sparred as she darted around the hunky douche of an immortal. He chuckled as he narrowly avoided a few of her well-timed leg sweeps.

Smirking, Frost retaliated, "Don't get all pissy with me. It's not my fault you have the coordination of a drunken moose."

The others gathered, cheering and chanting her name as Frost cockily ambled around her like he wasn't even the tiniest bit concerned. *He was in trouble now. She was taking this asshole down even if she had to think up a two-by-four and smoke him across the face with it.* She swung her leg, attempting to trip him again.

Chuckling while manoeuvring out of her way, he provoked, "Having problems, Princess?"

What would Lexy do? Kayn took him by surprise. She motioned like she was going to sweep his leg and launched herself at him, knocking a stunned Frost flat on his back. Pinning him like she pinned Zach, she added a more Lexy to it.

Looking up at her, he winked and teased, "Why… You're not really a princess at all are you Froggy? I'll be the first to say good job." He tried to get up. Kayn pressed down on his shoulders with her knees. *She would show him who was boss.* Frost shook his head at her, grinning.

Lexy walked by and said, "You took him down, impressive. Frost would never just let you pin him down. Would he Grey?" Lexy glared at her Handler. Grey shrugged and winked at Melody.

Scowling, Mel complained, "I want a rematch. I knew that was too easy."

Feeling pretty damn proud of herself, Kayn let Frost stand up. He leapt to his feet, still grinning. *Why was he smiling like that? She'd kicked ass and taken no names. She'd put that cocky asshole in his place.* She looked over and noticed the others saying their goodbyes.

Before he left, Frost walked up behind her and whispered in her ear, "Next time remember you're not wearing any underwear."

Her mouth dropped open. She whirled around. Grey, Lily and Frost were already walking away together. Frost glanced back, winked at her and they disappeared into thin air.

Lexy stood before the trio of Newbie immortals and cleared her throat a couple of times to make sure she had their full attention before announcing, "This portion of the training is a brain exercise. The Testing will tell the Third-Tier if you are a viable long term. A Second-Tier's biggest weakness is that their brain is trained to respond to situations as a human being. We can heal everything but your psyche. In order to have the ability to run full force into a hurricane, you must be able to shut down the need for self-preservation. You need to fully accept the fact that death is not a permanent state. The human brain has a little self-preservation switch. It wants to turn off once it's been wounded. It needs time to reboot. Some call it shock, others say it's a blessing, but your brain wants to protect you from prolonged agony. You break a limb and your brain shuts off the pain until the shock wears off. Our brains need to be able function in those moments after serious injury. Just because we can heal your body, that doesn't mean your brain will allow you to operate it."

Kayn could read the disclaimer at the bottom of this page. *This portion of the training was going to epically suck.* They followed Lexy obediently through the endless desert. There was a flash of light and the scenery changed. They stopped cold, standing right on the edge of a vast clay ravine with no greenery.

Lexy declared, "The three of you are only as strong as your weakest link. Hold hands."

Perched on the rock bluff, Kayn and Melody each grabbed one of Zach's hands. *Were they going to have to stop themselves from falling? They knew how to do that. What was the big deal about this exercise?* Kayn leaned forward and peered over the edge. *They wouldn't have much time to work up the adrenaline to stop. This wasn't thousands of feet. They entered the In-between from just above the cloud line. This drop would be fast. It would hurt like a son of a bitch if they didn't stop themselves.*

Lexy addressed the trio, "This game has only one rule. No matter what happens, you can't let go of each other's hands."

Kayn looked at the other two. *That sounds easy enough.*

Melody squeezed their hands, saying, "Don't let go. Let's do it on the count of three. One, two and jump."

"So, we're jumping on three then?" Zach confirmed.

With a deep breath, Mel answered, "I don't think it matters. We have your hands. When we jump, you're coming."

Melody began to count, "One, two and jump."

The trio sprung off the ledge without fear. When they each reached out a hand to slow their descent, it didn't work. She recalled falling into the In-between with Kevin. *Someone hollered, let go or you won't be able to stop! Oh, Crap! The order was do not let go of each other. So, they didn't.* Kayn squeezed her eyes shut a second before impact, cursing, "Shit!" There was an explosion of excruciating soul-altering pain, followed by nothing, then flickering light and steady humming. Everything was shaking. She felt weighted to the clay floor.

Mel's voice sounded like it was coming from the end of a tunnel, "Kayn. Zach. Wake up."

Choking while inhaling air into her lungs, Kayn gasped. *Her chest felt like it was scalded on the inside with boiling water all the way down her throat. It was on fire. It was burning.* She took another breath as it subsided and normalized. *Shit... That sucked.* Someone groaned beside her.

Writhing in pain, Zach thought back, '*You can say that again.*'

Kayn agonizingly rotated her head his way and noticed Melody was already standing. *She was fine. Why couldn't she be a Healer instead of this Conduit bullshit?*

Zach choked out, "Ditto."

As the nausea subsided, Kayn attempted to sit upright on the blood-splattered clay floor. She turned to Zach. He was sitting beside her.

Looking at the thirty-foot radius of blood splatter, Zach remarked, "Now, that's just upsetting."

Lexy called out from her perch on the cliff above them, "Well! What are you waiting for? Get your butts back up here and do it again!"

"Oh, you've got to be frigging kidding me," Zach groaned.

Always searching for a silver lining, Melody squeezed his shoulder, assuring, "There must be a way to do this. We just have to figure it out."

The three thought themselves back up to the top of the cliff. Kayn looked at Lexy and implored, "Come on, give us a hint."

"If you learn a lesson the hard way, you'll never forget it," Lexy replied.

Hesitantly, they took each other's hands and grimaced in unison. Kayn's mind yelled, *what in the hell are you doing?* They stepped off the ledge and plummeted towards the ravine's unforgiving clay floor. It ended with blinding pain and a revolting accumulation of visual blood splatter. They tried a few more times but there was no stopping their descent. Once again, they were ordered back to the ledge.

As they stood there mentally preparing to leap to their excruciating demise, Zach whispered, "Is she trying to actually kill us, because I think it's working."

Kayn took his hand and replied, "Yes, she quite obviously is."

"I would say that's her plan," Melody added as they stepped off the edge.

She'd ceased to count the number of times a while ago. What was the point of counting? There was no preparation needed for this insanity. Kayn closed her eyes before impact, and once again, there was an explosion of soul-altering agony as the trio splattered on the unforgiving ravine's floor.

The humming was back again, then the shaking sensation. Sweltering like a furnace, Kayn tried to suck in that first breath of air, but her scalded lungs were barely functional. She struggled to move. The landscape wavered. She could only look straight ahead. *Son of a bitch that bloody hurt.* As she fought to lift herself with her arms. Her mind began screaming, *what in the hell are you doing?* She managed to turn only her head towards the other two. Melody was standing already but Zach was struggling as much as she was to regain his bearings but managed to get up. He took her hand and pulled her up with him. With wobbling legs, the trio looked up at Lexy and thought, *No... No. Not again. Please don't make us do it again.*

Without mercy, Lexy hollered from her perch, "Let's try that again!"

From far above the landing site, they could see what they'd left behind. It was intimidating, to say the least. The morbid accumulation of brain matter and clumps of meat splayed across the floor bordered on a 'Texas Chainsaw Massacre' level of visual gruesomeness.

"Our bodies are in tombs. This is a test, just jump," Melody whispered.

Once again, they smoked the clay floor and painted it red. They never let go of each other's hands. After an even longer span of recuperation time went by, they struggled to their feet with their minds ringing and their lungs an inferno of torturous fire. Over and over, the trio stepped off the ledge. She made them keep doing it until they could no longer rise. Their minds were screaming in unison, *No More!* Even Mel was incapacitated.

Lexy jumped off the ledge and stopped herself from falling easily because she was alone in her descent. Standing above them, she ordered, "Stand the hell back up!"

Kayn tried, but her brain wouldn't allow it after being squished dozens of times with no decent amount of recuperation between splats. She couldn't even wiggle her toes. After a minute or two, she twitched her fingers, but the rest of her wouldn't budge. *She'd felt this way once before, but this time, she knew she was indestructible. Well, only temporarily destructible. There was no urgency to escape. It was the opposite. She needed five minutes before she killed herself again. They were attempting something meant to be impossible.* Kayn was certain there was no way to stop without letting go of each other's hands.

Crouching, Lexy threatened, "Stand up or I'll think up something terrifying to come and eat you, Brighton. Will that help you find the urgent need to stand back up?"

Damn her inner dialogue. Melody was up. Zach was trying to get up. Willing her body to move, it wouldn't. *She was giving it everything she had.*

Lexy directed her next statement to the two standing, "Just leave her here and you two won't get eaten." The crimson-haired immortal vanished, and instantly, she was on the cliff bluff above. Far out of the way of whatever heinous creation she'd thought up to devour her.

Melody frantically tugged on her arm, pleading, "Come on Kayn! Get up! You have to try!"

She understood the gravity of the situation. She just couldn't do anything about it. Kayn gasped, "I'm trying. I can't move. Just get out of here. I can take it." *Whatever it was. It would be over in a second. They weren't leaving her.* Barely able to breathe, she asserted, "Just leave me. Go." She heard ominous thundering clicks in the distance and managed to look. *Seriously?* A dozen enormous scorpions the size of buses were running in a spine-chilling herd towards them.

Zach lifted her into his arms, assuring, "I have you. Keep trying to move. We're not going anywhere without you." He swung around with Kayn in his arms and pressed her flush against the clay wall, putting his body between hers and the oncoming herd of terrifying scorpions. Mel stood in front of them. Neither left her there to be devoured. Preparing for the agony of claws and stings, they held their breath. The scorpions vanished into mist ten feet away. Zach put her down. Kayn could stand. *It felt like their loyalty revived her.*

Lexy proudly declared, "There might be hope for you three yet. Need a break?"

The surroundings flashed. They were in front of a familiar house, standing in a meadow of wildflowers. *It was Granny Winnie's house.* Kayn sprinted towards the house, shouting, "Come on, you two! It's Kevin's Grandmother's house! She practically raised me!" Kayn ran through the open door and skidded across the icy floor. The interior of the house was full of ice and snow. Kayn slipped around, struggling to keep her balance. Her breath pirouetted in front of her face. The kitchen cupboards, the table, everything was covered by ice. She danced from foot to foot on the icy floor. *It hurt.* Kayn called out, "Granny! Are you here?" *There was no answer. They couldn't even sit at the table. Their butts would stick to the ice. Bare skin on ice was always a bad idea.* Kayn dashed out, leaving behind the frozen wasteland. Warmth embraced her like an old friend the second she was out the door.

Leaning through the threshold, Zach peered in and said, "I don't think Granny Winnie lives here anymore."

Kayn thought of Kevin with her eating peanut butter and jelly sandwiches on the stoop. Her heart ached. She pushed the feelings down. *A frozen wasteland was all that was left of her childhood sanctuary.*

Zach held out his hand. Without the need for words, she laced her fingers through his. Mel took her other hand, and the three walked away from her past. They strolled through the seemly endless field of flowers until she noticed a patch of purple clover. Kayn bent to pick one.

"Maybe, you should leave that purple clover in the ground," Melody suggested.

It was far past the time to leave it in the ground. She knew it.

"Purple clovers are your past," Zach declared as he searched through the patch of flowers until he found one he could name. He plucked a daisy from the ground and passed her the flower. Kayn took it, smiling. He suggested, "Maybe your future is more like a daisy?"

"Maybe it's lavender instead of purple clover?" Mel said, motioning to a patch of heather."

Nudging her, Zach teased, "Maybe your future love interest isn't obsessed with flowers at all?"

Grinning, Kayn disclosed, "He wasn't obsessed. It was just a cute story about how we met as kids."

"We should find something that signifies our bond," Zach suggested, methodically plucking petals off a flower.

"Cherry Jell-O. That's my vote," Mel bantered, laughing.

Cherry Jell-O sounded wonderful. Kayn sighed, "All right. I vote for Swedish Berries." She kept walking through the field.

Zach shoved her, teasing, "Those Swedish Feet candies are better and pizza."

"Mmm… Spaghetti, or maybe lasagna?" Melody reminisced, wandering through the meadow.

With her arm around Mel, Kayn said, "Let's not use food. This conversation's making me hungry."

Glancing at his friends with their arms draped around each other, Zach teased, "Maybe it's a girl and not a boy?"

Kayn winked at Zach, baiting, "Maybe it is?"

"Maybe mine is too," Mel toyed, aware of his crush.

Zach dropped in the grass. Star-fishing gangly teenage limbs, he groaned, "Quit messing with me. It's not nice." They sprawled by him, laughing as he commentated with an announcer's voice, "One lone man destined to be perpetually lost in the friend zone with two beautiful girls... Forever."

Melody pestered, "The best way to get over someone is to..."

"Mel, our Kayn is an innocent flower. Leave your tarty suggestions for a lunch with Lily and Frost," he taunted.

Mel bounced around and declared, "What about Frost? You stare at him all the time. I've seen him staring at you."

Kayn glared at her and replied, "Everyone stares at Frost. How can you not? He barely speaks to me. He was in love with my dead twin. I think a part of him is angry Chloe didn't turn out to be the dominant soul. He can't stand the sight of me."

"Anybody but Frost, he's such a peacock." Zach groaned.

Kayn plucked a handful of grass and threw it at him.

He chuckled, "Oh, no. She's already defending him. Should I order your wedding cake right now? Carrot or lemon?" Zach yanked a bunch of grass out and started to cover her with it. Kayn flailed, fending him off. He pinned her and said, "You swing like a toddler." Melody dropped grass on her while Zach tickled her until Kayn was absolutely covered in it squealing, she was going to pee.

Lexy cleared her throat and sighed, "Seriously? Just when I thought you three couldn't possibly get any weirder?" Grinning, their crimson-haired afterlife coach teased, "Pee yourself if you must, we have to get back to training."

The next day was hundreds of versions of Lexy screaming, "Come at me!" They attacked her, and she killed them in increasingly creative ways. Lexy's skills as a warrior were unmatched. If you attacked her for any reason, you were going to die, and it was going to be extremely unpleasant. She took everyone out like swatting moderately annoying flies without breaking a sweat when they came at her armed. It was intimidating.

Lexy appeared to have no fear. It was more than that. She seemed incapable of it.

Three weeks were spent in the In-between, running through impossible scenarios. Twenty years in the future, they'd still be having nightmares of Lexy hollering, 'Come at me!'

During breaks from their repetitive, uber-humiliating beatings, Frost taught them how to be free-spirited. It would take the ability to balance good and evil to fulfil their future obligations to Ankh. Frost was the voice in everyone's ears, whispering, *I dare you to do it.*

Whenever they were ready to have a well-deserved breakdown, they'd have an hour or so with Guru Grey. Each of their roles had importance. Grey's was teaching spiritual survival skills. To find their way through a complete absence of daylight, they needed the ability to create a light within themselves. This light would serve as a reminder that the darkest of times didn't last for more than a second in the grand scheme of things.

They'd kept her so busy she barely thought about Kevin. They didn't require sleep while in the In-between. It was a much-needed reprieve from the beautiful dreams that haunted her.

All of their hands began to flash. The scenery blinked and they were standing in the desert. Frost announced, "Time's up. It's bound to be a bumpy ride. I bet Arrianna is exhausted... Lexy."

Time to begin the stomach-churning descent into reality. Disintegrating into the white sand desert, they appeared in the tombs. It only strobed a few times before going into a high-speed flat spin. *This was the worst carnival ride ever.* Bracing herself, trying not to hurl, she noticed the darkness. *No strobing. This wasn't good.* When the older ones began screaming for Lexy, she knew they were in trouble.

"Shit," Lexy cursed. She placed her palms in the prints on the ceiling. The tomb strobed with blinding light with Lexy screaming a primal shrill pitch as they spun at a stomach-churning rate.

Kayn wanted to see what she was screaming about but the light was too bright. Lexy kept shrieking as they spun in vomitus high speed circles until they abruptly stopped. *She'd never been so grateful to stop moving in her life.* Nobody was hooting or having fun this time. *They were probably all holding their hands over their mouths to stop themselves from upchucking like she was.* Waiting for the tomb to open, nothing happened. *This was weird?* Kayn turned to look at Lexy. *She was out cold. It was more than passed out. Her eyes were wide open and glazed over. She was lying next to Lexy's dead body… Awesome.*

Everyone was silent for a minute before Grey enquired, "Lex, how many times did you kill them today?"

There was an awkward silence before Kayn replied, "Hey... Um. You guys. I think Lexy's dead."

Grey groaned and said, "She can't die. It's only temporary. She had to use her own energy to operate the tombs. Which means, she got carried away with your training and killed Arrianna. How many times did she kill you guys?"

"Shit, I lost count, Zach replied. "I don't know. Fifty, maybe a hundred times?"

"Well, get comfortable everyone. It could be a while," Lily sighed.

Kayn looked at dead Lexy, asking, "How do we get out?"

Grey answered loudly from the tomb beside her, "Lexy just made Arrianna heal three people a hundred times in three hours. She's quite obviously dead. Lexy will wake up first, give her a minute."

"Can't we just open them?" Mel's voice enquired.

"Frost might be able to open his but the rest of us have two people per tomb. We're stuck in here," Lily responded.

Frost chuckled and said, "I'll wait a few minutes with you guys. I'm in no hurry. So, you guys got killed a hundred times in three weeks. That's hilarious."

Melody corrected Frost, "It was more like, a couple hundred times each."

Frost started to howl.

"That's so hilarious I forgot to laugh," Zach mumbled.

Grey addressed the group from within his tomb, "Sorry guys. I would have stopped her if I'd known she was going that far overboard."

Lily sighed, "Seriously Grey, we all knew she was going to go overboard. That's why we did it. Quit trying to be good cop."

"Thanks for that," Zach said to his tomb mate.

"Cut the comic relief, Zach, before I tell Lexy you made fun of her for passing out," Lily teased.

"Well, I'm going to take a nap," Grey announced.

They were all exhausted and fell asleep while waiting for one of the Healers to awaken. Kayn's last conscious thoughts were of how wrong it was to take a nap beside a dead body. *It felt a bit insensitive.* Her thoughts drifted to Kevin. *If his memory had been erased, he was dealing with a perfectly clean slate. He'd have no torturous visions of what they'd lost. He'd been given a gift.* She slipped away into a dream and after a short cat nap, Kayn opened her eyes to the welcome sound of the lids grinding open.

Lexy sat up and declared, "I come back from the bloody dead and you're taking a nap beside my corpse. How desensitized did I make you?" Lexy climbed out and teased, "Out or in Zena?"

Zena Warrior Princess. Ha, ha. Funny. Kayn got out. Lexy knelt in front of the last tomb and laid her hand flat against the side. *She'd never seen them being operated from the outside before. It was extremely cool.* Her hand glowed and the other tombs began grinding open.

Grey hopped out, looked at Arrianna's body on the ground and chuckled, "I hope it was worth it. She's going to be pissed."

Lexy crouched by her body as she replied, "When the Testing is over, we'll know."

Chapter 5

Sweet Dreams Of You

They were travelling South to Florida for their next job. It was a hell of a long drive and you could only play so many board games. Kayn spent a lot of time sleeping because it was the only way she could see him. Tonight, she was back at the house she'd grown up in, alone in the kitchen. She gathered what she needed out of the fridge and was slicing a tomato. Each movement of normalcy was so soothing. Somebody knocked on the door. She knew it was Kevin by his trademark knock. She raced down the hall, opened it and provoked, "Whatever you're trying to sell, I don't want any."

Kevin wandered right past her, teasing, "Oh, I already know you want it."

She beamed and continued the game, "Wait right here. I'll grab my purse." Kayn slowly scaled the stairs, glancing behind her every three or four steps. As she wandered into her room, she heard the soft rustle of his footsteps on the carpet.

He strolled into her bedroom and teased, "Don't you want to see what I'm selling first? I mean, who buys something without checking it out to see if it works?"

Kayn kept up the pretence as she sparred, "Well then, what are you waiting for? Show me how it works." He grinned as he kissed her gently on the lips. She taunted, "Never mind, I'll buy something from the next salesman." He kissed her again with such passionate intensity, she lost her balance when he released her from his embrace and fell backwards onto the bed.

"How forward of you," he baited. They playfully removed their shirts and hastily tossed them aside. He gathered her in his arms and while lost in the loving warmth of his embrace, he whispered, "I'm so in love with you."

Pulling away, she gazed into his eyes, tenderly caressed his face, and provoked, "I know."

He chuckled, "Oh, you know?" He started tickling her and they laughed, wrestling around until his tickles changed to kisses. He tenderly kissed the barely visible scar above her heart, gazed up at her and whispered, "Who are you?"

She awoke with a gasp on her bunk. *Well, at least this one had been about them together. She'd also been dreaming of him bedding other women. Those ones were more like nightmares.* Kayn swung her legs over the side, stepped off and strolled over to the fridge to pour herself a glass of juice.

The whole group was playing cards at the table. Frost looked up from his hand when she wandered into the room and asked, "Are you okay?"

She was a little shocked he'd spoken to her. She replied, "I'm fine," before wandering back to bed.

Frost followed her to her bunk, saying, "No. You're not."

Kayn sat on her bed as she answered, "It was just a bad dream. It's not a big deal, honestly."

Frost leaned against the bunks across the narrow hall. With concern in his eyes, he suggested, "Drink your juice and pass me your glass. I'll bring it back to the sink."

She drank her juice and passed him the glass. Their fingers touched. His voice cracked with emotion as he whispered, "I'll get Zach."

Kayn got under the covers. *That was strange.*

Zach appeared. He climbed under the covers with her and gave her a giant bear hug as he whispered against her hair, "You had a bad dream? Want to talk about it?"

Feeling safe in his arms, she whispered, "I've been dreaming about Kevin. They always start out incredible, then go…Bad."

"What do you mean by bad?" Zach whispered.

The warmth of his breath against her hair tickled. Kayn smiled before she began her confession, "Sometimes, I see him with someone else. In other dreams, he asks me who I am." She turned in bed to face Zach. *It looked like he wanted to say something. He didn't have to. She knew that's what Kevin was probably doing. It made her heart ache.*

Gently stroking her hair, Zach whispered, "You can't obsess over this anymore. It's not healthy. From what I understand, erased in Clan lingo is as good as gone. The guy you were in love with no longer exists but we're here and we all love you. He's moved on. You should too. I dare you to flirt with someone tomorrow. You have to try to move forward in life. Just take baby steps until you feel like you're ready to take normal ones." Zach snuggled up and didn't say anything else. They just went to sleep.

The next afternoon they arrived at a motel where they would all get a break from bunkbeds. Kayn was sharing a room with Zach and Mel. They ordered a pizza and watched movies until everyone decided it was time to go to bed. Zach was singing over whooshing spray while having a long overdue shower. Not ready to sleep, Kayn walked out into a starry night's welcoming breeze in a tank top and shorts. As she leaned over the railing with a view of the courtyard and saw Frost, hand in hand with a beautiful brunette. Pausing to whisper something in her ear, he arrived at the top before she could dive back into her room unseen. *Crap.* Frozen like a deer in headlights with every hair on end, she couldn't peel her eyes away even for the sake of being polite, as he kissed the curvy brunette against the building.

He opened the door for his friend. As she went inside, Frost noticed her. With a mischievous grin, he flirted, "You want to come?"

Wide eyed as her cheeks heated, she didn't have a comeback. *He was toying with her.*

Looking for her, Zach wandered out, asking, "Why are you outside?"

"I needed fresh air," Kayn explained, as Frost vanished into his room, closing the door.

Containing his smile, as he caught on, Zach whispered, "Don't let him mess with you, Brighton. He gets off on it."

She knew he did. With X-rated sound effects next door making it awkward, she slipped past, climbed into bed with Mel, and screamed into a pillow as Zach locked the door.

Laughing before she opened her eyes, Mel sighed, "Is Frost playing games with you again?"

"Our Kayn is a deep shade of burgundy," Zach volunteered, getting into the other bed alone.

"Frost needs a room on another floor if he's planning to entertain locals," Mel sighed.

"So, always then," Zach bantered.

Mel teased, "Don't smother yourself, Brighton."

That would be one way to get to sleep.

From the next bed, Zach teased, "Awe muffin. Did the big bad naughty wolf of Ankh turn you on?"

"Cut it out you two," Kayn grumbled into the pillow, trying to block out the visions of what Frost was involved in a few rooms away. *He drove her insane but it sounded like he was having fun.*

"Stop thinking so loudly Kayn," Zach mumbled. "I'm trying to pretend the girl's screaming my name."

"Don't be gross, Zach," Mel murmured.

Kayn giggled as he complained, "You girls are horrible for my ego."

Switching beds, Mel snuggling with Zach, saying, "You are incredibly hot. If we were allowed, I'd be into you."

Zach whispered, "Seriously?"

"Sure, why not?" Mel replied.

She was full of shit. They both thought of him as a brother.

"You're a horrible liar, Mel," Zach whispered.

Cuddling him, Mel whispered, "I'm sure Kayn would be into you too."

Zach turned to Kayn and she winked. Between Frost's hookup and Mel lying next to him, Zach was beginning to look uncomfortable.

He whispered, "All right, Mel. Get back into bed with Kayn."

There were glitches in their sibling-esque relationship. You could turn on a monastery with the sound effects coming from Frost's room. Zach was a teenage boy so it didn't take a lot. Covering her head with a pillow to muffle Frost's escapades, she went to sleep.

Adrift in Chloe's memories, she was sprawled in lush grass beneath a glorious ceiling of stars with Frost feathering lusty kisses on her stomach. Watching him make love to her twin as a participant blurred the line between Chloe's memories and her own secret desires. Goosebumps rose on every inch of flesh as he inched lower. She moaned as ripples of pleasure left ration in the rearview. A faint voice lured her out of the fantasy. Kayn awoke, humming with pleasure. *He wanted her. He wanted Chloe. She wasn't Chloe.*

Stroking her hair, Mel whispered, "You were talking in your sleep."

"Moaning. You were moaning in your sleep. Good morning, Brighton," Zach teased, tossing a pillow at her.

She squinted in the sunlight accosting her eyes as it streamed through the sheer curtains. *Was it seriously morning? Awkward. She knew what she'd been dreaming about.* Side glances spoke volumes as they packed in silence. *She wanted to say she didn't want him. It was her sister's memories. It was just a stupid dream. There was no point in denial.* Opting to act like it wasn't a big deal, she excused herself. *She needed a shower.*

Standing under the intense spray, imagining Frost behind her running soapy fingers all over her body, she snapped out of it. *What in the hell is wrong with me?* She turned the nozzle to cold. Squealing when it was colder than expected, she laughed. *All she needed was a cold shower. What a cliché.* Kayn got out and vigorously towel-dried her hair. Moist curls stuck to her back as she struggled into her shorts and tank top. Quickly putting on a touch of makeup, Kayn wandered out. Her friends were gone. Frost was sitting on the bed waiting for her. *Ignore him. Pretend he isn't even there.*

Grinning as she marched past without acknowledging him, Frost got up, offering, "I'm here to be a gentleman. Zach said you needed help with your bags."

Zach, you enormous asshole. Kayn turned around and provoked, "Now, that's funny. Using your name and gentleman in the same sentence." *She only had one backpack. She didn't need his help for anything.* Holding it up, she stated, "I only have one bag." He held out his hand, offering to carry it for her. Swinging it over her shoulder, she baited, "No thanks. I know where your hands have been." *What was wrong with her?*

"I washed my hands when I had a shower this morning," Frost toyed, grinning.

She fought the overwhelming urge to jump on top of him and beat him senseless with her backpack. *That dream messed her up. She was acting like a jealous ex-girlfriend. Theoretically, she was sort of a jealous dead girlfriend.* Looking in the mirror as she passed it, Kayn thought, *down Chloe.*

Glancing back at her, he said, "What did you just say?"

He'd heard her damn inner dialogue. Needing him out of thought range, she practically ran down the stairs to get away from him. They piled into the RV. Everyone stowed their bags under the bunks. *She felt jealous. Her inner Chloe reared her head for the first time, and she was pissed right off.* She manoeuvered by Frost in the hallway.

He grabbed her arm, whispering, "You're mad at me."

With her twin's pageant smile, Kayn coldly responded, "Why would I be mad?"

Without letting go of her arm, his grasp to loosened, slipping to her wrist. Pulling her closer, he whispered, "What did I do?"

Why was he touching her? He'd barely spoken to her. Smiling at his attempt to understand her hostility, she fought the urge to stomp on his foot.

His predictable inner douche teased, "You could have joined us."

Oh, that would have been the perfect first time.

Wide eyed, Frost blurted, "No way. I assumed you and Smith sealed the deal."

Damn her inner dialogue. She scolded, "Stop listening to my thoughts Frost. I need to get by you. Seriously, I have to go to the bathroom."

Intrigued by her behaviour, he taunted, "Go then. Nobody's stopping you."

What she truly needed was for him to let go of her. He was holding her wrist with one hand, gently stroking her pulse point with his finger. *What's going on? She felt like she was going crazy. He must be doing something to her with his gift. He was making her want him.* With her eyes glued to the curve of his lips, she remembered how they felt trailing kisses. Looking at the floor, she forced ration. *He wasn't kissing her. Those were Chloe's memories. She wasn't Chloe. She wasn't Chloe. They could never be together. He would speak and she'd end up smothering him with a pillow. Frost was a horrible idea. What was she thinking?* Suffering from an overabundance of common sense, kept her from having as much fun as the others. She forcibly pushed past him and he let her go.

Kayn shut the bathroom door. Catching her breath, where he'd been stroking her wrist was tingling. Caressing her pulse point with her thumb, she held her wrist to her heart, knowing Chloe wasn't going to stay dormant. *She wasn't going to be able to hide this. He was going to find out she had Chloe's memories. If he hadn't already put two and two together, he would.* Pointed a finger at her reflection, she scolded, "You're making this difficult, Chloe." Hiding until she calmed down, using the toilet as a chair with tires humming beneath her feet, she waited a decent amount of time before sucking it up and venturing out. Aware she wasn't even fooling herself anymore, she avoided Frost.

They drove for hours, only stopping for lunch and gas. Everyone settled into their usual routine of playing cards and watching movies. When they switched to gaming, she opted to read a book. Endless driving was painfully sedating. Finding it difficult to focus, she snuggled under the covers to recharge her battery and drifted off with Chloe's sexy time with Frost in the In-between playing like an R -rated movie.

Stroking her hair, Frost whispered in her ear, "You're talking in your sleep."

She awoke a deer in the headlights to his grin. *There was no time to hide her true feelings. He'd read them loud and clear. This* was *the moment that would start their seductive tango. There was one giant problem. Kayn couldn't dance her way out of a paper bag…*

After an awkward silence, Frost whispered, "You remember being with me, don't you?"

Kayn whispered her reply, "It was a dream. I could have one about Grey tomorrow night."

Reading on his bunk, Grey teased, "I hope you do. It sounded like a steamy one."

Shimming off her bunk, she took off. With limited places to hide, she yanked on the bathroom door, stammering, "Come on. Seriously?" Frost followed her. The door opened. Mel shimmied by with a giant grin. Kayn attempted to slink into the bathroom but Frost shoved her inside and shut the door. They stood there breathing and staring at each other. *Every nerve ending was screaming at her to close that space between them.*

Frost whispered, "Listen... I always manage to say the wrong thing where you're concerned. I know you're Kayn. I know you're not Chloe. I just want to know if you share her memories. Tell me you don't feel anything when you're with me and I'll never ask again."

Chloe wasn't a separate entity anymore. Confused about what her sister's feelings meant, she was desperate to keep her life as uncomplicated as possible. *She didn't want to have these feelings. Not for him. She wasn't stupid. In the dictionary under the word player, there was probably a smiling picture of him.*

Frost whispered, "Now, that's not nice. I understand why you don't want to care about me. Yes, it would probably be complicated, but I assure you my name is not under player in the dictionary."

Kayn asserted, "Stop listening to my private thoughts."

"We're in a confined space and you are thinking loudly," Frost sparred.

"I had a racy dream, that's all it was. It was just a dream," she explained. *She could tell he didn't believe her.* She looked at her feet, anything to avoid the gravitational pull of his eyes.

Touching her chin, he tilted it up so she was looking at him and disclosed, "You are far too intelligent to fall for me. I just didn't think you could want me back... As you. That's all I meant by that."

His lips hovered a breath from hers. *He was going to kiss her. She wanted him to.* He saw the desire in her eyes and grinned as he stepped away from her, opened the bathroom door and abruptly walked away. *Damn him.*

While rehearsing telling him off in the mirror, the ground began to shake beneath her feet. *They were driving on gravel. They must be stopping to eat. This was horrible timing.* Holding onto her rituals of humanity, she put her curls in a ponytail and applied some sparkle coconut lotion to her arms and legs.

Making her way down the tiny hall, she pushed her way out of the door into a cloud of parking lot dust. She coughed and covered her eyes, she followed the others, avoiding eye contact with Frost as she approached. *He was like a cat with a toy. She'd have to face this awkward situation head-on. He enjoyed teasing her. She couldn't help but wonder how far he would take it now that he suspected she wanted him back. How far did she want him to take it?*

Chapter 6

Burgers, Shakes And A Side Order Of Phobias

He was still grinning at her as they congregated at the entrance of the small highway diner to read the menu on the door. She looked away as a car pulled out of the parking lot. *They'd been travelling for days without stopping. It felt unbelievable to stretch her legs. She needed to go for a run.* She watched the cloud of dust flow behind the car as it disappeared into the distance. *The diner was similar to the one they had lunch at yesterday.*

"After you ladies," Frost announced, politely opening the door. They all walked through, except for Kayn. She turned to catch his amused gaze. "Don't even think about running, it's time to eat," Frost teased.

She should go for a run. What was he going to do? Chase her?

"You remind me of one of those finger traps. You're difficult to figure out," he confessed with a smirk.

She had no idea what he was talking about. Was that an insult?

"It's a compliment on your originality," he chuckled still holding the door.

Kayn purposely brushed by him as she passed, making eye contact without shyly looking away. She could tell by his fascination, he'd taken her forward behaviour as a dare. *It was like she was playing a game of chess and she only knew how to play checkers.* He walked behind her as she slid into the booth next to Lexy.

Frost left her at the table, saying, "You know what I want. I'll be right back."

Peering up from the menu, her thoughts flickering through memories of Kevin. *They were always joking about horror movies.* The ominous phrase, *'I'll be right back,'* was often said in retrospect to horror movie folklore. This token quote had been used in every B horror movie since 1970. It was far less ominous when you knew you could never die. The entire premise of horror movies gave her little to quiver over now. Kayn shifted in the booth. Wincing as her thighs stuck to the pleather bench seat, she glanced around, and inconspicuously pealed her legs off and shimmied over to give herself elbow room, so she could eat without taking out the person next to her.

Reading the names of dishes on the menu, she couldn't help but grin. This was one of those campy roadside diners that had downright weird and funky names for everything. Even the downright normal was made exciting and new with funny pun or play on words, The Hell of a Gut Bustable Combustible Burger. *Frost would order that one for sure.* Someone used a loud blender. *Something random always reminded her of the family she'd lost or Kevin. She wasn't the only one. Melody was staring at little boys across the diner eating ice-cream with their mother. It was an unspoken rule. They never brought up the moments before their Sweet Sleep. It was difficult to concentrate on the good in each day when you were busy soaking up every ounce of joy in your afterlife with the happiness sucking sponge of devastation and loss. There was no point in living in the past. It already happened.* Kayn glanced up as the waitress asked for her order. Being a creature of habit, she always ordered one of three things. She requested a Grill 'em Up Batterless Chicken Burger with a side salad and dill dressing.

Squirming in her seat, Lily declared, "Let me do it. I bet I can guess them all."

"Okay shoot," Grey chuckled, putting his menu down.

Lily raised her brows, scanned the page and began to speak, "Grey will have a Humongous Beef Brawler Steak Sandwich. He always says rare, but he wants it medium. He'll throw a hissy fit if it's still bleeding. He would like that with poutine and a beer, preferably honey ale. Mel wants a Funky Chicken Caesar Salad and one of those giant silver blender milkshakes that I see on the counter over there. Strawberry. Frost wants the grossest double burger patty, wiener filled heart attack in a bun on the menu. So, that will be the ..." She scanned the menu. "Oh, unquestionably, the Hell of a Gut Bustable Combustible Burger and a beer. He could care less if it's draft. Now, Lexy can be tricky, but she will order the same thing as someone else at the table. Okay, I know. She will have a Grill 'em Up Batterless Chicken Burger with poutine and a chocolate milk shake." They all burst out laughing.

She looked at Zach. He directed, "Oh, I'll have exactly what Lexy ordered."

"I'll have one of those too," Lily said, grinning.

Frost got side-tracked by a swooning girl on the way back from the bathroom. He managed to escape and make it back to the booth. He slid in next to Lily, kicked Melody under the table and stated, "I bet you three all got the same thing again?"

"Sort of," Melody chuckled and glanced at Lily.

Lily put her arm around Frost, gave him a half hug and revealed, "You got a version of your favourite burger." Frost was always on an endless personal mission to find the most incredible burger and pizza parlour in the world.

Grey made a plane out of the drink flyer and flew it at Frost's forehead, "It's my feet you are playing footsies with, by the way."

"Sorry to disappoint you but it's not me. I know you love it when I touch you like that," Frost chuckled.

A moment went by and Grey's eyebrows raised again. He threw a sugar pack at Frost, "Cut it out! You're creeping me out man!"

Looking up from the drink menu, Frost frowned, saying, "I'm not playing footsies with you, Chuckles."

Obviously Grey could still feel something tickling his leg. He glared at the next usual suspect and teased, "Listen Lily, no means no."

"Do try to get over it Grey. I'm afraid that ship has sailed," Lexy sparred.

"Okay, not funny. That was halfway up my leg," Grey accused as his eyes widened.

"Oh Shit!" he squealed and hissed, "Get out of the booth! Get out! Oh, my God! There is something furry in my pants!"

"That's what she said," Zach whispered.

Everyone was howling laughing as Grey began to squeal, "Oh crap! Oh crap!" To the other patrons' astonishment, he undid his pants, squeamishly struggled out, and left them in a bundle on the floor. Wearing nothing but sexy underwear, Grey squealed, "Oh, shit! Shit!" His pants moved and out from under them crawled the largest black rat she'd ever laid eyes on. Shrieking like a terrified child, Grey leapt on his seat with everyone hysterically laughing to the point of crying. "I'm out of here!" Grey stammered, "That grotesque creature was in my pants!"

"That's what she said," Frost chuckled.

The waitress picked up the rat, apologizing, "Sorry. It's the owner's kid's pet. He must have gotten out. It's not a wild rat or anything. It's just a house pet."

"Your pet was in my pants!" Grey hissed causing a sputter of laughter while everyone was trying to stop.

Zach whispered, "That's what ..."

Raising a hand, Grey threatened, "Finish that sentence, and I will kill you in your sleep."

As the waitress walked away with cat sized rodent in her arms, the Dragon of Ankh consoled her Handler, "Sit down, sweetie. The big bad rat is gone."

Remaining where he was, Grey mimicked, "Just a house pet." Intensely staring at the waitress, her skirt fell off. She squealed and ran into the backroom without letting go of the rat.

Lexy yanked Grey back down on the bench seat, scolding, "You're a grown up. Was that necessary?"

Innocently, Grey baited, "I'll give her a good tip."

Zach sparred, "Just the...?"

Scowling at Zach, Lexy stated, "I'll kill you my damn self if you finish that bloody sentence."

"That made my month. Hell, that made my year," Frost whispered, grinning.

Lexy shot him a dirty look. The waitress showed up with their meals and fully clothed. She handed Grey his meal first. He stared at his plate for a minute. Kayn suspected, he wanted to walk away and refuse to eat it but knew nobody was going to follow him out of the restaurant. They were all too hungry. Mental note: *All mighty and powerful fire making warrior Grey was deathly afraid of rodents.*

They finished lunch and took a minute too stretch their legs before getting back in the RV. Wandering to the back, Kayn sprawled on a pillow on the floor. Zach and Mel were quick to fling themselves down beside her. The vehicle began to move. While lying on the floor it was ten times bumpier. They giggled as their bodies shook with the rhythm of the uneven parking lot.

Melody let out a sheep like vibrato, "Ahahahaha."

They all immaturely copied her, laughing until they were on smooth pavement.

Zach grinned and said, "Should I say something, or do you want to Mel?"

They were going to give her crap for being in the bathroom alone with Frost. Kayn stared at Zach and prodded, "Well, spit it out?"

"Go take a look in the mirror," Zach whispered.

Humouring him, Kayn got up and wandered to the bathroom. Taking in her reflection, she smiled. *How does this always happen? She was covered in dust. It was stuck to her skin in clumps. There was even a streak on her forehead and across her cheek. Awesome. This is just perfect.* It didn't take much to deduce how she'd come to exhibit her comical appearance. *She'd put lotion on and walked out into a cloud of floating dust.* She cleaned it off with a washcloth and came out of the bathroom just as the RV went over a bump. She lost her footing and fell into Frost's arms.

He teased, "Stop hitting on me, Brighton."

She shoved him away and went into the back, mumbling, "In your dreams."

Frost chuckled, "No. In your dreams." He shut the bathroom. Kayn tossed a pillow at the door in the hallway.

Melody got up and grabbed the pillow, threw it back at Kayn and ribbed, "Do you know what this is? It's foreplay."

Zach smacked Kayn in the face with his pillow and said, "Don't do it man. Not that guy."

Joking around, Kayn propped herself up on her side, looked at Zach and comically enquired, "Why not?"

Melody butt scooted to a pillow beside her and whispered, "I'm all for it. Stop pining, start living." Zach sighed and added nothing else in response.

They drove for a few more hours before deciding to stop for the day. Kayn, Melody, Grey and Zach were sitting at the table playing Scrabble as Frost strolled by wearing a plaid shirt. They kept playing. Kayn was the Scrabble champion. She may pass out first but she was the one who got all of the Scrabble glory. Frost gave her an idea for a word as he strutted by and she grinned.

"Oh, watch out. Brighton's got a good one," Grey taunted.

Zach glanced up, looked at Frost and teased, "Do you have a plaid shirt I can borrow?"

While looking through the fridge, Frost glanced back, winked, and sparred, "Not everyone can pull off this shirt kid."

"Let me rephrase the question for you," Zach countered. "Why are you wearing that plaid shirt?"

"You mean you don't like it?" Frost chuckled. He held up a beer. Grey nodded, Frost opened it and passed it to him and added, "We're in cowboy country. Women love this shirt."

Kayn could appreciate the shirt. Frost tried to grab another one out of the fridge and it rolled onto the floor. He bent over to grab for it in front of Kayn.

Zach elbowed her. *Whoops, she was staring.*

"I have my word. It's peacock," Zach announced. He looked at Kayn and enquired, "What's yours? I know you have one."

Kayn turned her board around and they all laughed. Her word was… Superficial.

Frost leaned across the table and playfully threatened, "I should put you over my knee and spank you."

Kayn smiled sweetly and dared, "I'd like to see you try."

Frost teased, "Are you trying to flirt with me, Froggy?"

She had an almost cool moment for a second there.

In the weeks that followed, a plastic rat mysteriously showed up everywhere, in Grey's bed under his covers and in the shower of his hotel room. It appeared on his bunk in the RV and in the truck while he was driving. Eventually, Grey stopped squealing every time he saw it. He angrily launched it at Frost and Zach each time he came across it. It had never been Zach or Frost, it was her. Frost suspected her but couldn't prove it. *Kayn had one hell of a poker face. She used it every time she looked at Frost.*

Chapter 7

The Secrets We Keep

Kayn stared out the window as the tires whirled monotonously down the highway. There was off key humming to music from various headphones. Snickers as someone belted out a chorus into the almost silent air space. Shuffling of paper from turned pages. These sounds were as familiar as her Clan member's voices. With the clicking of the signal, the vehicle abruptly turned and the tires crackled. She guessed they'd arrived at one of a possible thousand convenience stores along the seemingly endless highway. A gas station perhaps, as she heard the ding from the pump. Before the RV had come to a complete stop Lily left the passenger seat up front and began fumbling with the lock on the door. It could be claustrophobic with the hours upon hours they spent together in close confines. There were only so many games of Fish, Twenty-one and Monopoly one could play. They took turns driving the two vehicles. That meant four people were awake at any given time, so they slept in shifts. If they were lucky, they had the opportunity to stop somewhere for the night so they could all have a semblance of normalcy.

As Zach followed Lily out, he hollered, "Does anybody need anything from the store?"

"We need more orange juice and cereal," Lexy answered.

Zach replied, "I'll look. If they don't have anything good, we'll stop at a real grocery store later."

She shifted the curtains aside to see where they were. She honestly couldn't tell. It was rather nondescript scenery. Usually there were mountains or flat for as far as her eye could see. She enjoyed people watching. There wasn't much else to do between jobs. Lily and Grey could be a downright comical combination. Grey had been her Mr. Right Now, not Mr. Forever. They passed each other in the parking lot, bags in hand. It had been a long time, but they still wouldn't even utter a simple good morning to each other. This was an excellent example of why dating a co-worker was a bad idea. It was still done though. They were together all the time and hormones happen. Only when the Clan's Oracle stepped in and said, 'No way' was it forbidden. Maybe Frost had been warned to stay away from her? Perhaps, over the course of a thousand years he'd learned to guard his heart diligently and it wasn't worth the risk? He'd worn his feelings on his sleeve during their conversation in the bathroom. Now, they had this weird passive aggressive thing going on. He'd continued flirting with her as per usual but hadn't pushed it further. He also hadn't been with anyone else since he found out she'd been dreaming of him. He'd left her alone with her thoughts and she had plenty rolling around her squeaky, empty hamster wheel of a brain.

Kayn glanced across the room. Melody was sitting there staring at her laptop, deep in thought. She'd spend hours looking at images of her old property. She read the online newspaper from where she used to live daily but never shared anything about it. They all had their strange rituals. The past was the past and they managed to leave it there for the most part. Mel smiled as she read whatever graced her laptop's screen. Lexy was sprawled on her bunk, mesmerized by a book.

The door opened and they all looked up. *It was Grey.* Looking exhausted, he smiled and tossed a bag of Ketchup chips at Melody. *That was sweet.* Mel looked up from the computer and smiled at him. Grey walked past the others without even speaking and collapsed on his bunk. *She was always a little disappointed when Grey opted out of speaking. He had the best accent in the world. Australian had been her first guess but occasionally, he sounded Scottish. There was a story behind that. She never tired of his voice.*

Lexy sat up, sighed, and made her way to the driver's seat. It was her turn to drive the RV.

Frost walked in, locking the door behind him. He handed her the bag with the juice in it. No cereal, but an enormous jug of orange juice. Kayn held onto it perturbed. *What the hell, Frost? He could have walked one foot and put it in the fridge by himself. She opted out of complaining because she hadn't learned how to drive yet.* He climbed onto his bunk, stretched out and smiled at her mischievously, before laying his head on his pillow and shutting his eyes. Kayn made her way up to the cupboard and grabbed glasses. She poured Lexy and herself a glass of orange juice, before putting the jug in the fridge and steadied herself as the RV began to pull out. The tires crackled through the gravel before whirling down the highway again. Kayn sat beside Lexy without words and handed her a glass of orange juice.

Lexy took a drink before placing it in the holder and saying, "Thanks, Hun."

This was the usual deal. Kayn didn't drive but that didn't mean she wasn't expected to keep the person who was driving comfortable. Kayn entertained Lexy with jokes from her cell phone. She spent a lot of time with Lexy but she was a mystery to her. Lexy was beautiful and as tough as nails in a fight. In day-to-day life, the Clan's infamous Dragon was a firecracker of comedy, not violence. Lexy always had a weird joke or hilarious story about something she'd seen online. A tale about someone she'd met in a store or randomly on the street. There was never guy drama where Lexy was concerned. Perhaps, she was just smart enough to know it wasn't the brightest idea to get into a relationship with someone you could never break up with. Literally ever, as Grey and Lily found out. Truth be told it was Grey and almost everyone else. Lily, Arrianna and Melody, if their brief half-hour-long fling even counted.

Kayn glanced at Lexy. *She knew Grey was Lexy's Handler but wasn't sure what that meant. She suspected their relationship was more than just friendship. There was real love there, she'd seen it.* She'd been tempted to ask on various occasions but always decided against it, afraid of accidentally inciting drama. She watched the scenery whirl by for a few more minutes. Kayn felt eyes on her and turned to see Lexy smiling. *Damn inner dialogue.*

They heard a honking horn. Zach was waving from the truck in front of them. *What a goofball. Zach wasn't the classically hot guy, but he had this strange mixture of likability and goofiness that made you want to be near him.* He overzealously waved. Lexy shook her head. Coolly unrolled the driver's side window, she gave him the finger. *Zach had a long hard road to forgiveness with her. The crimson-haired warrior was usually plotting a warped revenge scenario in her mind.* It always made Kayn smile. *It is always advantageous to have something to look forward to in life, even if that something is a wicked deplorable act of self-satisfying revenge.*

They went over a bump and Lexy's glass of orange juice was saved by Kayn's reflexes. Her act of orange juice heroism was followed by a smile from Lexy. She was surprised she'd caught it. *Her reflexes were usually more like a drunken circus clown than a stealthy feline.* She recalled Frost's taunts about her having the reflexes of a blind hammered moose. *She felt like that a lot. He'd been an asshole but he wasn't wrong.* She giggled aloud at her own thoughts.

Lexy gave her a strange look and chuckled, "I'm afraid to ask what you're laughing about. With you, it could be anything."

Kayn stretched in her seat as she replied, "I was imagining myself as a blind hammered moose."

Lexy momentarily stifled her smile. It escaped as she teased, "My point exactly."

The long miles of highway whirled at a stomach-churning rate in her peripheral vision. *She had to look straight ahead but something would always draw her attention to the blur. Wasn't that a perfect observation on life?* This was the calm before the storm. This time was about learning to embrace what she was destined to become, training in the in-between, long monotonous days of driving, sleeping and overthinking everything. *There was far too much time to think.* Her thoughts kept travelling back to the night Frost appeared all cocky and shirtless in her room. *He'd changed her life the night he'd branded her Ankh. He'd given her a ticket to this warped, magnificent rollercoaster ride. She kept telling herself everyone was attracted to Frost. It didn't mean anything. Kevin was another story. She couldn't shake the feeling that their love was now a mirage only she could see. He wasn't waiting for her. Waiting for him was beginning to feel like standing on the highway waiting to get smoked by a car. She could make a choice to get out of the way. Logic told her to stop romanticizing something that had no hope of becoming anything. She would see him again and it wouldn't matter. She wasn't a naive dumbass. Well, she wasn't a dumbass. She was tired of withering away holding onto memories of a person that was no longer. He was carrying on with no recollection of what they'd lost. She was beginning to accept Kevin's absence as irreversible. Perhaps, that was the first step in moving on.*

While lost in revolutions, the sun vanished, surrendering to dusk and it was time to switch drivers. With heavy eyes, Kayn wandered to her bunk. *Frost had to get up with Grey, it was their turn.* With her head on her pillow and only a few feet separating their bunks, she watched him, entertaining the idea. *Was the pull she felt just confusion over having her twin's memories? How was she supposed to know?*

Frost opened one eye and groggily whispered, "A penny for your thoughts?"

If he'd given one up, each time he recited that phrase, he'd owe twenty bucks. Kayn snuggled under the blanket, continuing to look into his eyes. He tossed something on her bed. She grabbed for it. *It was one of those fake rings from a bubble gum machine.* She held the ring up to get a good look and smiled as she said, "Cute. Where did you get this?"

He winked at her and replied, "In the gas station earlier. I also got a chocolate bar."

"You didn't get me one?" She teased, touched by his gift.

Frost responded, "I'm having a hard time figuring out what you want."

So am I. Kayn bit her lip and whispered, "Sweet dreams." She turned to face the other direction, staring at the plastic ring with a fake topaz stone. *He'd made her day.* She heard him quietly laughing.

Leaning over her bunk, Frost whispered in her ear, "It's my turn to drive. Sweet dreams to you." He tucked a loose strand of hair behind her ear and softly kissed her cheek. Her heart flip-flopped. Kayn didn't move a muscle until he'd walked away. She hid her smile with her hand. She wanted to squeal but knew someone would hear.

From the bunk above Frost's, Lexy's voice whispered, "For the record, that's an exceptionally bad idea."

Still grinning, Kayn whispered back, "I know." She stared at the ring. *It was her birthstone. He'd loved her sister. He would have paid attention to the little things. Her little things were the same. That had to be convenient. She had Chloe's memories. What if she was also feeling her emotions? Was she just lonely? Why did Frost have to be this hot?* She looked at the silly gift. *The ring came out of a machine. He probably stuck a quarter in on a whim. She was reading too much into this.* She held it to her lips. *Full grown adult men don't give girls bubble gum machine rings. It was just a cute gesture.* She drifted into one of her sister's memories. Frost was holding a buttercup to his chin humouring Chloe, seducing her with his eyes. He trailed his fingers seductively down the length of her arm, slowly along the soft skin on her upper thigh. She shivered and sighed.

"You're having graphic dreams again, Brighton," Zach chuckled.

What time is it? How long had she been asleep? Why had they stopped moving? She smacked Zach in the face with her pillow.

He climbed up on her bunk next to her and said, "Don't kill the messenger. I'm just trying to be a friend."

She confided in him, "I'm dreaming of Chloe's memories but it feels like they're mine, along with her emotions. It's confusing. It started that night at the hotel and hasn't stopped. I'm afraid if I give in to what she wants, she'll take over and I won't be me anymore. I love Kevin. Chloe loves Frost, but truthfully, I don't have any idea what I want. In a perfect world, I'd be with Kevin but Frost is… I'm…"

Zach massaged her shoulder, assuring, "You're trying to hold onto the person you were before you died. That girl's gone. Kevin's gone too Kayn. I was Triad. I've seen people have their memories erased. I'd never want to hurt you but I promise you, the guy you loved, he's long gone."

She knew that. She had to let Kevin go. She winked at Zach and teased, "Our platonic love can last forever."

Zach grinned and declared, "Always." He gave her a bear hug and with his chin resting on her shoulder, he sighed, "I'd never want to lose you or Melody. I know you ladies find me difficult to resist but you're going to have to find a way to control yourselves."

Grey leapt on top of them. He hugged them both, squishing them as he chuckled, "I love you too, man. Isn't this beautiful? All of this platonic love."

"Grey, I can't breathe. You're squishing me." Kayn laughed.

Zach choked out, "Grey that's my ass you're pinching."

"It's not my fault. You have a lady butt," Grey chuckled.

Zach socked Grey in the stomach and began wrestling with him defending his manhood. Kayn was giggling under a pile of guys when Melody wandered around the corner and piped in, "Trying something new?"

Grey grabbed her wrist and yanked her onto the bunk with them cackling, "Smart asses get platonically loved around here."

He gave her a birdie. In five seconds, it looked like she'd back combed her hair. They were laughing, trying to squirm away.

As Lexy shimmied down the narrow hall past flailing arms and legs, she sighed, "It's way too early in the morning for this crap." She dramatically slammed the bathroom door.

Frost paused by the group of idiots wrestling, shook his head and continued to the bathroom. He yanked on the door.

Lexy's voice called out, "It's busy!"

"I really have to go, Lex," Frost complained.

Annoyed, Lexy replied, "Go outside. We're camping. You're a guy. Pee on a damn tree."

Frost paused by the group of wrestling teens and remarked, "Should I even ask?"

Grey replied from on top of the dog pile, "It's a platonic love fest."

"Good idea, keeping it platonic," Frost teased and then added, "Does anyone else need to use the bathroom. I have to go look for another one."

Kayn piped in, "I need too." They rolled off her. She grabbed her makeup bag and got up. Wearing shorts and a tank top from the day before with a rather hilarious unkempt lion's mane, she slipped on her shoes and followed him outside.

Lily was setting up a tarp over the picnic table. She casually commented, "That's a good look for you hun."

Kayn clicked in and patted down her hair.

"Hold still," Frost instructed as he tried to tame her birdy, grinned and teased, "You need to wet it down. Let's go find the bathroom Froggy. You'll scare campers wandering around like that."

His nickname was never funny but at this moment she felt like a frog. She looked at him and sarcastically mocked, "Ribbit."

Cracking a giant grin, he asserted, "Give me your hand." He slipped the elastic band off her wrist and put her hair back in a messy ponytail. He caressed a loose tendril, his fingers brushed her cheek as he declared, "I always thought Grey had a wacked out sense of humour but you've officially won… Ribbit?" Frost shook his head and started walking.

Morning's welcoming rays shone through the branches, creating magical streams of sunlight. The birds sang their chorus from the trees and the slow rhythmic chirping of crickets came with every third step of their feet. *Just another one of those odd things you notice with heightened senses. His butt looked amazing in those jeans. Her attraction to him annoyed her almost as much as that condescending nickname. She wanted to smack him with a stick. Now was as good a time as any.* She bent down, picked up a stick from the trail and poked sexy Frost's butt.

He turned and complained, "What in the hell, Brighton?"

She enquired, "Is that how you see me? Chloe was the princess and I'm the frog."

Visibly offended, he revealed, "That's ridiculous. I shortened it. There was a sticker on your face when we met. It wasn't Chloe I was rooting for the night of your Correction. It was you. When it was time for the Clan to claim you, I didn't have a chance. You were already in love with somebody else. Do yourself a favour, stop selling yourself short. You're amazing. You always have been. Just as you are."

It was the most incredible thing anyone had ever said to her and it came from Frost.

"The bathroom is over there," he pointed it out, shaking his head as he disappeared into the men's washroom.

There was a wheelchair accessible sign on the women's door so she had to shove it. *It was weighted to close on its own, which made it more difficult for someone in a wheelchair not less. It was a pet peeve.* She looked at her refection. It was worse than she thought, even after being fixed by Frost. She smiled. *He'd been rooting for her on the night of her Correction.* She quickly brushed her teeth, washed her face, put on a touch of makeup, dampened her curls and rushed out before he left without her. *He wasn't outside. Maybe he'd already left?* She placed her ear up against the door to the men's room. She couldn't hear anyone in there. *She should make sure before just walking away.* As Kayn pushed the door, Frost hollered, "You're about to get an eye full Brighton."

She cracked it, apologising, "Sorry, I thought maybe you left without me." She leaned against it. *Just one cool moment, is that so much to ask for?* She stepped away.

He stuck his head out and provoked, "Quit apologising Brighton. So, you wanted to see me naked. Everybody does." He closed the door.

Kayn started laughing. *Just when she'd dared to think he was more than the pompous ass she'd always seen him as. He'd clarified the situation.* She started the trek back to the campsite, heard his footsteps but didn't turn around.

Frost dramatically sighed, "What did I do now?"

She kept walking. *What an ass. This was funny as hell for him.*

Frost started to laugh, "I was kidding. It was a joke."

She continued ignoring the insufferable ass.

Frost's voice teased, "Is it difficult to walk fast with that stick up your ass?"

Kayn stopped, swung around to face him and hissed, "I don't know. Do people chase you around with wads of toilet paper because you're a piece of shit?"

He held up both hands to show he'd surrendered and toyed, "Good one, Brighton. Truce?" Taking advantage of her flustered state, he grabbed for her wrist.

She scolded, "Let me go, Frost. I'm not in the mood for your games."

He rubbed his thumb in a gentle circular motion on her wrist and seductively whispered, "You're tying yourself up in knots for no reason. You're always trying to pick a fight with me, it's exhausting." He yanked her towards him and forcibly held her against him as he whispered in her ear, "Lighten up. Have some fun today. I dare you." He released her from his embrace when she stopped struggling against it.

He was right. She got bent out of shape every time he opened his mouth. This was confusing as hell for her. She wasn't sure whether she wanted to kiss Frost or smack him over the side of the head with a shovel. Both options felt equally appealing. Kayn sucked in her confusing urges and responded, "You're right, I haven't been fair to you. You haven't been fair to me either. You've barely spoken to me. Do you have any idea what it felt like to have you following me everywhere I went, never saying a damn word? You stalked me for an entire year."

Frost cautiously replied, "I had to keep you safe. You needed time to attach to Zach and Melody. I was warned, you'd become too dependent. It's a complicated situation."

He was right. He'd barely spoken to her and she'd used the mere sight of him as a security blanket. She'd always needed to know he was close by. He both drove her insane and calmed her down.

He held out his hand and vowed, "I won't ignore you again."

If this was Grey or Zach, she wouldn't have hesitated but she still wanted to punch pretty boy Frost in the head. *They were playing a game of chess and it was her move. She wasn't certain it was the right one but he was Ankh. She was supposed to show him trust.* She laced her fingers with his. *It didn't kill her. His touch had quite the opposite effect.* The birds were chirping and the branches of the trees were moving a slow waltz in the morning breeze. They quietly strolled back together. A part of her kept whispering Kevin's name until she let go of Frost's hand. *She felt guilty for holding it.*

"I've seen you hold Grey's hand fifty times," Frost teased. "I guarantee Kevin's done a lot more than hold someone's hand. You know that, right?"

"I know," Kayn responded.

"Fair enough, I won't be offended. I'll just assume you're a little flighty," he baited. He started laughing as he teased, "See, that was a joke. Lighten up. Sometimes you just like people with no rational explanation. Stop overthinking everything. Do me a favour, for one day just try to have fun. Have a good time without worrying about the consequences. Nobody's going to let you do anything you'll regret." He held his hand out, his eyes beckoning her to take it.

She took it, knowing she was playing with fire. *Being with him felt exciting and more than a little dangerous.*

He stopped walking. Lifting their interlaced fingers to his lips, he kissed her hand, assuring, "Nobody is going to let me do anything you'll regret either." He let go of her hand just before they arrived.

Grey attempted to pass Frost a beer. Kayn snatched it away and said, "Morning Grey," as she downed the whole beer.

Grey grinned and taunted, "Should I just start holding your hair back right now?"

Melody stepped out of the RV and sighed, "Are we drinking beer at eight am… Seriously?"

Grey took a swig of his and declared, "Kayn started it."

Melody tossed in some ration, "If you start drinking at eight in the morning, you won't make it past noon."

Kayn smiled and countered, "I'm just having one. Then, I'm going swimming."

Zach whipped his shirt off, agreeing with her plans with action, "That's a brilliant idea. I'll race you to the water."

Grey stripped his off. Kayn hadn't put on a swimsuit but Frost dared her to cut loose. *Fine, you think I need to cut loose, watch and learn.* She tugged her tank top off and tossed it aside, leaving only her sports bra and shorts on as she raced the boys to the water. They saw the dock in the distance and sprinted for it. She ran down the centre and leapt off the end into the water. She came to the surface. *Crap! It was cold!* The rest of them came strolling down the length of the dock with the cooler full of beer. Grey lured them over to the hot tub and pool. *It wasn't a nice lake to swim in. It was slimy on the bottom.* They moved their gathering to the heated pool and hot tub. Kayn dove into the pool and swam the length of it under water. She came up on the other side almost in Frost's lap.

Frost was sitting on the edge of the pool. He chuckled, "I swear I didn't plan that."

She pivoted and swam to the other end. She heard the splash as he jumped in but didn't look back. When she reached the other end of the pool, she held onto it.

He appeared beside her and provoked, "It feels good to step out of your box. Doesn't it?"

Kayn smiled at Frost as she admitted, "You're right, I'm overthinking everything. Maybe it's time to have some fun?"

Taking full advantage of her declaration, Frost dared, "If I beat you to the other side, you have to rub my feet." He took off without giving her a chance to answer.

She beamed as she hollered, "That's cheating!" Even though she had no hope of winning, she still raced him to the other side. He beat her, and she knew she'd have to pay up. They all sat in the hot tub as Kayn rubbed Frost's feet. She looked into the immortal's eyes as she teased, "I thought your feet would be hotter."

Frost splashed her from the other side of the hot tub and laughed, "What's wrong with my feet?"

"Nothing, but have you ever seen Shallow Hal? A girl gets dumped for having a longer toe like yours."

He fished around, grabbed one of her feet and held it up, flirtatiously sparring, "You have the same toes!"

Kayn smiled widely as she countered, "Hey, I never claimed to be the perfect specimen of manhood."

"I'm sure you meant womanhood," he baited. Instead of letting her foot go, he started to massage it. She chuckled and squirmed. He toyed, "Relax… Close your eyes. You are getting your feet rubbed by a perfect specimen of manhood with messed-up toes."

It felt so good. She tried to relax. *Frost was touching her. They were having a good time together. This was weird.* She opened her eyes to Melody and Zach's confused stares. *Mel thought Frost was a great idea. Zach looked like he wanted to punch Frost for touching her feet. He was taking his brotherly role too far.* Kayn winked, letting Zach know everything was okay. *It was more than okay. She was stepping outside of her box and having a good time.* They spent the day relaxing in the pool and hot tub. Frost kept finding increasingly creative ways to accidentally touch her. Other people got into the hot tub. He sat so intimately close he was grazing her thigh with his. *She pretended it wasn't on purpose. She didn't care if he was a stupid idea. He was making her feel alive again.*

Chapter 8

Just A Song

You take a moment of happiness in whichever way it presents itself to you. A beautiful moment can come in many forms. Sometimes beautiful moments are not found in obvious places.

There was nothing striking about this dive of a small-town pub. It was always something random that changed the average experience to memorable. She could tell this was going to be one of those nights. A gold star on her ever-expanding list of wild whacked out afterlife experiences to reminisce upon during their tediously long hours of travel. The smoke machine added something extra seedy to the ambiance. Kayn lifted her hand off the bar. *It was covered in dust.* She wiped it on her jeans. Dust drifted in through the large double swinging doors each time someone entered.

The guys were sitting at a table a few feet away, surveying the female patrons. She was watching the locals sing karaoke badly. *This was the best kind of karaoke.* Everyone in the establishment was clearly tone-deaf and possibly crazy, but they were all having the time of their lives. Tonight was about embracing the simple things like stopping at a random pub to allow the equally crazy boys of Ankh to school the locals. She would have liked to use the 'you're only young once' phrase but when you could be whatever age you wanted, that saying lost its ability to hit home. Shots kept being sent from a table of attractive cowboys. The ladies of Ankh raised their tiny glasses in salute as a thank you. She found her gaze travelling as always in search of Frost. He was grinning, more than a little intrigued by how much she was drinking. Another shot appeared in front of her and she drank it. *She'd made a few alcohol-induced decisions in the last five or ten minutes. She was jealous of the scantily clad girls hanging on Frost's every word. She wanted to walk over there, sit on his lap and stake her claim.* Each time she snuck a peek in his direction, she caught him watching her. She glanced away, afraid he'd be able to read her mind if their gaze held for longer than a second. *She was all but a few stolen glances and innocent brushes against him from ignoring her earlier plans to make good choices. He was thoroughly aware of it.* She could hear their conversation clearly from where she was sitting. It was becoming difficult to stifle her laughter.

Grey punched Frost's arm and reprimanded, "Don't be that guy."

"What did I do?" Frost laughed in his mischievous manner.

Zach shook his head disapprovingly. He looked at Grey and said, "He's not that much of an ass."

"Yes, he is that much of an ass. It's like you don't know him at all," Grey chuckled as he shook his head. He scolded, "I'll be personally disappointed in you. Don't you dare lay a finger on her while she's drunk."

All the girls were listening to the conversation now. Lily got up, wandered over to the guy's table and remarked, "Kayn can hear everything you're saying. Frost is not plotting to deflower her tonight. That would make him Satan and I'd like to hope I have better taste in friends."

"I'm just happy she's finally having fun," Frost replied.

"We wouldn't want her to regret her first night out in public drinking, would we?" She teased.

Frost whispered his response, "Oh Lily... Nobody regrets a night with me."

Kayn's cheeks heated up. She turned away and pressed her palm on her face as another shot showed up. She downed it.

"I was there when you were given that order Frost. It wasn't a suggestion," Lily chastised.

"I know, I don't need to be reminded," Frost replied.

She knew it. He wasn't allowed.

Lily caught Grey's eye as she left the table. His gaze followed her as she strolled away to the bathroom. Another drink appeared just as the boys were called up to sing. Kayn, Lexy and Mel stole their table so they'd have a decent seat for the gong show. As their tone-deaf rendition of a Mariana's Trench song began, Kayn couldn't wipe the grin off her face. *Zach was decent so was Grey. Maybe they were all horrible, and she was so drunk they sounded phenomenal?* They sang to every girl within flirting distance. Frost, of course, lost his shirt five seconds into the song and their performance turned into a karaoke slash Chippendales act. They laughed for a solid five minutes, nearly falling out of their chairs. They'd all lost their shirts by the time the song ended, attempting to one-up each other. The naughty trio came to sit down at the table. A still shirtless Frost scooted into the booth beside Kayn. She smiled at him and shook her head while actively trying to stop herself from ogling him but she was far too drunk to be coy. He casually slipped his hand over her knee and gently squeezed it. She picked up her drink and took a sip, trying to act like his forward behaviour hadn't thrown her. He didn't remove his hand. He left it there. Kayn smiled knowing it was a dare. He wanted to see if she'd scurry away like a frightened rabbit. She wasn't going to offer him the satisfaction of reacting to the placement of his hand. She could feel him smiling at her stubbornness without looking up. Desperate to think about anything else, she picked up a coaster and began reading it as his hand travelled a seductive path from her knee to her inner thigh. Aroused, she bit her lip and covered her mouth as she giggled. *She was going to lose this game of chess if she wasn't careful.*

Lily broke the tension as she ordered, "Put your shirts on before they kick us out."

Grey rolled his eyes and provoked, "Why must you always be such a party pooper?"

Zach was sitting on the other side of her. He snatched the coaster out of Kayn's hand and gave her a glare of disapproval. *He'd noticed the placement of Frost's hand. Awkward. Lexy was smiling so hard it was creepy. She'd done something.* Zach was called up to sing.

Zach smiled at Lexy and as he stood up, golf clapped and jousted, "Kamikaze karaoke...Touché Lex."

For a second Kayn had no idea which song it was and then it clicked. *Oh, that's so evil.* They were laughing hysterically as soon as the chorus started. It was, "The Woman in Me" by Shania Twain. If Lexy expected Zach to crack under pressure or storm off the stage mortified, she'd underestimated him. His sense of humour was just wacky enough to prove her wrong. Zach didn't flinch. Without missing a beat, he belted out the song and even serenaded the men at the tables around him. They were laughing so hard they were crying. Frost removed his hand from her knee to put on his shirt. *Moments like these were amazing. They didn't care if they made a fool of themselves. Why would they care? Every person that they met would only in the end be a blip on the screen of their existence.* Kayn got up to sing next and she wasn't half bad. One by one they took turns. When karaoke ended, the music began. The alcohol had loosened her inhibitions. She wanted to be wild and carefree even if it was only until her brain cells kicked in and staged a revolt. She shimmied closer on the bench and whispered his name, "Frost."

He whispered back, "What?" He was listening to Melody tell a story.

Zach rather abruptly grabbed her hand, yanked her to her feet and towed her to the dance floor, laughing, "You'll thank me later."

She met his eyes and sighed, "You don't need to protect me. I'm a big girl."

Zach pulled her closer and whispered in her ear, "I'm your friend and you're drunk. Things always seem like a way better idea when you're drinking. This is all new for you. Do you have any idea how badly I want to hit on Lexy? Does that sound like a good idea?"

"Not even a little bit," she chuckled.

Zach whispered back, "From what I've heard crazy girls are always incredible. Drunk me would totally be willing to risk the aftermath."

Someone bumped into them and then they were shoved by someone else. Eventually they were standing in the middle of the dance floor not dancing at all, just talking. Kayn laughed, "The whole two-stepping thing is a tad lost on me. I'm horrible at this. We should go and sit down before I hurt someone."

They swayed so they wouldn't stand out as Zach whispered, "I can't two-step either." He spun her around and they parted ways. They began doing the lawn mower and the sprinkler to the country music, powering through a list of hilarious dance moves that people who couldn't dance did to be awesome. It caught on and everyone started doing it. Zach grabbed her hand and twirled her around again. She hadn't had a chance to catch her breath when she was stolen mid-goofy twirl by Frost.

Zach started to laugh. He pointed at her and teased, "Behave Brighton." Without missing a beat, Zach had a new partner.

Everyone was crammed on a small, claustrophobic dance floor. She'd been out of breath before Frost pulled her into his arms. *Now, catching her breath felt impossible.* With nearly perfect timing, the song changed to a slow one. In a swift, skilled movement, Frost pressed the length of his body against hers. She remembered what it felt like to be in his arms and even though she was aware they were Chloe's memories, in this inebriated state it was undeniable. She relaxed with her head on his shoulder. Her hand was pressed against his chest as they danced. Just a hint of ration remained. She could feel the rhythm of his heart pounding against her palm. *He could make her forget about everything that ailed her if she allowed him to do what he did best.* She inhaled his scent and was swept away by it as she removed her only boundary and they fully embraced. *Everything about him made her want to let her guard down and just allow herself to be free. That's what Frost signified to her in one word... Freedom.*

"See, it's not that hard... Is it?" He whispered in her ear. She grinned at the innuendo. Kayn accidentally stepped on his foot hard enough for him to sputter, "Shit, Brighton. That actually hurt."

"I'm sorry. I might be drunk," Kayn apologised.

"You don't say?" The dangerously sexy immortal toyed as he tucked one of her wild curls behind her ear.

She thought he was going to kiss her and her lips parted in anticipation. *She wanted him too.*

Instead, he dipped her and chuckled, "You weren't lying about the dancing thing, were you? I thought you were fibbing. In my experience when a girl tells me she can't dance, it's usually because she just doesn't want to." He paused, and for a moment, they stood still while he whispered against her hair, "I'll put dancing on the list of things I can teach you."

They slowly began to move together. Heat rose within her as he suggestively caressed the base of her spine. She was tempted to push him further by saying, *What else is on the list of things you want to teach me, Frost?* She met his always mischievous eyes with her own, knowing he'd heard her thoughts even though she hadn't said the words aloud. *He was never thinking G-rated thoughts. His day-to-day thoughts would never even fall under the realm of Parental Guidance.* He towed her along rather suddenly as the song sped up. She was laughing as he began trying to teach her how to two-step like there would be a dancing miracle. This, of course, proved to be a terrible idea. They were both laughing hysterically by the time the song was finished.

He urged, "Be serious for a second. Watch my feet. Try to copy what I'm doing. I know you can do it. I'm sure you'll catch on quickly to almost everything."

He always managed to say something open to naughty interpretation. She wanted him to kiss her. The next song was a slow one. She gathered up the guts to tell him what she wanted, and just as the words were about to slip from between her lips, Grey swooped in and stole her away. Before the song was over the lights turned on, bringing on the harsh glare of two a.m. *It was closing time. The moment was lost.* They gathered at the front door of the pub and began their long moonlit walk back to the campsite. Kayn was silently walking beside Frost. Grey and Zach started to sing obnoxiously.

"My feet are killing me," Mel complained as she took off her heels and massaged her feet.

Grey bent over and suggested, "Hop on beautiful," offering her a piggyback ride.

Lily knit her brow and pouted, "My feet are killing me too."

Zach bent over and comically volunteered, "I shall be your mighty steed." Lily grinned and jumped on his back.

"Do you want a ride too?" Frost whispered in his usual naughty manner.

Kayn stammered, "No. I'm okay. I wore my running shoes." *I wore my running shoes… Why did she always have to be such a dork?* She felt like kicking herself for not having innuendo to say back.

"You are kind of amazing, Brighton," Frost whispered, looking at her beaten-up running shoes.

She grinned and teased, "I do try."

The seemingly normal group of wasted teens made it back to their campsite in one piece. She remembered taking off her shoes and tossing them by the picnic table. Grey whipped off his shirt and hollered something about the pool. They all followed suit. She could recall the refreshing sensation of the water and Frost swimming after her doing a drunken rendition of the Jaws theme song, "Da, Da... Da, Da." He trapped her against the side of the pool and caught her by hooking his thumb through her bra strap like a fish on a line. She felt his breath on the nape of her neck and the overwhelming yearning of wanting something to happen. She extended her fingers on the wet cement and parted her lips as he kissed her neck. She wanted to turn around to face him but he stopped her. He laid his pal on her bare stomach and slid his hand along the waistline of her panties. She gasped and arched her back against him.

"You're killing me, Brighton, he groaned. "I'm not allowed."

"Somehow, I don't see you as the guy who always does what he's told," she provoked. He moved her damp strands of hair out of the way and stroked his thumb across the crescent-shaped birthmark behind her ear. He rubbed her ear lobe seductively between his thumb and forefinger.

She felt the warmth of his breath against her ear as he whispered, "You can't afford to have me as a distraction. We'll be friends. I can wait."

Kayn remembered little after that…

In her dreams that night, she was adrift in a wildly churning sea of emotions. *First, she'd been dreaming of Kevin in someone else's arms. Guilt perhaps. She'd been seconds away from the same scenario. In her final moments of slumber, it was Frost's embrace she was tangled in, swept away by the incredible feeling of being wrapped in his muscular arms.* Kayn opened her eyes but didn't move a muscle. *She was sleeping next to Frost. It was more intimate than that. She was being spooned by him.* His breath rhythmically moved against her hair. The heat radiating from his bare skin caused the pit of her stomach to tighten. Her eyes widened as her head pounded a path to memories of the night before. She breathed a sigh of relief when she realised that she was fully clothed. Kayn quietly slinked away from him. She inched her legs over the edge of the bunk and slipped off. It took a moment for the RV to stop feeling like it was shifting underfoot. *Saying she felt gross this morning would be an understatement.* She grabbed a towel and her shower bag before sneaking outside into the crisp morning air. *She needed space between her and the situation she'd woken up in.* Using the public showers was a start. After a peaceful stagger through the woods, she arrived at the public restrooms. Kayn turned the cold, dew-covered metal handle and wiped her wet hand on her shirt. She turned on the light. It flickered as only half of the lightbulbs went on. *They'd yet to stop in a campground where the caretaker knew how to change a bulb.* She turned on the shower and adjusted the temperature to a shade less than freezing. *There was no hot water… Of course there wasn't. She needed an icy shower after those steamy dreams, even if the racy visions hadn't actually happened to her.* Kayn darted through the freezing water, shrieking. She laughed as she soaped herself down in preparation for the next icy dive through the frozen liquid stream. After rinsing off, she got out, towel-dried her hair and grabbed an elastic band from her bag. *She needed to remember to put product in it when she got back to the RV.* Naturally curly hair like hers was something you learned to tame at an extremely young age. She looked in the mirror. *Man, did she ever look rough this morning.* She gathered her toiletries and made her way back. They were all awake drinking coffee at the picnic table. She walked up to the group and stood beside Frost. *This was going to be awkward.* "I really have no idea what happened last night," she whispered. *It was probably best to just rip the Band-Aid off her alcohol-induced amnesia.*

Frost whispered in her ear, "You had a fantastic time. I was a perfect gentleman. I'd never lay a finger on you unless you were of sound mind and even then, you'd have to ask me to."

Every nerve ending in her body instantly became alert. *He always knew exactly what to say.* He was standing just a little too close, enjoying the effect his words had on her. Frost brushed against her from behind. Kayn shivered as an electric current of energy travelled through her entire body. He was her partner in this naughty tango.

He whispered in her ear, "I want you Frost. That's all you have to say."

Kayn struggled to keep a straight face as her pigment enflamed to brilliant rouge. *He'd ignited something inside of her she wasn't going to be able to ignore.* Kayn ran through her list of excuses. *It came down to the undeniable fact that she was a grown woman feeling the need to go against her grain. Was this her inner Chloe winning the battle for control over her heart or was this a normal teenage thing? How would she know?* N*othing about her situation could be misconstrued as normal. She could try to tell herself she was growing tired of fighting her sister's feelings. That's all this fixation on him was. That was a lie. She had feelings of her own for him. She had been trying so hard to deny something that now felt inevitable.*

"We'll be driving to the next location tonight. You can all have the day to relax and have fun tomorrow," Lily announced. She made eye contact with Kayn and winked.

There were whispers of the dark job that was coming as they pulled away from the small town and drove past the pub, they'd had such a fantastic time in the night before. There was unspoken anxiety brewing within the RV. *The phrase 'dark job' was not even spoken unless it would be crossing a line for everyone in some way. It was unusual for Markus to send them on this kind of job. There were certain things they weren't supposed to do until they were Enlightened.* The story of the job drifted out in conversation during the drive. It was a demonic possession. A man was destined to do the unthinkable. He would murder his wife and two children. They weren't allowed to intervene. Everybody knew the drill. They knew that there must be a reason. The act was going to cause a chain reaction that must be allowed to unfold.

Chapter 9

To Stalk And Protect

Sprawled on her bunk, Kayn listened to the humming of tires for what felt like hours. *She'd awoken on this day as she did on most, with the overwhelming urge to go for a run. Sometimes, she just needed to sprint her worries away.* The vehicle turned. They began driving down a gravel road. The noises as they arrived at their destination were always the same. *They were the self-proclaimed campground royalty of North America.* The vehicle came to a stop. She heard rustling outside. Kayn jumped up to get into the bathroom first. She heard the front door of the RV open. *Someone else tried to get into the bathroom.* "I'll be super-fast," she said. The door handle stopped moving. Kayn brushed her teeth and pulled her hair back into a ponytail. *She would go for a run and feel like she had a new lease on the afterlife.* She tugged on shorts and a tank top. When she came out of the bathroom, nobody was there. *They must have found another bathroom.* She fumbled with the door. *She was exhausted. What was she doing? She didn't even have the motor skills to open the door.* She stepped out of the RV into the crisp, moist air. *Yes, she needed this.* The isolated darkness of early morning may be an unappealing thing to some, but to her, it was like a rebirth. She was in her own little world. Nothing was more soothing to her than the rhythmic sound of her feet hitting gravel, pavement or a rubber track's surface. Gingerly, she leapt down and looked around. *It was still nighttime. Even better. It wasn't scary. It was exciting.* She loved letting her senses lead the way, her footing guided by nothing more than the instinct of self-preservation. *It was a magical feeling, this miracle of running blind into the midnight wild.* Missing the roots and rocks on the path was a challenge to her senses. As she began running the moist gravel road of the campground, she heard the matching steps of someone behind her. *There was a time when goosebumps would have emerged, but she'd changed.*

An all too familiar voice teased, "You're not even going to look behind you? What if I was a serial killer?"

"You mean you're not here to murder me?" Kayn provoked as she continued running without slowing down. *He was going to have to keep up.*

Already winded, Frost sparred, "Protecting you, would be the phrase used by someone who appreciated me."

"I don't need your protection anymore. I'm eighteen now," Kayn chuckled without breaking stride.

"Call it force of habit," he huffed from behind her.

"Whatever will you do with all of your spare time?" Kayn toyed as she opted to run the highway. It might have looked like she was taking pity on him. The truth was more twisted. She planned on running Frost until he dropped to his knees if only to prove a point. She knew ego alone would keep him going until she was almost ready to drop herself. *It was her turn to have some fun with him.* The two immortals ran towards the horizon as it burst into brilliant light. It was a miraculous sunrise. She slowed her pace a touch, allowing him to catch up. They'd been running beside each other for miles down the straight stretch of road before the first car passed by. Frost wasn't exactly inconspicuous. He had no shirt on, and no matter how sexy you were, it looked a little nutty. It wasn't particularly warm outside in the wee hours of the morning.

"Maybe, I like protecting you? Maybe, I don't want to stop?" Frost huffed from beside her.

She was wearing him down. She could tell. She was far past her endurance level already but couldn't help herself. She'd have to push him much further if she ever wanted to run alone. "At least you're talking to me this time instead of running behind me like a shirtless mime," she baited. They were soaked to the bone with perspiration.

"Maybe, I just love to run? Maybe, I'm into shirtless miming?" Frost teased. A blatant lie as he staggered.

A lie meant to make her laugh. "Not stalking of course?" Kayn sparred. *He was going to break her first if she kept using her energy to talk. There was no steam for talking and running at this point.*

"Oh, come on. A stalker doesn't bring breakfast, does he?" Frost taunted, patting his pocket.

"That's exactly what a smart stalker would do," Kayn laughed as a shot of adrenaline gave her a second wind and she found renewed ability to spar. She lost her footing and skidded before regaining her balance. *The universe didn't want to allow her a cool moment. It just didn't. It was a thing.* She picked up speed. When her feet had hit the ground enough times in a row at a steady pace, she jousted, "The question remains... Do you have duct tape in your other pocket?"

"Oh no, honey. I'm just happy to see you," Frost teased.

She couldn't help but laugh. A car swerved on the road. Forced to stop running for fear of the public's safety, she sighed, "You can come jogging with me if you put your shirt back on. I don't want to be responsible for any traffic accidents." More than a little annoyed that she had to break stride so he could put a shirt on, she couldn't stay mad as her eyes travelled his rippling abs. *He was insanely hot. Calm down. He's only a guy.* She started running back towards the campsite before he put his backpack on, so he'd be forced to catch up. *Her ego needed to win this one. It took everything in her to keep going.* They turned back down the trail to the campsite. As they ran the wooded trail, Frost went down in the grass, unable to run one more step. She cheered and did a victory lap around him with her arms raised in the air before collapsing in the grass beside him. They lay there together, thoroughly exhausted on the patch of lawn dividing turns into the campsite, laughing.

Flat on his back in the grass, he teased, "Do you want me to continue to stalk you today or should I go stalk someone else? There are cool cabins by the lake. I could stalk almost anyone. The options are endless."

Kayn sat up and wiped the sweat off her brow. He was sitting beside her. She admitted, "I think you've earned the right to stalk me for the day."

Frost grinned as he took her hand. Helping her up, he said, "I was hoping you'd say that. I want to show you the cabins we're staying in. They're spectacular."

On some days, it's just easier to give in once you've won the battle that matters to you. Kayn followed Frost down the winding trails, but now they were both walking. The campsite was alive with the sounds of creatures. They approached the front door of a rickety old cabin. He grabbed a key from under the mat.

Intrigued, she teased, "They just randomly leave keys under mats around here?"

"Yes, they do," he chuckled, "If you call ahead and ask them to."

Were they all staying in the cabins tonight or had he rented the cabin of her dreams to seduce her? But they weren't allowed? Kayn gasped as she walked inside and declared, "This is amazing."

He grinned as he answered, "It's pretty nice, isn't it?"

Saying it was nice was an understatement. It was incredible. There was a king-size bed and a giant hot tub right in the middle of the room. A kitchenette with a table. *It fell right out of her fantasies.* They didn't say anything to each other as they looked at the sink at the same time. They walked over, grabbed glasses from the cupboard and drank so much water they were laughing. She rubbed her protruding stomach.

He pulled his shirt up over his and said, "Want to feel my water baby?"

Kayn almost spit out her mouthful of water. *She'd used that line in her thoughts on many occasions when she'd eaten too much in one sitting.* She swallowed another gulp and lifted her top. "I have one too," she laughed. Her usually firm stomach rounded with the mass amount of water she'd chugged. He touched her stomach. It growled loudly on cue. *It was almost a sexy moment. No such luck*. "Did you say something about breakfast?" She asked.

Frost smiled as he removed granola bars from the backpack and plunked them into her hand. She laughed aloud, "Oh, fancy. That's exactly what I wanted. How did you know?"

"Oh, you just wait," he chuckled. He walked over to the fridge and opened it. There were bottles of two-million-dollar orange juice and a fruit basket. That was Ankh's long-standing joke about eating or drinking from the minibar. He pulled out a bottle of champagne and opened it with his mind. It shot the lamp and knocked it off the end table, smashing it onto the floor. "Um… Whoops," he laughed.

"That's what you get for showing off," Kayn teased as she got up to help him clean.

"No, leave it. I'll get it. You relax," Frost said, quickly cleaning up the mess. He came over with glasses of orange juice, champagne and the basket.

Oh, it wasn't just a fruit basket. There were Twinkies and Swedish Berries under the fancy wrap. He was pulling out all the stops to seduce her. She was both panicked and excited. She'd never been in this situation before.

His eyes crinkled as he grinned at her inner dialogue and assured, "I was going to ask you to stay with me. I just wanted to get to know you without an audience. You're safe with me." He sensed her hesitation and teased, "I dare you to stay with me, as friends of course."

It was easy to read between the lines. He was daring her to pretend she didn't want him back. He knew she couldn't resist a dare. She was playing with fire and it was exciting. She glanced at the bathroom and asked, "Do you mind if I jump in the shower then... Friend?" *She needed to buy time to think. Why did she have to have a brain?*

"Sure," he teased, "But you probably shouldn't jump, you might slip on the soap."

"Ha, ha, ha," Kayn sparred as she strutted to the bathroom, raised her hand in front of her and pushed the door open with her mind.

"Show off!" he called after her.

Kayn sauntered in and closed the door the old-school way. She stood there wondering if she should lock it. She left it alone. He told her he'd never lay a finger on her unless she asked him to. She fought the urge to hop on one foot in the shower for the bragging rights. *She'd hopped in the shower and lived to tell the tale. She was far too exhausted. There's nothing sexy about a concussion.* Hot water soothed her fatigued muscles. His seductive vow travelled through her mind as she lathered up. *This was crazy. What in the hell was she doing?* His words replayed. *Unless you ask me to. What would it be like to be the girl who asked someone to kiss her?* She came out of the shower into a steamed-up room. *She'd forgotten to turn on the fan.* She flicked the switch, hoping the hum of the fan would drown out her thoughts if he was attempting to listen. She wiped off the mirror with a facecloth and gazed at her image. She leaned against the counter. *Get a bloody grip on yourself. What are you even thinking? You're a smart girl. You are not a naive idiot. You have a brain.*

Chapter 10

Playing With Fire

Kayn emerged from the bathroom wearing a fluffy oversized bathrobe from the back of the door over underwear, a sports bra and a t-shirt. *It passed for swimwear. Sort of.* This place had everything under the sun but a hair dryer, so her hair was towel-dried sexy, and damp. She could tell by his expression that she looked fantastic. She heard clinking in the kitchen. *It was Lexy and Grey.* Lexy was sitting on the counter swinging her legs, eating an apple. Grey was breaking into the basket of snacks with a white plastic butter knife.

"We weren't interrupting anything, were we?" Lexy teased. She jumped off the counter and walked towards Kayn.

"No, you weren't. We were just hanging out. We went for a run," Kayn replied.

"Oh," Grey teased, "Just a run?" He'd opened a box of crackers but was struggling with the seal on the packet inside the box. Lexy shook her head, snatched it from him and easily opened it. Kayn grinned as Grey handed Lexy the jar of pickles without even attempting to open it.

"Just a run," Kayn repeated. Grey gave her a handful of crackers and she popped one into her mouth.

He chuckled, "Some energy for you my dear. You know, for all of the future running." He had a giant grin on his face. He wasn't buying it.

Lexy playfully swatted him and scolded, "Quit being an ass. This is kind of sweet. It makes me want to gag a little admitting anything Frost does is sweet. This is a lot of effort for him."

Arguing with them to prove her innocence was pointless. Kayn asked, "Which cabin are you guys staying in?"

"Everyone else is staying in the RV," Grey casually revealed.

She'd suspected that. She also knew this whole romantic seduction scenario was a lot of effort for a guy who didn't have to put in any at all. All Frost had to do was be in the room and he could have almost anyone he desired. Denying what was going on was also pointless. "Stay and use the hot tub," Kayn offered, meeting Grey's gaze.

"That's all you needed to say," Grey chuckled as he stripped off his shirt and got in. Lexy removed her clothes down to her underwear and climbed in with him. *The situation was becoming less romantic by the second.* Someone knocked on the door. It was Zach, Melody and Lily. Kayn opened it and they all just barged in.

Zach huffed, "I am personally offended. You guys attempted to have a hot tub party without me." They got into the now almost full hot tub.

Lily whispered in her ear, "I tried to keep them away but the idea someone might want time alone is like speaking another language."

It was true. Privacy in this Clan was a foreign concept. She should warn him. Kayn knocked lightly on the bathroom door.

"It's open. Come in," Frost called out.

She turned the doorknob and gently pushed the bathroom door open. *He'd answered from the shower.* The room was full of steam. She turned on the fan and leaned against the sink.

He pulled back the curtain, peeked out with a mischievous grin and toyed, "Want to come in and wash my back?"

Kayn caught herself entertaining the idea but rained on his parade by saying, "I thought I'd better warn you, they're all in the hot tub."

He stuck his head out and sighed, "Seriously? Everyone?"

"Everyone," she answered honestly as he vanished behind the curtain again.

"It's fine. That was bound to happen," he responded from within the shower.

Relieved, she was about to leave when his gorgeous water-dampened face peeked out and teased, "Sure you don't want to come in?"

With everyone outside. Right. Kayn laughed, "I'll see you in a few minutes." She heard him turn off the water and paused before reaching for the doorknob.

He flung open the curtains and flirtatiously enquired, "Can you pass me that towel?"

She looked away but not before she got an eye full. She threw the towel right at his face and stammered, "Frost… Seriously?"

Without looking back, she bolted out as he howled laughing. Her face was a brilliant shade of red as she untied her robe.

Grinning, Grey teased, "My dear, you are blushing all over... Everywhere."

"Give it a rest, Grey," Kayn scolded as her robe dropped on the floor. She climbed into the tub with the rest. Frost stepped out of the bathroom in shorts, looking nothing short of the glorious force of nature he was, and slipped into the tub across from her. *Everyone else was light years ahead of her life experience wise. I am eighteen for heaven's sake.* A few giggles erupted. She ignored it as the hot tub soothed her muscles. *She'd overdone it this morning.* Kayn closed her eyes and sighed as she sunk her aching body under the surface of the steaming water.

"You damn near killed me. I haven't been this sore in forever," Frost commented.

Kayn opened her eyes to everyone's shocked expressions.

"We went for a run. An extraordinarily long damn run. I am pretty sure she was actually trying to kill me this morning," Frost explained.

She smiled and shut her eyes again. *She had been.*

"I knew it," Frost laughed as he splashed her face.

She tried to kick him underwater, but her calf muscle tightened into an excruciatingly painful cramp.

Seeing her agony, Frost suggested, "I can fix that."

She smiled, knowing Melody and Lexy had the ability to fix what ailed her. *She'd invited the others on their sort of first date. With no dating experience she felt guilty.* "All right," she answered, stretching her leg towards him. He took her calf in his hands and began expertly kneading the knots out of her muscles. *It felt so incredible.* Forgetting they weren't alone, she groaned, "That feels amazing."

Lily stood up and announced, "I'm sure we need supplies from town." She gave everyone a look that was hard to miss as she got out. She tapped Grey on the shoulder because he hadn't moved.

He caught on and slyly remarked, "Oh yeah, sure, supplies. We should be gone for supplies for a few hours at least."

Kayn opened her eyes. Zach shook his head to show his disdain for her scantily clad player massage. Melody grinned at her and winked. She grabbed Zach's arm and towed him away. They all dried off, leaving them with not one dry towel, disappearing as quickly as they'd arrived.

It was getting far too hot in there for so many reasons. Frost rhythmically massaged her sore muscles, stopping just short of the tender flesh of her inner thigh. She'd forgotten everything but the pleasure of his skilled hands kneading her sore, aching muscles. He switched legs once she stopped grimacing in pain. *It felt phenomenal. She didn't want him to stop.*

"Want me to massage your back next?" He not so innocently enquired.

She wanted him to keep touching her. Kayn scooted up against him without thinking about what she was doing. He massaged her shoulders for a few minutes. *Everything in her was humming with pleasure.* Her mind was screaming, *say it. Tell him you want him.* Intending to do just that, she turned to face him and felt a bit woozy. Lightheaded, she reluctantly admitted, "I think we've been in here too long. I'm getting dizzy." She glanced over the edge. The towels were all sopping wet.

"I'll get you something to dry off with," Frost offered as he got out. She stood up and climbed out onto the pile of sopping wet towels. He brought her one of the terry cloth robes. They both put one on over their wet undergarments. Frost strolled over to look out the window. "It's pouring. We can take our wet stuff off underneath our gowns and hang everything up to dry. I can finish that back massage on the bed?"

Her cheeks blushed at the thought of his hands massaging her bare skin.

He gauged her reaction before assuring, "I'm kidding. You know I'm not allowed to take this further than close friends. Why don't we take advantage of the fact that we're already wet and go for a swim in the lake? It'll be a refreshing change from the hot tub."

Grimacing at the downpour, she said, "Do you really want to go swimming?"

He threw out another thought, "We can go back to the RV for supplies and clean dry clothes. If we put them in a garbage bag, everything will stay dry on the walk back."

Kayn stood beside him in the fluffy white robe. *Option one was tempting. Option two sounded like a scene from a chick flick. Swimming with Frost as the rain pelted down from above. That scenario was just as hot as the massage.* He smiled with weird timing and she knew he'd read her mind.

Hugging her from behind, Frost nuzzled her neck and chuckled, "I'm supposed to keep this PG, your naughty inner dialogue isn't helping. Making a run for the RV might be fun?"

He enjoyed watching her squirm and she was for various reasons. Kayn pulled her shorts on over her wet underwear. She was wearing a soaking wet t-shirt and she was cold. *He was staring at her. She knew the white shirt left little to the imagination.* He took his robe off and stood there in his shorts. Shirtless, he opened the door and held out his hand with the pouring rain behind him. She smiled and took it. They dashed out into the rain and ran through the trails until Kayn slipped in the mud. She looked up at him. He held out his hand again, and this time, her heart did a flip-flop. He tried to help her up and slipped, landing on top of her in the black tar-like mud. They both laughed. *Just one cool moment. Was that so much to ask for?*

"You've got some mud on you. Right there on your nose," He teased, purposely wiping a handful of mud on her face.

"You have some on you too. You should let me get that for you," she laughed as she smeared a handful of the gooey muck across his cheek, getting some in his eyes. They wrestled, covering each other with mud.

Their impromptu wrestling match ended with Frost on top of her. "Give up?" He huffed out of breath.

"Yes," her voice caught in her throat, making the meaning crystal clear. Time stopped as rain continued dancing through the branches. It picked up a touch as wind howled in the background. She imagined the trees were cheering in this truly magical moment. Kayn bit her lip and shivered. She was soaking wet and utterly frozen. *But that wasn't the reason she'd shivered. It was because every fibre of her being wanted him to kiss her.* His lips parted. They were only a millisecond from touching hers when a loud snort came from behind them. Once again, they were frozen a breath away from each other.

His lips grazed hers as he whispered, "Don't move."

"Tell me that's not what I think it is?" She whispered back. *It sounded like a grizzly.*

He covered her lips with his hand and spoke to her using only his mind. *'You know the drill BC girl, play dead. I'm going to move my hand slowly. You need to bite it hard enough to set off my symbol. Don't draw blood. It'll get Yogi all excited.'*

The salivating creature was directly behind him as she responded with her thoughts, *there isn't time to mess around. Throw something at him. Hit him with a tree.*

'That will only piss him off. We're not supposed to hurt him. We must subdue him without seriously injuring him. Those are the rules. Bite me and someone might show up before he finishes us off,' He answered via thought. She bit his hand. Frost smiled in the face of the hungry Grizzly as he thought, *'You are going to have to bite me a lot harder than that to set me off.'*

'Even now, Frost... Really? He was plying her with innuendo in the face of being eaten by a bear. She thought, *what if they all really went to town?*

'They were just leaving us alone,' Frost responded with his mind as the bear began to sniff his legs. He flinched in preparation as he bit his hand.

She felt her symbol heat up and it started to glow, which only intrigued the Grizzly. Her adrenaline began pulsing through her and she forgot she was supposed to think it, not say it, "Bears can't run downhill."

"Who told you that?" He mouthed and flinched as the bear grunted and gave his leg an excruciating swat.

We can't die. We can't die. She squeezed her eyes shut.

"Screw the rules. I'll roll off you and draw him away. You run," Frost mouthed to her. The king of the wild had waited long enough for his snack. The bear's jaws clamped down on the back of Frost's thigh and yanked him off her, towing him mercilessly across the forest floor. "Run!" Frost yelled as the ferocious beast swung his head and tossed the mighty immortal into the air like a rag doll.

Kayn froze... *The bear had flung Frost out of the way in favour of her.* It lunged at her, gnashing its terrifying jaws, and let out a deafening thunderous roar, spraying her with hot, foul-scented bear spittle. With barely enough time to regain his faculties after being thrown, Frost swept his hand across the ground. Mud flew into the

Grizzly's eyes, startling him. He whimpered and zeroed in on Kayn again. She scrambled out of claws' reach, but her attempts to flee her carnivorous assailant were hindered by the sticky mud beneath her. Bushes rustled and twigs snapped, signalling someone's arrival. The beast cocked his head and snorted loudly as Grey burst through the bushes.

"Oh, come the hell on. A frigging Grizzly?" Grey complained as he cautiously backed away. The Grizzly cocked his head inquisitively and lumbered at the lively, spirited snack.

With the Grizzly's attention on Grey, Kayn scurried to Frost. His leg was torn wide open. Blood was gushing from the wound. *Damn it. He was going to pass out.*

The critically wounded immortal commanded, "Give me your shirt."

Kayn gapped out, stunned by the sight of the blood. "My shirt?" She questioned.

He repeated with more urgency, "Your shirt! Quickly! Before I bleed out!"

She took her shirt off and tossed it to Frost. He tore it in half and tied it around his leg above the wound. He grabbed a twig, slipped it through the knot and twisted it a couple of times, tightening it.

Grey was comically explaining in considerable detail the reasons why the beast should choose to eat him. His hilarious, one-sided rant was a heroic attempt to distract the salivating beast from the scent of the blood streaming from Frost's thigh. Trying to use Pyrokinesis, Grey couldn't make a spark. Occasionally, the bear replied to his shenanigans with a snort.

Kayn tugged Frost to his feet as he hissed, "What are you waiting for? Burn that son of a bitch Grey!"

The time for being politically correct in front of her had passed.

Grey was managing to keep the bear's attention. Frost grunted as he pulled a stump, complete with a tangle of roots, straight out of the ground. He ordered, "Think of him as an enormous stuffed teddy bear. Just burn him enough to scare him away. The sight of the flame might even do the trick."

Grey was so amped with adrenaline his gift wouldn't spark the tips of his swaying fingers. "It's not going to work!" He hollered during his comic conversation with the confused bear. Grey almost lost his footing, backing away.

"Run down the hill!" Kayn yelled. The bear turned and grunted at her but kept walking towards Grey.

Grey stammered, "What! Why in the hell would I do that?"

"Bears can't run down hills!" Kayn shouted.

Frost grabbed Kayn's arm and ordered, "Run back to the cabin. We've got this."

"I'm not leaving you two," she asserted. *They didn't have anything under control.*

Frost repeated, "We have this. Go."

There was no point in attempting to argue. This was not the time or the place. Kayn pretended to run away. She stopped just out of their line of site.

Towering on his back legs, the beast bellowed a thunderous roar. It chased Grey, who ran down the hill, screeching, "Bears run down hills! Bears run down hills!" Frost ran after the bear wielding a branch. Kayn ran after Frost.

In a moment of absolute hilarity, Lexy's voice boomed, "You are a naughty bear! Bad! You get the hell out of here! Go! Get! Bad bear!"

The bear let out a couple of wails, yelps and cries as he lumbered off into the bushes. *Lexy didn't touch it. She just stormed up with a raised hand like she was about to slap him square on the nose and scolded it.* Everyone paused, shocked. They looked at each other and doubled over laughing until they were in tears.

Kayn hugged Grey and said, "Thanks for taking one for the team buddy." She walked back to the campsite with her arm around him.

"Bears can run down hills," he mumbled.

Kayn sheepishly responded, "Yes, I saw that. I was obviously misinformed." She glanced at Frost. Their eyes met momentarily, and he winked. *He'd always been there, even if he hadn't uttered a word.* His actions spoke volumes. Her heart gave her another gentle tug towards him.

Lexy casually touched Frost's arm. He understood and began slowly hobbling beside her. She put her arm around him, healing his injury. After a few seconds, he began to walk normally.

Chapter 11

Learning To Be Your Own Hero

The others had really gone into town. Thank goodness a few stayed behind. The black dust-covered truck peeled into the campsite with everyone in a blind panic as they made it back to the RV. They ended up spending the afternoon at the picnic tables under the weathered awning and stayed for dinner. Grey regaled the highly elaborated harrowing tale of their escape from the bloodthirsty thousand-pound bear. With the creativity to stretch the truth to its absolute limit and still have it almost believable, Grey's accent always made everything more exciting. The story, of course, was complete with Lexy's newly discovered skills as their Clan's Grizzly bear wrangler. Frost and Kayn were caked in mud from head to toe but nobody mentioned it. After the tales had been told and their stomachs were full, they gathered dry clothes and began the lengthy, dimly lit walk back to the rustic cabin, certain the bear wouldn't dare make a second attempt after its volatile run in with Lexy's badass dominatrix skills.

It stopped raining. Moonlight streamed through the trees along the path. Light flickered each time the breeze made the branches dance. It was a peaceful sight marking the end of a long, dramatic day. They each knew what the other looked like, so it wasn't necessary to mention it. They walked in silence back to the cabin with a few stolen glances and utterly exhausted smiles. *Fate stepped in every time they had the opportunity to begin. There must be a reason, but she was too tired to question anything.* An owl began to ask, "Who, who?" *That's how it sounded in her subconscious. It felt like another sign to take pause. She was a chicken. A giant immature mud-covered chicken. Kevin was gone. He wasn't coming back. Frost was here and he had real feelings for her. This was sort of their first date, and they'd been attacked by a grizzly bear. Frost looked like he was carrying a dead body through the bushes in a plastic bag.* She chuckled, thinking of the jokes during their morning run. *She'd always had a messed-up sense of humour.*

Frost glanced back, questioning, "What's so funny?"

She was o*vertired. Everything.* They trudged back to the cabin with their feet sticking in the mud and arrived bear attack free. He opened the door and motioned for her to go first. *She envisioned being carried over the threshold by someone.* She slipped into the bathroom first. She looked at her reflection in the mirror and began to laugh. *She was thoroughly covered in mud.* She turned on the shower and listened to the pleasurable, calming water humming before stepping in. The streams of liquid revitalization feverously pelted her skin. She felt revived enough to stay awake for a while longer. She had to wash her hair four times before the water at her feet ceased to be discoloured by mud. She stepped out and noticed he'd come in while she was showering. *Her pajamas were on the counter beside the marble sink. Her choice in sleepwear was an attempt to keep things from going too far.* She slipped on the giant baggy red t-shirt and matching oversized bottoms as proof of her PG-rated mindset. She looked in the mirror and decided to leave her towel-dried curly hair loose and flowing. *How much had he seen when he dropped off her clothes?* She took a deep breath, silently preparing herself for what came next. It was then that she noticed hundreds of initials lovingly carved on the back of the wooden bathroom door. *They were the other couples that stayed in this place.* She ran her fingers across the painstakingly engraved etchings of love. *It was an incredibly romantic tradition. The owners of the cabins hadn't removed them.* She imagined carving her initials in the door on her honeymoon and coming back year after year to see them still there. *Things were different now. She'd never have a honeymoon. Nobody would ever have a reason to carry her over a threshold.* She grabbed the doorknob and twisted it, leaving romantic notions of door carvings and nuptials behind her.

"Use this robe, it's almost dry," Kayn said, strolling over and handing it to Frost. Their fingertips brushed as their eyes met.

"Thank you," Frost replied, grinning as he sauntered away.

His rear view was a spectacular site to behold. He ducked into the bathroom. She heard the steady humming of the shower and all she could think about was how badly she wanted to join him. *She needed a distraction.* She tried flipping through a magazine on the nightstand, but her mind kept feeding her steamy images of Frost soaping up. She got up and the mattress squeaked in protest. *She'd better grab a glass of water if she planned on drinking anything else.* Kayn snagged some crackers off the counter. She spied the snack bag and tossed a few Twinkies onto the bed along with a full bag of Swedish Berries. She sat on the counter and flipped through the local newspaper. Frost emerged from the bathroom wearing shorts and nothing else. *Why did he have to be this ridiculously good looking?*

He retrieved a surprise bottle of wine from the bag, removed the cork and asked, "Do you need a glass?"

"I'm from Vancouver Island honey. Everyone knows you're supposed to drink it right from the bottle when you're at the lake," she teased. She strolled over and sat down next to him on the giant luxurious bed.

"I thought you didn't drink?" Frost baited. He pulled it away in jest and grinned before handing the bottle of wine to her.

"That is just what I've heard," Kayn replied with a wry smile. She took a giant swig and passed the bottle back.

He drank some and provoked, "Right… I'm on to you Miss Brighton. You've been playing with me, haven't you? I bet you used to drink every weekend with that Kevin kid." He instantly regretted his slip and winced.

Her mind flashed an image of Kevin valiantly attempting to open a bottle of wine with an umbrella. *If she wanted to move on with her life, she'd have to be able to survive conversations about her past. Not freaking out when Kevin's name was mentioned would be a significant first step.* "We stole bottles from our parents on occasion. Doesn't everyone sneak their parent's alcohol in their early teens? I thought it was a rite of passage?" she sparred.

He drank some more and revealed, "I was fighting in a war at nine years old in Rome. We were allowed to drink as adults but we were also allowed to die as adults." He passed the bottle back.

She was feeling the effects of the wine already. *The spirits had taken the edge off. She couldn't overthink the situation if she tried.* "That's really messed-up," she replied. As she handed the bottle back. They brushed fingers and her breath caught in her chest.

"Back then it was normal," he chuckled.

She grabbed a Twinkie, ripped open the packaging and chomped off the end. She stuck her finger into it and took her time licking off the cream.

Frost choked, swallowed what he hadn't spit all over the white sheets and offered the bottle to her. It was only after seeing his reaction that she realised how suggestive her Twinkie eating must have been. *It was unintentional.* Kayn accepted, wrapped her fingers around it and held it to her chest. *She had so many questions. It was hard to wrap her mind around his real age when he looked to be in his mid-twenties.* She tipped the bottle up, taking an extra-long swig. He tried touching his own face, hinting she had cream on the corner of her mouth. She tried to lick it off but kept missing.

Frost grinned as he leaned in and seductively toyed, "Let me get that for you." He wiped the cream off her face with his finger and erotically licked it off without breaking eye contact.

Oh yeah, that was hot. He caught on to her arousal and winked. Kayn casually harassed, "Don't you feel like a dirty old man, flirting with a girl nine hundred and eighty years younger?" *Her filter was officially off.*

Visibly impressed by her alcohol-induced ballsy comeback, he taunted, "Do I look like a dirty old man?"

She met his naughty expression as she countered, "You're a dirty something." *He wasn't going to deny a damn thing.*

"I want whoever I want and do whatever I want to do. It's an immortal thing," Frost bluntly provoked.

Kayn took another swig. *There were far too many comebacks to filter through.* She laughed, "You have to let me make you an online dating profile. My name's Frost and this is the testosterone show. I want whoever I want and do whatever I want to do. It's an immortal thing."

Frost shook his head, snatched the wine out of her hand, took a drink and placed the empty bottle on the magazine. He grabbed a Twinkie out of the wrapper and took a giant bite. She pouted. *It was the last one.* He offered her the other half. She attempted to take it and he mischievously teased, "Open your mouth."

That was a brilliant move. He assumed she'd be scared off by his advances. She opened her mouth. He slipped it between her parted lips. She chewed it up and swallowed. *There wasn't really a seductive way to chew a Twinkie.* Frost licked the leftover cream off his finger and tucked one of her damp curls behind her ear.

He slowly ran his fingers all the way down one of her ringlets until it slipped from his fingertips and whispered, "You have to stop trying to seduce me, Kayn. I'm supposed to behave."

Every nerve ending in her body was humming. *Her mind had been feeding her slivers of her twin's sensual memories for months. A part of her felt like they'd already been together. It was hard at first to tell the difference between what she was feeling and what her sister once felt. She wasn't trying to seduce him. Truth be told, she had no idea what she was doing.* Kayn stared into his devious eyes as she dared, "I don't recall asking you to behave." *Did she just say that out loud? What in the hell was wrong with her?* There was a pained expression on his face. Torn between what he should do and what he wanted to do, his lips came closer, and as he shifted his weight on the bed, the empty bottle rolled off, making a loud clang as it hit the floor. Startled, she dodged his kiss and toppled with an ungraceful thud onto the unforgiving hardwood floor. Guilt and confusion ached in the pit of her stomach. She planned to make light of her reaction by climbing back onto the bed. *It was a cruel game her mind was playing. This wasn't right. Her first time was supposed to be with Kevin. She was pushing her heart past where it was ready to be. This rustic cabin… all of this had been planned in her heart with someone else. What was she doing?*

Resolve passed over Frost's face as he spoke, "Don't overthink another word. I was already taking a risk pushing the limits of my orders."

Kayn moved closer and quietly said his name, "Frost."

Shaking his head, he disclosed, "You think if you put your heart somewhere else the pain will go away. I have real feelings for you. I know better." Frost abruptly got off the bed to put distance between them.

She tried to explain, "I need to know for sure that Kevin's gone. I think I have to see it with my own eyes." She saw the hurt cross his expression. "That came out wrong. It's not that I don't want you. I'm just not ready to give up on the idea of..." She'd tried to save it, but she could tell by his face she'd punched him in the stomach with words.

"I understand," Frost answered curtly. Walking away, he glanced back and confessed, "For the record, I just wanted to be here with you, eating Twinkies and drinking cheap wine. I wanted the memory." He attempted to smile before excusing himself.

He'd walked away from her. She didn't blame him. She couldn't bring herself to let go of the fantasy that Kevin would remember her, and somehow, the obstacles between them would disappear. She was holding on to their imagined reunion and wasn't ready to let go. She'd demanded Frost let go of his fantasy of Chloe, lured him in and thumped him out. She blinked to avoid the embarrassment of tears. *Had she destroyed her chance for happiness blindly waiting for something that might never be?* She sat on the bed awkwardly waiting for his return.

Emerging with an understanding smile on his face, he sat beside her and clarified, "I want you. I'm not going to pretend I don't. It would be an insult to your intelligence. I know where you are in your head right now. I've been there. A word of advice. Try to prepare yourself. It won't stop your heart from being demolished, but maybe you can manoeuvre your way through your first run-in with him without coming off like a complete psycho."

She was afraid to respond, certain there was no way to stick her foot in her mouth any further.

Frost's eyes softened as he spoke, "You still have lessons to learn and strangers to kiss. You need to know how it feels to be lonely." He took her hand as he disclosed, "I don't care if I'm your first. I don't care when we happen but when we do. I don't want to be a choice. I want to be an inevitable fact. The Oracle was right. I won't be around to play your saviour. You have to learn how to be your own hero. Concentrate on the bond you have with Zach and Melody. You need them. They need you and I need to get out of your way."

The infamous Testing was coming. Only two words came to mind as Kayn responded, "I understand."

He turned to walk away and paused. He turned back and said, "After the Testing is over and you three make it out, if you ever decide you want to be with me and only me... You tell me. Just promise me one thing. Don't ever say those words to me or to anyone else just because you're afraid of being alone. You tell someone you love them when they leave the room and it runs out of oxygen. I don't want to play second fiddle to some kid. You stay here tonight. I'll send someone back to spend the night with you." Frost stood there for a second, staring at her like he had more to say. Instead of speaking he strolled out the door, leaving her feeling strangely empty inside.

Kayn lay in bed, rethinking every second of the night until she felt sick to her stomach. *He'd been so sweet.* Lily was sent to the cabin to keep her company.

Lily sprawled out next to her and said, "He'll stay away from you for a while, but he'll come around. He needs some time to get his emotions in check. He was warned to stay away from you. He was told to keep your relationship G-rated. I should have stopped this little sleep over. I was curious to see how far he'd push the boundaries. We aren't free to do whatever we want."

Kayn fell asleep replaying those words in her mind. *We aren't free to do whatever we want.*

She awoke the next morning with a pulsating headache. She staggered groggily into the bathroom, splashed cold water on her face and stared at her reflection. *She'd definitely made a mess of things. He was going to ignore her again. This time she deserved it. Demanding he forget about Chloe and then pushing him away because of her unresolved feelings for Kevin. She wanted him. That wasn't a lie.* She heard someone come in. *It was Zach and Melody.* Her eyes wandered to the carvings on the back of the door. *Frost had carved their initials. When did he do that?* She sat on the floor and traced her fingers over the freshly carved initials F + K 4 ever. *She wanted to take a picture to look back on the sentimental act. She had to allow him to let her go. She decided to pretend she hadn't seen it.* He spent the next day avoiding her as she'd anticipated, but this time, she only had herself to blame.

Chapter 12

Only A Fool Isn't A Little Afraid Of The Unknown

She was going on this next job with Zach, Melody, Lexy and Grey. *She was nervous. She'd been warned jobs involving the undead rarely went as planned.* The Clan's Oracle had only given loose details this time. The house was on a rather isolated piece of property. It was a murder-suicide. The family's bodies wouldn't be discovered for weeks, so there was plenty of time to do what needed to be done. It was a basic angry spirit removal detail. *They were supposed to make sure the family moved on. It sounded far too easy.* They'd taken the truck and left the other two to pack up the campsite. As they drove down the remote stretch of forested road, it occurred to her that this was the first job she'd ever done without Frost. *She was going to have to get used to it. He was going to avoid her like the plague now.*

Zach slipped his fingers through hers and asked, "You okay?"

She nodded as she replied, "I'm fine. I'm just overthinking things."

Zach squeezed her hand, and teased, "Never try to have an emotional conversation while drinking. Filters are important."

Kayn leaned over and whispered, "He told you?"

"I overheard his conversation with Grey," Zach whispered.

Grey heard his name mentioned and assured, "Don't worry about it. We've all done and said things we wish we could take back. It's part of life. You have lots of time to fix it."

Kayn watched as the trees flashed by her window. She glanced away, knowing that if she kept looking, she'd be queasy before they arrived. *She wouldn't be able to help anyone if she was barfing in the bushes. It was stupid to be worrying about this stuff right now. She was on her way to her first job involving a murder-suicide. What would it take to kill your own family? There were so many unknowns in this job. This would be another first for her. She might have to see a dead child. They kept looking at her. It was unnerving. They expected her to snap and bawl at the slightest trial. They didn't think she was as strong as the rest. Dead children wouldn't be a small thing to see. She could handle it. She'd come a long way. Her Clan needed to cut her some slack.* They passed by several gravel roads with street numbers on posts. It was a long time before they hit an unpaved driveway into the dense forest. They turned and drove down the long rural road for a good ten minutes. *This was why the bodies wouldn't be found for such a long time. The property was so isolated you could stand outside and scream at the top of your lungs, and nobody would hear you. It also meant nobody would see as they attempted to right evil's wrongs.* The farmhouse was oddly shaped. It was covered in ivy with dark green weathered shutters. *They were all closed like they were preparing for a storm. Had they sensed something coming? Had the wife woken up that day feeling sick to her stomach without knowing why? Had she known what her husband was capable of?* Kayn grabbed the handle and struggled with it before realising it was still locked. The doors unlocked from the front. *Lexy hadn't let them out.*

Lexy looked at her and cautioned, "There's no hurry Brighton. What we're walking into can't be unseen."

She wasn't an idiot. After a deep breath, Kayn replied, "You guys really have to stop treating me like I might emotionally implode."

"Everyone else has seen a dead child. You shouldn't walk blindly into this situation," Lexy advised.

"I can handle a few small dead bodies," Kayn argued. She gave the door another frustrated yank as a hint for Lexy to stop babying her.

Lexy opened the glove compartment and pocketed tiny bags of salt while explaining, "Spirits can be hostile when they've been murdered by someone they trusted and loved." She unlocked the door when she was finished saying her piece.

Kayn got out, and as her feet hit the gravel, she shivered. *A warning of what was to come. Good times.* She didn't say anything as she followed the group up the worn wooden steps to the large double doors. *They'd been left ajar.*

Grey raised his hand and waved it slightly, opening the door without touching it. He declared, "For the record. I hate this spooky ghost shit."

The doors slowly creaked open the rest of the way, revealing a dark hallway to the left and a set of stairs to the right.

Zach calmly observed, "No bodies visible from the door."

"We always check the bedrooms first. Children are usually killed in their beds," Lexy disclosed.

That made sense. At the first sign of danger she would have hidden beneath her covers as a child. Kayn asked, "What are we going to do after we find the bodies?"

Lexy casually responded, "We have to account for everyone in the household. I'll try to draw the souls back into their shells then we'll send them to the In-between where they'll be recycled through the Hall Of Souls."

"That sounds easy enough," Zach chuckled.

Grey exclaimed, "Angry, brutally murdered souls rarely go willingly. If you have unfinished business and that business is revenge, that's how some species of demon are created." Kayn reached for the switch. Grey snapped, "Not yet! Leave it off!"

Kayn yanked her hand away and glanced at Zach. *Why didn't he want her to turn on the lights?* The group began slowly scaling the stairs. A wave of nausea lit up that part of her mind that told her she wasn't safe.

While climbing the dangerously steep staircase, Zach ran his hand along the textured, old fashioned wallpaper. He whispered, "I had wallpaper just like this in one of the houses my family lived in growing up."

Kayn caressed the silky wallpaper. *This house was strangely stuffy. Yes, the windows had been shut but the door was cracked open. There was an indefinable putrid scent.* "What's that smell?" she whispered to Zach.

He scrunched up his nose and whispered, "Dead people and bleach."

She'd recognized the scent of bleach. It had a distinct fragrance. It almost stifled the potent stench of the recently deceased, but not entirely.

Glancing back at the two stragglers, Grey whispered, "Close your eyes and open them. Scan the room. Tell me what you see and feel."

After taking a deep, rancid breath, Kayn shut her eyes, and as they opened, a dark presence flickered on the ceiling in the corner. It vanished so she closed her eyes and opened them again. A dark haze above her ominously loomed. *What in the hell is that?* She whispered, "Every time I close my eyes and open them, something dark flickers above us on the stairs.

Grey winked her way and said, "I'm going to turn on the lights. Once we add electricity to the mix, the shit will hit the fan. You three, take a close look at the family portrait on the wall. Keep that image in your mind. We're here to help them. Try to imagine them as they were. Trust me, it helps."

Kayn looked at the picture as the staircase lit up. *It was a beautiful family portrait.* The children's innocence was preserved within that frame even though it had been stolen from them in life. They were girls. One was a toddler with wispy wild chestnut hair and the other was maybe five or six-years-old with deep-set doe eyes. The mother was dark featured with similar stunning pools of chocolate brown. In her imagination, she envisioned the little girls running down the stairs together unaware of their fate. Their father seemed out of place in the picture. He was a frail man much older than his spouse. Kayn took note of the goosebumps as they formed on her arms. Her pulse began to race as shivers crept up her spine.

Grey whispered, "Awe shit. Here we go. Did you guys feel that?"

The temperature in the room was dropping rapidly. It steadily declined until it was frigidly cold. A gossamer mist appeared from between everyone's parted lips with each breath they exhaled. Kayn's body hair prickled on her exposed skin. *This can't be good.* The temperature continued its descent until her nose began to run. She raised her hand to wipe it, felt the stiffness of her skin and glanced at the others. Everyone's lips were quivering and turning blue.

Lexy gave Grey's cold shoulder a comforting squeeze. She whispered, "Calm down. This isn't your first dunk in the dead pool."

Grey snickered, "Blind panic fuelled by adrenaline always warms the blood."

The lights flickered ominously. *That can't be good.* The glass fogged and exploded on all the pictures. Kayn shielded her eyes from the shards. The urge to vomit was now an uncontrollable need to rid her system of the poison filling the air like a putrid toxin. Each time she inhaled, her lungs clenched and burned. She looked up…*It was hovering above her.* The hazy entity was now a visible dark cloud with thousands of thread-like, swaying arms.

Avoiding its grasp, she almost fell backwards down the stairs. *Oh… Shit!*

Grey caught her, cautioning, "Careful. Those threads sting like a son of a bitch."

Lexy grasped Melody's arm and questioned, "Have you done this before?"

Mel grimaced and sighed, "Yes. I've had the displeasure."

Lexy addressed the group, "Back up. Get out of the way." The tentacles had begun to stretch down the stairs, multiplying and aggressively blocking their path to the top. Everyone who wasn't a Healer backed down the stairs and away from the reaching arms of the ominous entity prohibiting their ability to reach the top.

Unfazed by the madness, Lexy looked at Melody and rather bluntly offered her a choice, "Sucked or stabbed?"

"Sucked," Mel replied as she stepped into the swaying grasp of the writhing demonic arms. They attached to her and began to drink from her being. Thousands of horrifying veins sank beneath her skin and attached to her own. Melody's veins became visible as the demonic entity began to suck the life from her body. She twitched as her feet rose off the stairs while attached to thousands of black strings like a demonic marionette. Suspended in mid-air by spindly veins, her eyes rolled back into slivers of white. They fluttered and closed. Lexy stepped in, clutched Melody's legs with both hands, yanked her back from the place where she floated and fought against the threads aggressively suspending Melody.

Lexy yelled, "Do it!"

Grey sunk his blade into Lexy's back. A surge of healing energy pulsed through her, travelled up Melody's legs and exploded from her torso as a yellow burst of light. The hovering entity evaporated into a fine tar-like mist.

Melody dropped to the stairs, landed on her knees and groaned, "Well, that sucked." Black beads of the entity glistened on her skin.

"Literally," Grey chuckled as he helped her up.

Struggling to regain her bearings, Mel whispered, "You're a funny guy."

Obviously concerned, Zach offered, "You can have my shirt to clean yourself up."

"It's all good. I'm soaking in what was stolen from me." Melody disclosed.

Lexy got up and brushed herself off. There was a blood stain on the back of her shirt from where Grey stabbed her. At first it looked like her limbs might not support her, but it only took a breath to regain her balance. She cracked her neck and announced, "Well, that was round one. Let's get upstairs before round two starts."

Kayn touched her lips. The air was warm again, but her lips were dry. She took a deep breath and followed the Healers up the stairs. *That was crazy.*

Zach poked Melody. She turned to look at him as he declared, "That was badass."

Melody giggled as she replied, "I try." She was visibly exhausted but it didn't stop her from jogging up the last couple of steps.

Kayn smiled at her badass friend as she followed. *The layout upstairs was remarkably similar to the home she'd grown up in.* The others looked in the first room. She kept walking. Instinct told her which room belonged to the little girls. As she pushed the door open, she noted it was abnormally cold. *Here we go again.* She held her breath for the unthinkable but the room was empty. There was a crib in one corner and a toddler bed in the other. She went to reach for the light switch and opted out. *The temperature was already dropping.*

Grey's voice interrupted her train of thought, "Zach, go check the closet out."

Two of the others were in the room with her now. Kayn's heart panged. *The oldest child hadn't even been tall enough to be switched to a normal bed.* Kayn rubbed her hands together to warm them as Zach looked in the closet. She walked slowly to the crib. *Dead babies… The sight of the crib made it real.* She took the pink knit blanket out of the crib and held it to her face for warmth. *It still smelled like baby powder. The scent of a well taken care of toddler lingered even through the putrid scent of death.* She held it against her chest. *She could take it with her for warmth and use it to cover her eyes when they found the bodies.* Kayn placed it back into the toddler's crib. *If the toddler could still see it, perhaps even after death, it offered the child's soul solace.* She pressed the button on the ocean themed mobile. It began slowly rotating on its own, playing a haunting rendition of "Under the Sea." Her eyes teared up as the song played. *She'd always loved this song.*

Grey turned the power off and whispered, "We're here for a cleanup and disposal. Don't make it harder on yourself. Don't personalize this. Shut your emotions down. Shut the blanket sniffing sentimental fool inside of you off."

Kayn stepped away from the mobile. It began to play the song again with the power turned off. *Well… That was super creepy.* Even though she'd frozen in place, she wasn't afraid because she suspected the ghostly culprit might be one of the sweet little girls from the family portrait. *They were only attempting to make contact. Those poor babies must be so scared... So alone.*

Grey's voice said, "Spirits can communicate through the electronics in the house... Watch this." He unclipped the mobile from the bed and took out the batteries. It began to play while in his hand before he'd finished reattaching it to the crib.

"That's amazing," Kayn whispered. In awe, she touched the plush rotating fish on the mobile as it turned.

"You just wait princess," Grey replied. "In situations like this, amazing can change to messed-up in five seconds flat."

The monitor screeched as they left, startling them. Intrigued, Kayn went back into the bedroom alone. The others lingered in the doorway. She couldn't help it. Utterly amazed, she picked it up and whispered into the monitor, "We're here to help. Who are you?"

Lexy's voice piped in from behind her, "Oh, sweetie. You don't want to know the answer to that question. We'll be in the next room when you've unromanticized this."

They were all so jaded. Without looking back to see if anyone was still there, Kayn whispered, "They might be trying to tell us something?" She heard a whisper come from the monitor. She held it up to her ear.

A child's crackly voice said, "I know how your skin comes off." Kayn dropped the monitor, sprinted out of the room and raced to catch up with the others. Visibly shaken, she grabbed Grey's arm.

He chuckled, "They communicated with you… Didn't they?"

"Some kid knows how my skin comes off," Kayn stammered.

"That's not a kid. For your skin's sake, don't wander off alone," Grey warned as he gave her shoulder an assuring brotherly squeeze.

Melody overheard their conversation and instructed, "Just pretend you didn't hear that."

They were behind Zach and Lexy as Zach pushed open the door to the parents' room. The scent of death was overpowering. The bed had been slept in but they hadn't been killed in it. There was a blood stain on the carpet in front of the closet. *They'd found the bodies.* Grey hesitated before opening the closet but did it. The foul scent that wafted out was almost incapacitating. In the closet was the mother's body. She was wearing a robe drenched in blood. *Even in death, she was protecting something.* There was a tiny arm hanging out. *It was her babies. She'd died protecting them from their father's rampage. It had been her final act of love. She hadn't succeeded but died trying.* The interior of the closet was covered in a fine mist of red. There were larger sprays of blood in places. On the inside wall, there was a symbol written in blood. It looked like an abstract painting. Kayn's eyes blurred with tears. *She was going to vomit. The scent of decay was overpowering.* Her stomach lurched again. She looked back at the doorway. *She wasn't going to be able to stop it.*

Lexy began to speak, "Okay, we know where the victims are. If they're all here it will simplify things a touch. We're going to leave them for a minute. We need to find the father's body. The scent of bleach is highly suspect. It means someone tried to clean this up. Nobody cleans up a murder-suicide. Everyone must be accounted for before we start sending off souls. We don't need any surprises."

Grey closed the closet out of respect. As the folding doors shut another burst of sour putrid air was released. Kayn couldn't take the vile stench. She bolted out of the room, knowing the urge to vomit wouldn't cease until she got away from the scent of decomposing flesh. She closed herself in the upstairs bathroom and knelt before the toilet, battling the urge to vomit. The scent of the dead clung to her nose hairs. *She couldn't escape it.*

Grey leaned past her and opened the shower curtains. He rubbed her back while sternly warning, "Always check behind the shower curtains." He patted it, instructing, "Pull yourself together. You need to stay with the group." He reached into his pocket, took out a small flat container, removed the lid and put some on under his nose. He offered it to her. She did the same. "I wanted to give you some of this before we came in here but you needed to know what decomposing corpses smell like."

The vapour rub blocked the assault on her senses. She leaned back from the toilet and took a deep breath. The urge to purge her stomach's contents left her. She got up and followed Grey out of the bathroom. Zach was offered scent relief as they ran into him. Their scent saviour wandered off to find the others, leaving the two newbie Ankh alone. The lights flickered. Kayn grabbed Zach's arm. They laughed nervously.

Zach elbowed her and chuckled, "You were pretty tough a minute ago... What happened?"

"I was going to puke from the smell," Kayn whispered.

"That happened to me the first time," he replied, giving her shoulder a reassuring squeeze. "How are you doing other than that?"

"Only a fool isn't a little afraid of the unknown. The voice in the monitor threatening to skin me alive didn't help," Kayn replied.

"How zen of you. Just so you know, if someone plans to skin you alive, they'll have to go through me and Mel first," Zach assured.

Kayn grabbed ahold of the worn wooden railing and ran her hand down it as they descended the stairs. She felt a twinge of pain and paused to look at the sliver in the heel of her hand. She held up her wounded palm for Zach to see and whispered, "This family wasn't terribly safety conscious. Look at the size of this sliver."

Zach took her hand in his and said, "Oh, for heaven's sake."

It looked like he was planning to kiss her hand as he plucked the enormous sliver out with his teeth. She grinned as he spat it out. *A brotherly act of kindness he'd used on his siblings in his last life.*

"Quit messing around," Lexy scolded, coming down the stairs.

Once they'd all reached the bottom, they made their way down the hallway to the kitchen as a group. The scent of bleach grew stronger as they entered. The kitchen cupboards were painted yellow with white glass see-through ones where dishes had been placed away in perfect order of size and shade. Keepsakes and knick-knacks were on the windowsill with a few cactus plants.

There were white lacy curtains with green trim that perfectly matched the shutters. *This family took pride in their home... When they were alive.* Kayn noticed something behind the curtains. She pulled them aside, revealing a symbol similar to the one in the closet. A shiver trailed her spine. *This meant something significant.* Her stomach curdled again. *This was nowhere near over.* Kayn motioned to Lexy. The crimson-haired immortal looked at the symbol and was expressionless as she concealed it with the curtain. *There was a spotlessly clean murder weapon in the sink. The father had tried to rid the house of evidence… But why?* Instinct whispered, *you shouldn't be here. It's a trap. You need to leave.* Kayn peered up from the large butcher knife in the sink and met Lexy's concerned face.

The fearless immortal whispered, "I know... I feel it too."

Lexy's nervous. This can't be good. There was only one place left to search… The basement. They all had the same apprehensive looks on their faces. *This was going to be messed-up.*

Zach broke the uncomfortable silence by clearing his throat. He questioned, "Are we certain Daddy's dead?"

"Oh, I guarantee you he's dead. How did he die? Now, that's the question that remains unanswered. He attempted to clean up after his little murder spree. Why would he do that? This doesn't scream murder-suicide, does it?" Lexy responded while pointing out the obvious.

The dishes were done. The kitchen was spotless. If the father managed to dispose of the bodies and the house was clean and tidy, it would look like the family had simply gone on a holiday. But why hadn't he finished the job? Grey turned a doorknob in the kitchen. There was a steep set of stairs leading into darkness. It led to the basement. They heard the shuffle of tiny footsteps.

"Tell me I didn't just hear that." Lexy sighed.

Grey looked directly at Kayn and Melody and barked, "Go upstairs! Check underneath mom! We need to know which child's missing!"

Kayn's heart leapt. *One of the children might still be alive. There was hope.* She darted towards the basement door and was roughly blocked by Lexy.

She ominously cautioned, "Oh, sweetie. Trust me on this one. You do not want to go down there."

"It might be one of the children," Kayn asserted. *They'd lost her. Why were they not running down the stairs to help?*

Grey dramatically rolled his eyes while saying, "Skin coat, Brighton. Do you want to be a skin coat?"

"I'd honestly like to skip the whole skin coat thing if that's at all possible," Kayn answered. *She got it. Something moved in the basement. It didn't necessarily mean that something was alive.*

Grey calmly repeated his order, "Please, go upstairs and check the bodies so we know the size of what we're dealing with."

Zach couldn't help himself, "I thought size didn't matter?"

"Anyone who foolishly allowed you to believe size doesn't matter is a dirty liar," Lexy proclaimed. She chuckled as she opened the fridge.

The fridge was crazy full of raw meat and nothing else. Lights flickered ominously as they stared into the fridge.

The crimson-haired Dragon of Ankh said, "Shit."

Oh, that's just lovely. The hitman is concerned. Kayn gawked at the creepy display of red meat.

Zach blurted out, "Who needs this much red meat?"

Grey shoved past him. Peering into the fridge, he repeated Lexy's curse, "Shit." He placed his hand against the fridge and closed it.

On that note, Kayn and Melody decided to go upstairs and check the bodies.

Grey and Lexy looked at the ominous pastel blue, worn wooden door that led to the basement. Somebody had carved that same symbol on the door.

"What does that symbol mean?" Zach asked as he ran his fingers along the grooves in the wood tracing the symbol.

Lexy smacked his hand and scolded, "I don't have a frigging clue. It's not a Tri-Clan symbol. That's an Abaddon symbol. Never… Ever… trace any symbol with your finger. Something epically bad may happen."

Zach probed, "So, neither one of you know what it means?"

Slowly nodding his head, Grey answered, "I know it's an Abaddon symbol, and someone in this house was preparing to feed something that requires a crazy amount of raw meat. That's all I need to know to want to get the hell out of here."

Grinning, Lexy disclosed, "There's one of those symbols inside the closet with the bodies and another by the kitchen window." She strolled across the kitchen and pulled the frilly curtains aside to reveal the symbol. "I'm starting to think our Oracle's reading was not entirely accurate. We may have walked into a trap."

Grey grimaced as he began his rant, "Are you kidding? Isn't it obvious? Yes, it's a trap. Look in the fridge! We're the damn fresh meat delivery service!" The livid immortal opened the basement door again. They stood there, staring into the darkness together.

With glorious comic timing, Lexy sparred, "Well, they've ordered from the wrong place now, haven't they? They aren't going to like us much. There's usually a light switch at the top of the stairs. It could be one of those in the kitchen by the door." She walked over and flicked them. Nothing happened.

Zach added his two cents, "Maybe the lightbulbs are just burnt out?" The light flickered and came on. It gave a touch of brightness to the stairway for a second before it flickered and went out.

"Of course," Grey sighed. He stretched up to mess with the lightbulb itself. It was tightly in there. Nobody loosened it. They heard the pitter-patter of tiny steps run across the room in the darkness. Grey jumped off the staircase and slammed the door.

Lexy commanded, "Don't go down there until I get back. I'm going to check on the girls."

Grey chuckled, "No problem. I'm willing to put off having to attempt to catch whatever that is until I have a clue what we are dealing with."

Chapter 13

Rabid Little Angels

Kayn and Melody raced up the stairs, down the hall and into the parents' bedroom. *After seeing that thing on the stairs earlier, neither one planned to take their time.* Mel opened the closet to reveal the brave mother's corpse huddled in the corner. Kayn's mind whispered, *you left the group. That was stupid.* Kayn was shaken by the imagery. Without the putrid scent, the visual itself became more disturbing. There was no need for bravado. Melody had the ability of an Empath, as well as a Healer. Kayn wasn't going to be able to hide her feelings from her. They were alone. There was no one else to block the flow of emotion. Kayn's eyes filled with tears.

Her friend wasn't a newbie in many ways. Mel protectively asserted, "I'll do it." She gently attempted to shift the mother's body, but it was rigid as stone.

This was rigor mortise. She'd heard about it but never seen it. She wanted to help Mel, but her body wouldn't budge. It felt wrong to move this body. It felt as though they were defiling a sacred resting place. In death, she was still protecting her offspring's remains. Melody tried to move her with a little more force and the corpse wouldn't budge an inch.

Mel whispered, "You're going to have to help me do this. I'm sorry Kayn. I was hoping to involve you as little as possible."

Kayn knelt before the mother. Her heart ached. *The last moments of her life must have been horrible. The desperation she must have felt as she covered her offspring with her own body.* Kayn shuddered as tears began to flow without restraint. *Shut it down. She had to shut her emotions down.* Kayn followed Melody's lead. She'd never intentionally touched a decomposing body. She slowly moved her finger to the neck expecting to feel skin. Her fingers sunk into a mushy, cold neck wound. She yanked her hand away and decided to try to shift her by moving her arms. It was also her first experience with rigor mortis. There was a strange, unnatural stiffness and resistance to movement. They had to forcibly move the mother's body. The lifeless body of the five-year-old was curled up in the fetal position. Her tiny torso was brutalised by a blade. Kayn moved the matted hair out of her open eyes that stared through her into oblivion. Tears streamed down her face as Mel gently touched her shoulder.

With her heart breaking, Kayn whispered, "Can you imagine the kind of evil it would take to kill a child this tiny and defenceless."

Mel replied, "I was forced to be a party to ending a young life. I was in Trinity at the time and I couldn't do it. Someone else was forced to do it for me. I understood then that sometimes, terrible things must happen for the right reasons. It's all in your perception of right and wrong."

How could something like this ever be anything but wrong? Kayn shuddered with emotion as she thought of the little girl's smiling face in the picture on the stairs. *How?* It was then that they noticed something bundled in the mother's arms. She'd died clinging to a blanket. Mel managed to pry it from death's grasp. *There was something in it.* Kayn was plagued by an ominous feeling. *Oh, no…It wasn't…*A stiff newborn lay wrapped in the blanket. They gasped in unison. The infant's eyes were glassy and in the centre of the newborn's forehead was a distinct smear of blood.

Lexy's voice came from behind her, "Is there a crescent shaped birthmark behind the infant's left ear?"

Mel looked and whispered, "There is a birthmark. What does it mean?"

Lexy answered, "The baby was a demonic vessel. It means that the father going crazy and killing them all may have a just purpose. He may have been possessed from either side, meant to help or to stop the birth of this child. I need to grab something. I'll be right back." Lexy disappeared from the bedroom.

Sick to her stomach, Kayn disclosed, "I have a crescent shaped birthmark behind my ear."

Melody looked and replied, "I don't think you have to worry. Your birthmark is on the other side."

Chloe had a birthmark on the opposite side. She was a part of her now. What did that mean?

Melody observed the tiny deceased being, "There doesn't seem to be any physical signs of violence. Maybe it was stillborn? It's possible the mother accidentally smothered it, trying to keep it quiet."

Kayn took the infant's tiny hand. She touched its teeny, stiff fingers, "Please stop calling the baby… It."

Lexy appeared in the doorway. She came to the closet, got down on her knees by them and declared, "Grey and Zach are blocking the stairs so whatever is in the basement doesn't get out. We'll deal with whatever is down there after we've dealt with this."

She had the knife from the kitchen sink in her hands. That's what she needed to get.

The lights flickered again in protest as Lexy cut the palm of her hand and began marking the foreheads of the deceased with her blood. After double-checking the mark behind the infant's left ear, Lexy said, "I hate it when our Oracle misses something this crucial. It can happen when dealing with dark things. The symbols around the house blocked what was actually going on inside of it."

Respectfully, closing the mother's vacant eyes, Lexy whispered in Greek. "Εγώ ἱερός ἄμβροτος αἷμα νόστος." The lights flickered in the hallway.

Kayn leaned closer to Melody and whispered, "What do those words mean?"

"Something along the lines of, my sacred immortal blood return home," Mel quietly responded.

Lexy shifted closer to the child. She closed the little girl's eyes and whispered the exotic words once again. Colour returned to the child's cheeks. She became limp instead of stiff, and in the blink of an eye, her vessel was empty. Kayn was blown away by what she was seeing. *It was a beautiful duty. She'd been a party to forcefully making sure the living passed on but didn't know they also made sure spirits found their way home. She'd been expecting one to put up a fight and go all Amityville horror on them. Yes, she'd seen horrible things. She'd been threatened but they'd gone willingly to the other side.*

With creepy timing, Lexy remarked, "The toddler's missing."

The boys stood in front of the closed basement door. They heard the pitter-patter of little feet. It was usually a cute but not today. A child's laughter was also a beautiful noise but not this time. Not tonight, coming from a dark basement. Grey frantically began searching the cupboards for salt. There was nothing. "I just know it's going to be the toddler," Grey complained as he slid down to the floor in front of the door, putting the full weight of his body against it.

Zach smirked as he declared, "Toddlers are small. Open the door. We can just go and get her."

Grey chuckled and disclosed, "You've obviously never fought an amped up evil child, have you? They have a low centre of gravity and they're a hard-core pain in the ass to catch. There's also that pesky guilt factor. They are so tiny and cute. Just because they are little that doesn't mean they're not psychotic carnivorous depraved little fiends. Lexy needs to be the one to kill it. If a child kicks my ass again, I'll never live it down."

Sitting beside Grey with a smile on his face, Zach baited, "Oh, for heaven's sake it's a child. Are you seriously concerned a baby is going to kick your ass?"

Grey rolled his eyes and remarked, "This is going to be bloody humiliating. Somehow Triad always finds out about this kind of embarrassing shit. It's a baby possessed by a demon. It's not a cute cuddly kitten. It is surprisingly hard to fight back when your instincts are screaming, don't hurt the baby!"

On the other side of the door, they heard a soft knock. A child's voice sobbed, "I have to go pee. I don't want to hide here anymore. It's too dark mommy. I'm scared."

They both leapt up. Grey dramatically threw himself in front of the door, blocking Zach's path to help the child. Grey wasn't budging an inch.

Panicking, Zach asserted, "Open the door! What's wrong with you? The mother obviously hid the toddler in the basement!"

"Oh, you can't possibly be this frigging stupid. You were in Triad," Grey groaned.

Desperate to help, Zach insisted, "My instincts say this is just a scared child. Isn't part of your duty to teach us life lessons through cause and effect? I'm willing to take the chance on this one."

The toddler was sobbing on the other side of the door, "Daddy, don't hurt me. I just have to go pee."

Zach spoke sweetly from the other side of the door, "Sweetie, are you okay? Is someone else down there with you?"

"My Daddy's down here with me. He fell down the stairs. Can I go pee? Where's my mommy?" There was a thumping sound like the child had fallen down the stairs.

Zach got in Grey's face and threatened, "Open the bloody door right now! I'll kick your ass and a baby will be the least of your worries!"

"All right, kiddo. Go be the hero. You just let me know when you've had enough," Grey chuckled as he stepped out of the way. Zach ran blindly down the stairs into the darkness. Grey stood at the top of the stairs and listened to Zach as he called out for the child.

A sweet demonic voice answered Zach in the darkness, "I know how your skin comes off."

Zach yelped, "Oh! Shit!" There were a few loud thumps, followed by high-pitched psychotic laughter and shrieks of intense pain. He started shrieking, "Burn it! Kill it!"

"What was that you were screaming?" Grey sang from the top of the stairs.

Zach screamed, "Enough! I've had enough!" There was a loud smashing sound, followed by the rattling of chains.

Grey stood at the top of the stairs smiling before saying, "Oh hell, kid." He made his way down the pitch-black staircase.

He was halfway down the stairs when a creepy child's voice whispered, "I made something for you Mr. Grey."

Something moist was placed in the palm of his hand. *Crap.* Grey lit up a small flame with his free hand and looked at what had been placed in the other one. *It was a large slice of Zach's skin. When a demonic toddler skins your friend alive and places his flesh in your hand, I don't care who you are, it's bloody difficult to keep your shit together.* In his peripheral vision, Grey saw the father's skinless corpse and the pathetic tiny flame he'd created puffed out. He only had time to say, "Oh, crap... How do you know my name?" Before the rabid demonic toddler mercilessly attacked him. After being clubbed by something large, he was launched into the cement wall. *He couldn't see anything. It was pitch black.* He struggled to his feet as the tiny rabid demonic beast began gnawing at his shin.

It tore a large mouthful of flesh from his lower leg, cackled and spit it out, "Too salty your flesh is… Mr. Grey."

Booting the child away with his feet, Grey spun in a circle, hearing scampering feet. *What in the hell was it doing?* He dropped to the cement as the toddler bound his legs. He tried to ready himself for the agony of being consumed but lost it as he usually did while experiencing the torture of his flesh being torn clear off in long people jerky strips. After strip ten, he became groggy. As glorious shock set in, the pain dulled, and all he could hear was the heavy panting of an excited predator. Light flashed at the top of the stairs. Grey faded in and out of agony. His ears filled with the screams and gasps of his Clan member's torture. There was a high-pitched squeal as the room exploded with blinding light.

Lexy stayed upstairs to finish the job and sent Kayn and Melody down to tell the others what they were up against. She gently closed the newborn's eyes with her fingertips. As she chanted the words meant to draw the spirit back in, its tiny heart began to beat. The infant's skin became pink. Its open empty eyes returned to dark blue liquid pools of innocence and she turned to a puddle of mush. *She always overshot the healing energy on infants.* A newly born infant only needed a touch, or it would come all the way back once its soul returned with no grace period to send them forward to the next life. There was no way to see humanity in its purest form and not die a little inside as you took it away. Lexy checked behind the infant's ear, needing to be certain she was doing the right thing. *The brand of the damned was there. This wasn't a choice.* She held the infant close as its tiny heart fluttered and stifled a sob. She wrapped it back up in the blanket. Something possessed the father to make sure this child would never take its first breath. She contemplated placing it up in the attic but starvation was a horrible way to die. She had to cover its tiny mouth and nose but couldn't do it. The infant grasped her finger with its tiny hand and squeezed. It's trusting eyes bore into her soul as she pulled her hand away. *There are some dark acts even a Dragon can't do.* Lexy looked above her and implored, "Please, don't make me do it." *Her emotions wouldn't turn off. They always turned off.* She pled, "Please… I can't." She was blinded by incapacitating white light. The world went dark.

Lexy awoke what felt like moments later to find Frost and Lily standing above her.

Frost slowly shook his head and sighed, "You guys went off the plan again, didn't you? What in the hell happened?"

Lexy scrambled to her feet and looked for the baby but it vanished into thin air. She whispered, "The others are downstairs fighting a possessed toddler."

The immortal trio cautiously entered the kitchen. Lexy showed them the contents of the fridge.

Lily giggled, "This was totally a trap. You guys were dinner."

Grinning, Lexy thought about her conversation with Grey. The light to the stairwell turned on. Sensing the evil had been dispersed, they descended the stairs without reservation. Their friends were strung up by chains and mounted on the basement wall. They'd all been beaten to a pulp and were missing long strips of skin from their legs and torsos.

Bound to the wall, Zach raised his head and croaked, "Well, that was an extremely unpleasant experience."

Grey scowled while struggling to free himself and scolded, "I warned you, didn't I? Next time I tell you not to do something, entertain the idea that I've been around for forty years and I know what I'm talking about. Lily can you please unchain me from the wall?"

Frost's eyes were full of unhidden amusement as they took in the creatively depraved medieval torture devices in the basement. "Who in the hell was this family?" Lexy unchained Grey as Lily helped the others. Frost couldn't help but tease, "Did you let a tiny toddler kick your ass Zach?"

Zach grumbled, “That was not a toddler. That was a tiny rabies infested superhero.”

As Lily unchained Zach, she said, “Getting beat up by a toddler once is a lesson learned. Grey has no excuse for being this epically stupid.”

There was no sign of either the infant or the toddler as they made their way to the front door. Kayn was missing a large strip of skin down her leg. The exposed meat burned in the slight breeze. *She’d been wounded and Frost barely looked at her.*

“Are you alright?” Melody whispered.

Kayn quietly replied, “A demonic toddler peeled the skin off my leg. I’m not fantastic.” She couldn’t help but chuckle.

Melody’s delicate skin had already returned to pristine ivory. Grey disappeared for a while and reappeared with the scent of smoke as the house began to burn. He set the entrance ablaze on his way out the door. They got into the truck. Parked beside it was a motorcycle Frost and Lily borrowed from the campground.

“I guess we have to take that back, don’t we? Lily laughed.

Frost teased, “Better not leave someone’s bike at a murder-suicide. That’s just mean.”

“Want to go for a ride with me Grey?” Lily asked.

Grey’s eyes lit up a touch as he replied, “I should heal the pesky strips of missing skin before I attempt to go for a ride with you. Maybe later?” He flirtatiously smiled at her.

Peace between the two was right around the corner. Kayn allowed a knowing smile to escape as she shimmied into the backseat. Lexy started to laugh.

Grey questioned, “What’s so funny?”

She tossed a bag of salt at Grey.

He rolled his eyes at his partner in crime as she removed the rest of the bags from her pockets and put them back in the glove compartment. Grey scowled at Lexy as he reprimanded, “You asshole! You had those in your pocket the whole time!”

Lexy giggled before apologising, “I’m sorry. I forgot.”

Throwing his hands up, Grey hissed, “I got beaten up and skinned alive by a rabid frigging toddler!” He muttered under his breath the whole ride back to the campground. “It’s bloody humiliating.” Each time her Handler complained, Lexy grinned, and everyone snickered. After twenty minutes of under his breath bitching, Grey was ready to snap. He threatened, "You all think this is funny? I'm going to drive this truck right off the frigging road. Then we'll see how funny it is!" By the time they reached the campsite everyone had their lips pressed together, desperately trying to stop themselves from laughing. Grey got out of the truck, dramatically slammed the door, and stormed past Frost and Lily.

Getting off the bike, Frost said, "Who pissed in his cornflakes?"

Lexy comically raised her hand, revealing, "I had bags of salt in my pocket the whole time. I forgot they were there." Everyone laughed again. Lexy sighed, "I'll go kiss up to him."

They finished packing up the campsite. Kayn noticed Frost heading in the direction of the public bathroom. *He hadn't even acknowledged her presence. Not a damn word. She hated this.*

As she stared after him, Zach whispered in her ear, "It's his loss."

She appreciated the solidarity but knew she'd created the mess by stringing him along. Kayn started helping again by methodically moving the blocks around the tires and placing them back into the storage. She kept glancing towards the public bathrooms awaiting his return, knowing their situation was far too complicated to blow off by merely saying she'd strung him along. *A part of her longed for him, but it wasn't fair to lure him in any further… Not until she'd dealt with her unresolved past.* She felt a hand on her shoulder and turned around. For a split second, she caught herself hoping it was Frost. *It was Grey. He'd obviously calmed down enough to let the drama from earlier go. He was quick to lash out but also quick to forgive.*

Grey enquired, "Are you okay?"

"I need to go to the bathroom to wipe the Vicks out of my nose," she replied.

Grey knowingly probed, "What's stopping you?" It was then that Frost reappeared. He caught on, "Oh, I see. Give that time. His ego is wounded. He'll get over it."

Frost walked past her without even glancing in her direction. *It hurt. It felt like he was trying to hurt her.*

Grey hugged her, consoling, "Awe, Muffin. These things always have a way of working themselves out."

She felt bad for laughing.

They went into the RV, closing the door on another adventure. Grey handed her a flamingo wine glass. He tempted, "Shall I fill it up?"

Utterly exhausted, Kayn replied, "Why not?" *Today had been epically shitty. She'd seen vein-drinking demons and helped put dead children to rest. She'd been chained up and skinned alive by a rabid toddler and was being coldly ignored by someone she cared about. If ever there was a time to down the contents of a flamingo wine glass… It was right now.*

Chapter 14

Awkward Days And Field Vermin

The following weeks were a mind-numbing blur. Frost had been making a spectacle of himself with an endless sea of women. *She understood why. She'd seen what was beneath his armour and spent time with the guy who carved initials on the backs of doors. His flamboyantly shameless conduct was how he was dealing with what she'd done to his heart. Yes, she'd stomped on it a little. Even though she fully understood the reason behind his behaviour, he was beginning to piss her off. It wasn't like she didn't care about him at all.*

They'd been taking Melody with them on jobs, leaving her and Zach behind. *It made sense. Mel was a Healer. Concern ate at her, but she said nothing. The Testing had been brought up frequently in the weeks after the demonic toddler incident. The infamous Testing that nobody would go into any detail about. Neither she nor Zach had any battle-worthy abilities.* They were sitting at the table playing cards. Kayn studied her hand, successfully stifling the urge to bring up her concerns. *She couldn't shake the feeling that they were running out of time.* The sound of the truck's tires signalled the end of their card game. Zach gathered up the cards and put them back in the cupboard. Kayn gave his butt a playful swat as she walked by. He chased her out the door, trying to slap her back. They stopped horsing around the second their eyes met Melody's. *There was a vacant look in her eyes. Whatever they'd done must have been an emotional stretch. It wasn't the time to be joking around.* They solemnly helped pack up the campsite. When Zach wasn't asked to drive, they knew they were being left to tend to the emotions of their third. Melody climbed up onto her bunk. They joined her knowing sometimes all an injured soul required was a moment of peace, wrapped in the arms of the people they love.

Each night, the endless span of darkened highway whirled past the windows until the sun emerged from its hiding place in the distant horizon, signalling dawn. Eventually, everything melted together into one endless stream of monotony.

Kayn was in a deep sleep when Grey's melodic voice whispered in her ear, "Time to wake up, Brighton."

She ate a granola bar on the fly, rather excited they'd parked somewhere. Everyone else must have been up for a while. They were all waiting for her outside as she emerged from the RV. She glanced at Frost, who looked right through her. Every time he dismissed her, it made her both miss their friendship and feel like smacking him across the face with a household appliance. When she looked at Mel or Zach there was always a smile in return. *Those two were her saving grace.*

They strolled together in the golden morning hours through the thick brush and slid down a steep ravine. Kayn was always intrigued by these side trips. They rarely discussed where they were going with the new Ankh. They just knew they were supposed to follow the others unless they were told not to come. Kayn was thrilled to feel the loss of control as she slid down a dusty hill in pursuit of them. Her eyes always gravitated to Frost, who hadn't even bothered to look back at her. *It was difficult for her to be emotionally blackballed by him like this. They'd had a real connection. She had to get over it. He'd obviously left their almost romance behind.*

They were standing together on a small slab of dusty earth that jutted out from a steep drop above a teal river. *This was glacier water. It was a beautiful yet isolated feeling place.* Kayn smiled at Grey. *This morning's excursion seemed like one of his joy finding ideas.* "It's absolutely beautiful." Kayn decreed in Grey's general direction. The others began to chuckle. Everyone laughed except for Zack and Melody, who'd assumed the same thing. Lexy glanced back at the three with scarlet hair rippling in the wind, looking hauntingly beautiful. She dove off the ledge in one graceful motion into the icy teal liquid below. *Oh… Crap.* Kayn glanced at the other two, knowing they were meant to follow her. Grey glanced behind him and winked as he dove in next. Lily followed suit.

Frost didn't look back as he said, "Do try to keep up. The water is freezing. If you get lost in one of these underwater caverns and

I'm forced to come find you, I'm going to be pissed." He leapt from the rocky perch into the teal liquid below.

Melody laced her fingers with Kayn's. She held out her other hand to Zach. He squeezed his eyes shut as he took it, and the trio leapt into the freezing water. As they hit the icy liquid death below, there was an explosion of mind-scrambling agony. They sputtered to the surface. As they regained focus, they swam after the others who vanished beneath the surface by a trickling waterfall. *The thought of opening her eyes in the icy water made her want to scream. She had to maintain the illusion of strength, but right now, she just wanted to tread water and cry. There was no choice. They had to keep up with the others.* They swam as a group underwater through a bubbling maze. She followed the movement of swirling legs and feet ahead of her. By the time she came to the surface, her brain felt ready to explode. She gasped in the much warmer air, following the others to the rocky cavern's shore. *Her chest hurt.* Kayn made eye contact with Frost. *For a second, it looked like he wanted to help her out of the water.* He turned away and left her, struggling to get onto the ledge. Her chest tightened again. She managed to pull herself out. Lying there shivering with her chest burning, her limbs wouldn't work. She attempted to move again. *Nothing.* Her mind whispered, *Go to sleep. Close your eyes and go to sleep.* Exhausted, she shut her eyes. *Everything dissolved into peaceful nothing.*

She heard Chloe's laughter and cautiously opened one eye. *Why was she standing in a corn maze?* She opened both of her eyes and looked at her hands. *They were tiny.* She recognized the corn maze as Farmer Bill's. Her family used to go on hayrides and get lost in this maze every year around Halloween. *It was a labyrinth of seemingly endless choices and a rather ironic place for her mind to have travelled.*

Chloe yelled, "I bet you can't find me Kayn!"

Kayn began to run in the direction of her twin's voice while listening for the rustling of her sister's footsteps ahead.

A hand grabbed her from behind. Her brother's voice yelled, "I gotcha!" Kayn turned and hugged Matty. He tried to squirm out of her grasp. "Auch… Yuck! Let me go, you dirty field vermin," her brother dramatically choked.

Allowing him to struggle free from the unwanted bear hug, her bottom lip trembled.

He took her hand and said, "Don't cry. I'll help you find them."

They raced through the maze together. Her heart leapt as she saw a familiar mass of dark, wavy hair in her peripheral vision. The younger version of Kevin darted past her into the maze. Suddenly, she was all alone. Nobody was holding her hand and it was no longer the size of a child's. *No! She didn't want them to leave her!* Tears swelled in her eyes as she stared at her adult fingers. Kayn yelled, "Matty! Don't leave me! Chloe! Come back!" She was listening for their footsteps as a clammy hand covered her eyes. She knew who it was and gasped, "Kevin, is that you?"

The scenery changed and she was sitting on a pile of stacked hay. Kevin was sitting across from her. They were being towed by a tractor. They were on the haunted hayride. She looked behind her as students dressed as ghouls came running out of the corn maze. They squealed and laughed. Her best friend had the biggest grin on his face. She wanted to move across to where he was seated and hug the endearingly awkward preteen version of him. He had a genetically unfair amount of acne. Kevin squealed as someone attempted to grab him through the spaces between the boards that served as rails. Entranced by the memory of him, she was ignoring the devastating number of fake zombies attacking the hayride. He gave her a strange look and she knew she'd better play along. She dove into the centre of the wagon. Kevin was there with her. They were laughing hysterically as they swatted away their classmates pretending to be undead. Everything exploded to white around her. She clung to Kevin, desperate to stay lost in the memory. *She'd missed him so much.*

She heard Grey's voice in the distance and felt the sting of his hand on her butt. "Wake up, Brighton!"

With a sudden deep breath, she was returned to the here and now. She scowled at her butt-slapper as he helped her up.

With an unusual amount of patience, Lexy announced, "For future reference, having a nap after being in water that cold is a bad idea."

She wasn't cold anymore. She felt surprisingly warm and glorious but Lexy was looking a little rough. *It didn't take a brain surgeon to figure out what happened. Shit. She must have died.* "Sorry Lexy," Kayn whispered.

The exhausted Healer replied, "Do try to stay alive long enough for me to recuperate."

Kayn smiled sheepishly as the part of the group that stayed behind to bring her back walked into darkness until the cavern narrowed to a slit of the cave, resembling a half-smiling mouth because it was wide on one side. Kayn climbed through, following the others. *She didn't like this. She felt extremely uncomfortable with the idea of climbing into anything resembling a mouth. Her imagination was still on overdrive.* The cavern was cramped for about thirty feet before it widened enough to allow some range of motion. She crawled on her knees, manoeuvring through the tight space. A light was flickering ahead, beckoning them forward. The air had become humid and oddly muggy as laughter in the distance caused her to pick up her pace.

Grey spoke from ahead of her, "You're about to get a chance to do something extremely cool. You are in for a treat."

The two in front of her climbed out, granting her a clear view of the opening, just as claustrophobia was about to win the tug-of-war inside of her. Grey yanked her the rest of the way out. Relieved as her feet hit the stone, they felt like Jell-O for a minute. A torch flickered on the wall of the cavern by a pool of steaming water. *It was a hot spring.* The trio stripped to their undergarments and joined the others. Kayn noticed tombs alongside the pool. Lexy threw her stone. Her tomb materialized. Another one appeared when Grey tossed his.

That was always cool. Kayn stepped into the steamy pool. Gasping as the warmth enveloped her, she rested against the ledge of natural stone. Stretching out, her leg brushed against someone. *It was Frost. She knew it without looking.* Purposely pushing his boundaries like he always pushed hers, she kept her eyes closed while maintaining contact with his skin. Not so innocently sliding her leg against his, she snuck an eye open just in time to see him get out of the water. *He was determined to avoid her. That chicken shit.*

Zack leaned over and whispered in her ear, "You always want what you can't have. It's the natural order of things."

Kayn smiled and nodded, knowing it was the truth. *She hadn't died for the opportunity to sit in a hot spring, had she?* Her eyes were drawn to the rearview of Frost in his underwear. *It was difficult to look away. Shit, she was staring at him. She was not playing it cool.*

Turning to face everyone, Frost announced, "All right everyone. Out of the water and into the tombs. Party time is over."

They climbed into the tombs in pairs. *She wanted Frost in a confined space. Held captive where he couldn't look away and pretend she didn't exist.* Grey motioned for her to come with him. She nodded and climbed into his tomb wearing her smiley-face underwear. *It was like being in an uncomfortable situation with your brother. At least she was wearing the least sexy underwear on the planet.*

"Nice red and yellow happy face panties, Brighton," he teased.

It was the old rule of thumb. Never wear your ugly underwear. If you get into an accident everyone will see them. Well, she'd actually died in her ugly panties today. "I'm throwing these out the second we get back," Kayn stammered. *Brotherly figure or not, Grey was hot and shirtless. All she could think about was how uncomfortable it was.* In awkward silence, the tombs clicked, shifted and shut with the familiar grinding of stone on stone. Grinning at each other as the tomb pulsed and light strobed, they were shot up into the air with stomach-churning velocity. As they twisted, spun and whirled, Grey hooted.

Everything paused as the tomb exploded with a blinding light. Kayn squealed as they dropped. In a heartbeat, the tomb was gone. Understanding there was nothing to fear made passing through the cloud barrier with wind and condensation on her flesh like a rebirth as they burst out into the sunshine. Free falling into rapidly approaching desert, they slowed themselves. Landing squatting in the silken sand, they rose in unison wearing short, ivory sarongs and loincloths.

Smiling as she wiggled her toes in the warmth of the sand, Kayn noticed there were no diamonds in it. *This was the place between life and death that those who were Clan could visit but never pass through. There were no diamonds in the sand because they had nobody left to lose.*

Frost began to speak, "Okay, we still have a few things to go over. Get ready for a refresher in otherworldly situations." With that, they disappeared, leaving the newest of the Ankh alone in the desert.

Chapter 15

To Catch A Phobia

To her, the arrival site was an exquisitely beautiful place. Kayn grinned at the feeling of the warm luxurious grains of sand between her toes. Above her, it looked like someone had melted every shade of blue in a jumbo box of crayons in the sky. Kayn looked down at her toes and noticed that someone had written something in the sand. It was a symbol of some kind.

"Hey… What do you think this means?" Mel asked, concerned as Zach knelt and traced the pattern in the sand with his finger. She warned, "I have a feeling you shouldn't do that."

Zach replied, "Okay, I don't mean to be captain obvious here, but everyone keeps saying don't trace the symbol. We probably have a symbol in front of us so we can trace it to experience cause and effect."

"That makes sense," Kayn agreed as they waited for the sky to explode or a monster to come flying at them from out of nowhere, but nothing happened. Kayn shrugged and suggested, "Maybe we all have to do it?"

Always their sense of reason, Melody replied, "I don't like this. I don't think this is what we're supposed to be doing. Maybe, they put temptation in front of us to see if we have the presence of mind to leave it the hell alone?"

That also made sense. Kayn stopped tracing the symbol with her finger and looked up. *Well, it was obviously too late now.* She asserted, "Come on, we might as well just finish what we started. Aren't you the least bit curious?" Something caught her eye and Kayn didn't finish. *Weird. There was a random seashell in the sand.* She held it up to the others and asked, "Why would there be a seashell in the middle of the desert?"

They looked at the shell grasped between Kayn's fingers and lightbulbs appeared over all three heads at once. They all looked up and to the East far off in the distance, there was a hint of blue on the horizon.

Zach sighed, "Oh, crap."

They ran in the opposite direction as fast as their feet would carry them with no time to speak, nor the breath to yell obscenities at each other. Their hearts pounded uncontrollably, and adrenaline drove them forward as the thundering echo of the approaching bone crushing wall of water pursued relentlessly. *They could see it. The edge of the sand.* The trio dove into the air with arms outstretched to push themselves further out of the incoming waves reach. *They cleared it.* Behind them was the sound of the water rushing over the edge of the cliff as they plummeted towards the forest floor. *They'd done it. They had outrun the wall of water.* The water whooshed over the edge like a waterfall and rushed through the forest between the trees like a destructive otherworldly tsunami. It passed beneath as they slowed themselves down for impact with the forest floor. *A forest floor, no longer there. Oh, crap! They hadn't thought that far ahead.* There was only a split second to make up their minds. *In which way, did they want to die?* They looked at each other. *This was going to suck…*

She hit the surface and was sucked into the flow. All Kayn could see was churning water and bubbles as the current surged through the trees flopping her body around like it was nothing more than a rag doll. The water was too deep and the tops of most of the trees were not tall enough to grasp onto. Kayn struggled to keep her face above the surface to breathe. The unforgiving force felt like it was grabbing at her legs, attempting to pull her under. Her flesh was savaged by submerged debris. *She couldn't breathe.* Sputtering and choking as she fought for a breath but each time she made it to the surface, she was pulled back under. The white froth around her bubbled red as she bobbed up again. *She was alone. The others were gone.* She grasped for anything, attempting to slow herself down while the unseen pummeled her from beneath the rapidly moving water. *There was a large tree coming.* The plan was to grab hold of it to stop her violent journey. *She was approaching it too fast.* With a blinding flash of excruciating pain, the suffering was over…

Well, that sucked. Kayn's body had come to rest on solid ground. *She heard rhythmic roaring waves. Was her mind playing tricks on her? Was she still close to the water? She knew she wasn't in the water.* She kept her eyes shut as she twitched her fingers on smooth, unmalleable surface. *There was stone under her fingertips.* She inhaled a giant breath and glorious air travelled into her lungs. She opened her eyes and pushed herself up with exhausted arms. She had a sense of foreboding for the physical pain she'd undoubtedly feel while attempting large movement and was relieved when there was none. Her mind struggled to process her surroundings. *Where were Zach and Melody?* As she got up and looked around, she realised she was on an island at the mouth of a cave. They usually ended up in the same place each time they were killed in the In-between but in every other direction, there was nothing but endless churning sea. *There was no other way. Come on… She was going to have to climb into the tight fit of the cave's opening and face her new-found fear. Well played, Karma… Well played.* She hesitated at the darkened opening and called out to her friends. *They didn't answer.* Her skin began to crawl. Sensing something behind her, she spun around. Her jaw dropped. She knew better than to make lots of noise before thoroughly checking out her surroundings. A monstrous arachnid was crawling up from the water's edge. *Never make lots of noise in a strange place. You never know what you are calling. Come on. She'd already done her time with spiders, but this one was the advanced version of the first spider involved horror movie she'd endured.* She slowly backed away from the vehicle-sized arachnid. *It was far too big to fit through the mouth of the cave. The enclosed space was the lesser of the evils. Hell, she would have chosen an enclosed space over a tiny house spider.*

Kayn dashed into the cave. When she reached the point where it narrowed, she shimmied between the stone. Relief washed over her, knowing the enormous arachnid wouldn't have a crack at her. *Maybe there was a way through to the other side of the island?* It gradually became a tighter fit until she found herself wedged precariously between narrow walls. She continued working her way through until it was hard to breathe. When she glanced up, there appeared to be more space between the stones above her. *She'd have to move further up to manoeuvre her way through but if she slipped, she'd be seriously stuck.* With no choice, she climbed upwards. *Either she'd been wrong about what she'd seen from that vantage point or the walls were becoming tighter on their own.* Kayn paused, only able to take short, quick breaths. *The cavern appeared wider above her.* She needed to climb up higher. *It was her only shot at making her way through.* The opening became wider near the cave's top. *She was right!* Relieved, she gingerly shifted her way through. She glanced down. The walls were now touching beneath her. *Tell me I'm not about to be sandwiched.* Feeling more than a little squeamish for some reason, she peered up… A mass of something was moving on the ceiling. *Crap!* The dark blur dropped on her, and suddenly, she was covered with thousands of tiny spiders. *Oh, shit! Shit!* Having already learned the lesson on noise, she stifled shrieks of terror. *They weren't biting her. She felt no pain.* They'd blanketed every inch of her skin. Her stomach convulsed as her body shook with uncontrollable shivers of adrenaline. *This was one of her worst fears.* If she panicked, she'd slip and become wedged between the walls. *She would lose her ability to move.* Panic wracked her brain but her mind persevered. It fought for control of her limbs and she continued to inch her way through the cave even though what she wanted to do was to pass out cold and awaken somewhere less terrifying. *Somewhere where countless prickly arachnid legs weren't scurrying a wickedly torturous path across her flesh.* She heard Chloe's voice in her mind. Her twin talked her through the horror, 'T*hey're tiny spiders, Kayn. They are insignificant, bothersome flies. You are a giant to them. You are an insurmountable mountain. Keep going. You need to keep moving forward.'* Kayn repeated her sister's words in her mind. *They are insignificant, bothersome flies. I am a mountain.* She would have spoken it aloud but had to keep blowing air out of her nostrils to obstruct the entrance of the spiders. *The last thing she needed was a hundred rushing into her mouth. She did not need to make a bold affirmation that badly. If spiders scurried into her mouth, she'd lose her shit.* Kayn kept shimmying until she felt a breeze. She felt a hand brushing the millions of scurrying legs off her skin. Her senses breathed a giant sigh of relief as she fell into Zach's arms.

"It's okay. We've got you," he affirmed.

She felt soft hands brushing the remaining spiders from her skin. Mel consoled, "It's okay. You can open your eyes. They're gone."

No! No! She couldn't! They were going to get in! She couldn't. Her body continued convulsing.

Melody embraced her, whispering, "It's over. They're gone. I wouldn't be hugging you if you were still covered in spiders."

That made sense. Kayn opened her eyes in the safety of her friend's embrace and choked out, "That sucked. That scared the shit out of me." Once she'd regained her bearings, she realised she hadn't made it out the other side. They were in a large open space but still within the cave, with a pool of water. She glanced back at the opening Zach yanked her out of and sighed, "Please tell me that's not the way out."

Zach weakly smiled, replying, "You may wish it was in a minute."

Still shivering while noting it was unusually cold, Kayn answered, "I highly doubt that. My chest feels like it was a second from exploding. I think I was about to have a spider-induced heart attack."

Nervously tucking her shoulder-length chestnut hair behind her ears, Melody pointed out, "It's getting colder by the second. We'll freeze in here within the hour, even if we keep moving. To make things worse, swimming out isn't an option." Crouching on the cold cave floor, Mel reached over and placed her finger into the frigid water. She removed her painfully frozen finger and shook her head.

Zach shivered as he asked, "So, there were only small spiders when you came into the cave from that side?"

Kayn wrapped her arms around her chest. Her lips quivered as she answered, "Only thousands of tiny spiders while I was inside the cave but I was chased into it in the first place by a frigging enormous one. A spider so big it couldn't fit through the cave's opening. I need you to tell me there's another way out."

He was shivering as he replied, "Yes, there's another way but it's definitely not any better."

Kayn knelt to touch the water just to see for herself and only stuck her finger in for a split second before yanking it out. *It was about ten times colder than the water she'd died in far too recently to try that insanity again.*

Melody began to explain, "We woke up in the forest. There was no water on the ground. It wasn't even wet. I called for you and thousands of wasps swarmed us. They chased us into this cave but wouldn't come in. It was strange, they just hovered outside the entrance. Peek, if you want to. We were stung so many times, I passed out after healing Zach. He had to wait for me to wake up. The temperature in here started out normal and then began to drop. It's still going down. We don't have long to decide which direction we want to go."

Pacing back and forth, Zach prompted, "Brains over brawn. What would Markus do?"

Melody slowly shook her head and said, "The spiders are scary as hell but not deadly. The big one, we can deal with when we get to it. I'm not sure we have time for that option. We'll freeze before we can wriggle our way out and the way we came in has a wall of wasps ten feet deep. We'd have no skin left after five seconds. Whichever way we go, there's no option of survival here."

She had an idea. Kayn quizzed, "The cave wasn't this cold ten minutes ago?"

Zach replied, "No, it wasn't. What are you thinking?"

Kayn's quivering lips turned up into a smile as she replied, "I'm thinking of science class and the ice skating on a pond rule. If we jump through that ice right now, we may die but at least we go out trying to survive. I say we choose the freezing water. Once we've broken through the thin layer of ice on top, we'll keep swimming down until the water gets warmer."

"You died this way less than an hour ago," Melody stated.

Kayn smiled and said, "There's no time to debate this." She took the lead and stepped out onto the thin layer of ice. *This was going to be painful.* She fell through the surface, and sure enough, it was less painful five feet under. *She was right. It was tolerable.* Water rushed around her as they both leapt in. There was a shimmering light in the distance. She motioned them to follow, hopeful it was the way out.

In moments, the trio surfaced. *They did it! They'd made it out!* They paddled side by side as they looked back at the island.

There were easily a dozen giant spiders above where she'd entered the cave. *Now what?*

"What are we supposed to do now?" Zach called out, doggie paddling in now lukewarm water.

"I'd rather drown," Kayn declared, swimming in place.

The sky exploded with blinding light. They were warm and dry, standing in the desert with the rest of their Clan. Grey was doing a slow clap.

Chapter 16

Invasion Of The Body Snatchers

In the following weeks, Kayn kept reliving the moment she learned Tiberius was Kevin's biological grandfather. That revelation altered both of their paths. *Had he made a conscious choice to leave her?* There were so many unknowns, but her mind never attempted to alter history as she relived the highlight reel of the reasons why they could never happen. *She missed the steamy dreams of Frost. At least they'd made her feel alive. They'd urged her to move forward instead of stagnantly dwelling in the past.* She lay on her bunk, listening to the steady hum of the tires. *The sound had become strangely soothing. It meant they were moving towards a place she'd never seen or experienced.* She always had Zach and Melody, but Frost's emotional absence hung thick in the air. *She had to hand it to him. He'd done a brilliant job of switching their roles around. It was now her longing for him, but it wasn't fair to string him along until she was sure. She needed to be certain it wasn't loneliness speaking… Or Chloe. She needed to see Kevin. How long would she have to wait for her heart to find some sort of internal resolution? You want what you can't have… Zach had been right about that.* She shifted around to face Frost's bunk. *He wasn't even sleeping there now. He was acting with self-preservation. She understood that much.* Kayn threw her legs over the side of the bunk and wandered to the front. *Frost was driving.* She sat in the passenger seat next to him and said, "How long are you going to avoid me?"

"Well… I was avoiding you but of course, here you are," Frost mumbled, staring at the road ahead without even looking at her.

It was dark out with no streetlights, so she stared at the yellow line on the endless highway that lay before them. *It was a symbol of their life. It was a long line. There would be twists and turns but no dead-ends for either of them.* She couldn't stop the selfish words from slipping from her lips, "I still need you as my friend. Please stop acting like you hate me."

Frost's eyes softened as he whispered, "I don't hate you." He kept his eyes on the road.

She whispered, "You once told me all I had to do was tell you how I felt, and that would be enough for you."

He didn't answer right away. There was a long pause in the conversation before he repeated part of his earlier speech, "You need to learn to stand on your own."

He kept staring at the road but she could tell she'd gotten to him. As she stood up to leave, she felt his eyes on her as she attempted to balance in the moving vehicle, valiantly trying to get back to her bunk with her ego somewhat intact after being blown off by him. The flash of a big rig's lights flickered through the RV. She glanced back at Frost. In front of the RV was a giant moose with wide, terrified eyes. Frost swerved to avoid it and hit the soft shoulder of the road. They crashed into the ditch and rolled down the embankment. She was flung against the bunks. Something cracked in her chest. Kayn slammed against the other side as they flipped. Her arm snapped. Her ears rang as her head smoked the roof. They came to an abrupt stop upside down at the bottom. The others were flung from their bunks in their sleep.

"What in the bloody hell!" Grey bellowed from the back on the ceiling where he'd come to rest. His leg was broken and his body bruised.

"It was a moose! You never hit a damn moose!" Frost yelled back. "It would have totalled the vehicle! Is everyone alive?" He hollered. They all answered except for Zach, who remained silent.

Grey began to rant, "How in the hell do I drive the damn vehicle for forty fricking years and never get into an accident! I avoid every damn animal crossing the highway but not you, Frost! Not you! You hit bloody everything!"

"You know what? Kiss my ass, Grey!" Frost shouted back, but Grey had already started to laugh.

Kayn heard the approaching sirens. She glanced down at her broken arm and fought off the panic. She'd had multiple broken limbs in the last six months of her life or death, depending on how you looked at it, but it never stopped her from freaking out a bit when it happened.

Frost started barking out orders, "Melody! Heal Zach! He's dead! Everyone with broken bones, you'll have to go through the motions with the paramedics! They're already here!"

Kayn was gapped out, staring at her severely mangled arm as Frost knelt and whispered, "I'm sorry. I've been dealing with this situation badly." He shoved open the window. Melody was positioning herself to heal Zach. Frost stopped her, urging, "There's no time, Mel. Your legs are broken. Take the energy you need to heal yourself. You'll be healed before you're casted. It'll be too obvious."

With Zach already deceased, Kayn offered Mel her hand. She felt the warmth of her life force as it travelled up her arms into Melody.

The first responders were already at the window. A voice called out, "Is everyone all right in there?"

"We need help," Frost answered, even though they didn't.

There were too many civilians. Their vehicle had to be fixed. They would have to let it all play out.

Kayn awoke in the hospital with the strangest sense of déjà vu. She saw Kevin's face as she attempted to focus on where she was through the blinding white. She recalled the first time she'd woken up in a gown like this, surrounded by white. This time, it was Frost beside her bed. He got up as her eyes opened. Kayn chuckled when she felt how heavy her arm and leg were. The cast went right up to her waist. She felt the bandages on her stomach. *Did she have surgery? She was as high as a kite.*

Frost kissed her cheek and lovingly whispered, "Sorry. You're going to have to play along. Enjoy the Jell-O. You're staying here until we've fixed the RV."

"How's everyone else?" Kayn whispered, still groggy from the sedation.

"I'll give you a quick rundown. Melody is healed. Lily and Lexy are fine. Grey has a broken arm and Zach is in the morgue, which complicates things a touch. The accident was caused by a moose. There are no charges for the Aries group to deal with. I need to leave because we have to stop Zach's autopsy and steal his body." He squeezed her sheet-covered leg. "Avoid another X-ray. You'll be healed by tomorrow. It freaks the mortals out."

She couldn't help but grin as Frost left, knowing he was going to steal Zach's body from the morgue. She giggled until a nurse stuck her head into the room and scolded her.

It would take them little to no time to steal Zach's body from the morgue. They'd done it more times than any of them could count. They all had their usual body theft duties. Frost and Lily were the distraction. Lexy would take care of the cameras while Grey prepared to set off the fire alarms if shit went South.

Grey nudged Mel and instructed, "Come with me. We'll follow Frost and Lily. One will distract the coroner while the other clears the exit. Watch and learn."

They took the stairs to the basement. Frost shoved the door open, glanced back at Melody and asked, "Have you ever done this before?"

Grinning at the immortal, she replied, "Yes. When I was with Trinity."

"Good to know we're not the only Clan with the Aries Group on speed dial," Lily said as their steps echoed down the deserted, dimly lit basement hallway.

The four immortals peeked through the foggy glass on the door labelled morgue. A man was just about to start Zach's autopsy. Lily was up to bat. She tried the door. It was locked. Poised to knock on the tiny window, she covered her mouth, stifling laughter. Zach was awake! He'd opened his eyes. The coroner was too busy preparing his work area to notice.

Seeing Lily through the glass, Zach mouthed, "What in the hell?"

Ready to start the procedure, the coroner stated the date, time and description of Zach. As he turned around with the scalpel, the doctor's eyes met with his live patients.

Zach comically declared, "I sure as hell hope you're not planning to use that on me." Terrified, the doctor dropped his instrument and slowly backed away from the table. Their pale, recently deceased friend sat up and said, "Calm down. I can explain."

The man began yelling, "Help! Don't eat me! Help!" Pausing mid-sentence, he dramatically clutched his chest and collapsed.

"This royally screws up a perfectly good plan," Grey sighed. He backed up to take a run at the locked door.

Clearing her throat, Mel said what should have been obvious,

"Let's just ask Zach to open it." She winked at Grey as she rapped loudly on the door.

Confused, Zach slipped off the metal gurney. He wandered over to the door and unlocked it, saying, "I think the doctor died."

"He was the coroner," Lily explained as she knelt to check his pulse.

"Well, that explains his reaction," Zach chuckled. Watching everyone do their thing. He asked, "If I was dead, how did I wake up?"

Strolling out of the bathroom, Lexy explained, "My bad. It took me five seconds to deal with the cameras. I was going to play musical toe tags to confuse the paperwork until the Aries group had time to erase the evidence. I switched Zach's toe tag with someone else's, thinking I'd have plenty of time to wake him and walk him out. The coroner showed up. I had to improvise."

"Which drawer did you take it from?" Frost questioned.

"This one." Lexy answered as she opened the drawer and pulled out the body of a white guy with flaming red hair.

Zach shook his head, pointing out, "I'm brown."

"Oh, come on. It'll be weeks before anyone looks at the paperwork. The coroner's dead on the floor. He had a heart attack. Someone's going to come in and say, oh no..." She crouched to read his name tag. "Phil, had a heart attack."

"He does look like a Phil, doesn't he?" Melody comically observed.

Grinning, Lexy said, "Wait. They record the autopsy." Patting Phil down, she found the device and took it out of his pocket. She erased everything and put it back.

"You left fingerprints, Einstein," Zach teased.

"I don't have fingerprints, Zach," Lexy countered as she grabbed the deceased coroner's can of soda off the counter and popped the lid.

Checking out his hands, Zach said, "Holy crap! I don't have any fingerprints either."

They all laughed as Lily piped in, "We should get out of here."

Zach was beside Lexy as they strolled down the dimly lit hallway away from the morgue. He whispered, "I bet he thought I was a zombie."

"When you wake up during your autopsy, they always think you're a zombie," Lexy chuckled.

As they approached the stairs, Zach asked, "Can't we heal him before we leave?"

"He has to die. If he's remotely observant, he knows you're not a red-headed albino and he'll have zombie tales to tell. When a mortal's time is up, it's up. We're not allowed to heal mortals. You know this. If you mess with the grand scheme of things and get caught, there's big bad medieval punishment."

Mel joined the conversation, "I healed a person and a horse."

"They allow you a mistake or two before you know what's going on. Look up the person you healed. I guarantee you, he's dead. Any alterations we make in a mortal's life path will be Corrected. Life lesson one hundred and four, you can't change the road. You can make it easier or harder by the choices you make. That's all you can do. The end result is always the same."

That night a highly sedated Kayn vaguely recalled being cradled in Frost's arms while leaving the hospital. By midnight they were on the road heading towards their next adventure.

Chapter 17

Diabolically Evil Fish

The jobs became increasingly disturbing as the days went by. Kayn suspected it was in preparation for the infamous Testing. Tonight, they'd be waltzing with the devil while attempting to come out unscathed. This was the first job involving the death of a serial murderer. She'd read stories and watched movies about them, but the idea of running into one on purpose this evening had her tingling with nervous energy. She was almost looking forward to this one. She was both frightened and excited. It was like watching a scary movie that might suck you into the screen. They were Correcting the most horrific kind of human. There would be nothing to feel guilty about in the aftermath. Each one of Fate's prior attempts at this maniac's life had been thwarted by the Legion of Abaddon. The Ankh were being sent in to set things right. Tonight, Kayn would feel proud to be a part of a just Correction.

The glare of fluorescent lighting made her squint. Lexy ordered her to keep her eyes open so she could finish applying her eyeliner. So, she opened her eyes as wide as a Black Moor fish. Her crimson-haired makeup artist rolled her eyes. *There was distracting buzzing coming from the lights above the bathroom mirror. It was irritating her way more than it should. She'd learned to tune things like this out, but tonight she couldn't.* Lily was straightening her hair. She having fun so Kayn allowed her to do it without giving much thought to the emotions it might pull to the surface. *Chloe always took the time to straighten her curls, but she'd never bothered.* Lexy carefully applied brilliant red lipstick to her lips. Kayn glanced in the mirror at the finished product. Her hair had been straightened to a silky sheen. It was quite the contrast to her daily messy ponytail. *Her reflection was disturbing. It could have easily been Chloe.* Lily passed her a bottle of gin. Tempted to take it, Kayn opted to be smart instead of emotional, "I'll pass. I'll be sick later."

Smiling at her, Lily urged, "Humour me." She dabbed gin on Kayn's neck like an expensive perfume. "You need to appear to be an easy target."

They'd all been given the backstory this time because tonight, they were Correcting someone who would fight back. A man so undeniably evil that the word 'dark' was a grave understatement. There was a twenty-five per cent chance it would be her, coming face to face with a mortal more heinous than the one responsible for her own brutal Correction that fated night in the forest. They were bait. The lure on the line the others would use to reel the darkness in. Kayn filled her plastic glass with water from the tap and inhaled the scent of the musky room before drinking it. *This was a sketchy motel. Maybe it was all in her head?* It was then that she noticed the green shag carpeting. *Kevin's parent's living room had the same carpet.* Kayn squeezed her eyes shut, attempting to turn off the thoughts of the past. *Sentimentality served no purpose tonight. She'd lose what little edge she had.* She opened her eyes. Lexy was standing beside her, extremely proud of her makeover. Lily adjusted her blouse, opening the top buttons to reveal a subtle hint of skin. Lexy was wearing an outfit that screamed, take me now! It gave merit to the quote: you can't judge a book by its cover. *Lexy dressed the part but didn't act it… Not in the least.*

Mel was sprawled on the bed, angrily flicking through channels, scowling at her choice of fuzzy shows. "We never end up in a hotel with a TV that works?" Melody complained, tossing the useless remote on the seventies mustard-coloured sheets. "I've been in two different Clans and not once in two years have I watched any of the shows I used to watch. You'd think there would be working cable in one of these shitty hotel rooms," Mel mumbled.

Lexy reached into her purse and tossed a chocolate bar at Mel like a man whose wife had nasty P.M.S. Mel said nothing. She just smiled happily and ate the candy bar. Lexy wandered over to the sink. Mel followed. Passing Kayn, she offered her some. Kayn leaned forward and took a bite while noting the personal evolution it took to do it. *She would have never even shared a pop with her twin.*

She'd always been germ phobic. She was the hand sanitiser queen. She had no problem with dirt on her face, but Heaven forbid she touch her food with unwashed hands after using a bank machine. Checking her teeth for remnants of the chocolate bar in the mirror, Kayn caught herself staring at Lily as she applied the finishing touches to her makeup. *It was hard not to. She was inhumanly beautiful.* Aware she looked pretty with sleek, straight blond hair and freckles, Kayn felt way out of her league standing beside these three. *It was enough to give her a complex. Her ability to blend into the background might work in her favour. Maybe she wouldn't be the one who caught the serial murderer's attention?*

When they were ready, Mel draped her arm around Kayn as they strolled out of their room, announcing, "Let's get this show on the road!"

While appearing to be normal girls ready to go clubbing, they knocked on the guy's room. Frost opened the door shirtless with his chiselled chest and abs. Feigning shock, his jaw dropped. He smirked, and you just knew something extremely naughty was about to roll out of his sexy lips. "I had a dream just like this. Come in, ladies. Hop in my bed."

Caressing his cheek as she strutted by, Lily provoked, "I'd rather pull my own teeth out with rusty pliers."

"Not likely," Lexy sighed, socking his arm.

Grinning, Frost teased, "It's not a solid no, then?"

Lexy wandered away, rolling her eyes. Almost every word that came out of his mouth was thinly veiled innuendo. If everyone hit Frost every time he uttered something inappropriate, they'd have permanently sore wrists.

Distracted by the base vibration beneath her feet, Kayn almost walked right into him. Taking in her serial killer bait makeover, his gaze travelled up her legs to her recently pierced belly button. *A choice made solely by her.*

Running his fingers over soft flesh close to her piercing, Frost flirted, "It suits you. Maybe you should just go with the naughty thing for a while. Have some fun?"

His touch scrambled her brain. Wracking her mind for a comeback, Kayn had nothing. *Silence was the best move. What was wrong with him? Why couldn't he ever wear a damn shirt?*

Lexy reappeared, saying, "Let me guess, Grey had to dance?"

"I was going to tell you they were downstairs at the club waiting for you high maintenance ladies, but you barged in," he teased, trying to ruffle Lexy's hair.

Lexy swatted him away, threatening, "I will kill you… Dead!"

He grinned and winked at Kayn. *Guess he was flirting with her again? He smelled amazing.*

Steering her away, Mel whispered, "You're staring at him. Let's go before you light this cheap hotel on fire with the heat from those cheeks. That bedspread looks flammable."

Touching her cheeks as they left, they were burning up. *She felt like an idiot. He was flirting with everyone.*

Frost caught up and took Lily's arm. They strutted past a huge line like royalty. The bouncer lifted the rope. They strolled into the club like their entourage. Music pulsated, luring them to the dance floor. They needed to make a spectacle so their prey would bite one of the immortal hooks they were dangling. Making a spectacle was Kayn's speciality, but not in the sexy, cool way. About to descend the stairs, she tripped over her own feet. Scrambling to grab for the railing so she wouldn't tumble down the stairs, she launched herself over and ended up dangling from it, cursing. *Nobody flinched.*

Lily, the beacon of genetic perfection, yanked her back over the railing, quietly reprimanding, "Really, Kayn? You have to learn to walk in heels."

"I know... I know," Kayn sheepishly mumbled. *There were only three steps leading to the dance floor. Why did this crap always happen to her? I'm such a dork.* They were joined by Zach, who was still laughing at Kayn's good-slash-bad luck. On an endless mission to regain Lexy's favour, Zach started dancing in front of her. She coldly shut him down and walked away, leaving him standing there. Without knowing what the mark's triggers were, she unknowingly volunteered herself as the victim.

Hugging Zach, Melody assured, "She'll get over it once she's had the opportunity to get even."

"Yeah. That's what I'm afraid of," Zach chuckled in her embrace.

Pitchy squeals startled them. A mortified girl was on the dance floor in her underwear, covering herself with both arms. Her dress was on the floor. Kayn shook her head. *Every time Grey got the chance to telepathically whip off a button-up dress or shirt, he did it.* Without missing a beat, Mel towed Zach into the crowd. Swaying to the music, Kayn watched her friends dancing. A waitress handed her a fruity slushy from her tray. She pointed at Grey. S*he accepted it because she was thirsty*. He gave her a thumbs-up sign. *Guru Grey was trying to make her more comfortable.* Smiling, she sipped the drink. *It was delicious!* People watching, she drank it too quickly and gave herself wicked brain freeze. Scrunching her face, she rubbed her tongue on the roof of her mouth to dull the pain. As alcohol numbed inhibitions, Kayn danced with the bass, keeping time with the rhythm of her heart as multicoloured strobe lights and smoke whirled. She shivered as her pulse raced with a surge of adrenaline. Blowing it off, she confidently danced, embracing the freedom. Her eyes searched for him as always. Surrounded by a flock of adoring women as per usual, Frost caught her staring. *Oh, shit! He was coming.* She peeked from under her veil of lashes as he manoeuvred his way through the writhing herd of scantily clad bodies with the fluidity of a sexy exotic jungle cat. Unsure of what she should do, Kayn stared into her drink. *He was supposed to stay away from her. Don't look at him. Don't look. A* hand slid across her bare shoulder. Ready to blow him off, she saw him leaving with his arm around a curvy brunette. *He was toying with her. Cats love to play with their prey.*

They weren't allowed to take off in the middle of a job. Frost was someone's backup. Kayn glanced around the room. *Her Clan disappeared. Where did they go?* She wandered through partying mortals, blissfully unaware a serial killer was hunting in their midst. *They'd all taken off without her. What in the hell?* Shoving through the crowd congregated at the door, she was met with a cool blast of oxygen-rich air. *It was disgustingly stuffy in there.*

Time to get kidnapped by a serial murderer. Where in the hell did they go? Who was her backup? Wishing they let her know they were leaving, Kayn began her unsupervised jaunt down the street lit by flashing neon, casually strolling towards the first alleyway she came across. *This was the obvious place to get kidnapped.* Listening to her heels mistimed clinks, she stumbled. *She really did have to learn to walk in heels.* She gave herself a peep talk. *Act sexy. Sway your hips. You've got this.* Turning the corner into the alley behind the club, she caught a glimpse of a shadow and sensed Frost's presence. *She knew what he'd been doing… Who, he'd been doing.* With conflicting emotions, she walked away. *She had no right to be upset. Having feelings for Frost was nothing but a messed-up emotional rollercoaster ride. He was so much fun until his behaviour made you sick to your stomach.* Hearing footsteps, she caught a whiff of Frost's addictive pheromones. *He was her backup.* Kayn stopped. *So did the footsteps. Why was he following her tonight?* She continued down the alley. *First, he all but ignores her for a year, then attempts to start something, and when she doesn't fall over with her legs in the air, he ignores her again. Then, she bares her soul to him. He hits a moose and tells her he doesn't hate her. They still weren't allowed to be together. Frost was a slutty, self-centred douchebag.* Turning down an adjoining alley, she felt him watching each step she took. Acting like she couldn't care less, Kayn strutted away. Graphic, sensual visions involving her twin began flooding her thoughts. *Not now!* Her hand slid along an icy railing, descending stairs. She almost had cool moment until she realised the stairwell was a dead end. *Where in the hell did she think she was going to go?* She stood there contemplating the merits of banging her head against the cement until she knocked herself out. *She could start fresh tomorrow.*

From the top of the stairs, Frost teased, "Is there a magic tunnel down there?"

"I thought I saw something," Kayn replied, wincing and clutching her forehead. *She sounded like an idiot. She'd trapped herself at the bottom of a damn stairwell. She didn't know how to come back up without looking like a complete dork. Rip the band-aid off.* She mustered up a confident smile as she scaled the stairs. *He wasn't blocking the top as she'd expected.* Looking in both directions, she didn't see him. She heard a noise in the darkness to her left, so she went right with rhythmic clicking heels echoing on the cement, each step beckoning him to follow her. *He was hiding in the shadows.* She felt his gaze.

Refocused on the job, she was aiming for Jessica Rabbit but hadn't learned the art of being subtly sexy. *Walking in three-inch heels wasn't as easy as it looked. Her feet hurt.* Kayn turned the corner, strolled into a narrow extension of the darkened alley and realised she'd backed herself into a corner. *The danger was exciting. Fate would take its natural course and she was along for the ride. Would it be her? A small part of her wanted it to be.* With each click of her heels, the echo chanted, *I dare you. Come get me. I am all alone.* They were all walking the streets that night as baited hooks for a diabolically evil fish that they had the honour of reeling in. A fish had been hooked by one of the four Ankh women the second he'd laid eyes on her.

Chapter 18

Slaying Dragons

It had been over an hour since Kayn had begun to wander dark alleyways, trolling for a serial murderer. She stopped mid-high heel click, laughing with an extremely unsexy accidental snort. Frost stepped out of the shadows and startled her.

Frost provoked, "Do you think it might be possible to aim for a more sexy, less standup comedian?"

Scrunching up her face with distaste, she whispered, "It's been hours. My feet are frigging killing me. Why in the hell do women wear these things? I couldn't even imagine working in an office wearing these torture devices." Kayn took off the heels and stood there saucily with them dangling from her hand.

Acting the part of a John soliciting her services, Frost leaned in and quietly teased, "Okay Froggy, giving up is not an option."

"Enough with that nickname," Kayn countered under her breath with her back almost against the building. He seductively stepped forward causing her to press her back against the brick. Her lips parted in anticipation. As his finger grazed her bare skin, she realised he was only fixing her strap.

He quietly teased, "But it's an adorable nickname."

She'd completely misread his intentions.

They felt the heat of their symbols at the same time. Neither, needed to take off their glove to look. The warmth of their hand travelled up their arms to their hearts, creating a surging pit of fear. Frost began to run. Kayn chased him with her heels in hand. The panic the brand induced when one of her Clan was in danger was difficult to describe. The Ankh appeared from various directions and met in the middle of the street.

Sometimes, you just knew who was in trouble, and other times, you used the power of deduction. Everyone was accounted for but Lexy. Oh shit. Did that serial murderer ever pick the wrong girl. As their eyes met, it was obvious everyone was thinking the same thing.

"This sick bastard is going to get his ass handed to him in a seriously epic way," Grey chuckled.

Lily shook her head, saying, "We have to find her before there's nothing left of this guy to process."

Pulling up in the truck, Frost unrolled the window and rushed, "We have no time to waste. Get in."

She hadn't even noticed he'd left. Kayn squeezed into the backseat. They sped down the road and turned with their Ankh symbols acting like a gut driven homing beacon. Kayn looked at Grey and whispered, "You don't look worried at all. What if he hurts her before we can get to her?"

Lexy's Handler casually said, "If you're ever kidnapped-by-a-serial-murderer, the rules are simple. Pretend you're unconscious. They need you awake so they can see the fear in your eyes. They want to enjoy your pain. They get off on it. You buy time by not giving them the satisfaction of seeing you squirm. Once they know you're awake you can buy more time, confusing them with your lack of fear. Lexy's survived places none of us could even imagine. She has strength I could never dream of. She'll not only be fine, but we'll be lucky if the dude is still alive. She might kill him before we get there. Lexy's only issue is her lack of control. Where logic steps in for most of us, she becomes lost. She's gone once rage takes over. Like every one of us, our greatest strength is also our greatest weakness."

Dragon Versus Serial Killer

Wake up, Lexy. She didn't open her eyes. *She knew better.* Lexy wasn't sure how long she'd been out. She kept her eyes closed, knowing the deal behind these sickos. *He'd wait until she woke up to begin his torture. He would want to watch her squirm. He'd want to place his hand on her chest and feel her heart as it palpitated with fear. The longer she kept her eyes closed, the more time she'd buy. Aware she could opt out of the pain, she was far too curious. She desired the full experience. She wanted to know what he'd done to his victims. This was going to be fun.* She used her other senses to prepare for her surroundings. Lexy could tell that she was lying on a cold floor. Perhaps it was a table. She knew this without opening her eyes. She felt a breeze across her skin. Goosebumps rose in response. *She was naked. What did she smell?* Scanning through the list of foul fragrances in her memory, she recognised the tinny scent of blood combined with paint and gasoline. *Was she in a garage? These were all things she could tell without opening her eyes and giving away her return to the land of the coherent. One odour in particular, haunted her subconscious. The metallic scent of blood had always stimulated her inner Dragon. She knew Ankh would come. When, was the question? She was buying them time by pretending to be out cold for as long as possible. Time to save the serial murderer from her Dragon's wrath. If she killed him before they arrived, they wouldn't have the opportunity to mark him and send him to where he needed to go. Markus would be furious with her. She hated disappointing her surrogate father figure. Skippy the serial killer had chosen the wrong girl to play his wicked games with tonight.* O*nce their game began it would be difficult to play nice. He wasn't going to buy it much longer. She could feel him there.* Without opening her eyes, she could sense his excitement. *She loved this part. She had a seriously warped sense of humour, but she owned it. Ah hell,* she thought. *Curiosity won the battle over good behaviour.* She opened an eye to sneak a peek. The room was covered in plastic. *Of course, it was.* She contained her smile. *He was one of those guys.* Lexy tried to shift her hands. They were only bound with duct tape. *This was going to be hilarious.* To her left was a silver sterile-looking table full of silver instruments. She could smell a hint of bleach. *He took the time to bleach between murders. Isn't that sweet? The metal table was such a cliché. This tool was watching too many late-night horror movies. His prior victims would have been terrified.* Lexy found predatory monsters amusing. She smiled and thought, *oh, this is going to be fun. It felt like some good old-fashioned vengeance was in order.* She would settle the score for all who'd been on this table before her. A smile burst through her cheeks as she chuckled aloud. The contemptible excuse for a human appeared. She didn't bother turning her eyes immediately. *It always drove these ones insane when you didn't react.* She super casually glanced in his direction. *His curiosity was peaked. She could see it in his eyes.*

"You're not afraid of me?" He questioned, standing before her with a knife glinting in the stream of light through the taped window.

"Surely, you're not serious?" Lexy provoked. She coolly gazed into his eyes and goaded, "Why would I be afraid of something like you?" Intrigued by her lack of fear, he moved closer, knife in hand. He was perspiring so heavily his glasses slipped down. Her supposed assailant slid his spectacles back up on his nose. He gripped the knife and hovered it above her skin at her collarbone. *He was waiting for a reaction. She gave him nothing. Shuddering, he* traced his blade along the tender ivory flesh between her breasts, lightly slicing her skin. A sliver of blood seeped from the wound, trickling almost artistically across the gossamer palate of her skin. Lexy didn't even flinch. "What do you think you can do to me with that tiny knife? Please explain and don't leave out any details. I'd like your punishment, to fit the crime," Lexy taunted. *She'd always had a hysterical sense of comic timing.* Her wound had already healed. He was too busy acting out his sick torture ritual to notice. He traced the blade down her leg from her groin to her big toe on either side. She felt the burn of each slice, but it was only an irritation. *She was a Healer, flesh wounds healed quickly.*

Giddy with excitement, the hideous excuse for a human whispered, "In your worst nightmares, you've never imagined what I plan to do to you."

"Yes, that's what all my dates say," Lexy sparred. *She wished someone was here to hear these comebacks. They were priceless. She was on fire tonight.* She heard the laugh track from an old comedy in her mind as he slid the knife into her stomach. Lexy commented on his murder skills, "My liver was a little to the left. You missed it by a hair. Do you need a moment to figure this out? Pass me my cellphone and I'll google it for you?"

He viciously knifed her twice in the gut and hissed, "Shut up bitch!"

It was always exciting in the moments before a psycho realised the tables had turned and the hunter became the hunted. He stared at the table, methodically picking up weapons, gaging her reaction to each one. Lexy teased, "Oh sweetheart… You're going to need better weapons than those. Nothing on that table will keep me down for five minutes. Don't you have a gun or something? It's way more fun for me when it's a bit of a fair fight."

He whispered in his own special brand of mockery, "You are a piece of meat to me, nothing more. Speak again and I will cut out your tongue and eat it right in front of you."

Lexy grimaced and shook her head. This sicko talked a good game but she didn't need the visual of this scrawny, creepy guy devouring her tongue. She watched him choose his instrument of torture. He looked rather pleased with himself as he turned around to find her sitting up on the metal bed, casually tearing the duct tape off. She sighed, "You know duct tape sticks to the hairs on your arms. You have no self-preservation skills. How have you gotten away with killing people for this long? You're not the sharpest tool in the shed. Are you? Think about all of that pesky D.N.A. evidence you're leaving behind." His eyes wandered to her healed wounds. *There it was… Bingo.* He looked confused for a split second before running at her with his weapon of choice. She casually smacked it out of his hand, then slapped him across the face. Lexy hissed, "Simmer down cupcake. Trust me; you don't want to see me upset."

He grabbed another weapon and lunged at her again. Lexy stood there, allowing him to stab her stomach. He got creative, twisted the knife, and her hand began to glow. *He got sidetracked.* She smacked his hand away, removed the blade and chucked it on the floor.

Lexy sighed, "It's not that I don't find your psychotic rants moderately entertaining. I really do appreciate your love of the kill. Once you've heard one serial killer's rants, you've heard them all." The pale-faced, perspiring middle-aged waste of oxygen began to back away. Lexy walked slowly towards him, past the table of weapons, without attempting to grab one. *Lexy didn't need a weapon. She was the weapon.*

He backed up until an axe was within reach and hissed, "What are you?" He swung the axe in a laughable attempt at fending her off.

Lexy manoeuvred out of the way. Grabbing it with only one of her hands, she cautioned, "Okay, muffin. Your little twisted deal here is done. By twisted little deal, I mean your mortal life, darling. We can do this the easy way or the hard way." He started throwing random weapons from the table. She swatted the objects away without touching them, using only energy. *She wanted to snap his neck and be done with him. They'd better hurry up.* She stopped walking and sighed dramatically. He was quite the sight, cowering against the wall. When he noticed she'd stopped moving, he stood upright. *He wanted her to lose control. She could see it in his eyes.*

He whispered, "I did things to you. Things you haven't even dreamt of."

Lexy stepped closer. He began rifling jars at her from the wooden shelf on the wall again. Lexy grimaced. *That thought was disgusting.* Lexy coldly lured, "I can think up a few things, you've never dreamt of." He tossed a can of paint while her mind was on his perverse admittance. It smoked the side of the head. She lost her cool and punched him in the jaw. He dropped to the floor like a sack of stones. She stood above him, taking a moment to calm down. *Markus wants him alive.* He had another knife. The creep took a swing at her ankle, cutting the strap of her shoe. "You stinker!" Lexy scolded. She glanced at Lily's destroyed strap and spat, "I borrowed these shoes! Asshole!" She stood on his shoulder to make him drop the knife. *He was pissing her off. He wouldn't let go of it.* She glanced away from what was annoying her and looked at her surroundings to calm the Dragon within that wanted to finish him off. *This was a bad idea. It had the opposite effect. The blood stains on the plastic tarp told the sadistic stories of his past victims.*

Without letting go of the blade, he shrieked, "You Whore! I'm going to cut you to pieces!"

"Well, we can't have that. Can we?" Lexy goaded. She stepped harder on his shoulder to shut him up. When that didn't work, she grabbed his wrist and tried to pry the knife from his grip. *He still wouldn't let go.* So, she stepped harder on his shoulder while yanking on the wrist, clutching the blade. *He was ticking her off.* She felt her ability to control her rage disappear. Lexy reefed on his arm and accidentally ripped it right off. He began shrieking as his blood spurted across the room. *Whoops.*

"I've gutted dozens of whores! You're nothing! You are nothing!" He shrieked.

His vile words of contempt set her inner Dragon free. She saw flashes of women he'd tortured in his plastic-covered den of horrors. The terror they must have felt as they prayed for salvation. *Their prayers had gone unanswered. They'd be answered in this moment by her.* In a blind rage, she beat him with the wet end of his own dismembered arm as vile images flashed through her mind. That was when the rest of the Ankh showed up.

The whirling strips of storage containers and abandoned buildings by the docks slowed outside her window. Kayn could tell Lexy was close. *It was truly miraculous how this gift worked.* They pulled up to an inconspicuous rundown warehouse, jumped out and sprinted to the building led by something greater than themselves. *Well, that... and the male high-pitched screaming.* Frost waved his hand. The door blew open revealing a visual instilling such awe they all required a second to comprehend what they were seeing. It was a scene from a horror movie. Plastic-covered walls with blood and matter sprayed everywhere. *This guy was seriously messed up.* In a wildly unstable rage, Lexy was beating a shrieking man with his dismembered arm, screeching, "You sick! Pathetic! Twisted! Freak!"

As stunned as the rest, Frost didn't move a muscle.

Grey comically chimed in, "Well, this is new." Lexy's Handler walked towards his bestie, calmly soothing, "Honey... Hey, darling. You can stop beating him. He's almost dead. We need to do a little ritual to make sure he goes where he is supposed to go. Come with me, sweetie. Let's get you some clothes. Perhaps a shower? I bet you could use a nice cup of tea?"

Lexy abruptly dropped the dismembered arm, stepped over a sick pile of human hearts and whispered, "That does sound lovely." She went willingly with Grey and allowed him to guide her out the door to pass her off to those not involved in the clean-up.

Frost whispered to a stunned Zach, "That's the girl you lost tonight because you were too busy flirting with Lily to notice. Let's hope she got all of her pent-up aggression out." He walked over to the man, who'd lost enough blood to calm his screaming. Frost cut his hand, causing it to glow and placed his palm dripping with immortal blood on the evil man's forehead.

The man murmured, "What are going to do to me?"

Frost coldly assured, "You did this to yourself." He spoke in Greek.

Kayn recalled the words but suspected he was delivering this soul to a slightly different destination. With a last wheezy breath, his shell became still. The air felt clean again.

Grey returned to stand beside them and urged, "Check on Lexy. I usually do this part myself."

Kayn watched as Grey ripped the electrical outlet out of the wall. He exposed the wires, held his hand over and began to heat the wires until they burst into flames. It was always best if the cover-up looked like an electrical surge.

The older Ankh had seen this kind of blind rage in Lexy before. The three newest had only ever heard about it. It would be easy to become lost in the darkness if you could shut down emotionally. Grey was Lexy's tether to the light. They could withstand time's ticking hands if they moved through eternity together. Tonight, she'd need Grey close so he could lead her back into the light. This was his gift. He was the yin to her yang. The light to her dark. They fit together like an immortal puzzle. They watched as Grey walked from the burning building towards Lexy. He gently lifted her chin so he could look deep into her eyes. She'd shut her emotions off. This was how she kept reality at bay. There was no fight left in her vacant eyes. There was nothing there at all.

Grey vowed, "I'll be there faster to protect you next time, I promise." He pulled her into his embrace.

Lexy's rigid frame loosened as she nestled into the crook of Grey's neck. He stood there with her, rocking back and forth. Life appeared in her eyes. She whispered back, "I will protect you."

Grey stroked her silky hair lovingly as he whispered back, "Whatever you want my love."

They drove straight back to the hotel. Grey came to their room and climbed into the bed next to Lexy. Exhausted, she curled up in his arms and fell asleep. *She slept a dreamless sleep free of Dragons, for she had slain them once again.*

Chapter 19
Focus

Things become peaceful after a storm. The clouds clear. The dust settles. Futures come into focus.

Travelling North through the familiar scenery of British Columbia, the humming tires were a soothing lullaby. As they reached their destination, Kayn was far too excited to sleep. As soon as the sun crept over the horizon, she threw her hair in a ponytail and washed up. The biting chill of an early morning run in an oxygen-rich environment would clear her mind of everyone and everything. Kayn fumbled with the door. *She was home. She was finally home.* Stepping outside, she inhaled the sweet crispness of dawn. They were parked in an almost deserted campground. She imagined the trees in the rugged wilderness were waving hello. Her heart sang out with pure joy as her feet began breaking twigs on the trails. A sound that once incapacitated her with terror now brought her to the brink of elation. She knew someone was coming by the crackling of twigs behind. She glanced back and decided to hide. Frost jogged around the corner and slowed to walk when he didn't see her. She leapt out of the bushes.

"Woooo… You scared the crap out of me," he teased.

"I'll get you one day, wascally wabbit," she joked. Frost grinned blankly. *He'd missed the joke completely.* Kayn ribbed, "Not a fan of Bugs Bunny?"

Thoroughly amused by her dorky behaviour, Frost taunted, "You do realise you're an adult making references to a cartoon."

Kayn winked, baited, "Everybody likes Bugs Bunny and I thought you weren't allowed to stalk me anymore?"

"The world doesn't revolve around you, Miss Brighton," he sparred. "I was just going to check something out. I dare you to try and keep up." He took off.

She couldn't refuse a dare. It was one of her afterlife rules. She was also aware daring her to come in Frost code meant he wanted her to. He couldn't ask her to because it would destroy his 'he didn't care what she did anymore' stance. She raced after him as he darted through the overgrown trail. A branch flew back and whipped her in the face. She staggered backwards. *Ahhh. Right in the eyes... That stung.* He was too far ahead of her to notice. She shook her head. *That's going to leave a mark.* She sped up and caught up. He abruptly stopped, and she almost ploughed into him.

Wiping perspiration from his brow, he announced, "I haven't been to this place in five years. I know it's somewhere around here."

"If you tell me what we're looking for, maybe I can help you find it?" Kayn teased, following him towards a small entrance to a cave that only a tiny animal could live in. "I'm pretty sure we won't fit," she laughed.

"We don't have to. Watch this," Frost answered while running his hands along the rock on the inside of the opening. Finding what he was looking for, his face exploded into a dimpled grin. He placed his hand in the grooves on the inside of the opening. The ground disappeared, revealing stairs descending into darkness.

"Okay, this is extremely cool," Kayn whispered, in awe of the hidden Crypt. *This must be the Ankh Crypt hidden in the British Columbian wilderness. She'd heard Lily talking about it.*

"We have them all over the place but this one is different. This Crypt has a special purpose. Do you have a lighter?" He asked.

"Why in the world would I have a lighter?" Kayn laughed, hearing him searching for something.

He glanced back at her, smiled and added, "Don't worry about a thing beautiful. There's usually one hidden in here." He disappeared down the stairs.

Every time Frost added the word beautiful to the end of a sentence, it felt condescending. The corridor lit up with the first torch's vibrant flame. Kayn cautiously followed him. As she stepped off the last stair, she heard the entrance to the forest grind shut behind her. *They were alone.* Frost lit the torches down the long corridor. A pathway of warm flickering light revealed the Ankh Crypt. As he strolled back down the long hall towards her in the glimmer of torchlight, she felt her elastic band snap. Her blonde curls cascaded down her back. She felt in her hair for it, then scanned the floor. When she looked up, he was right in front of her.

He plucked the broken piece of elastic out of her hair, slipped it into his pocket and questioned, "Ready to pay attention?" She nodded as he began his history lesson, "This is one of the original Ankh Crypts. There are only a half dozen on each continent. This is our sanctuary in the North."

It didn't look like much of a sanctuary. It was just an open area with old dusty pillows on the floor and mats. Kayn whispered, "This place looks like a breeding ground for spiders. I'm not a fan." She stepped on a pillow. A cloud of dust released into the air. Waving t away, she coughed.

Frost patted her back, casually saying, "I'm leaving. I'm going to the Summit in a couple of days."

He was leaving her. Kayn turned away from him and stared at the carvings on the walls, trying to focus on the ornate, dusty tapestries to sidetrack her mind so the panic didn't register. *Testing was sooner than she'd thought.* She fought her urge to shoot a thousand questions at him. *What was the Summit? Was he coming back? She was far too dependent on him. He'd been right about that. Hearing* his 'he wasn't doing her any favours' speech in her mind, she changed the subject. *She had to act like his absence was no big deal.* "What are these carvings about?" She whispered as she traced her fingers along the surface of the stone.

He shook his head and laughed as he brushed her fingers away without attempting to reply. The carvings were of one woman and three men. She raised her hand to the stone again. He brushed her finger off the wall and taunted, "You seriously have me worried sometimes. It's like you're a glutton for punishment. Never touch the carvings unless you are looking for something messed-up to happen. You already know this."

Kayn could feel him standing behind her as she took in the pictures but didn't feel them this time.

Frost answered her earlier question, "It's just an old story about three brothers who fell in love with the same girl."

She felt him rest his hand on her hip. Every nerve ending in her body stood on end. She leaned back until she was almost touching him as she asked, "Who did she choose?"

"Her choice didn't matter in the end. They never got to be together," Frost replied as he cupped her hips with both hands and shifted her closer.

Intimately relaxed against him, she felt the absence of his hands. She heard the Crypt grinding open and turned around. He was gone. *Come on… Seriously? This passive-aggressive bullshit made her certifiable. What was with the disappearing act? Had she leaned just a little too close?* She caught her hand halfway to touching the carving on the wall again. *It was surprisingly difficult to resist the urge. She would have to ask someone about that. You didn't have to be a brain surgeon to figure out what the carvings were about, but she'd always wanted to hear Frost's version of the story. She knew he was one of the original Ankh. He was one of the three Brothers Of Prophecy. Kayn couldn't help but wonder why Frost gave control of the Clan to Markus. There was a story behind that.* She lowered her hand again as it raised to touch the wall by itself. *He brings me here to tell me he is leaving, and then he takes off without saying a word?* She caught herself touching the carving of one of the three men while actively trying not to. *Her hand was stuck to the wall! What in the hell?* She tried yanking it away but it felt like it was glued there. Her pulse started to race. She yanked her hand away. *That was weird.* Kayn made her way down the long hallway of flames towards the stairs, scaled them and instinctively figured out where to place her hands to open the hatch. It slid open. She squinted in the blinding glare of the sun's rays. *It felt like it was later in the day. Strange? How long had they been down there?* M*agical place time-lapse?*

There was a bright side to their excursion. She'd finally have a chance to run into the wild without knowing where she was or where she was going. To anyone else, that would sound strange, but in Kayn's mind, it was as exciting as winning the lottery. She pulled the spare elastic band from her wrist and put her hair back in a tight ponytail. This always made her feel like she was preparing for a battle. *A personal battle with her need to feel freedom. The only battle she could win.* Sprinting into the bushes, her heart beat in unison with her feet. With fluid footsteps as agile as a predatory animal, she raced through winding trails until she found her way out of the wild and hit the highway with a vengeance. Her running shoes pounded the pavement in a soothing rhythm.

She had been running wide open for at least twenty minutes when a school appeared in the distance. *Was it a high school? Nope.*

It wasn't. She saw the college sign and smiled. *They would have a track.* She wanted to run where she could shut her mind down and not think about her footing. *That was what she needed.* Kayn could tell by the sparse amount of students lounging on the lawn eating sandwiches that there wasn't much of a summer program. *Sandwiches. It must be lunchtime.* She strolled past, imagining what it would be like to be a college student. *Right now, she'd be on her way to the track for a lunchtime run after class.* She walked up to the fountain and took a drink, splashed water on her face and adjusted her ponytail. It snapped. *Lovely. She was running out of extra elastics on her wrist today.* She wet her hair and left it untameable curls. Looking like a normal girl with freckles and a golden tan, Kayn Brighton strolled past a cluster of teens on her way to the track. *She would have been in college right now.* She pulled her hair into a tight ponytail without missing a stride, thinking about nothing but the freedom of the run that lay ahead of her. She lunged and stretched at the start line, then sprinted away, kicking up dust. With her heart beating at the pace of her feet, she felt as untameable as her wild mane of curls. Nothing mattered but the thrill of the run. Grinning as she passed a group of teens on the sidelines. *They were staring. Was she running too fast?* Rounding the corner, she looked at the gawking teenagers. Her heart almost stopped in her chest. *Was that Kevin?* She lost her footing, skidded and slid across the ground on her knees, feeling the sting of the road rash and the embarrassment of the fall. She squinted in the sun's glare. It blinded her for a second and as her eyes focused, there he was standing above her. *She'd imagined this moment so many times.* She held her breath for the version where he remembered her.

Kevin held his hand out towards her, enquiring, "Are you okay? That was quite the wipe out."

She gasped, "Kevin... Is that you?" *He looked incredible. He'd filled out in the last year.*

Smiling, he said, "Do I know you?"

She couldn't speak as he looked at her palm. Intimately stroking her symbol of Ankh with his thumb, he smirked and said, "I'm sure someone from your Clan can fix your knees."

She couldn't bring herself to let go of his hand. He was looking a little uncomfortable, so she let go. He stepped away and smiled before he left her standing there in shock. With her feet cemented in place, she watched him walk away.

She heard Grey's voice behind her, "Was it everything you dreamt it would be?"

Frozen in place with her lips slightly parted in shock, Kayn couldn't speak.

Grey reworded his question, "Did he remember you?"

"No," Kayn quietly admitted. *She'd been waiting for so long to see her best friend again. He hadn't known her at all.* Her mind struggled to wrap itself around the obvious. *She wanted to chase after him.*

Kneeling to check out her road rash, Grey whispered, "You just met for the first time." He sweetly kissed her skinned knees.

Grey always made her feel like she still had a brother. That's who he was to her. A surrogate big brother.

"Lexy will fix that right up when we get back to the Crypt. Come on, munchkin," he teased with his always adorable accent. He placed his arm around her and gave her a half cuddle as they walked away.

He really was an outstanding guy when he wasn't making a pompous, chauvinistic ass of himself. Kayn randomly asked, "What nationality are you?"

Kissing her head, he laughed, "You, my dear, are the queen of random questions. I'm Scottish, but my family moved to Australia when I was twelve."

Trying to think about anything else, she replied, "Well, that explains it. I couldn't decide where you were from. You use slang from both places."

As they passed a cluster of people, a male voice called out, "My brother from down under! How's it going? Who is this enchanting, extremely sweaty vision of loveliness?"

Holding her shoulders so she couldn't turn, Grey whispered, "Be charming. Don't react. This is going to freak you out. Trust me and lay whatever girly crap you can manage to fake on this guy. Lay it on thick."

He let go of her. She turned to face a group of strangers. One of the men looked exactly like Kevin's entombed brother Clay. The look-alike was obviously Tiberius, the infamous leader of Triad. He was a hot, well-dressed version of Clay. She sucked in her reaction and then couldn't help herself, "You do look exactly like Clay. It's kind of amazing." She took his outstretched hand, smiling. *She was going to need a full bottle of Lysol to make her hand clean again.*

Tiberius flirted, "You're a feisty one. I love that... A challenge. You know the original is always way better than the copy."

Kayn decided she'd need more than one bottle. *Hell, she was going to need to buy shares in the Lysol Company.* She saw Frost in Tiberius. That dark, attractive quality. Naughty boy vibes.

"There's something I need to do," Tiberius flirted as he reached over and slipped the ponytail out of her hair. He smiled as it fell untamed down her shoulders. Rubbing a smudge of track dust off her cheek, he seduced, "Oh, I love that. I can picture you with nothing on but that wild mane of loose curls."

He was toying with her. Two could play at that game. Flirtatiously touching his nose, she provoked, "I'd picture you naked, but I left my microscope and tweezers at home."

Sputters of laughter from the Triad turned his smirk to a scowl. Kayn made eye contact with Kevin. He was biting his lip. This was something he'd always done while trying to be serious. *That meant he wanted to smile.* He winked at her. *Did Kevin just wink at her?*

"Well, it seems our lovely Kayn does come quite well armed for your always entertaining battle of wits," Grey commented. Looking directly at Kevin, he said, "Kevin... Nice to see you again kid."

Kevin looked at Grey, knit his brow and glared at Tiberius.

Tiberius sparred, "Cute… Really cute. You shithead."

Knowing during the Summit there was no violence between the Clans, Grey patted Tiberius' shoulder, teasing, "That's 'Sir Awesome Shithead' to you."

She couldn't stop staring at Kevin. *He'd winked at her.*

Grey grabbed Kayn's hand and towed her in the opposite direction, calling out, "Bye, Kev! So good to see you again!" Once they were out of earshot, he chuckled, "Microscope and tweezers? That was awesome. He's going to be obsessed with you thinking he's not packing any ammo. You just wrecked his whole week. He'll be accidentally flashing everyone in Triad for a month."

Kayn glanced back at Triad. *He was still watching her walk away. Maybe he could remember her? He just didn't remember yet.*

"You just wait until you see the three brothers in the same room together," Grey said. "You just made it change from merely entertaining to a gong show!"

They casually strolled through the woods hand in hand towards the hidden Ankh Crypt in peaceful silence as streams of sunlight filtered through the trees on the trail in their path. Billions of floating dust particles danced in each ray making the forest appear to be a magical place. Almost beautiful enough to deter her thoughts. *Twelve years as best friends and he didn't remember her. They'd all been right.* Grey squeezed her hand in solidarity without uttering a word. *She didn't need him to say anything. She just needed time to let it sink in.*

They entered the Crypt. It was empty. As they left, the glare of the sun brought her back to the track... *That first meeting.* She'd waited all this time for a lacklustre moment. Thier *reunion had done nothing but leave her feeling raw, lost and even more confused. His memory had been erased. That was a fact.* But as she relived their first meeting in her mind, she felt it. *Erased or not, there was something undeniable between them. It was still there in the touch of his hand... In the look in his eyes. She'd need to see him again to be sure.* She was off in la, la land when Grey cleared his throat to catch her attention.

"You have a lot to process," Grey acknowledged.

Did she ever. Kayn replied, "I thought when I knew for sure, once I could saw for myself that his mind was erased and he didn't know me, everything would become clear, but all I want to do is smack him senseless until he remembers me."

He took her hand and said, "If fate gave us a clear life path to walk down, we would never wander off in the wrong direction. What fun would that be?"

"I can't wander off in the wrong direction now. You'd bring me back," she laughed.

Grey chuckled and replied, "You would be surprised how often I have wandered off in the last forty years, even with supervision. Choose your roads with wisdom, not emotion and you can take a few wrong turns out of the equation."

Her heart warmed. *Guru Grey was back.* Kayn sighed and teased, "Why do I have a sneaky suspicion all I'm going to get from you are fortune cookie readings if I keep asking questions,?"

He gave her hand another brotherly squeeze and declared, "If I knew I wasn't going to get into trouble for answering your questions, I'd answer every one without hesitation."

"I know," she answered as they wandered down the path. Streams of sunlight wove through the trees. They paused in the hovering light, basking in the luxurious warmth of the rays. She let go of his hand, moved to stand in her own magical beam of heavenly radiance and smiled as the warmth caressed her face. *He was an excellent guru. She felt much better.* She whispered, "It's pretty wonderful, isn't it?"

"Amazing," Grey agreed. "This is one of my favourite things."

"Do you know what I like best?" Kayn replied.

Grey squinted in the sun to look at her and teased, "Does it have something to do with running?"

"Well, that too… But this one's really good," she confessed. Kayn knelt by a stump and opened her hand. A furry black and orange caterpillar strolled onto her palm. She allowed it to circle her hand as she stood up and nodded at Grey.

Grinning as it meandered from her hand into his, he said, "I say we go for lunch and then just spend the rest of the day doing cool peaceful things. Forget about ex-boyfriends with amnesia. We can allow all of our problems to melt away with the setting of the afternoon sun."

That might be just what the doctor ordered. She watched him set the caterpillar free on a flowering dogwood as she replied, "I think that's a great idea." The two happiness seekers strolled off hand in hand through the forest. They were almost back at the RV when they heard the crackling of tires in the distance and knew someone had probably been sent back to the camp to pick them up.

"I'll race you there so we can add running to the moment," Grey laughed as he took off on a dead run through the foliage.

She gave chase but let Grey run ahead of her. She wasn't in the mood to fight for the lead. They broke through the bushes laughing right in front of the truck. Lexy stomped on the brakes and scowled at them through the window.

Grey chuckled, "Good thing Lexy knows how to use the brakes because, for the record, being hit by a truck also sucks."

Chapter 20

Long Overdue Introductions

Kayn's ears were accosted by hundreds of clinking dishes and the thick echo of chatter. The restaurant was beyond packed. There were still four seats at the end of the long table they were sitting at. *Who else was coming?*

"Did you have a good morning?" Frost whispered as she shimmied into the empty seat beside him.

Dazed, she replied, "Not so much. My mind's a melted pile of goo. Is it coming out of my ears?"

Frost grinned and teased, "Not yet."

Grey told the rest of the Clan about their crazy morning. The whole table erupted with laughter over Kayn's microscope and tweezers comment. Her heart clenched. *Had Frost known she'd be seeing Kevin today? His expression was impossible to read. He was looking at everyone else but her.* The table paused as the door jingled announcing new patrons. Markus and Arrianna walked across the room and joined the table. *That was an explanation for two of the four extra chairs.*

Lily's face erupted into a grin. "Father!" She said, getting up to embrace Markus. Lily looked around. She'd announced father loudly and Markus looked less than ten years her senior.

The bells rang for the diner's door again. A strikingly handsome blonde stranger approached the table.

Frost leapt up and joyously embraced him, "This is Orin everyone. Orin, this is Kayn, Zach and... Melody."

Reining in her shock. Mel peered up at the man with the name of her biological father.

One more chair. Who was the next surprise guest? The door jingled again. Everyone's eyes lit up as a beautiful girl with kind eyes and shiny chestnut curls came to their table. Her dimpled smile immediately put her at ease. Orin was staring across the table at

Melody. *He obviously knew she was his daughter.* Frost, Lily and Markus all stood up out of respect.

"Jenna... How are you here?" Markus asked, hugging her.

"I thought I'd better come back before you guys messed everything up," Jenna teased as she embraced Lily.

Orin looked as shocked as she had been when she ran into Kevin.

"Jenna," Orin acknowledged her presence.

Holy tension.

Jenna responded with one solitary word, "Orin." They stared at each other as their waitress came to take their order.

This was awkward.

As soon as their server left, Jenna said, "Melody. It's a pleasure to meet you."

Overwhelmed by emotion, Mel took Jenna's hand, whispering, "You look exactly like my mother

Jenna gave Orin the dirtiest look. She held out her hand towards Zach.

Leaning across the table, Zach gallantly kissed her hand, saying, "Nice to meet you."

When Jenna laughed, everyone smiled. She held her hand out to Kayn, and as she shook it, Jenna grinned like she knew the colour of her panties. Smiling, Kayn welcomed her, "It's a pleasure to meet you."

Keeping ahold of her hand, Jenna replied, "I've wanted to meet you for a long time. I've known your mother forever. She's one of my best friends. You look a lot like your mother too." She elbowed Frost and shook her head. Grinning at Frost, Jenna whispered, "I see you are still being led around by your second brain. I'm not sure if that's endearing or just pathetic."

The sibling relationship with Frost was funny.

Frost leaned over and whispered to Kayn, "Jenna left Orin a couple decades ago for the opportunity to be the Guardian Azariah's right hand."

Jenna whispered in Frost's other ear, "I'm sitting right here."

"You knew she was sitting right there when you accused me of being led around by my junk," he whispered.

With raised brows, Jenna reprimanded, "I have every right to be pissy. You haven't been respecting my orders."

The two immortals continued their sparring match. Kayn just sat back and watched the drama unfold. Mel met her genetic sire. *Orin was traumatized by Jenna's presence. Maybe they hadn't told him his ex was going to be here? Just like nobody had bothered to inform her that her ex was going to be here.* Kevin's reaction to her Ankh symbol flashed through her memory. She blinked away the tears forming in her eyes. *He was here. She needed to go to the washroom to get her shit together.* She quickly finished her lunch.

Grey grabbed her chair, abruptly pulled it out and said, "It's time to go kids. These boring old people need to have some alone time."

"Where are we going?" Melody questioned as she stood up.

"Here and there," Grey answered. "Don't worry about it. Let's go."

Knowing Grey had their back, they left the bell jingling behind them.

The Ankh at the table began to talk about deeper, more intensely important subjects once the Newbies were out of earshot.

Markus addressed the group, "So, only one of trio has been Enlightened?"

"I have been trying to trigger one myself for months," Frost chuckled as he took a sip of his drink.

Lilarah kicked him under the table.

Jenna spoke, "I gave Winnie my seat at Azariah's side. The next time any of you decide to disobey a direct order, do try to remember it will be Winnie who will be choosing your punishment. She doesn't know you so there's no sense of guilt in causing you pain. I'm sure I don't have to tell you she's not your biggest fan, Frost." Jenna glanced at Orin, saying, "I know every one of your dirty secrets and naughty acts over the last twenty years."

"See anything you liked?" Frost teased.

Jenna sighed, "Oh, please. Put a cork in it, Romeo. I'd rather commit suicide by eating something off this menu."

They casually sipped their coffees while talking about life-altering events.

Lily addressed Jenna directly, "Do you feel like the three of them are ready? Do any obvious mortal fears still linger? Anything we've missed?"

"Aren't there always?" Jenna responded.

Pushing it a little further, Lily probed, "I'm asking you if you believe there is a chance this group will survive the Testing?"

Solemnly, Jenna replied, "It has been a long time since our sacrifices have had a chance at surviving the Testing. This group is going to survive. I can feel it. If we think it, the Third-Tier are already preparing for it. Testing is psychologically unbeatable if too much of your humanity remains. If there is anything that still needs to be covered. Grey and Lexy must cover it during this next trip to the In-between." Jenna paused before continuing, "The faster they become Enlightened during the Testing, the better their chances are. Their souls need to be broken down to be built. The farther they fall, the stronger they'll become. I've had visions about one of them. I have an idea."

After swallowing a gulp of coffee, Frost questioned, "What's the idea?"

Jenna replied, "We'll arrange to have Kevin kill Kayn."

There was deafening silence for a minute.

"That's seriously messed-up, but a good idea. We might even be able to get Tiberius to help us," Orin replied.

Markus nodded and said, "If we're upfront about wanting to trigger Kayn with Kevin, he might appreciate the irony."

Lily shook her head. She placed her cup on the table and began tracing the rim with her finger.

Jenna addressed the group, "The Summit starts in a few days. Orin, you'll need to stay behind to run the tombs. I'll help you run the re-enactments of their Sweet Sleep. I don't have to ask you to keep quiet about what we've said here today... Do I?"

"No, I got it. No bonding talks with Melody," Orin answered.

Jenna looked at Lily and ordered, "You will be the one that talks to Tiberius about what needs to happen."

Lily mumbled, "Of course."

Chapter 21

Unpacking The Baggage

They spent the day doing random things. They took turns telling each other about uncomplicated times they cherished. There were certain moments it was always best to avoid. They passed the elementary school and paused briefly as the bell rang. *School was out for the summer. The bell was still running on a timer.* Kayn saw a vision of her brother Matt walking in front of his little sisters. Chloe was running behind him, repeating his name. He was ignoring her. *It was a strange thing to feel sentimental about. Her family was in the back of her mind... Always. It killed her to know that, in the grand scheme of things, her family's lives had been inconsequential to everyone but her.* Mel paused as two little boys ran by her, followed by their mother. *They were all the same. They'd all lost everything that mattered most in becoming Ankh.*

Grey unlocked the doors with the keypad. Loud beeping snapped her out of her stupor. Lexy got in the front. Everyone else squished into the back. They pulled away from the elementary school and drove in silence.

Trees whirled by the window of the truck until they turned down the road to the campground. They parked and strolled down the road to the campsite. Seeing a grassy meadow full of buttercups through the trees, Kayn said, "I'll just be a minute." She scaled the barbed wire fence surrounding the field and stood there in the sea of yellow buttercups. She bent to pick a flower, feeling Chloe's spirit inside of her. *She wanted to stay here and watch the furry bumblebees, but her heart just couldn't take it. This was one of their favourite things. Her twin was a part of her. Kevin was as good as gone. It felt like they'd taken pieces of her soul when they left.* She touched the buttercup to her chin and smiled a secret smile. She closed her eyes to listen to the humming of the bees. *She had to get back to reality. Where were the Triad staying? When would she run into Kevin again? Could they still be friends even if they could never be anything else? Maybe he did remember her? What if he was only pretending that he didn't?* She opened her eyes and willed the glowing sun to fill her with the peace of mind she so desperately needed. She climbed the barbed wire fence and managed to catch up with the others.

They walked down the side gravel trail in silence. In the distance through the woods, they could see the water. Zach hooted and raced down the trail to the water's edge like their hyper younger brother and waited. There was a dock and from a tree hung a rope swing. Grey glanced at Zach. They raced to the swing, peeling off everything except for their underwear.

"Hey! That water is still going to be frigging freezing you guys!" Kayn yelled.

Zach swung off the swing and dropped into the icy water with a giant splash. He shrieked, "Oh crap! Oh crap!" He swam to the dock and climbed out, as they all gutted themselves laughing at his reaction to the cold. Grey went next. Always one to do just what the boys were doing, Kayn stripped down to her sports bra and underwear, catching the swing as Grey hit the water with a high-pitched squeal.

Melody seemed spooked. She hollered at the others, "I need to use the bathroom!"

"Sure, you do!" Grey teased from the water.

Mel called out, "I saw a big public one where we parked, I'll be right back!" She walked away.

Suspecting something was going on with her friend, Kayn declared, "I have to go too." She followed Mel quietly to the bathroom and paused outside because she heard her speaking to someone.

The unfamiliar female voice disclosed, "Thorne will want to see you. I thought he was going to lose his mind when I came back without you."

Kayn recognised the name Thorne. *He was the leader of Trinity.*

As the girl's voice said, "I'd better go. It's so good to see you." Kayn decided to make her presence known. She pushed open the bathroom door and strolled in. A dark-haired girl smiled at Kayn as she walked past her out of the bathroom.

Startled by Kayn's sudden appearance, Melody questioned, "How much did you hear?"

"Enough to make me curious. There's a lot more to you than meets the eye," Kayn probed, leaning against the counter.

"The Thorne situation is complicated. It only really started the day before I left Trinity. I guess I didn't think it was worth mentioning," Melody confessed.

"We all have baggage." Kayn assured, "If you ever need some help unpacking it, I'm here. I'm always willing to listen."

As Melody went through the motions of washing her hands, even though Kayn knew she'd never actually gone to the bathroom, she replied, "I just need to get through seeing him again. I'll be fine. Being together isn't even an option now."

Kayn flashed back in her mind to when she'd begged Melody to help her say goodbye to Kevin. *Mel was Trinity.* She'd said the words, *you have no idea what I am giving up to do this. She now understood the gravity of her selfless act.* Kayn promised, "I won't tell anyone."

Smiling, Mel affirmed, "I know."

"I can't believe you had a fling with rival Clan royalty. That's amazing," Kayn sparred.

"You almost had one with his brother," Melody teased while drying her hands on her shorts.

"Almost," Kayn replied as she looked at the door sensing their time alone was coming to an end. "You know hiding in here all afternoon won't stop Grey and Zach from throwing us in the lake," she laughed.

"I know. I needed to talk to her. We used to be close. She was my friend. I haven't bumped into him anywhere since I've been with Ankh. I needed to know if he was here. I just wanted to be prepared," Melody answered back.

"You could have told me. I would have understood," Kayn said as the girls embraced. They heard the boys coming. *There was no time to run.*

Grey marched in, flung screeching Melody over his shoulder and comically proclaimed, "Don't fight it sweetheart. I am going to get you so wet."

Mel laughed, pleading, "Let me take my clothes off first. Come on you guys!"

"That's what she said," Zach chuckled as he grabbed her bottom half.

They carried a squirming Melody down to the end of the dock and threw her off the edge. They had no mercy. She was still wearing her shoes. They all jumped in after her, howling, shrieking and squealing. *The water was frigging freezing!* Kayn surfaced. They were no longer alone. Kevin was on the dock with a boy and a dark-featured girl with her hand possessively on Kevin's shoulder.

Kevin turned to his friends and introduced the Ankh, "The blonde girl's Kayn. Apparently, we know each other. I met Grey earlier. I'm sorry, I don't know anyone else, but I can hazard a guess that the hot girl with the red hair is the infamous Lexy."

While dog paddling in the icy water, Grey teased, "You did pretty well, but you also know Melody."

Mel laughed while treading water, "I only brought you back to life once upon a time. It was no big deal."

"There are a few gaps in my memory." Kevin admitted, staring at Kayn.

The sound of his voice made her heartache. She was trying to convince herself to stay in the freezing water versus climbing out almost naked. Kayn replied with her lips quivering from the cold, "Yes... You seem to have a few." He met her eyes. She looked away and trained hers on Melody, who gave her an understanding smile.

The blonde boy standing with them declared, "I just have to say it. Are you all frigging insane? That lake has to be freezing."

She was curious about this guy. He was a little chubby. Definitely not the usual Triad stereotype.

"Don't knock it till you try it," Grey chuckled, playfully splashing the trio on the dock with lake water.

Kayn's lips were blue but she continued treading water, where she was as the rest swam to the dock. They helped each other up. *Ah, hell. She had to get out.* Kayn swam to the dock. Grey helped her out. She saw his roguish grin just a second too late. "Don't you dare!" She hissed as he shoved her back in.

They all howled as Kayn sputtered to the surface. She swam back to the ladder and began climbing out again.

Patrick gave her a hand up. "I won't push you back in, I promise," he vowed.

Oddly enough, she believed him and didn't hesitate. Kevin was only there because of his grandfather, but this Patrick guy was immediately likeable. The girl shifted closer to Kevin, who couldn't seem to tear his eyes away from Kayn's barely clothed state even for the sake of being nice. Kayn was nicely ripped with womanly curves and round, subtle hips. His eyes drifted to her belly button ring. Stephanie angrily elbowed him. *Their dynamics were easily interpreted. They were obviously in a relationship. This girl was skin her alive jealous. As tiny and helpless as she looked, she had an evil streak a mile wide.*

Patrick gallantly took off his shirt and passed it to Lexy, "Your lips are blue."

Lexy, who would have thrown it back at anyone, took it and asked, "Haven't you heard of me?"

With a genuine smile, Patrick responded, "Of course I have. You're Lexy of Ankh. The one Tiberius is afraid of."

"He is going to kick your ass for saying that!" Stephanie spat.

"It's the truth though," Patrick countered. "You're cold, give it back to me later. Apparently, we'll be at this campsite for the next week together."

Kayn was stumped as Lexy put on the chubby kid's shirt and even smiled at him. *It was a little bit adorable. Patrick was a sweetheart.*

"You have dry clothes over there Lex. You just got that kid's shirt wet for no reason," Grey reminded, pointing to the pile.

"I'm sorry, I forgot," Lexy sweetly apologised as she took his shirt off and handed it back slightly damp.

Why was Kevin grinning like that?

Grey nudged her and whispered, "Your headlights are on."

Headlights? She peered down. *Her white bra was see-through. She was cold.* Embarrassed, Kayn dashed after Mel and Lexy with her arms concealing her blessings. She whipped her clothing on.

Grey broke the awkward silence by addressing the kind blonde boy directly, "Nice to meet you, buddy. My name's Grey." He shook Patrick's hand and gave him a giant smile.

Patrick stammered, "Patrick. My name's Patrick. I've heard about you too."

"All good stuff I hope," Grey chuckled as they strolled down the dock together. Grey stopped in front of the girl, blocking her stride and questioned, "And your name is?"

"Stephanie," she repeated with attitude.

Stephanie was extremely unlikable. The Kevin she'd grown up with wouldn't have wanted anything to do with that girl.

Grey extended his hand, "Nice to meet you Stephanie. For the record, if you even entertain a one of those thoughts running through your mind, I'll take it personally in the future when we meet without a cease fire."

Stephanie ignorantly responded, "I am Triad and you are Ankh. It doesn't matter what you think. Your Clan is insignificant. We win against you, every time." She turned on a dime and strutted away.

Lexy marched up behind Stephanie mid-strut and tapped her on the shoulder. The bitchy Triad swung around to face her. The Dragon of Ankh cautioned, "I've taken on your entire Clan all by myself, including the fearless leader you so admire. When people are ignorant to my friends it upsets me."

"Is that supposed to scare me?" Stephanie haughtily provoked.

"It should." Grey declared. He strolled up and stood beside her.

This girl was a complete moron. Nobody messes with Lexy.

Kevin placed his hand on Stephanie's shoulder and bluntly directed, "That's enough, Steph."

Livid, Stephanie glared at Kevin and asserted, "Don't you dare try to tell me what to do!"

Lexy directed her attention to Kevin and remarked, "She's a bit of a handful."

Kevin pressed his lips together as he'd always done when embarrassed. He stared the ignorant Triad down. In a hushed tone, he reminded, "There are no sides this week. Try to act like a reasonably sane person or just do us all a favour and leave."

Shooting daggers with her eyes, she grumbled, "You can't tell me what to do."

"Probably not," Kevin admitted.

Stephanie mumbled something they couldn't make out and stormed away, tossing Kayn into the shrubbery as she passed.

Kayn landed inside of a bush. *Seriously?*

Giggling, Zach helped her up, brushed her off and teased, "It looks like you've made a new friend."

"Sorry about that. She's a little territorial." Kevin apologised.

"Also, a little bit certifiably insane but she grows on you." Patrick added with an apologetic smile.

She looked at Kevin and asked the question on the tip of her tongue, "Is she your girlfriend?"

Kevin bluntly stated, "Hell no. I'm not a girlfriend kind of guy."

Not a girlfriend kind of guy. This cool act was hilarious. He really didn't know her. He was curious about her, but he didn't remember who she was at all. Kayn couldn't help herself as she questioned, "You really don't remember me?"

Melody put her arm around her, saying, "Alright… We have a few things to do. See you boys later." As she led Kayn away from the dock, she whispered, "You're doing good, hun. Just keep walking away." As they strolled back to the RV Melody quietly assured, "Now, you can move on with no guilt. His memory was erased. He's fine. He seems happy."

He wasn't fine. He wasn't himself. Kayn didn't say a word. She just kept walking away. *What was there to say? She knew where they stood. They'd tried to prepare her for this.* They reached the RV and she silently followed Melody inside. Frost, Markus and Orin were sitting at the table together having a drink. They abruptly stopped laughing when they walked in. Orin gave Melody an uncomfortable smile as they walked by to the bunks. *Her friend's awkward, 'who's your daddy' situation was a little bit comical.* Kayn announced, "On the bright side, your dad is smoking hot."

Melody laughed, "That's gross, Brighton. Almost as gross as the fact that I know he broke up with Jenna and impregnated her mortal double."

Kayn stretched out by Melody on the bunk and pointed out, "I'd imagine a break up after a thousand years would be a bit of a gong show."

"They can hear everything we're saying," Mel hinted.

Kayn stared at the bunk above as she teased, "Awkward. I just called your dad hot in front of Frost."

The bathroom door opened and Jenna appeared with a grin. *Once you've embarrassed yourself to a certain degree you might as well just go for gold.* "Apparently, I also called your dad hot in front of his ex-girlfriend," Kayn laughed.

"Orin's always been hot," Jenna teased. "Yes. I knew about Melody's mother and our breakup definitely was a gong show." Jenna sat on the bunk across from them.

Melody couldn't stop staring. She apologised, "I'm sorry. I miss her and you look just like my mom. Almost identical, every detail right down to the dimples in your cheeks. You're younger than she was of course."

"Feel free to stare," Jenna replied. "You'll probably catch me staring at you too. You're a part of him and your mother looked like me so it stands to reason if I had a child with Orin, she would have looked just like you. I never had a baby, but for hundreds of years I wanted it more than anything."

As Kayn observed Mel and Jenna, she knew they'd have no problem pretending to be mother and daughter. She suspected their hearts had already begun to fall into the roles. *Melody was a lucky girl.* Kayn sighed as she rested her head on her pillow and drifted off to sleep, listening to their laughter as they talked about Orin.

She stirred as she sensed him. It had been a while since she'd awoken to find Frost sitting beside her like this, watching her sleep. Without even opening her eyes, she knew it was him by the way he tenderly stroked her hair. She usually felt warm and secretly adored but today her dreams had been of Kevin. *They hadn't been romantic… They'd been about innocence lost.* They were running around the cherry tree in Kayn's yard with homemade weapons. Chloe was perched in a tree and they were protecting her. Her sister Chloe had always been a princess in every game they played for as long as she could remember. *She'd never been envious of her sister. She had never coveted the role of princess as a child. She'd always dreamt of being the hero.* She kept her eyes closed until he left her side. *She knew he still cared, even though he was trying to act like he didn't. She could feel it in his fingertips.*

Chapter 22

This Is Not A Fairytale

Night came once again, christening the landscape with shades of pink and orange painted artistically across the horizon. Kayn raced through the trails with her hair pulled back in her usual messy ponytail. She'd wanted to look like she was only going for her run, but in truth, she had other plans. *She'd been overthinking everything. The way he'd been looking at her earlier. Was he still in there somewhere or was that just wishful thinking? She needed to think. It was difficult to allow her thoughts to revolve around Kevin when she knew it might hurt Frost.* Kayn sprinted down the road towards the track, desperate to go for a run unencumbered by twigs and roots of trees. As she arrived at the college, she was relieved to find not a soul in sight. She needed to run wide open to feel her blood coursing through her veins. She wanted to run fast enough to match the beating of her own heart with the rhythm of her feet. She'd always done her best thinking this way. *For her, a good run could be easily compared to an evening at the spa.* She took off with everything she had and ran until she was surprised by the arrival of darkness. Night crept across the isolated track as daylight faded. She pictured the shadows reaching out for her, grasping at her ankles. This vision drove her powerful legs harder and faster until she was running blind in the total absence of light.

Timed flood lights turned on revealing a presence. Kevin was walking towards her in the pathway of light streaming from above. She didn't have time to be nervous as she slowed and wiped the perspiration off her brow. *Why was he here? Why did he look upset before either of them had even said a word?* Her eyes clouded with unintended tears. *It was like she'd loved him in another lifetime.* There were a million intelligent things she could have said, but instead, she walked into his open arms. *Maybe he wouldn't speak and she could pretend he was still her Kevin?* She felt him uncomfortably patting her back. Holding him tighter, she whispered against his neck, "Don't say anything. Let me pretend it's really you. Please… For a second." He stiffly allowed her to embrace him as he leaned in and, if she wasn't mistaken, smelled her hair. She felt his entire being soften as he melted against her while touching her hair. She shuddered against him as sobs slipped out.

Tenderly stroking her hair, he whispered, "Hey… Don't cry. Please, don't cry. I asked Tiberius if he erased my memory. He told me the truth. He explained why he did it. His actions made perfect sense. He didn't want me to waste my days pining away for someone I can never have. We can't be together. I don't see the point in trying to remember you."

Kayn pulled away. *His brutal honesty stung.* She was biting her lip, trying to think about what she could say to get him to want to remember her. She searched his eyes for what had once been there as she recited just a touch of their story, "We met when we were five years old. We've been best friends our entire lives." She stepped closer and caressed his face tenderly with her hand, desperate for him to see how much he meant to her. *How much they'd meant to each other.* Her mind whispered *you are not what's important. You know he left you to save his family.* Her heart clenched in her chest. She lowered her hand, knowing spending a week with this version of him was going to break her heart. *This fantasy she'd been holding onto had been just that... A fantasy.* Tears began streaming from her eyes. She tried to blink them away.

Kevin began to speak, "I don't think I'm the same person I was when you knew me. I'm sure we've both changed. The guy I am right now thinks you're incredibly hot. How could I not want you with that wild messy hair and those adorable freckles? This guy would suggest we lock ourselves in a hotel room for a few days and try to figure this mess out. I know it's not what you want from me but that's all I have to give you."

Tempted to take him up on his offer, she tried once again to explain her tears, "My whole childhood. Everything I miss and love is tied to memories of you."

Kevin's demeanour changed and his voice became colder as he replied, "We're not Romeo and Juliet. We're not going to live happily ever after. I know my life is not by any stretch of the imagination a fairytale. I don't know about your life but mine is like a damn horror movie. I know my story doesn't have a happily ever after ending. My life is all about who dies next and what kind of pleasure I can find myself to make my existence tolerable. I'm just trying to survive here. Let's not make this awkward. The last thing I need is for you to be hanging off my arm sobbing for a week. If you want to try to hang out and see if I remember, I'm all for it. If you can cut the girlie water works."

His dialect, his tone of voice, everything was different. He sounded a lot like Tiberius. Kayn guffawed, "You have got to be kidding. Don't do me any favours." *He didn't remember her at all. Girlie waterworks. She should punch him in the damn stomach. He'd remember her then.* Kayn sensed a new presence. She turned to see Lexy walking towards them in the stream of light.

Their Clan's crimson-haired Dragon spoke, "Hi again, Kevin. Kayn, you need to come with me. I'm sorry… Oracle's orders."

With a spiteful last look, Kayn fought the urge to punch the new and definitely not improved version of Kevin in the throat before walking away. *What a douche.* Deciding to take the high road, Kayn curtly said, "I'm sure we'll see each other again."

Kevin quietly responded, "It's a small campground. I'm sure we will." He disappeared into the darkness as he stepped out of the beam of light.

They walked back silently until Kayn glanced at Lexy and tried to explain, "I didn't go looking for him."

Lexy replied, "I know, hun. You got to see him. He is all in one piece. Winnie has his back. She'll take care of him."

Kayn stopped walking. "This isn't who he was. How do I just let him go?" Kayn answered, staring off into the almost starless night sky. She glanced back at the deserted lighted track. *Her version of Kevin was gone.*

"He's already gone," Lexy replied as they made their way back to the others. After a moment of awkward silence, she assured, "Everything works out just as it's meant to. I promise it does."

She knew that was the truth. He's already gone. Her best friend was now a testosterone filled Tiberius wanna be. He'd actually given her the 'let's not make this awkward' speech. You'd think they'd slept together.

After a walk through the woods in darkness, they entered the Crypt lit by soft, calming light of torches. Her carefree Clan were lounging around, reminiscing about days gone by. Glancing up at

Kayn, Jenna smiled as she walked by. *She needed to be alone.* Kayn turned around to hollow footsteps behind her.

Jenna touched her should, saying, "Humour me. I might be able to help." She placed her hand into the grooves on the wall. Stone slid away to reveal a small private room. Their Oracle sat on a dusty cushion in the corner and signalled Kayn to join her.

Curious, Kayn strolled over and sat down.

Jenna began to speak, "My best advice in this situation is, if you do what's right, the right things will come to you. I know you'll attempt to spend time together while we're gone. You need to remember he's on a different path. His adjustment makes it possible to save his family. If he doesn't at least try your separation was for nothing. You can't tell him about his mother and brother. That discussion is out of bounds. He's not strong enough to do anything about it. Timing is everything. You, my dear, have an important path all your own. You need to travel your road and he has to travel his. The two stand no long-term chance of coming together until you've found yourselves. You're still in the process of becoming who you're meant to be. So, concentrate on being happy in the here and now. There's only pain in wanting someone incapable of loving you back the way you need them to."

Kayn nervously fumbled with the corner of one of the pillows. She knew the Oracle was right. *She had a question in the back of her mind. She was having a deep conversation with an Oracle. Why not make it count?* Kayn asked, "Kevin had his gift before he left Ankh a year ago. When do I get mine?"

Smiling, Jenna responded, "You only get your abilities once you've demonstrated control over your mortal side. You need to be capable of separating emotions and duty. Think back. Kevin made the right choice that day. It was a painful decision but it was the right one. He chose the harder road, having faith that he'd end up where he was meant to be. You need to find that kind of faith within yourself. Trust in the process."

Kayn understood what she was saying. *Kevin had taken the road he was meant to take. He'd chosen the path hardest on her. With his memory erased, what did he lose?*

Jenna laid her hand on Kayn's heart. Grinning at a vision, she whispered, "I have to confess, I was curious as to how the mix between the two would happen, but you've combined seamlessly. It's extraordinary."

Realising she was talking about her twin sister, Kayn replied, "Extraordinary isn't the word I'd choose. Confusing is more like it. She's an inner voice, a feeling. I have her memories. She urges me towards what she wants."

Intrigued by her declaration, Jenna questioned, "Towards what she wants?"

Who she wants. Kayn answered truthfully, "I dream about Frost."

Jenna smiled affectionately and patted her lap. Kayn rested her head on it. Maternally stroking her locks, Jenna disclosed, "Let me tell you something about relationships. Imagine you're building a puzzle and all the pieces fit perfectly. You put new pieces in each day and then one day, when there are only a half a dozen pieces left, you can't seem to find a single piece that fits anymore. Now, if those pieces aren't meant to fit in that puzzle, it doesn't matter how hard you try. You'll never complete it. If you want the satisfaction of completing the puzzle, you must take all the pieces apart and put that old puzzle back inside its box. You'll have to close it and put it back up in the closet, so you don't get the pieces mixed up when you open a new box and start to build a new puzzle. I think you still have some pieces to put back in the box."

As Jenna continued stroking Kayn's hair, her eyelids became heavy. She was mentally drained from the events of the day. *She did have to put the pieces of Kevin's puzzle back in the box.*

Jenna's soothing voice whispered, "I'll stay here with you until you fall asleep."

So exhausted she couldn't even bring her mouth to open to thank her for her kindness, Kayn rested her head on a pillow.

Their Oracle whispered, "Sweet dreams till sunbeams find you."

She heard the door grind open and then close. After that, Kayn heard nothing.

Chapter 23

Rise And Shine Princess

In the morning, Kayn awoke after the most amazing sleep with Grey standing above her obnoxiously clapping his hands, "Rise and shine, princess! We're training in the In-between today! Woohoo!"

Kayn groaned dramatically and then grinned because she loved Grey's accent. That, mixed with his comical smile, instantly lightened her mood. He held out his hand and helped her up. She felt something tickle her foot and looked down. *Maybe it was nothing?* Kayn shivered as a spider scurried across the floor. She swallowed and squeezed Grey's hand tighter. *She hated spiders.*

Having his big brother role down to a tee, Grey nonchalantly said, "Spiders drink from your tear ducts when you're sleeping."

With full body shivers, Kayn wrinkled her nose, sparring, "Thanks for that."

Grinning back, Grey replied, "Just doing my best to keep you informed." He began spouting details, "The Summit rented the entire resort for a telekinetic study retreat. There will be no staff on site that isn't from the Aries Group."

Kayn didn't know a lot about the Aries Group except that they were an organisation whose staff was trained to deal with the unusual. Tri-Clan had a deal with the Aries Group.

Grey continued his speech, "The corner store will be run on the honour system. The kitchen staff will be on site each morning and evening for two hours in the main meeting room. They are also from Aries Group. So, feel free to pass the salt to someone with your mind."

Melody appeared beside her. She whispered, "Did you actually sleep in the Crypt last night?"

Kayn nodded. Melody grimaced. *She still had the heebie jeebies over the fact that she'd slept on the floor in there. Spiders probably had been drinking out of her tear ducts.* She shivered while silently following the growing group through the bushes to the conference room. *That little tidbit of useless yet utterly mortifying information was going to stick with her. She was starving.* She was aware it was strange timing for that thought. *Spiders drinking out of her tear ducts, and she was hungry.*

Zach appeared out of nowhere. He poked her in the ribs.

Kayn glanced at Zach. *It looked like he hadn't slept a wink.* She questioned, "Where did you end up last night?" He grinned without responding. *She knew what that meant. That was code for, 'he was up to no good.'*

Mel shoved him, teasing, "Zach, were you fraternising with the enemy?"

Grey chimed in, "Don't knock it until you try it. No lines between the Clans this week. There's only one more trip to the In-between after breakfast, and then you have a whole week to relax."

They were usually gone for an hour Earth time, but it would be over a week in the In-between. Grateful for a way to avoid Kevin as they arrived at the hall, she realised she may run into him right now. Grey opened the door. *Please don't be here. Please.* Kayn held her breath as they walked in. *Kevin wasn't there. It made her morning. They'd both changed due to circumstance and self-preservation, but she needed to believe she still had a future to design. This was an adult revelation much bigger than a childish list of broken fantasies.*

After breakfast, a dishevelled Lexy appeared and snagged a few pieces of bacon before they left. They walked back to the Ankh Crypt. When they arrived, Jenna and Orin were already there. They followed Grey down the long corridor to the end, where there seemed to be nothing but a wall of stone with no grooves or ridges. Zach ran his hand across the wall. Grey stood back as he tried to figure it out.

Zach chuckled, "I'll bite... How do you open the wall?"

"It doesn't open!" Orin hollered from down the length of the corridor. "You have to run through it!"

Zach backed up and ran at the wall, smoking into the stone.

Scowling as Orin howled laughing, Jenna scolded, "That was completely unnecessary."

"Oh, I had to. At least once. Come on, admit it. It's a little funny," the blonde immortal chuckled.

Kayn was trying not to smile in solidarity with her friend.

"After we make it so you can. Way to jump the gun, kid," Orin teased.

Embarrassed, Zach got up and brushed off his pants while scowling at Orin, who was still grinning as he placed his hand on the wall. Grey positioned his hand next to Orin's, and so did Lexy. The wall became almost transparent.

"Do you want a redo now? One where you don't look like an idiot," Lexy teased as she glanced back at Zach.

Zach put his hand in first and then edged his body through the hazy, see-through wall. They walked through the stone, following him into the large open room on the other side with four tombs much larger than any they'd seen before. Each one could easily fit three or four people side by side.

Kayn stated the obvious, "These tombs must be for more than one person."

Grinning, Orin explained, "These are the original offerings from Azariah. There are four giant tombs at each Crypt, hidden well over a thousand years ago for travel to the In-between. They're only accessible by the hand of an Ankh. These tombs can never be moved or used anywhere but here."

"This training will show us how much you've grown," Jenna explained. "This is your opportunity to redo your original Sweet Sleep. Call it a quiz for the final exam."

Opportunity? Really? They knew what happened. They were brutally murdered. They bargained away their mortality. Their mortal demise was as permanently seared into their souls as the brand on their hands.

"I'm guessing this isn't optional?" Zach muttered under his breath.

Orin didn't bother with a response as he placed his hand on a tomb. It opened. *They were going in the same tomb. How was that going to work?* The trio of would-be immortals looked at each other one last time before taking the bull by the horns and climbing into the large open tomb together. Without a word, they lay in silence as the lid closed ominously above them. Kayn wanted to keep her eyes open as the last seconds of the real world disappeared. The rose quartz walls hummed to life. *There were tiny handprints engraved on the lid of the tomb.* She counted eight before the tomb began strobing with light so blinding, she had to squeeze her eyes closed to stand it. She braced herself for the stomach-churning sensation of being launched upwards at light speed. *She did this each time, but it always seemed to happen a second before she felt prepared. How could you ever be prepared?* The tomb launched into the air. It lurched, twisted and turned until she felt like she couldn't take it anymore. Usually, there were squeals of laughter and excitement at this point, but a redo of their Sweet Sleep was an experience nobody wanted. They began their rapid descent into the In-between with the scenery of incoming desert, and everything went black.

What in the hell? "Hello? Did we stall?" Kayn whispered into the darkness. *Maybe they were back in the tomb?* As she raised her hands to feel for the lid and the smooth rose quartz sides, her body did a cartwheel. She was weightlessly suspended in midair. *What was this?* The tomb was gone but she wasn't falling. She tried to move again and her whole body began to spin. *She couldn't stop.* She could not see a thing in the complete absence of light. *Where in the hell was she? What in the hell was this?* She wanted to call out into the darkness for Zach and Melody but knew she shouldn't. *Calling out into the darkness was almost always a bad idea. Could there be something more terrifying than her fear of being left alone? Were the others in this place with her? It felt like they might be.* She was tempted to bite her hand and turn on a light so she could see where they were. The sensation of floating on invisible water was a unique one. It was like a calm silence absent of any form of control. There was nothing to see and nothing to hear but there was sensation. She was hovering close to patches of icy air while moving slowly. First, only a leg would feel icy, and then, only her face. A chill crept across the surface of her skin. *She wasn't alone. She had the sense others floated in the darkness with her.* A light turned on in the distance. *It was either Zach or Melody.* Her symbol strobed in response. In the span of nothingness between them were hundreds of hovering sinister entities. One was a mere foot from her. The form turned to gaze into her eyes with deep soulless empty sockets where life should have been. She started to panic. Her heart began to palpitate. She'd been set adrift in the unknown. It was a terrifying place. The breath escaping in short gasps from her lips pirouetted into dark nothingness as a fog in front of her face. In her desperation, her mind cried, *put out the light! Cover the light! Tortured depraved faces with hollow eyes were everywhere. Was this hell? She shouldn't be here. She shouldn't be seeing this place.* She screamed in her mind at the Clan member also drifting in the dark sea of ominous souls. *Put out the light! Please! She didn't want to see this.* She suspected her eyes were not ever meant to see this place. She squeezed them shut while trying to calm herself down. *Breathe in… Breathe out,* her mind recited as she placed her hand over her symbol to conceal her mark of Ankh, afraid it would go off again in response to her panic. Terrified it would illuminate the darkness and show her wicked things mortal eyes were never meant to see, Kayn began to spin in the direction of the hand she'd clutched as she squeezed her eyes shut. She heard a sick, hollow gasping and realised it was the sounds she'd made during her brutal demise, echoing through her mind, taunting her. *Torturing her soul.* A child's voice called out to Melody in the darkness in a pitch reserved for agony and terror. The child sobbed out Melody's name again. Kayn's heart fought the urge to swim through the sea of floating dead towards the source even though the child wasn't calling for her. *What was this place?* She heard crackling flames and inhaled the unforgettable fragrance of burning flesh. There was rhythmic cracking of twigs and the repetitive soft thud of her bare feet. She felt the cool whistle of an after-downpour breeze and smelled sour skin mixed with cedar. *It was time to take her heart somewhere else. She tried to think of happy things.* She envisioned Kevin as a child and his laughter freed her mind from the dark place it was trapped in. She travelled back in time to a beautiful memory. She was crouched in Grandma Winnie's overgrown lawn with Kevin squatting in the grass beside her. They were plucking dandelions out at the root, making wishes and blowing them into the wind with puffed cherub cheeks. After a while, they changed the game. They ran around the yard, spinning and waving the flowers in the warm summer breeze. *The dandelion seeds looked like miniature celestial beings in parachutes as they floated across the sky.* Kayn's father struggled to rid their yard of dandelions. He'd lose his mind every time they picked one and blew seeds around the yard. Kevin's grandmother didn't mind. At Kayn's house dandelions were only weeds and wishes caused more work. At Kevin's grandmother's house, they were magic and capable of reaching the heavens above. Kevin's grandmother was relaxing on the stoop as they experienced the playfulness of childhood unencumbered by ridiculous grown-up rules.

Chapter 24

The Sweet Sleep Redo's

The four stood in silence knowing the horrors the newest Ankh were about to endure. Grey and Lexy had been there not long ago in the grand scheme of things.

Grey suggested, "Orin, you shouldn't watch this. You'll see everything that happened to her and hear every thought she had."

"It's not optional," Orin answered.

Lexy touched the tomb and it strobed twice. Melody was the first to find her way out of the darkness into her worst nightmare. In front of the tombs was a pool of water from a natural underground spring. They all submerged their hands in the liquid to create an emotional and physical link between them. Jenna knelt before the pool and moved her hand across the water's surface. They would all be there within her being, reliving Melody's Sweet Sleep with her.

Melody's Sweet Sleep

Melody winced as she yanked the car's backdoor open. *Her stomach had been hurting all day. She'd been plagued with nervous energy.* She chucked her school bag on the floor in front of little Stevie's car seat, avoiding his swinging legs. She kissed her baby brother's pursed lips. His face illuminated with joy. She lovingly greeted the toddler, "How's my sweet baby today?" Her other brother was ten and also in the back. Both boys were adorable with ash blonde hair and deeply set dimples. Melody smiled as she asked, "Did you have a good day at school, Kevin?"

Always trying to push her buttons, Kevin scowled, baiting, "You'd know how my day was if you ever came home after school."

They had the token sibling love-hate relationship. She wasn't in the mood for his crap today. Her stomach cramped again. Little Stevie was laughing and wildly swinging his legs, kicking the back of her seat, trying to keep her attention focused on him.

Her mother complained, "Must you always slam the door?"

"Sorry." Melody apologised, meeting her mother's frustrated gaze. Even when she was angry, her mother was stunning, with vibrant auburn hair and wide, gentle smile framed by deeply carved dimples. She was a beautiful woman with the softest green eyes, so gentle her soul looked almost breakable. You just wanted to give her a hug and protect her. With almost identical features, Melody's chestnut brown hair was shoulder length with a whimsical wave, which she always wore tucked behind her ears.

It was pouring when her mother announced her father was going to be late at night. She succumbed to the chanting chorus of ice cream coming from the backseat. They made a unanimous decision to stop at the diner on the way home, where they each ordered giant ice cream sundaes. Stevie had it literally everywhere by the time they were done. Melody smiled as Kevin entertained the table with his outrageous sense of humour. She took a moment to appreciate her mother's easy laughter and calm demeanour during Stevie's ice cream face painting fiasco. Her mom, all smiles, chose that moment to tell her they had another baby on the way and that she was well over four months along. It was a happy surprise. "Can you feel the baby moving yet?" Melody enquired as she ate another mouthful of ice cream.

Her mom replied, "Yes… I can."

Melody asked, "Can I feel the baby?"

"You can give it a try." Her mother answered sweetly.

It was fluttering as Melody laid her hand on her mom's rounded stomach. *It was truly miraculous.* She didn't want to take her hand off, but she did.

As they stood up to leave, her mom whispered a secret in her ear, "It's a girl."

She watched her mom walk away from the table to pay for the sundaes. Once again, she felt a strange wave of apprehension ripple through her. Melody clutched her stomach and grimaced. *She was a little concerned.* Her baby brother squealed as he winged his sundae cup on the floor. Crouching with a napkin to clean it up, Melody mumbled, "Seriously Stevie?" She heard her mother rustling above her at the table.

Her mom said, "Thank you, honey."

Grinning as she got up, Melody replied, "No problem." She followed her family out to the vehicle. *Their footsteps were humming in her ears. She was having a strange day.* She shook her head. *Maybe I'm coming down with something?* She was grinning in the car as they drove home, thinking about how much she'd always wanted a sister. While staring out the window, watching trees whirl by, she had to turn away. *She was dizzy. Motion sickness had never been her friend.* The car swerved on the road. Startled, she laughed, "Mom. What the hell?" She glanced at her mother. *She'd passed out in the driver's seat!* Melody panicked. With no time to think, she took off her seatbelt to reach for the steering wheel. The car swerved in one direction, then another and lurched into a shallow ditch, leaving the rear of the car exposed to oncoming traffic. With an explosion of pain, Melody's body flew through the windshield and toppled limply down a steep embankment, coming to rest in high grass.

Stunned, she tried to comprehend the severity of her situation. *What just happened? That didn't just happen. This wasn't real.* She lay bleeding in the foliage by the side of the road, taking small, laboured breaths, unable to move. *Did that just happen?* She could hear her baby brother's desperate, haunting cries, "Mommy! Melody!" His voice crackled through eerie silence in the frigid night air. Smoke was billowing above the car. She lay there twitching, incapacitated. Her wrist was in her line of vision. A bone had pierced through her skin. She felt the hot, sticky sensation of blood pooling beneath her with her head twisted sideways. She blinked away the curtain of blood tinting her vision. Stevie was sobbing with his hand against the window, imploring her to help. Trying to move, she couldn't. A voice inside of her mind kept whispering, *go to sleep, Melody. It's time to go to sleep.* Her little brother's cries kept her eyes straining to stay open. *She had to stay with him until she was sure he was safe. She couldn't allow her eyes to close. She couldn't succumb to the voice in her mind. Not until she knew somebody was there to help him.* Melody focused on his tiny, outstretched palm on the window. She could remember what it felt like to hold it and how the feeling of her baby brother's hand in hers made her heart surge with love. *She felt no pain. She was only thinking about him.* Melody was silently praying as a big rig turned the corner and ran directly into the back of the vehicle. She lay there in horror as her little brother's cries were silenced by crushing metal. What was left of the vehicle high-pitched scraped down the road as a sandwiched pile of rubble. There was soul-shattering silence, then an echoing explosion, followed by a crackling fire, but no screaming. Not a single cry, for they'd all been crushed on impact. She screamed from within her broken being, over and over until she succumbed to her mind chanting, *go to sleep. Just shut your eyes… Go to sleep, Melody.* A final thought trickled through her broken mind, riding on the last current of life as she bled out into the frigid, unforgiving earth. I*f they are gone, please let me die. The heartbreaking vision faded to black.*

She was so cold. Where was she? Her eyes opened. Foggy images came into focus. Leaves were all around her. *Where am I?* She could hear the steady humming of passing cars. She sat up. As she took in her surroundings, she realised the sound of the vehicles was coming from above her, up the grassy hill. She looked at her hands and touched her face, confused as to how she'd come to be lying in the grass down a ravine. The morning dew was glimmering droplets on the tall grass surrounding her. It was strangely magical. It looked like daylight stars in a sky of lush green foliage. Her hands were smudged with mud, as were her clothes, but she felt alright. *What was she doing by the side of the road?* Flickers of ice cream at the diner, a baby sister and her little brother's hand pressed against the backseat window, but nothing solid. *Had she gotten lost? Had she been kidnapped or attacked on her way home, walking from somewhere?* She wiped the dirt off her hands onto her clothes. She felt woozy while trying to stand but quickly found her balance. She stood at the bottom of the hill in moist thigh-deep grass thinking, *what happened?* As she tried to remember again, she was met with a piercing headache. It pulsated beneath her scalp. Her mind seemed to be saying, *just leave it alone. You don't want to know.*

She climbed up the side of the hill on all fours, clutching onto long, thick strands of grass with unexplainable strength rippling beneath the surface of her skin. When she reached the top, she rose to stand by the side of the road with her feet on half gravel and half cement. She noticed she was missing a shoe. *That's weird.*

Why would I only have one shoe on? Thoughts raced through her mind. *There was something she needed to remember.* She had a flash of memory… *There were diamonds in the sand. She was standing barefoot in the sand with her toes in the warm, luxurious silky grains.* As she recalled brilliant light and a beautiful woman, she felt more than a little delusional. *She must have hit her head?*

Seeing teddy bears and a memorial at a tree by the side of the road, she slowly walked towards it. She felt a sense of foreboding as she approached the shrine. Pictures of her family were on the tree, surrounded by flowers and toys. A cheerleading picture of her was also on the tree, as well as a picture of her on her horse. *Did I die?* She thought, still unable to remember anything solid. Confused, she picked up a bouquet of flowers from someone named Michael and read it. *Great loss of Melody and her family. My condolences. Was she a ghost? Had they all died in a car accident? That's why people made these shrines by the side of the road.* She dropped to her knees before the makeshift shrine. Looking like an angel kneeling at the bottom of a perfect ray of light that shone through the dense forest like it extended from heaven to guide her way home. *Why was she still here?* A car pulled over. Trying to process everything, she didn't hear it.

Her father spoke her name in disbelief, "Melody?"

What? She turned. Her heart leapt as she looked up at him. *Maybe angels came to guide you to heaven in the form of someone you love.*

Her father shook his head in disbelief as he took a step closer. His voice cracked with emotion, "Is that really you?"

Angels wouldn't cry. Her heart leapt. "Daddy?" She whispered, "Can you see me?"

Her father knelt before her. She was afraid. *What if this wasn't real, just a cruel, taunting nightmare?* He reached out and touched her shoulder. *He was real.* Her father opened his arms, and she sprung into his loving embrace.

He cradled her, sobbing, "How… How are you alive? How are you here with me?"

With tears blurring her vision, she whispered, "Are mom and the boys with you?"

"No," her father answered, "They're gone. I thought you were gone too?" They clung to each other, sobbing.

They were crying in each other's arms by the side of the road when a police car pulled up. An officer got out and gasped, "Oh my God!"

Looking up with his eyes overflowing with tears of joy and his daughter in his arms, her father replied, "Exactly."

After experiencing Melody's first death and resurrection as a Healer, they moved through her immortal experiences to the day of her Correction. When the Correction had come for her, Melody had been afraid, but instead of succumbing to fear, she'd blown up her house while blinded by fury. None of them had seen the dark side of Melody, but now, they knew what she was capable of. When it was time to redo the events, they all watched as she made the conscious decision to remove her seatbelt once again and allow the scenario to unfold as it was meant to. She was ready to battle in the Crypt. She'd chosen to keep everything the same. Melody grasped the concept of immortality. She was emotionally advanced beyond her years, but this was a common trait for a Healer to possess.

Zach's Sweet Sleep

The school bus dropped Zach off, temporarily blinding him with dust from the rural road they lived on as it pulled away. His three younger siblings were walking behind him with backpacks in tow. They knew better than to accost him with chatter. *He'd smack someone with his bag in a heartbeat. School wasn't easy for him, and home life consisted of a household of siblings with not a speck of personal space. He hadn't even come close to learning to appreciate what he had before it was taken away.* His yard was a scavenger's dream, adorned with shells from trucks amidst thigh-high weeds. His younger siblings raced past him into the front door as Zach chucked his bag on the sundeck and made himself comfortable on the porch swing. Treasuring silence, he swung slowly. All there was for miles were cornfields and blue sky. *Chills crept up his spine, followed by a nagging sense of foreboding. Something felt off. What was that scent in the air? He'd felt strange all day.* A murder of crows took off from the field. *Was something out there? Maybe he should go check it out?* He decided against it and continued enjoying the peace and quiet. His mind prodded, *murder of crows. Anything could be hidden in that field. It was probably just their dog. Wait a minute… Usually, their dog met them at the bus.* He stopped the repetitive creaking swing. *Where was their dog? It was too quiet. There was no commotion. No familiar laughter. His siblings weren't squabbling. There was usually something to irritate him, but today, there was nothing. It was both wonderful and unnerving.* Zach had three older siblings. *The middle child was never in charge of anything. Why did he have this nagging feeling he should be paying attention today? It was weird. His younger siblings never left him alone for his porch swing ritual.*

Zach spent a good hour daily on this rickety old porch swing, daydreaming of his future. *Right now, he was just a scrawny sixteen-year-old with moderately passable grades who dreamt of getting on a Greyhound bus and leaving this place forever, but a part of him secretly feared he'd be stuck here with no options for the rest of his life watching this empty cornfield. He lived with six siblings, his grandparents and his mother. He was the only unattractive one. Even his grandfather was better looking than he was. A girl at school today said it best. He could get an afterschool job standing in people's yards scaring off crows.* A dozen crows suddenly lifted off in flight from the field. *Again? That was a weird thing to happen twice. It was probably the dog.* He thought about calling the dog's name but decided against it. *If he made it known he was out here relaxing, the silence might stop.* Once again, he noticed the lack of noise coming from the house but chose to ignore it. The phone started to ring. It rang ten times. *Nobody was picking it up. Frig, ten people are inside and not a damn one can get off their asses and walk five feet to answer the damn phone.* It stopped ringing and started again. *Oh, Come on!* He let it ring out of sheer stubbornness and kept swinging, steadily creaking. *I'm such a rebel.* The phone was ringing again. *The quiet murmur of instinct whispering something isn't right became louder.* As he got up, an ominous wind whistled past, whooshing through the field of corn. An empty juice box tumbled across the wooden deck and hit the front door. *One of the kids left the door slightly ajar… That was strange.* As the phone began to ring for the fourth time unanswered, he went in and answered the phone on the table,

"Hello?" *It was his mother's boss wondering why his mother hadn't shown up for her shift at the diner.*

He looked around the empty living room as he responded, "I just got home from school. I'll check and see if she's here." *She must be deathly ill. She never misses work.* Zach carried the phone with him, calling, "Mom!" As he ran up the stairs, they creaked underfoot. He pushed open his mother's bedroom door. *She wasn't there?* He placed the phone to his ear and said, "She's not here. I have no idea where she is, but she'd never miss work unless it was an emergency." *Her boss seemed genuinely concerned, not angry.* He asked Zach to call back so he'd know she was alright. Zach kept walking through the house. *Where in the hell did everyone go?* He checked each room. *Nobody was there. Where are they?* His mother's purse and car keys were on the counter. The house was ominously empty.

He ran outside and jogged to the back of the house. The field rustled. *Could they be hiding? His mother wasn't skipping work to play a prank. What was the other option? They all disappeared for no reason? Her car was there and her purse. She could have forgotten her purse. Maybe one of his grandparents had to go to the hospital? The car was still here. Where was everyone? This didn't make sense.* The cornfield rustled again in the distance. *There was someone out there. He was sure of it. There had to be an explanation. Carbon monoxide leak? There was a logical explanation for everything.* He felt sick to his stomach as shivers raised every hair on his body. *Oh, no. He found us.* He sensed someone behind him, but before he could turn, he was hit over the head. His vision wavered, his ears rang, and it went black.

He came to, being dragged into the cornfield by his legs with his head bouncing in the dirt. He remained limp as survival instincts from years of abuse kicked in. *Play dead. He'd been through this before. He wasn't strong enough to fight back. Play dead.* His blood ran cold as he heard shrill screaming but kept himself from stiffening in response to the pleas. *One of the older, stronger ones would help. His job was ugly whipping post, not saviour. No matter how far they moved. He'd always found them. His father despised him.* The older three and younger three were his, but another sired him during a time when they successfully escaped. Once the adorable baby vanished, the child that wasn't genetically his became visible. *He was a constant reminder that she could find freedom. Things escalated until they ran again.*

He found them again. This became a cycle. They never stayed hidden for long. His mother was six months pregnant the last time they ran. *He'd learned to play dead, for this was the only road to survival.* Pulled deep into the field, he remained limp while kicked into a hole. He rolled into it, still playing dead. *If he moved, it would only bring pain.* He'd come to rest on his side. *There was the scent of rich manure. He'd been tuning out something else, smoke so thick it burned his nostrils. The screaming had stopped. He hadn't allowed himself to think about why they were screaming. It was only now in the silence that he wondered if his father could be heinous enough to burn his own children alive. He wouldn't do that. Why search for them and then kill them all?* Something heavy was thrown in the hole with him. The weight and size was jarring. He was paralyzed with fear. *This was no longer the stealthy wisdom of survival. Someone else's body had been thrown in. If it was one of his older siblings, they might be playing dead. The beatings were usually reserved for Zach and his mother. Something light was thrown over them. A blanket? Maybe his father didn't want to see what he was burying?* Under the blanket, he opened his eyes. *He was facing away from his grave companion.* Zach felt the trickling weight of earth and the repetitive shovel. *God, please help us,* he prayed, trying to remain calm. *If he moved his chest or breathed too heavily, the gravedigger would know he survived. He was being buried alive. They were being buried alive.* His mind whispered, *don't move. No matter what. Do not move. He doesn't have time to do anything more than cover us up. If the house is burning, someone will see it and come to save us.* The dirt hushed the outside world. *Voices. Was there more than one voice? He was sure it was more than one. He had a headache. They were almost out of air. Nobody would find them until it was too late. The house was too big a distraction. If he didn't dig himself out, they'd die anyway.* He whispered, "Who's in here with me?" *There was no answer. He could smell cologne. It was Johnny. A year older, he was the only one who wore it. Why would he hurt Johnny? He was his favourite. Maybe Johnny tried to save him? He tried to stay positive. He was out cold. It was up to him.* He'd count to one hundred before moving. At about forty, panic set in. *Please be gone.* Zach reached the edge of the blanket and began clawing at the earth. Shielding his face with the material, he vigorously clawed the ground. *Help us! Please help us!* He was going to have to move the only thing keeping the pocket of air. *It had to be done.* Zach peeled the blanket from his face. Dirt slid into the gaps, smothering him. He was attempting shallow breaths, but there was no air. He was breathing in the putrid soil. *This was it. He tried.* Right as his head was about to explode from lack of oxygen, someone broke through the dirt and tugged him out. Zach was gasping for air, sputtering out soil, choking out his brother's name, "Johnny." Covered in mud, Zach saw the strangers who saved him. He didn't have time to discover if they were friend or foe as he frantically dug his brother out and pulled him free of the shallow grave. The whites of Johnny's eyes were open and speckled with putrid-smelling earth. *His brother was gone.* Zach began shaking him, begging, "Wake up! Wake up! No! Please, no!"

It was Triad that saved him from his grave. Tiberius asserted, "He's gone, kid. Long gone. We need to get out of here if you don't want to join him."

"I can't! What about everyone else?" Zach panicked.

In an almost sensitive voice, Tiberius revealed, "They're all dead. Trust me, even if they weren't, you'd be coming with us."

"No. They can't be, no," Zach stammered as shock set in. He stared at Johnny's body, asking, "Why did you save me? Who are you?"

"We're Triad," Tiberius explained as he tore open Zach's shirt and branded his chest with his ring.

The sensation of melting skin stunned Zach momentarily, but he didn't scream. *He could turn most pain off, for sadly, he was used to it. His oxygen-deprived mind reeled through the horrific events. Dead. They can't be.* Dazed, he mumbled, "Is Triad a biker gang?"

Amused by the question, Tiberius disclosed, "Sorry kid, no such luck." Triad's leader unceremoniously snapped his neck like a brittle twig. *The vision faded to black.*

"Call this a hunch but I have a feeling he'll attempt to redesign these events and blow it. He's never had closure," Orin declared.

Once they had all experienced the end of Zach's life, they each knew that the boy had endless possibilities if given the proper guidance. The survival instincts from his years of abuse would come in handy down the road.

Jenna looked at Lexy and declared, "He might be the sleeping Dragon."

"What do you mean by that?" Lexy enquired.

Jenna smiled and explained, "I have it on good authority that if one becomes a Dragon in the Testing, they'll come home."

"I'm betting on the dark horse. I'll change my vote. I say the boy lets it all happen as it went down," Orin wagered.

Zach had seemed unimportant until they'd seen the end of his life. He did as Jenna suspected. During the redo of his Sweet Sleep Zach tried to change it all. He would find out that even if you endeavour to revise a few of the chapters, the ending to the story always remained the same.

Chapter 25
Kayn's Redo

It was Kayn's turn now... Lexy placed both hands on the tomb and it burst two times with brilliant light. She instantly returned from the void to the safety of the tomb. Jenna ran her hand through the puddle of water so they could all witness her original Sweet Sleep.

As they pulled up in front of her house, she leaned across the seat and thanked Kevin's dad with a hug. She opened the door and took a deep breath. *The air smelled like wet cherry blossoms. It must have been raining while they were eating dinner.* She stepped out of the car into a puddle and twisted her ankle. *Of course.* With a soaked foot, eggs, and school bag in hand, she hobbled up the driveway towards the front door. She lived in a wooded, somewhat isolated area. Normally, she would have darted from Kevin's dad's car into the house, but her ankle stung each time she put pressure on it. As she came closer, she noticed the door was partially open. It was *a* little *windy* out and quite normal for the door *to be* unlocked. *Maybe it was left ajar and opened by the wind?* She heard tires on gravel and turned just in time to see Kevin's father driving away. Kayn felt off, apprehensive as she made her way up the gravel driveway to the door that seemed to have a life of its own, shifting from cracked to closed with the breeze. She dug out her phone to look at the time. *Quarter after eight. She was fifteen minutes late.* The door moved again. She shook her head and laughed. *This was obviously a prank. They'd left the door open and entrance lights off to freak her out. Chloe was probably hiding around the corner. Practical jokes were a daily occurrence in their household.* Slivers of light from the moon flashed through branches as they swayed in the wind, and for a moment, it felt like they were waving her away. *She was being silly.* She shoved her cell into her pants, accidentally pocket-dialling Kevin.

"I'm home!" Kayn yelled, kicking off her shoes and dropping her backpack. She flicked on the light and nothing happened. *The power wasn't out. The lights were on upstairs when she walked up the driveway. It's just a burnt-out lightbulb.* She massaged her ankle. *Great, there goes the track meet.* Kayn tried to take off her wet socks. A stab of pain from her freshly twisted ankle caused her to place a hand on the wall while attempting to balance. Her hand slid off as she struggled to tug off a sopping wet sock. "Kevin's mom gave us eggs," she called out, realising she was alone. *Where would they go at this hour? Her mind sorted through scenarios. Something wasn't right.* "Mom… Dad?" She said, answered by silence. She went to close the door and felt something wet. A faint sliver of light was streaming through the doorway. She stepped into it and held out her hand. Her palm was covered in blood. *Whose blood was this?* Paralysed by fear, adrenaline coursed through her like thousands of tiny spiders running on the surface of her skin. A dark figure loomed at the end of the hall. *Who was that?* She gingerly stepped backwards.

In a primal shrill pitch, Chloe shrieked, "Run Kayn!"

With survival instinct on fire, Kayn fled with the bag of eggs. Rattled, she ran with no rhyme or reason, slipping on the wet grass. Scrambling forward, she sprinted for the trails, pitching the bag to slow her attacker. Fuelled by panic-induced impulse, she burst through overgrowth, ignoring pain as blackberry brambles tore her flesh, running with everything inside of her as twigs snapped behind her. Rounding a corner, she slipped in mud, skidding not falling, losing her half-second lead with her heart thudding wildly as athletic legs propelled her body through winding trails. Rocks on the path brutalised her bare feet as sharp, reaching branches and twigs slashed her limbs.

'You have to run faster, Kayn! Run faster!' Her sister's voice screeched in her terror-driven mind. *He was inhumanly fast.* Lights from the neighbour's house peeked through the trees. *She was going to make it. She was almost there. Almost to safety, just over the creek.* Her feet hit the wooden bridge as the darkness pursuing her kept pace, panting. *Almost there. She was going to make it.* About to burst through the bushes, she felt the elation of victory as something hot was driven into her back. Her eyes widened in terror as his knife seared a molten trail of agony. He muffled her cries as she

sunk to her knees in disbelief and crushed her larynx with python strong arms so she couldn't scream. At the brink of strangulation, he revived her with his tortuous blade. *Why was this happening?* Propping her up to see the salvation she wouldn't be granted, there was someone in patio lights through the trees. *Help me. See me. I'm right here.* Kayn's mind begged as he knifed her. *He's killing me. Please,* her soul pled. Her vision blurred with tears as blood sputtered from her lips. The competing rhythms of their hearts and his rapid breathing made her stomach churn with revulsion. His quiet laughter echoed in her mind as blood soaked through her clothes, trickling down her arms. *She was going to die.* He released her, whispering in a language she didn't understand. She slumped forward and tried grasping the ground with her fingertips, but no matter how hard she struggled from within the confines of her mind, she couldn't move. A soothing voice in her mind whispered, *sleep. It's time to go to sleep.* As she closed her eyes, she heard Grandma Winnie's final words to her, *'You survive. You fight hard.'* She screamed from within, clawing at the soil, forcing herself up to her knees. There was a blinding explosion of pain across her face. The lights flickered and went out. *In the woods lay a bleeding angel in all her glory. Her arms posed gracefully above her head, her hair soaked in the mud, blood, and faeces in which she lay. Dying, fading into the other realm, her form was christened by rain as the trees wept upon her for the brutality she'd endured.*

Kayn awoke in frigid darkness to the fragrance of damp moss, tree sap and the sweet metallic taste of blood. Images from her childhood flickered through her mind as pain recycled in waves until it dulled to become a tolerable numbness. *She was so cold. Where was she?* Her body involuntarily shuddered as her mind fed slivers of the inhuman savagery she'd suffered until she understood where she was and how she'd come to be dying in the forest all alone. *Maybe if she kept her eyes closed, he'd believe she was gone? She could slip away peacefully and become one with the forest.* Soothing raindrops tapped on the branches above her. *Maybe he was gone*? She opened her eyes and imagined the lush green branches of the cedar trees above as giant arms capable of offering her protection from the elements. At first, the image was nurturing and beautiful, but the trees came to life.

They cackled and mocked, "You're going to die, you silly bitch," as they waved their branches to haunting, rattling raindrops and the howling of the wind.

Kayn's consciousness snapped back to reality. *She'd lost a lot of blood. None of this was real.* The forest floor was alive with a dancing mist that seemed to add thickness to the tapping raindrops. Writhing in the mud as her essence moistened the ground beneath her, Kayn willed her body to move. Her fingers clawed at the soil until she was spent. She lay still like a half-dead animal waiting to be finished off by a hunter. With her eyes gazing to the heavens, she watched a stream of light from the moon that made it through the cover of rain clouds and branches. *It felt like she was breathing through a pinched straw.* She concentrated on each breath. *In and out, a little air.* The glimmer of light vanished, leaving only cold, isolating darkness and the flickering of blurry, confusing images. *Help me.* The only answer to her soul's plea was the crackling of rain. What vision she had clouded with tears as excruciating pain returned. She screamed from within the confines of her mind. As the wave of agony passed, she sensed his presence and tried to focus through the glossy film of her tears. His dark shadow ominously loomed as it had in the hallway, watching her. *Please. No more.* She willed herself to grasp at the moist, cold earth with her fingers but was unable to move. *Her body was nothing more than a broken shell. How cruel for her mind to desire life at this point.* As his form loomed above, she thought, *why are you doing this?* Involuntarily shuddering, she realised she was exposed to the elements. *Why was she naked?* Her eyes filled with tears. *Why was this happening?*

The dark mass of her violator knelt and leaned in. She smelled his putrid breath as it moistened her face. There was an electrical current between Kayn and the man in the dark. Every hair stood on end as he ran a finger over an exposed breast, disclosing, "You were never to be born, this situation had to be corrected."

His knife glinted in the moonlight as he raised it above her chest. *Yes. Let it be over.* She closed her eyes as he sliced into her flesh and opened them with acceptance. *She felt no more pain.* She stared into his eyes as hers filled with tears.

With a voice thick with emotion, he declared, "From this life unto the next."

He carved a symbol above her heart. She lay limp in his arms, conscious of what was happening, as he cradled her like a baby, rocking her broken, violated flesh, stroking her blood-soaked hair, sobbing as though he were repentant for how he'd tortured her.

As her vision flickered one last time, the man was gone, and in his place was her mother. Her eyes were filled with so much love it released her from pain and fear as it had when she was a child. Safe in her mother's arms, she was at peace. *Mommy.* Her heart sang, *you're here to save me.* The warmth of her mother's love enveloped her tortured soul. She gazed into her mother's eyes as she lovingly caressed her face, singing a song she'd sung to her every night when she was small. *Sleep, sweet sleep till the morning. Just dream away and close your eyes. My love, you'll be safe until the morning. Sleeping in my arms all through the night. Although bad dreams come to scare you. My love will scare them all away. My heart…*

The lights flickered, the pain went away, and her mother was holding her, singing, "Sleep, sweet sleep."

They sat in silence with no words. Kayn Brighton's redo began without a pause to catch their breath.

Kayn was standing in the shower at her old high school with water pleasurably beating down on her. Covered in suds and slightly confused, she rinsed herself off. She found her clothes, put them on and stopped to look at her reflection in the mirror. She noticed a bobby pin on the counter and tried to move it with her mind but couldn't. She glanced at her hand. *There was no scar. Interesting. This must be her redo. Lovely, she was in this day.* She shoved on the changeroom door, and there Kevin was with his mouth open wide, looking up at the sky. Her heart felt like it was about to explode. She wanted to say, catching flies as she had in the past. Instead, she decided to change things up a bit. *She'd always wondered what would have happened if she'd just walked up and broke their friendship façade while he was still the dorky, stubborn, endearing version of himself.*

With a strange look, he asked, "Is something wrong?"

"No," she replied. "I didn't realise how perfect everything was until now."

Kevin grinned, teasing, "Meaning me, of course. I know my perfection has always been utterly overwhelming."

"That it has," Kayn replied as she looked at her feet instead of into his eyes. *She wanted to stay with him but couldn't go lay in the grass and watch the clouds, knowing her family was being slaughtered. She'd felt it when her twin was being stabbed. That's what that sharp pain in her stomach had been. Maybe there was still time to change it.* Kayn stopped midstride and gave him a partial truth, "I can't come for dinner tonight. I need to go home. It's a Chloe emergency." Everything inside of her screamed, *kiss him! Kiss him just once!* As tempted as she was, she stopped herself. *No, he'll follow you home. Just tell him you'll see him tomorrow.*

"Alright, you'll be missing out," Kevin teased as they strolled away from the school.

This was one of her last moments of peace. It was hard to know that and enjoy it. Kayn took a last look at Kevin, wanting to remember him like this. *How had she not seen him clearly?* Under her breath, she gave him a response, "Not this time." She was about to walk away when she realised it didn't matter what she did, everything had already happened. Unable to help herself, she gave him a quick kiss on the lips before walking away. When she looked back, he was standing there with a shocked expression. *Hopefully, he wasn't going to follow her home like a confused puppy in search of an explanation. There was no time to worry, and it didn't matter anyway.* She jogged till she reached the alley before the woods and then sprinted through the trails to her house, slowing her pace to text her sister four important words, *lock the bathroom door.* She pressed send. *Maybe she'd have the chance to see her twin one last time. If she didn't have a plan, she'd just be showing up in the middle of the slaughter. Brains before brawn.* She grabbed a sturdy stick from the trail and chucked it, shaking her head at herself. *That would never work. Think Kayn. Think. Chloe was killed in the bathroom, her mother in the doorway and her father in the carport. She suspected by only one man.* Almost there, she walked. *What was she capable of changing?* She doubled over in agony. *It was too late. The*

Correction of her family had begun. For a moment, the nervous energy paralysed her. She fought to see through the fog of her mortal emotions. *She was going to be sick. Just breathe.* She crouched behind bushes to conceal herself. *Just breathe.* She heard her mother's car pull up. *She wanted to see her mother again so badly. Her emotions were all over the place and they couldn't be. Her mother would be killed two seconds after she walked in. It already happened. This was a test. The past had already happened. It couldn't be stopped. What did she need to move on? She needed to see the face of the man who destroyed her life. She needed to look into the eyes of the man responsible for the excessively brutal Correction.* She snuck through the backyard alongside the house and noticed an open window. *That's how he got in.* She stealthily climbed through it without a sound. She heard her mother's voice as she announced she was home. Instinct began screaming for her to try to save her. *Brains before brawn. Use logic, Kayn.* She heard the struggle at the front door and then eerie silence, followed by the creaking of the assailant's footsteps on the stairs. *He was going to finish her sister off.* Kayn tiptoed against the wall down the hall to the kitchen, knowing exactly where to walk so the floor didn't creak. She slid a medium sized knife silently out of the holder and crept back down the hallway. *She couldn't stop anything that was meant to happen, but she could use this opportunity for good old-fashioned vengeance on the being who murdered her family and cruelly tortured her without reprieve before violently ending her mortal life.* She was not going to pocket-dial Kevin this time. As she entered the living room, she dialled 911 on her cell and whispered, "3131 Falls Rd. He's killing everyone. Help us." She ended the call, cranked her dad's eighty's metal on the stereo and harnessed her inner Lexy. *She'd make him come to her.* Kayn clutched the knife as her heart pounded vigorously. She allowed the rage to swell inside until she felt the energy of her fury crackling beneath the surface of her skin. *He'd appeared to her the first time as a shadow in the darkened hallway.* This time there was no lurking in the shadows. He walked into the room with an intrigued smile.

Chloe's voice whispered in her mind, "Let's kill him, Kayn."

"What do you think you can do to me child?" He chuckled, leaning against the china cabinet with eyes as black as night.

There was no visible white at all. Her Correction hadn't been done by Tri-Clan. The Legion of Abaddon had done her Correction. This revelation changed everything. She wasn't strong enough to fight this being. She hadn't been Enlightened. She was going to be brutally slaughtered all over again. Crap! She was going to have to run, but that hadn't worked the last time. Had it? She needed to contemplate her next move. She couldn't beat him. He had the strength of ten of her. In her mind, she heard the words, *brains before brawn.* She had to make it past him to the kitchen, so she amped herself up. *He killed your family. Think about your mother, your father, your sister... Think about Chloe. What would Chloe do?* Kayn met his black pool eyes and vowed, "Someday, I'll kill you but today, I'll settle for pissing you off." She began rifling everything in the room at him. Laughing at her show of strength, the devious being didn't try to stop her as she darted past, down the hall into the kitchen. He casually strolled after her like a killer from a horror movie. *Brains before brawn.* She grabbed the heavy bag of salt from beside the sundeck door. Its purpose had been to keep the doorways from getting icy, but today she was changing shit up. Kayn slit it open with her knife and spun around as she tore it, spraying salt all over the Abaddon. He shrieked as it scalded his flesh. Like a badass, she plunged her knife into his liver, booted him in the stomach and sent him flying backwards. Buying herself precious moments, her shaking hands fumbled with the lock as the demonic entity in mortal disguise struggled to his feet. *He was losing a lot of blood.* She caught the scent as she slid open the door and ran. She leapt off the sundeck like a superhero and sprinted across the back lawn, tossing what was left of the bag of salt at the mouth of the trail for old-time's sake. He staggered after her to the sound of approaching sirens. Her eyes kept darting back to her mortally wounded foe. She smirked as she kept her eyes on her snail-paced assailant while pressing redial. She dramatically gasped, "Help. I'm in the trails behind my house." He paused, shaking while hunched over. *She'd beaten him.* He straightened up. She realised he was laughing. *Well, shit! She'd stabbed him in the damn liver, how was he still alive?* He grinned and began chasing her at full speed. *Crap!* She sprinted through the trails and across the bridge, this time with shoes on. Her heart was pounding wildly with the knowledge of how this played out. Kayn saw the light on the man's porch. As she was about to break through the bushes, she braced herself for the inevitable burning explosion of pain. The knife plunged into her back. She saw the flashlights flickering through the trees and heard voices. He had her in his arms, brutally squeezing the breath from her chest. She felt her ribs snapping. *How was this asshole still alive? She'd stabbed him in the liver. His shell should have died before he made it off the damn sundeck.*

The dark being whispered in her ear, "Until we meet again," as he released her, yanking the blade from her back.

The fire that lit a path through her core ceased. She harnessed her rage, kicked back and booted his shin. His knife dropped as she swung around and drop-kicked him in the groin with everything she had. He doubled over in agony and staggered backwards. She fell to her knees with a giant grin on her face as he ran away. She whispered, "You can count on it." She felt the warmth of her blood as it soaked through her shirt. *He'd made that one wound count.* Kayn knew what he was now and she would count the seconds until the next time he crossed her path. *When she was Enlightened, they would be fighting on even ground.* The lights flickered and went out.

Grey smiled as Kayn's redo ended. He looked at the others and whispered one word, "Wow."

Jenna spoke aloud, "We may have underestimated Miss Kayn Brighton. She was Corrected by Abaddon and in her redo, she fought back knowing she couldn't win. Go into your training knowing the two girls are close to being emotionally prepared but Zach needs a few lessons in anger awareness."

"Maybe the redo was enough," Grey piped in. He climbed into one of the remaining tombs with Lexy. They'd help them lick their wounds first before putting them through the ringer one last time.

Jenna peered into the tomb at the two and ordered, "Work them hard. This is the last chance to help them conquer those fears."

As the tomb ground closed, Lexy and Grey stared at each other and smiled. Sometimes it didn't seem like much time had passed since they went into the Testing with Arrianna. They'd also been three Ankh against six in each of the other Clans when they'd earned their tombs. Lexy took Grey's hand as she whispered, "This group might survive the Testing like we did."

"I'd be willing to bet on it… Now," Grey replied as the tomb started to pulse with blinding light and they were shot up into eternity.

Orin and Jenna were alone with each other for the first time. As she attempted to leave, he grabbed her arm and asked, "Stay here with me for a while. I can't go anywhere. I have to run the tombs and we need to talk."

Jenna met his eyes as she answered, "We'll have time to talk after the Summit. We ended a long time ago. There's not much left to say... Is there?"

He kept ahold of her arm as he said, "You know there is."

"There used to be," she stated. "I'm not the same person."

Orin released his grasp. She started walking away and he called after her, "This is me you're talking to! It doesn't matter! You know we belong together!"

Jenna stopped walking. She turned and stared into his eyes so there would be no misunderstanding as she disclosed, "That's just it… We don't."

Chapter 26

Clarity

Kayn awoke to a soothing trickling brook, the steady humming of bumblebees and the tune of a bird's enchanting serenade. The world around her was still slightly blurred as her mind struggled to find peace after reliving parts of her past best left buried. *The redo of their Sweet Sleep was complete.* Melody lay next to her, appearing to be asleep in the vibrant green bed of lush grass. Mel opened her eyes and smiled back. They lay in the still of the moment, just breathing as visions of tortured souls with vacant eyes hovering in a sea of loss kept trying to sneak past the barrier of the warm sunshine. Kayn tried to focus on the humming of the bees and the scent of life in the air. Emotionally depleted, they stared at the vibrant shades of blue swirling above. *It really did look like someone had just tossed cans of paint into the sky staining the heavens.*

"Well, that really sucked." Melody whispered.

Kayn quietly replied, "That was messed-up."

After a brief interlude, Melody tried to find her way back to the here and now by saying, "The sky in this place always reminds me of a kid's painting."

She was just thinking that exact thing. "Me too," Kayn casually responded, giggling. Mel snickered as the stress of what they'd endured catapulted them both into hysterical laughter.

Zach materialized out of nowhere, standing above them in the lush, almost teal-hued grass. Curious, he questioned, "Is something funny?"

They admitted, "The sky" in unison and pissed themselves laughing again.

Zach stood with his mouth agape, staring at the magical hues above as he exclaimed, "I hope this insanity is only temporary."

Kevin used to do that. The mouth thing, not the insanity thing. Her inner dialogue was having a discussion with itself. This can't be good.

He said, "On the bright side, this last week of training will be fun. Hell, getting chased by Jason through the woods with an axe would be shit loads of fun after what I just went through."

Zach was preaching to the choir. Kayn grabbed a handful of grass and tossed it at him while lying on her back. It landed on her face. She laughed as she blew it off her nose with a puff of air.

Zach grinned and teased, "See, had it not been for this thing called gravity, you might have gotten me good with that dangerous handful of grass there."

"Lay down with us and quit being such a pain in the ass," Melody sparred back.

He grinned and obediently sprawled in the grass next to them. Zach smiled as he spoke his observation aloud, "It is kind of nice, isn't it?"

There was a long moment of silence as each new Ankh's mind travelled back through the events of their Correction and redo. A light breeze whispered across the top of the grass, making the blades dance a little. The chirping of what Kayn determined to be a cricket added to the magical ambience. She closed her eyes to listen for the humming of bees again and heard the off-key deep croak of a toad instead. She took a breath and exhaled. *Breathe in and breathe out until you calm yourself.*

"I think I did everything wrong today," Zach confessed.

She understood the feeling. Part of her felt like she'd done the right thing, but she knew the point of the redo wasn't for her to get a chance to see the face of the monster who murdered her family.

"I didn't change anything. Well, almost anything," Melody added, wistfully staring at the swirly blue sky.

"I didn't save anybody. I knew they were already gone. I fought this time and I saw his face," Kayn reminisced. She wanted to add, 'it was a Demon that did my family's Correction.' She decided to keep that to herself for now because she wasn't sure what it meant. *They'd all done something different. Had any of them done the right thing?*

In response to Kayn's inner dialogue, Melody said, "Maybe it's only about closure? Maybe there is no right or wrong?" Mel grinned as she yanked a giant handful of grass from the ground and threw it at Kayn.

Kayn took the handful of grass in her face as a silent cue that she didn't want to speak about the redo anymore. *She knew Melody was right.* Zach's face lit up as Melody launched another handful of green into the air. Kayn sat up and playfully teased, "So, that's how you want it then?" She giggled while grabbing a handful of grass and launching it back at Melody.

When Grey and Lexy finally graced them with their presence, they were perplexed to find the three Ankh fresh from their emotional re-enactments of their Sweet Sleep rolling around face washing each other with grass. Their faces were comically green smudged.

"Seriously kids? Act your age," Grey playfully scolded.

That sentiment coming from him added to the hilarity. They all tackled him. Lexy just stood there shaking her head. They carried on wrestling in the grass for another ten minutes before Lexy cleared her throat and said, "I was certain we'd find three sobbing teens distraught over the redo of their Sweet Sleep. Instead, we came upon the three of you wrestling in the grass like a pack of sugar-loaded children." Grey tossed a handful of it directly at Lexy's face. She waved her hand, blocking it without touching a blade. It travelled away in the wind. Lexy glared at Grey and sighed, "Make that four kids." She stared at her Handler until he stood up with an enormous childlike grin. Lexy ordered, "Enough shenanigans! Get up and brush that grass off. We have a lot left to cover and only a limited amount of time."

Always ready with smart assed commentary, Zach provoked, "Do I get a spanking if I misbehave?"

Without succumbing to laughter behind tightly pursed lips, Lexy repeated, "Get up!"

The grass-covered, messy-haired playmates scrambled to their feet and tried to maintain a straight face. *They'd been through the wringer. They wouldn't retain anything without time to process the redo of their Sweet Sleep.* With the attention span of a squirrel, Kayn noticed a mosquito on Zach and slapped his forehead.

Stumbling with his hand on his head, Zach hissed, "What in the hell?"

Whoops, she'd done that without even thinking. "Mosquito." She explained, grinning.

Zach stood quietly for a second before hauling off and smoking her rear. Kayn scowled, cupping her nearly bare butt cheek. Grinning widely, he taunted, "Mosquito."

Grey glanced at Lexy and said, "It's going to be pointless to try to get them to do anything before they've had the chance to recharge those unhinged brains."

Lexy sighed and gave in, "Why don't you three take the rest of the day to think, dream, have a good scream. Do whatever you need to do to get your sanity back."

Without another word, Grey and Lexy wandered away from the trio of mentally unhinged Newbies. Out of nowhere, Grey smacked her behind. She scowled as he provoked, "Mosquito."

They walked about ten paces before Lexy snatched Grey's legs out from under him. Wielding his body in the air as effortlessly as a blanket, she whirled him in a circle by his legs and smoked him against the ground. Grey was gasping with the wind knocked out of him. Lexy leaned over her Handler and whispered, "Mosquito." She casually strolled away.

Once he'd managed to catch his breath, Grey scrambled to his feet and raced to catch up with her.

They were all dead silent, each of them a tiny bit afraid that if one Lexy-induced giggle slipped out, they'd be forced to play the 'come at me' game with her again.

Lexy was still laughing as they vanished into the vast space of the In-between.

Kayn declared, "We really need to learn how to disappear."

"She's so awesome," Zach whispered, in awe of the crimson-haired immortal.

Grinning, Kayn asked, "Where do you think they went?"

"My guess is far away from us crazy people," Mel chuckled, keeping the conversation lighthearted.

With nowhere to be, the trio sprawled on the grass together.

"We have good cause to be emotionally unstable," Zach pointed out, staring at the fluffy clouds that appeared in the sky. His honest insertion was followed by a long, drawn-out silence as their need for laughter subsided.

The gravity of the upcoming events was beginning to set in. With their minds reeling from the redo of their Sweet Sleep, they understood on some level that their darkest moments were nothing but teasers for what was to come.

Melody broke the silence with a question, "What do you think the Testing is going to be?"

While keeping his eyes on the fluffy white clouds above, Zach replied, "I always pictured an old school gladiator fight in a Colosseum with a two-headed monster or a mythical Medusa-like creature."

Everyone she'd loved had been collateral damage to her destiny. If she didn't survive the Testing, her family's Correction would be for nothing. She'd allowed herself to be claimed by Ankh and survived until the age of eighteen. She'd falsely assumed permanently becoming Ankh was the end of her mortal woes, but it hadn't guaranteed her survival. There was one more T to cross. A final hoop to jump through in this immortal game. Kayn glanced at Zach and responded to his jest, "We could kick Medusa's ass."

"I bet Lexy could kick Medusa's ass, all by herself," Melody countered.

Zach chuckled and jousted, "Lexy could kick Medusa's ass while hogtied."

Grey had referred to surviving the Testing on various occasions. Why hadn't the enormity of it registered? Kayn whispered, "I think our Testing is going to be soon. I don't know what it is or where it is, but I do know that I don't have the mental capacity to deal with anything else today." Kayn scrambled to her feet and asserted, "We need to take this relax and recoup offer seriously. Lexy is liable to be the one kicking our asses later." She looked either way across the wide span of never-ending grass. *There was nothing substantial in either direction. No mountains. No buildings. Not even the smallest hill.* She looked at her arm. *A mosquito was feasting on her. Where did the mosquitoes come from? Which one of them thought of mosquitoes and caused them to become a part of the In-between? Maybe it was her? She'd started the mosquito joke.*

Zack got up and helped Melody to her feet. As they began to walk together through the massive field of green, he questioned, "How do you guys want to spend the afternoon?"

"From what I understand, this place is whatever we want it to be... Right?" Mel said.

Zach baited, "I have an idea. We can play a game of hide and seek. We can call it Where's Kayn? It's just like Where's Waldo but with a stubborn uncoordinated hot chick?"

Kayn socked his shoulder and said, "Mosquito."

He tackled her to the grass, singing, "Mosquito."

They wrestled, tickling each other until Melody harnessed her inner Lexy and cleared her throat. They scrambled to their feet and attempted to pay attention as Melody suggested, "I know a beautiful place for us to decompress. I might even be able to find the way back."

With their curiosity peaked, they each took one of Mel's hands. They were going to one of Melody's places, and neither one wanted to get lost. The scenery flashed with bright light and they were standing by the shore of a peculiar swimming hole. It looked like a tidal pool with colourful starfish and glistening white sand but it was out of place in this location. Lakes did not have sea creatures, and the lush greenery of the countryside did not surround tidal pools.

"I can't believe that worked," Melody exclaimed.

"Okay, this place is cool," Kayn whispered, in awe of the orbs swirling like fish under the surface of the water. *She'd seen those lights before.*

Wading into the pool, Zach declared, "Amazing, is the word I'd use."

Melody knelt at the water's edge and ran her hand across the surface as she explained, "When I left Trinity after Markus made me Ankh again, this is where I ran into Grey."

Zach splashed her, teasing, "I remember this story."

Melody winked and said, "I'd just tanked my afterlife and he was there."

Kayn sat on the grassy shore. Picking up a small teal stone, she began rolling it between the tips of her fingers. *It was perfectly round.* There were rose-hued ones and white stones with speckles. They were all smooth to the touch with no sharp edges. *Everything around this pool was aesthetically pleasing.* She ran her hand across the grass and felt each strand separately caressing her palm. *What is this place?* Kayn winked at Melody and baited, "Grey's gorgeous. You were alone with an insanely cute guy in a dream... Why not?" Kayn got up with a handful of stones, wound up and skipped a teal pebble across the water. It skimmed the surface a couple of times on its path and bounced over Zach without hitting him. Beaming, Kayn announced, "I'm usually horrible at this! I've never been able to do that before!"

Zach piped in from his spot in the pool, "You ladies aren't planning to sit up there and throw rocks at me, are you?"

Mel picked up a rose-tinted stone and grinned as she pitched it. The pebble touched four times across the pool's surface. Mel disclosed, "I did this all the time. Back when skimming rocks across the surface of the water was a formidable life skill."

The fragrance of apples wafted through the air. Kayn looked behind her and noticed an apple tree that hadn't been there a moment before. *Since when did apple trees smell?* She leapt up and wandered over to stand by it. The tree was ideally shaped with branches chock full of flawless red delicious apples. *Red delicious apples were usually bruised. These were perfect specimens.* Kayn picked one. She had eaten one of these at the copy of Granny Winnie's house in the In-between shortly after she passed on. *It was delicious. It had been an incredible apple. The best one she'd ever tasted. She'd thought about it with every bite of an apple since that day.* Holding it in the palm of her hand, she smelled it. She motioned to Zach that she was going to throw him one. He was relaxing, floating in the pool. He reached up and caught it in midair. Zach looked before taking a giant bite. Kayn threw one at Melody and then plucked one off the beautifully sculpted tree for herself. After swallowing the first bite, they felt relaxed. She sat with Melody on the shore, eating delectable fruit and skimming stones. Melody stood up to grab more apples and shrieked, wrecking the exquisite calm. Kayn whirled around to see what had startled her. A giant snake was twisting around the trunk of the apple tree. Kayn got up and made her way to Melody's side. *She wasn't afraid… She was entranced. It was more than that. She felt mesmerized by the reptile's docile, nonchalant manner.* It slid around the trunk until the length of the enormous reptile encircled it completely. *She was certain it was looking into her eyes. It knew she wasn't afraid.* Kayn's reflections travelled to tales from her childhood. *Was this the Garden of Eden? Had she just given both of her friends an apple?* She shook her head and decided that was a ridiculous notion. *This was the In-between. This meant something to one of them. It wasn't literal. It was figurative. The Garden of Eden was a lesson about temptation.* Kayn grinned, suspecting she'd deduced the purpose of the pool. *It was to expose temptation.* The snake disappeared when she glanced back at the tree. Kayn asked, "Where did the snake go?"

"It just vanished." Mel whispered.

Kayn touched her shoulder and urged, "Let's go swimming. Just forget about it. It wasn't real. One of us must have been thinking about snakes and brought it here, just like I started the mosquito population earlier."

Zach admitted, "That might have been me. It did cross my mind that I was grateful there were no snakes here."

"Snakes usually hide in the tall grass by the edge of a path. It may have crossed my mind too. I'm just glad it's gone." Melody confessed, visibly relieved.

Kayn smiled again. *She'd been reading far too much into the snake and apple situation.* As she watched Zach splashing around in the pool, she found him strangely hot. Kayn glanced at Melody and noticed she was also staring.

It only took a moment for him to notice they were ogling him. "I knew both of you secretly wanted me," Zach teased.

Kayn winked and sarcastically sighed, "How did you know? I've been trying to hide my overwhelming passion for you since we first met." He playfully attempted to grab for her legs and pull her in. Kayn gently kicked him back into the water. He went under. She grinned and jumped into the pool. As he surfaced, she doused him with fresh spray. Zach splashed her back and she lost her footing. When she came up for air, strange lights scattered and weaved between her legs. *It was beautiful.* Zach splashed her again, almost wrecking the blissful moment until the lights whirled past her legs underwater once more. She chuckled as she jumped out of the way. Melody joined them in the pool, and they relaxed together, floating in the soothing warmth of the liquid heaven. She was fighting the urge to touch a starfish decoratively clinging to the speckled stone ledge but sensed something coming. She swung around to look just as snakes began dropping from the branches of the tree. Kayn whispered, "You two should probably get out of the water."

"Why? What are you looking at?" Mel asked as she turned.

It was a disturbing visual for someone with no reptilian phobia. Slightly confused, Kayn said, "There are hundreds of snakes falling from the branches of that apple tree. Are you telling me neither of you can see this?"

Zach replied, "If there are, I sure as hell can't see them."

"Well, knowing you see them is enough to get me out of the water," Mel declared. She scrambled out on the opposite side.

Zach also evacuated the pool. Curious as to where this vision was going, Kayn stayed put. *Why couldn't they see them? She wasn't afraid of snakes.* She'd caught buckets of them as a child with Kevin. One time, she'd even attempted to smuggle home a cardboard box containing dozens of snakes. When they arrived home, the snakes were missing. They'd escaped in her mother's vehicle. Her father had taken out the bench seats while searching but never found any. He'd told her they probably escaped through a hole in the floor and warned her that he had to tell her mother a little white lie because if he didn't tell her he'd found the snakes and disposed of them, she'd never get in her car again. *That was the day she'd learned the distinction between a noble lie and a bad one.* The others were upset by the snakes' presence. *If she was the only one who could see them, this wasn't about fear. There had to be a point to this involving only her.*

"Aren't you going to get out of the water?" Zach questioned.

Far too curious to get out, Kayn stayed put. *What was the purpose of this creepy visual?* "No. I'm the only one that can see them. I'd like to figure out what it means," she answered as the first one glided across the surface of the water towards her. She extended her palm and it slithered around her fingers. Kayn raised her hand, looked him in the eye and then placed it back into the water. The reptile slid off her fingertips and disappeared under the surface as the rest began to enter the heavenly pool in mass. She allowed herself only one squeamish millisecond as they slithered and slipped past her thighs. Kayn didn't budge, wanting to know the purpose of this visual madness. The pool rapidly filled with snakes, and before Kayn knew it, she was standing in a writhing mass of slithering reptiles. *Thank goodness this wasn't happening to Mel. She would have lost her damn mind. Why was this happening to her?* She caught on to the hidden meaning. *This hadn't just happened. She'd chosen to stay in the water. Everything was a choice.* They didn't constrict. *Breathe in, breathe out.* They just slithered around her with a slick, leathery rhythm.

She didn't react. When she didn't venture to leave, they abruptly vanished, and she was left standing in the luxurious warmth of the tidal pool. *Her mind wrapped around the moment as she struggled to figure out what it meant. Was this about temptation? Kevin and Frost were her temptations. The apples had reminded her of Winnie. She didn't need to guess the why anymore. She needed to talk to Winnie.* She swam to the ledge and climbed out of the water.

Curious, Zach asked, "Aren't you going to explain?"

"It's not necessary, it was a hallucination. I know what it's about though… There's someone I need to see," Kayn replied as she strolled away from the others. As they attempted to come with her, she slowly shook her head and asserted, "I need to go alone."

Zack hollered after her, "We shouldn't split up!"

Kayn shouted back, "I won't be long! I promise!" She glanced back after walking for a few seconds, and she was fifty feet away. *Wild.* Led by nothing but instinct, she kept walking. *Where are you?*

Chapter 27

Vampires, Dragons, Zombies And Oracles

The scenery flashed around her and she was back at the clean slate desert. Knowing they wouldn't wait long before they attempted to follow, she sprinted away barefoot through the silken sand, imagining herself as a wild stallion galloping through the desert wild and free. Her feet made no sound as they hit the silken earth. Her hair, free from the restraints of her usual ponytail, had become a glimmering mane of gold flowing behind her. *Left foot, right foot, faster and faster.* Kayn saw the cliff's edge up ahead. Smiling, she raced for it, needing to feel indestructible, even if it was a fallacy. *They were physically indestructible, yet emotionally each of them was a train wreck. Spiritually, they could all be slaughtered. She needed to disregard her vulnerability. Her internal weaknesses kept taunting, he doesn't remember you. He will never remember you.* She blinked the thoughts away as she felt the sand disappear from underfoot. There was the cool sensation of nothing but air. Her world sped by around her as she plunged into nothingness. Her mind cruelly reminded her of when she'd clutched Kevin's hand as they'd fallen together. *It was in this place, but another life. He was gone.* As she passed through the clouds, she felt baptized by the humidity moistening her skin. *The darkened clouds of her afterlife were working up a storm.* Her heart tightened. *That's what it felt like fate had in store for her...A storm.* As she continued her semi-controlled spiral towards the rapidly approaching terrain below, she spread her hands to either side of her, using the emotion that ached in her chest to stop herself seconds before making a crater in the forest floor. She landed on her hands and knees but remained frozen in place. *Her mind had been asked to swallow an incredible amount of bullshit. She wasn't sure she could swallow the presence of this version of Kevin. How was this beneficial to her training? She'd wanted nothing but a moment alone with him until she'd received one.* She whispered, "Winnie, I need you." Her surroundings flashed with an explosion of blinding white light. The afterlife paused, including her body's ability to breathe as the hollow agony of loss came flooding back. *She didn't think it would hurt this much to know he was really gone. She'd thought it would help her move on but couldn't keep her mind focused on anything but him. Every fibre of her being needed a good loud scream.*

"Why don't you then?" She heard a familiar voice say from behind her.

Kayn's heart leapt in her chest as she peered up. There stood the elderly version of Grandma Winnie. Kayn dove into her arms. As Kayn clung to her, Winnie's appearance altered to the version of her youth.

Winnie stroked Kayn's hair, "Cry child, scream, hit something. Do whatever you need to do. I'm here."

Kayn sobbed into her shoulder, "You must think I'm horrible, crying over Kevin. I know you saw my connection with Frost."

Winnie warmly cupped Kayn's face in her hands and assured, "There's not a horrible bone in your body my child. It's completely normal to want to move on. It's also normal for you to feel confused when you can't." The elderly woman had always loved like her own granddaughter. Winnie gazed into Kayn's eyes as she added, "There's something you need to do for me before we can keep talking."

"Anything," Kayn whispered, keeping her eyes locked on Granny Winnie's.

"I want you to scream as loud as you can," Winnie ordered.

Kayn stifled a nervous laugh as she questioned, "Seriously?"

"I promise, it will make you feel a million times better," she lovingly assured as she released her hold.

"Okay," Kayn agreed as she stepped away and released a wimpy scream.

Winnie knit her brow and laughed, "What was that? Trust me on this, you need a good emotional release."

Yes, that was pathetic. Kayn took a deep breath and screamed again, but it was still only about half of what she was capable of.

With empathy in her eyes, Winnie provoked, "Let me set this up for you. Kevin doesn't remember you. You just had to relive the worst night of your life. You didn't ask for any of this. Life isn't fair. Death isn't fair. You don't have any abilities yet. The

Testing is coming and you don't know what that means. Now scream. Scream at everyone and everything that has hurt you. Scream at anyone that will ever hurt you. Scream at fate for taking everyone you love from you. Scream with all that you are for everything you've lost along the way."

Against her will, her eyes filled with unshed tears. Kayn blinked them away as she took another deep breath and screamed with everything she had. She kept screaming, over and over, until she began to feel lightheaded. Utterly exhausted, she sunk to her knees before Winnie.

The youthful version of Granny Winnie knelt beside her and enquired, "Now…Doesn't that feel better?"

Kayn couldn't help it, half out of the comedy of the moment, and half from embarrassment, she began to giggle.

Their eyes met as Winnie winked at her and asked, "What do you need my help with?"

Everything. "Don't you already know?" Kayn teased, knowing she was psychic so that made her privy to everything.

"You want to know if Kevin will remember you or if your feelings for him are hopeless. Those pesky forks in the road of life make it difficult to choose a direction…Don't they? Well, I can't tell you anything for sure. I've seen several versions of your road. Everything changes day by day, based on your decisions. I know where you need to be in the end. I wish I could tell you all about it but I'm not allowed to. You choose your own adventure. You can do things the easy way or the hard way. I'm supposed to help protect the Clan from imminent danger. I'm not supposed to give forced love life recommendations."

"You gave Frost a forced love life recommendation," she teased, referring to the ban she'd put on a physical relationship between them.

Winnie chuckled as she quipped, "I knew you would call me on that." She placed her hand on Kayn's shoulder and attempted to explain, "You needed Frost to allow you the room to tie up loose ends. He wasn't helping you. The good version of your future had altered and I was forced to step in. In the altered versions, you three didn't make it out of the Testing. That version of your future had never been seen before and it caused us a little bit of a panic. You have no idea how important you are. You need to learn to be autonomous. Happiness is only ever wrong if it comes at someone else's expense. My grandson doesn't remember you. The harsh reality is that you are not in the same Clan and attempting to be with him now can only bring you both pain. Spend the next week tying up loose ends within yourself. Find closure so you can move on. This is important to your personal growth. Kevin has much more important things on his plate right now, as do you. If you are meant to be together, one day you will be."

She understood what Kevin's grandmother was saying but she didn't want to. Kayn pleaded, "Just tell him everything about his mother and his brother. You could show him where Tiberius is holding his family."

"He has to be ready to hear it and strong enough to do something about it or future events won't play out in his favour," Winnie explained. "Right now, he has little to no control over his abilities and there's an important chain of events that led up to him making a stand. So, if you want to spend the next week telling him about all that you were to him, go for it. Just heed this warning, speak of nothing else. If you want to talk about me, that's fine. He's used to hearing my voice directing him in his head. Say nothing about the rest of his family. Shut him down if he tries to pump you for information. Say what you need to say to find closure. You both need to be able to move on."

Jenna had already given her this speech. "He's my best friend. How do I just let him go?" Kayn whispered.

"You don't have to let go of the friend, but you have to force yourself to let go of the need for more than friendship," Winnie advised softly.

Kayn knew what she was saying was the truth.

Winnie continued to speak, "By all means, spend the next week or so proving it to yourself until you come to terms with it. I know the teenager in you wants to rotate your life around these feelings and make him the centre of your existence. You need to mature faster than that as a matter of survival. This is my best advice to you for the years ahead. Make yourself the centre of your existence. There are so many amazing things to experience. Be that stallion from your fantasies and run free."

Kayn smiled at the reference to how she'd imagined herself earlier. *Psychics could be creepy sometimes.* She'd grown up with Granny Winnie. She had one more question to ask, "Kevin was a Psychic. He found the talents from his grandfather's side and they seemed to change him. He doesn't appear to have that ability now... Why?"

"Well my dear one…Immortal brains are like processors. They can get overloaded. He must have subconsciously chosen one ability over the other. He doesn't know he's a Psychic. It doesn't mean it's not there, it just means it's dormant. It still could be delivering him dreams and visions of the past. The gifts he inherited from his grandfather are the ones he needs to master. His Psychic ability, if it endures on some level, is built on instinct."

Kayn stared at Winnie and asked, "How bad is the Testing going to be? Can you tell me anything?"

Winnie's expression changed before she had the opportunity to hide it. The elderly woman had an expression similar to the one she'd had on the night of Kayn's Correction. She gave her the only advice she could, "I want you to remember the word...Stand. You need to stand up. You must keep going. No matter what happens, remember to stand. People are always so much stronger than they believe themselves to be."

With a weak smile, Kayn responded, "That doesn't sound ominous at all." She could hear her name being called as an echo in the horizon.

Hugging her tightly, Winnie whispered, "They're looking for you. I love you child. You remember to stand back up."

She didn't have time to overthink as the scenery around her exploded with glorious blinding light. Kayn opened her eyes and she was standing in the grass beside the tidal pool of water. *Zach and Melody had been here with her not too long ago. How long had she been gone? They weren't here anymore.* Kayn was startled as a large amount of monarch butterflies took off around her. *She'd thought they were orange flowers.* The bushes separated ahead. *Something was coming… Something large.* She smiled as a honey stallion with a muscular torso moved through the bushes towards her. Its mane was the colour of her hair. A defining moment, for it symbolized her desire for freedom. *She wanted to be free of guilt, free to experience her afterlife with reckless abandon.* She moved closer to the majestic being with an outstretched hand, in awe of the moment, understanding it was a gift from Winnie for her alone to experience. As she attempted to touch the magnificent creature, her hand passed right through. She knew what this majestic being's significance was. *This was what she was meant to be. Wild, untameable and free.* The voices of her friends cut through the silence and the honey stallion vanished as they walked right through it. Kayn was standing there with her hand outstretched and a goofy grin on her face as they approached. She understood what Winnie was trying to tell her. *She wasn't meant to be pining over anyone. She was stronger than that. She was a stallion ready to run through a sandstorm.* Kayn Brighton would face whatever came across her path in life, living by the words of her favourite poem, *with her head held high with the grace of a woman, not the grief of a child. With every goodbye, she would learn.*

"What in the hell are you doing?" Zach chuckled as he took her raised hand in his own and lovingly pressed it to his lips.

Kayn answered, "Nothing... I was just trying to find you two." *She wasn't fooling him. He hadn't missed her dodging the question.*

"By doing magic spells?" Melody snickered. Mel waved her hands, wiggled her fingers and sang, "Bibbidy boobidy boo."

Zach shook his head as he said, "I hope you had the chance to see who you needed to see. It's time to start training. We had to run interference." He still had a hold of her hand as he gave her a knowing smile and began towing her along through the bushes. Melody kept wriggling her fingers at Zach. "There's no such thing," he chuckled as they met up with Grey and Lexy.

Curious, Lexy enquired, "No such thing as what?"

Zach rolled his eyes as he replied, "Witches."

"Of course, there are Witches." Grey declared. "Why wouldn't there be Witches?"

Mel strolled beside Grey, probing, "Vampires, Dragons and Zombies?"

Grey chuckled and sighed, "Don't even get me started. One form of necrophilia should be outlawed but the other is a lot of fun... Right, Lex?"

Lexy choked while laughing. Grey patted her back. *She suspected the dig was aimed at one of Lexy's prior flings. Maybe someday she'd hear the story behind the comment? She'd always thought the premise behind vampirism was sort of hot.* Kayn grinned while attempting to think about zombies in a sexy way. She pictured one with missing chunks of flesh hanging off its face and the nasty scent of decomposing flesh. *It wasn't a sexy thought. Dragons were sort of a bestiality thing.* She was tossing around rather messed-up thoughts when Grey asked her what she was thinking about.

"Grey?" Lexy teased, "You've known Brighton long enough to not even ask what's going on in her weird inner dialogue. Do you really want the answer to that question?"

Kayn winked at Lexy as she taunted, "In theory, if we had sex, it would be necrophilia."

Out of nowhere, Grey placed her hand on his chest. As she felt the warmth of his skin, she also felt the immediate need to yank her hand away as her blood raced in response to the thudding of his heart.

Grinning flirtatiously, Grey toyed, "We're living, breathing beings. Our hearts beat like any mortal. We heal a little faster. A lot faster if it happens to be your gift. That is why some of us can't end up in the hospital without freaking everyone out."

"I accidentally freaked someone out so badly they died the last time I ended up in the hospital," Zach chuckled.

Grey grinned, rolled his eyes and said, "Because Lexy healed you. I'm just trying to make a point to Brighton."

He'd definitely made it. Kayn had been avoiding eye contact with Grey since he'd placed her hand on his chest. *He hadn't missed her response. These Ankh boys were all the same. He wouldn't be able to resist teasing her a little now.*

As she'd predicted, Grey took her hand as he continued his little speech, "Every reaction to any stimulation is precisely the same as a mortal." He rubbed his finger slowly, rhythmically in circles on the soft skin of her wrist while gazing into her eyes with his intense blue pools of seduction. With his sandy blonde wavy hair swept across his brow, sometimes Grey reminded her of an angel. *A naughty angel that threw temper tantrums with a sexy accent.*

"Oh, for heaven's sake Grey, cut it out!" Lexy reprimanded, "We have things to do... Focus!"

Kayn exhaled slowly. *Something was going on.* He stepped away from her, grinning like a cat who'd just swallowed a canary. The lack of contact allowed her to regain their bearings. Everyone was enjoying Kayn's confusion over her reaction to Grey's touch far too much to explain it was the pool of water making her weak in the knees.

Melody poked Kayn's arm and said, "I bet Grey hangs out by this pool every time he comes to the In-between hoping to find emotionally distraught pliable girls."

Kayn lunged over and punched Grey's arm. He was grinning as she scolded, "You're such a jerk! I forgot where I was standing!" He had a case of the giggles as they strolled away from the tidal pool of seduction. Kayn smiled at Grey. *How can you stay mad at someone who is giggling like a child?*

Melody poked her and said, "You couldn't have reminded me of that tiny tidbit of information before you left me there alone with Zach?"

Grey's giggles turned to full-on laughter as he enquired, "Did you seriously fall under the tidal pool's spell again?" He winked at Mel and ruffled her hair as she attempted to swat him away. Grey playfully warned, "Be good to her or you'll have me to answer to."

Looking at the mischievous immortal with wide, innocent eyes, Zach disclosed, "I know better. I never touched her."

With an arm around Melody, Kayn whispered in her ear, "I think Grey's jealous."

Mel scowled, whispering, "He's just a big kid splashing girls with water. I have a feeling he's never really serious about anyone.

As they wandered ever-changing scenery of the In-between, Kayn was secretly relieved they hadn't started something. *They were going into the immortal Testing together. They didn't need romantic complications… They needed to survive.*

Chapter 28

Being the Lion

Lexy threw a cold bucket of water on the conversation with her words, "So, what do you all think your Testing will consist of?"

Zach answered promptly, "An old school Colosseum with the grandstands full."

Grey stepped back into the conversation, enquiring, "Tell me, Zach. Do you like video games?"

"I will have you know, I was the Halo champion of my family," Zach replied as he shuffled through the long grass.

Grey's eyes lit up. Apparently, that was a good thing. Again, with the damn video games. Kayn was listening to their conversation, not watching where she was walking and almost bailed in the thigh-high grass. Lexy grabbed her and gave her a disapproving look as she released her grasp. Kayn piped into the conversation, "I was never much of a gamer, but I did alright swinging a lightsabre playing Star Wars at Kevin's house. Trivial Pursuit Unhinged was my family's game night thing. I have amazing deductive reasoning skills."

"I'm good at board games," Mel added.

Grey carried on speaking, "As you know, fear can stifle your abilities. There is no need for fear. You can die repeatedly during your Testing. It will be just like playing a video game. You will be healed and sent back into the game. No death, no matter how violent, will be permanent. You need to leave sentiment outside of the Testing. Emotional connections will only leave you vulnerable... Kayn."

She understood what he was saying. Kayn nodded without looking at him.

Zach stopped walking aimlessly through the grass. He sighed and said, "No matter how violent ... Great. I was right, wasn't I? It is an old-school Colosseum, isn't it? Are we battling people? Third-Tier? Will the three of us be together?"

Lexy stopped walking. Turning to face them, she explained, "We aren't permitted to tell you everything. Melody, you'll be able to heal quickly. This is an advantage physically but a disadvantage mentally. Zach and Kayn, you'll most likely be Enlightened during the game. You'll have to stay on task. I assure you, it won't be easy. When you are first Enlightened, you'll react like an addict, craving whatever fuels your ability. You'll need to help each other through this."

With sympathetic eyes, their blonde immortal instructor addressed Zach, "Your pain level may need to be heightened to an absurd point to trigger your Enlightenment because of your tolerance as a mortal."

Kayn observed a look that passed between Lexy and the male member of their trio. *Their Dragon's eyes had forgiveness in them. Zach's Correction must have been horrific. She'd never asked him about what happened. She should have.*

Lexy drew her attention away from Zach. She addressed the group, "There will be weapons to use. You'll find them in random places. There'll be swords, knives, clubs, arrows, and salt. So, our first lesson today is on arrows. Trinity will have an advantage over other Clans. Arrows are their preferred weapon. Mel should be alright but there isn't enough time to even you two out with their skill level, but we can teach you how to evade them. The arrows will be drugged as I'm sure you know. It doesn't matter if it only nicks your arm. The poison will take hold and you'll go down."

Kayn's mind flashed back to her brother Matt's final moments. *He'd been drugged by one of Trinity's arrows. It didn't seem like the worst way to go. Memories of her family now left her feeling hollow. When she walked down the hallway towards her bedroom in her thoughts, the pictures on the walls were no longer there. That life was gone. It felt like she'd died alongside her family. That version of her didn't exist anymore.* While she was lost in her thoughts, bows appeared in her immortal trainer's hands. Scenery flashed with brilliant white light and they were in the forest.

Comically, Grey announced, "We're counting to twenty... I'd run if I were you."

"Are you serious?" Kayn questioned. She stepped back as Lexy began to count. Without hesitation, Zach and Mel sprinted into the forest. Kayn heard their bows being readied. Realising they were really planning to shoot them, she took off after the others. The ominous pounding of thunder overshadowed the all too familiar rhythmic noise of feet snapping twigs as she raced through the woods. *What twisted new version of hell was this going to be?* The sky dimmed and a violent downpour erupted from the clouds above. Adrenaline coursed through her veins in response to the sound. Lightening clapped with an explosive crackle in the bushes close by. *There was going to be lightning, too? What in the hell?* Rain vigorously pelted her skin as rocks brutalised the soles of her feet. As she skidded over loose gravel, her past flashed into her mind. *She was going to slip and fall.* She ignored her fears and sprinted, rapidly closing the distance between herself and the other two.

Lexy's voice hollered, "Twenty!"

Brains before brawn, Kayn reminded herself as she sped past the others and veered off in the opposite direction leaving the other two eating her dust. Competitive by nature, her eyes scanned her surroundings for somewhere clever to hide until the arrow-wielding immortals passed. She noticed the entrance to a cave ahead but chose to keep running. *That was too obvious.* All she'd accomplish by hiding in a blatantly obvious place was to become trapped like a caged animal. *She wasn't about to be caged. She was a lion.* Kayn ran past it and climbed upwards through the brush concealed by bountiful shrubbery, knowing even if they saw her, they wouldn't have a clean shot. She clutched the branches and roots of trees as she struggled her way up the side of the mountain, knowing it was best to stay where there was no trail. When she reached even ground, it felt like she'd been running for hours without even a glimpse of anyone. With her legs scraped, battered and bruised, she carried on running until she burst through the bushes into a thicket. Exhausted, she crouched in the security of the tall grass. Unable to catch her breath, she laid down, deciding to hide in plain sight. She would wait here until she heard them pass and then double back to where she'd started. After only a minute or two of rest, she heard voices approaching. Kayn shut her eyes, pressed her lips together and attempted to steady her breathing. As the voices trailed off into the distance, she thought, *what would she do if she couldn't find someone? Brains before brawn. She'd find a higher vantage point. If one of them climbed a tree, she'd be clearly visible, wearing white in a background of green. She could just run for it. If they suspected she was hiding in the thicket, they might just be waiting for her to pop up to see if the coast was clear. An arrow to the forehead did not sound appealing. What should she do? Should she stand, run and hope for the best, or stay hidden?* An uneasy feeling urged her to move. Instinct was a truly miraculous thing, but she hadn't yet mastered the art of listening to her intuition without questioning it. Kayn's intuition was telling her something right now. It was whispering, *be careful, Kayn… Something's coming.* She quieted her mind. Listening to the falling rain, the rhythm was slightly different twenty feet from her. It was accompanied by the gentle rustling of something moving through the thicket towards her. With the nagging sense that something was stalking her, she took a chance. Kayn poked her head up just enough to see the high grass parting ahead of her. She caught a glimpse of something tan. *Cougars were about that size. If it was a cougar, it was already too late to run. Brains. Use your brains.* She sprang to her feet and sprinted directly at what she'd avoided on her way in. Once again, she was in a position where there was no time to look back to see what was pursuing her but she heard something large rustling through the high grass behind her, increasing in speed. *Whatever it was, it was chasing her now.* With grass whooshing in one slick noise after her, Kayn shielded her face with her arms and ran head-on into a blackberry bush, forcing her way through with prickles slicing her flesh. *Wild animals would avoid the prickles. The prickle bush wouldn't hide her from Grey and Lexy.* Without even pausing in the middle, she burst through the other side, bleeding profusely. *She hadn't thought this out. Cats were intelligent hunters. The cougar would be able to track her by the scent of her blood. She'd have to give it options. Ironically, it was now in her best interest to find her hunters.* Kayn bolted down a hill without the option of using branches and roots to slow her descent. *There was no time for that.* She tripped and tumbled down the muddy embankment, smashing into jagged boulders and roots until her body abruptly came to a stop. *That sucked.* Her ears were ringing, but she was now muddy enough to be camouflaged. Kayn smiled as she realised the mud had naturally bandaged her wounds. She felt dizzy as she struggled to her feet. There was a burning sensation in her ankle. As she looked, she knew her ankle was broken. *It was a superficial break. It wasn't a game-changer, but it was going to be irritating as hell.* She appeared to have lost the cougar trailing her. *Perhaps meat was less appetising when covered in mud?* She took in the area. *She'd found her way back to the cave. She was so tired. It would have been searched already. That would have been the first place they looked.* The rain was washing off the mud she needed to stop the bleeding. She limped for the opening, stopping outside long enough to slather more dirt on her arms and legs. Kayn stumbled into the darkness. *She'd wait for it to quit raining and then she would leave. Hopefully, the mud would also disguise her scent. Why was she so sleepy?* It was a struggle to keep her eyes open.

What she didn't know was that she'd slit her wrist with the prickle bush. Between the sensation of the mud and the confusion of the situation, she hadn't noticed. It occurred to her that there might be something wrong as her eyelids grew heavier. *She didn't care. She was too sleepy. She needed rest.* Her eyelids grew heavier until she allowed them to close.

Kayn awoke in the darkness with a gasp. It took her a minute to remember where she was. *She was in a cave in the In-between. Lexy and Grey were hunting her for sport. Well… And a cougar hunting her for dinner. She'd better not forget about him.* She felt her way around the cave, unsure of the direction she'd come in. Vision wasn't an option, so she moved towards the current of fresh air. As Kayn found the exit, it only added to her confusion. *It was dark outside. It was nighttime. How long had she been asleep?* She felt her skin. *The mud was gone. She was clean and injury-free.* She squeezed her ankle. *It was fine. There was only one way to heal this fast during training. She must have died. How had she died? She didn't remember dying? Maybe that hungry cougar found her while she was sleeping?* Under cover of nightfall, she peeked out. *The coast appeared to be clear.* She pondered the merits of waiting until daylight to leave but heard voices, and they were coming closer. *She'd be trapped if she stayed.* She bolted to the left and up the embankment she'd tumbled down. The rain had ceased but the terrain was slick mud and guck. Kayn wedged her feet sideways to avoid a repeat performance of mud mania. She was leaving blatantly obvious tracks but hoped they'd go unnoticed until first light. Instinct was leading her back to the thicket. Hopefully, it wasn't also taking her back to the cougar. She closed her eyes as she burst through the bushes into the open space, thinking, *Please, let there be no cougar. Please, no cougar.*

Grey's voice called out, "There she is!"

They were right on the other side of the shrubs. She started to run. Kayn was halfway across the field when she was taken out by a gopher hole. *Son of a…* She'd twisted her ankle again. *Obviously, this was going to be a thing.* Kayn steadied her breathing and remained still, hoping they'd pass her by. A few minutes passed. Their voices drifted away in the distance. She stealthily peeked over the grass. *They were gone. She could head back in the other direction. Go back to the cave and repeat the same scenario. Well, minus the falling down the side of the mountain part. There was no possible way to win these training exercises, but you were given props for being the hardest to kill. She'd killed herself once already, but it didn't count. They hadn't done it.* Kayn stood up and winced at the pain from her ankle as she hobbled to the edge of the thicket. A blur of sandy beige streaked at her. All she had the time to say was, "Crap!"

The cat launched itself into the air. Kayn dove out of its path, hitting the ground with a thud beside a large rigid stick. The terrifying, salivating feline regained its footing and was immediately upon her. At the last second, she grabbed for the stick and swung it in front of her. The enormous cougar roared a spine-tingling pitch as it sunk its teeth deep into her shoulder. *Crap!* Its jaw slackened, releasing its grip. *The cougar impaled itself when it pounced on her. No way.* The cat looked confused as it slumped on its side. *She couldn't believe it. This kind of thing only ever happened in movies. She'd killed a cougar with a random stick. She was awesome.* She struggled to her feet, holding her shoulder. There was a lot of blood streaming down her chest. It already soaked her sarong. The mind was a protective thing. *Why was there so much blood? Why didn't it hurt?* The cat had torn a chunk from her throat. *This was not awesome.* She stood there stunned for a moment before falling into the thicket comically close to the mountain lion that killed her. In the thicket in the realm of the In-between, her inner lion slept tonight.

Kayn could smell the sweet scent of morning dew on the purple clover before opening her eyes. Inhaling oxygen-rich air, she didn't stir while cracking open an eye. Envisioning a cougar waiting to pounce as she sat up, she grinned. *Two times she'd died, but neither version was from an arrow shot by a Clan member. It had to be a little impressive that she'd managed to avoid them for this long.* Kayn looked around. She was alone in a field of purple clover and buttercups. She smiled as she picked a clover, plucked a thin petal out and put the sweet end on her tongue. If she had shoes, she might have stuck it in one for luck. She heard a whoosh as an arrow sailed past her head, missing her by inches. *They found her. It was time to run.* Relieved to be running in soft grass, she bolted for the end of the field, needing the cover of the trees. The moment her feet hit the dirt, her mind took her into the past. Adrenaline rippled across her skin. *Run faster, Kayn.* Her muscular legs carried her into the brush with only a second to deduce the most favourable getaway. *She was fast. This was one of her gifts. She'd bought herself only a moment. Uphill or down? She made the decision to go up. If she made it to the peak without being hit, it would buy her time.* Kayn climbed the steep embankment, pulling herself upwards using the ferns and roots of trees. An arrow whizzed past her. *They'd already caught up.* Another whooshed by, narrowly missing her leg. She scrambled upwards as she heard it again. An arrow pierced the back of her thigh, burning. Ignoring the pain, Kayn made it to the top of the embankment and tried to run full speed. Her vision wavered. *Oh, yes. There was poison in these arrows. She had to pull it out.* Stifling a scream, she snapped the end off and yanked it out. Hobbling away, she recalled Frost and the bear. B*lood loss.* Kayn ripped a strip of material off what she was wearing, tied it around her thigh and persevered until the scenery spun. Kayn dropped to her knees as the poison took effect. *She hadn't seen either Zach or Melody since the exercise began. The colours were so pretty.* Lying in the dirt, she saw Zach's body not far from hers. *Was she hallucinating?* Wanting to know if he was real, Kayn reached out. Stretching to touch him, the light flickered and went out.

She awoke, gasping for air with her lungs and throat on fire. This time, as she got up, there was no sneaky ceremony. The In-between had deposited her somewhere new. With only forest as far as she could see in every direction, she elected to climb a tree for a better idea of where everyone was. She scaled the first tree with an easily accessible, low-hanging branch. *It had been a long time since she'd climbed a tree.* She occupied her mind with thoughts of childhood as she gripped branches while scaling the massive tree. When the branches became too thin to hold her weight, she found a solid perch and gazed upon the exquisite beauty of the In-between. In the distance, she saw Zach and Melody running through the woods with Lexy right behind them. A branch snapped below her. *You've got to be freaking kidding me.* Her salivating feline nemesis appeared to be smiling as it cagily scaled the tree below her. *This mountain lion was relentless. She had nowhere to go.* She'd have to try to jump to the next tree. She cautiously shimmied out onto one of the branches while holding onto the limb above her. There was no way she was going to be able to make the jump. *Either way, this was going to hurt.* The loudly purring cougar had almost reached her when an arrow whirled through the air. The enormous feline wailed as it dropped from the tree. Relieved, she exhaled as she glanced down to see Grey standing below her beaming widely with his bow extended. Once again, she only had time to say, "Crap," as Grey's arrow penetrated her chest. A direct hit to her heart, she dropped from the tree, smoking multiple branches during her descent. Before losing consciousness, she saw a flash of the cat in the fetal position beside her as the lights went out.

She had an excruciating throbbing headache as she stirred in the dirt. *This training was painfully monotonous.* She sat up, scrambled to her feet and sprinted off into the woods. The Newbie Ankh ran away from Lexy and Grey for almost an entire week, replaying each scenario countless times. *The theme of the week's training was... Run.*

They were way past emotionally spent when they returned to the land of the living. The tomb slid open. They climbed out in a daze. As Grey opened the Crypt, bright sunshine flooded into the darkness. *It felt like she'd been gone forever, but in truth, it had only been a little over an hour.* Kayn trudged through the woods behind her equally spent Clan to the RV. Following the others inside, she quietly climbed on a bunk and slipped beneath the sheets.

Chapter 29

The Brothers Of Prophecy

Kayn slept until her mind regained its ability to function. She opened her eyes and saw Zach awake in the bunk directly across from her. He smiled at her. Kayn shut her eyes again. The plan was only to sleep for a moment longer. She heard the rustling of people getting ready and felt someone stroking her hair. *She didn't have to open her eyes to know it was Frost. They were all getting ready for tonight. She should get up.* She drifted off to sleep.

Lily's voice asserted, "Brighton, get up. We're supposed to be there in half an hour."

Kayn groggily opened her eyes and yawned. *It felt like she could sleep for a year.* The other girls appeared to be ready to go, and the guys were nowhere to be seen. Kayn shimmied off her bunk, knowing she desperately needed a shower. After a speedy one, she blow-dried her hair and wandered out of the bathroom in her underwear. She hauled her backpack out and stared into it. *She had no dress clothes. Nothing that wasn't sporty. She didn't have anything fancy.* She wanted to climb back onto her bunk, close her eyes and finish that dream. *She'd been having a wonderful dream.*

Lexy pulled back the curtain to the bunk area and took charge, "Let's get her dressed for this thing. Lily, can you look through the suitcases in the closet in the backroom and find her something to wear. Her elevator doesn't appear to be making it all the way to the top floor."

Yes, the hamster wheel between her ears was squeaking rather loudly. Her brain felt like a pool of slushy goo. She obediently put on the slinky silk top and short black skirt she was given as they did her hair and makeup. She ended up looking like a studious, sexy version of herself. *She was glad she was going now. She was curious about the Brothers of Prophecy thing. Frost was incredibly gorgeous. Tiberius was deviously hot. What was Thorne like? Mel looked stunning. She'd be seeing her old love interest tonight. This promised to be an interesting evening with the Clans in the same room.* The ladies of Ankh strolled towards the banquet hall arm in arm. Kayn whispered to Melody, "How are you doing?"

Mel whispered back, "I wasn't going to be able to avoid this situation forever. How about you?"

Kayn smiled while replying, "Other than the fact that I feel like I couldn't tie my own shoes right now... I'm fine."

"I'll tie them for you," Mel teased.

Kayn's jumbled mind prodded, *you'll be seeing Kevin. Ignore him. There's no point.* Her thoughts were distracted by the humming of conversations as they approached the large log cabin hall. Kayn squeezed Mel's arm in a show of solidarity as they climbed the stairs and entered. A guy was standing with Tiberius, Frost and Markus. *That must be Thorne.* If there was any doubt, the expression on his face when Melody walked in clarified it. The brothers were standing in a makeshift receiving line with Markus. *Markus was probably there to make sure they behaved.*

Tiberius chuckled, leaned closer to Thorne and provoked, "You, my brother, have the worst poker face I've ever seen and it's been a long damn life."

"I can think of worse qualities than the inability to lie," Thorne countered, stepping away from his younger brother Tiberius like he'd tainted his air space.

"Touché," Tiberius jousted with a knit brow, making it clear he hadn't missed his older brother's body language. With a wry smile, Tiberius casually pushed his buttons, "I bet Frost tapped that."

Under his breath, Thorne uttered, "Quit trying to fluster me you jackass."

"Who even uses the word flustered anymore?" Tiberius ribbed.

"Keep it up. The next time we capture you, I'll shoot a dozen arrows up your ass little brother," Thorne vowed.

"Promises, promises," Tiberius teased with a smirk.

Kayn fought the urge to grin. *They were hilarious together. It was incredibly entertaining.*

Lexy strolled right past Tiberius without making eye contact, taunting, "Charmed as never."

Tiberius called after her, "Satan... It is so nice to see you again. Glad you could make the trip to hang with us mere mortals."

"Well, isn't that the pot calling the kettle black?" Lexy sparred.

Markus took Lexy's hand. He leaned close and whispered in her ear, "Do try to behave tonight. Might I politely suggest that you sit as far away from Tiberius as you can?"

Kayn slowly shuffled along with the group, content to stay hidden in the background. She was busy listening to Markus as he warned Lexy to behave when she found herself standing beside Melody in front of Tiberius. Melody politely took Tiberius' outstretched hand.

He ignorantly remarked, "You're exactly Thorne's type, aren't you?" Melody accidentally stomped on his foot. Tiberius abruptly yanked his hand away as she gave him an innocent smile. He leaned in close and whispered, "A cease fire means you're not allowed to do that sweetie."

Mel winked and replied, "I'm so sorry. I seem to have two left feet."

Tiberius met Melody's eyes as he teased, "You look all sweet and innocent, don't you? I love it when dangerous presents are wrapped in inconspicuous boxes."

She wasn't sure if he was insulting her friend or complimenting her. Frost and Tiberius were a little more alike than either one cared to admit. Mel was standing in front of Thorne. She hesitantly took his hand.

He raised it to his lips and tenderly kissed it. "Melody," Thorne whispered with his voice full of emotion.

"Thorne," Mel whispered as their eyes locked.

It felt voyeuristic watching so she looked away. *That was the moment she'd hoped to have with Kevin but hers had been one sided.* As Thorne let go of Melody's hand, her heart broke for her friend. She was brought back to reality by the sound of Tiberius' voice.

The mischievous immortal flirtatiously taunted, "Well, don't you look lovely this evening…Like a naughty librarian. Humour me." He touched her hair.

Kayn froze, unsure of what he was up to. He slipped the pins out of her hair and it cascaded down her back in a loose pile of curls. She scowled at him.

Tiberius teased, "Now, that's much better. You look like the lion you were meant to be. You aren't meant to be a mouse."

He had a way of complimenting you, with an underlying insult. She wasn't honestly sure which he'd just given her. He was so familiar, an exact duplicate of Kevin's brother Clay. A part of her had to resist the impulse to hug him in greeting as another part was resisting the urge to slap him for what he'd done to her hair.

"Touch her again and I'll show you what a Dragon is capable of," Lexy threatened.

Tiberius glanced at Lexy and provoked, "I dare you."

Lexy met Tiberius' gaze with a fiery one of her own as she took Kayn's hand and whispered, "I'll fix your hair, it'll only take a second. Ignore Tiberius, nothing he says is important." Lexy pinned her hair back up and pulled out a few tendrils around her face. She smiled and said, "See you inside."

Almost having a sexy moment strutting away, Kayn stumbled in her heels and fell into Frost's arms.

Frost whispered in her ear, "Way to be inconspicuous love." Tucking one of her loose ringlets behind her ear, he propped her up, assuring, "Ignore my brother. Tiberius knows nothing of lions. Sheep are his cup of tea."

Tiberius teased, "Don't knock it till you've tried it brother."

"I'm hot enough to stick with my own species," Frost declared.

Thorne rolled his eyes and muttered, "Oh, for the love of everything sacred, you two are over a thousand-years-old. Your immaturity level is actually painful."

Grinning, Tiberius jousted, "Mr. Monogamy doesn't find my shenanigans funny. Oh, thank God. If you did, I'd have to chuck it all and join a monastery."

"You'd never be able to stop talking long enough." Thorne bickered.

Boisterously laughing, Frost piped in, "He'd light on fire as soon as he stepped through the gate."

"Right alongside of you," Tiberius provoked, patting Frost's shoulder.

"Touché," Frost chuckled. "You have me there."

They abruptly stopped laughing. Kayn didn't need to turn around to know who'd graced their presence because you could smell her intoxicating scent in the air before you saw her.

Thorne addressed her first, "Long time no see, Lilarah."

With genuine smiles, they greeted each other as old friends, embracing as she replied, "It's good to see you again Thorne."

Lily stood in front of Tiberius without attempting to touch him. Tiberius flirtatiously prodded, "What? No hug for me?"

The breathtakingly gorgeous immortal with shimmering black hair smiled and flounced away. *She was brilliant.* Kayn could tell it drove Tiberius crazy that Lily had opted out of speaking to him. Witnessing these strangely interwoven relationships was like watching someone slowly put together a puzzle. So far, two of the Ankh women had strolled right by Tiberius without even offering up a well-mannered attempt at a greeting. *One would think Tiberius would be upset. He was far from that. He appeared to be intrigued.* Tiberius caught her staring. He winked at her. Kayn quickly turned and followed the group.

The décor reminded her of a low-key wedding reception. There was white linen, crystal and candles at every table but no personalised wedding favours. Kayn kept her eyes trained on the girls in beautiful dresses walking in front of her. *Don't look for him. Do not do it.* She slipped into a seat next to Mel and Zach. She sensed Kevin's presence but kept her head from turning, knowing the mere sight of her best friend would create havoc on her heart. *Her emotions made her appear weak.* She thought of the humiliating speech he'd given her at the track. Each time she replayed his uncharacteristically brutal words in her mind, she managed to calm the urge to glance his way. *Heaven forbid she give Kevin, or guy that looks like Kevin, a reason to think she'd give him the time of day.* A squeal from the mic at the small wooden podium up front startled her. Jenna and two others she didn't know were standing at it.

Looking stunning, Jenna spoke, "Some of you are probably wondering why you are here. I'm sure your Clans have already made you aware that your authority figures will be leaving you alone for the next week. There has always been a prearranged cease fire between the Clans while the leaders go to the Summit. The older members of your Clans that have already gone through Testing are permitted to leave. The untested Clan must stay within a five-mile radius of this campground. This happens roughly every five years. Anyone who disrupts this week of peace will be entombed. This event is brought to you by The Aries Group. Enjoy your dinner and spirits."

Kayn asked for an Earl Grey tea as the waiter passed by her seat. When she glanced at the waiter to smile and thank him, she saw Kevin. He was sitting at the table directly behind her with a few girls. They were intently listening to his every word. *Times had changed.* Kayn quickly turned around so he wouldn't catch her looking. As she looked around the table, it felt like everyone was waiting for her to do or say something stupid.

Zach leaned closer and whispered, "You're doing fine. Those feelings are all in your head." He placed his hand over hers. "I've got your back."

Immediately at ease, she looked at Zach's hand on hers. *She was being silly. She was overthinking everything.* Kayn smiled while looking into Zach's eyes and said, "I know you do."

Grey excused himself from the table and made his way to the open bar at the back of the room. *Lexy looked as uncomfortable as she felt.* Kayn smiled at her. Lexy stood up and began to make her way past the table full of Triad behind them.

Tiberius blocked her path with his leg and teased, "We should finish what we started this afternoon."

Lexy smirked, baiting, "Oh, honey. You couldn't handle me even if I came with blow-by-blow instructions."

Tiberius whispered something Kayn couldn't quite make out. She looked at Zach. *He was also watching the steamy interaction.*

Zach gave her a nudge and whispered, "It's like watching a train wreck."

Tiberius brushed a thumb softly against Lexy's inner thigh. *It was hard to tell whether Lexy was turned on or repelled by him.* Out of nowhere Lexy cuffed Tiberius across the face. Grey was on her, a second too late. Grey towed her away. Lexy glanced back at Tiberius. He was smirking and rubbing his jaw. *That dirty dog. He loved it.* They sat down at the table. *It wasn't often that you got a front row seat to Lexy and Grey uncensored. The three of them sat quietly, attempting to pretend they weren't listening to every word.*

Grey scolded, "Seriously? You hit Tiberius five minutes into the damn banquet!" Lexy sat back down, smiling. Grey grilled, "What in the hell did he say to make you have selective amnesia? We are in a cease fire and you bloody hit the leader of Triad? You could be entombed!"

Lexy chuckled as she replied, "I'll tell you what Tiberius said, but I'm sure you'd prefer to leave this one alone."

Grey took a drink of his wine and probed, "Tell me what he said?"

Lexy rather bluntly disclosed, "I was going to look for you. He blocked me with his leg and suggested we finish what we started this afternoon. I told him that he couldn't handle me even if I came with blow-by-blow instructions. Then, he told me he was going to make me scream his name until I lost my voice. He touched my thigh and I liked it, so I hit him."

Confused, Grey repeated her words, "You liked it?"

"I'm not sure why I'm defending myself. He touched me so I hit him," Lexy whispered.

Grey's tone became dead serious as he quietly said, "Not Tiberius Lexy. Anybody but Tiberius."

"You can't seriously think that would ever happen? He was just teasing me like he always does. It was no big deal," Lexy whispered.

Grey tenderly caressed her cheek, softly kissed her lips, and implored, "Please don't."

Lexy looked upset as she excused herself from the table. Kayn watched her make her way through the crowded dance floor.

Zach whispered in Kayn's ear, "I knew there was more than friendship going on there."

She heard Frost's laughter. It drew her gaze. *Frost was being Frost, cavorting with one girl after another without even the slightest glance in her direction. Good for him.*

Melody held up her glass, declaring, "Have a sip of this wine. I swear this is the best wine I've ever tasted."

Kayn shifted her attention to her friend and chuckled, "I don't think adding alcohol to my messed-up situation tonight is a great idea." Kayn felt a tickle on the back of her neck, followed by the warmth his hand on her shoulder. She grinned and shook her head. Frost's breath was sweet scented from the wine he'd been drinking.

He whispered in her ear, "I'm going to be flirting with Mel. Evidently my brother Thorne has a thing for her. It will drive him nuts. Try not to read anything into it."

All hail the reigning master of mixed messages. He didn't owe her an explanation. Frost could do whatever he wanted. Kayn looked down at the little pot of tea as it arrived and thought, *on second thought, maybe I will need a drink.*

Sitting beside Mel, Frost whispered, "I had you pegged all wrong as a prude."

"I'm not in the mood for your cryptic mind games Frost," Mel mumbled.

The gorgeous immortal took the glass right out of her hand, swallowed every drop, and teased, "Well, just in case you want to know, Thorne hasn't been able to take his eyes off you."

Glaring at Kayn, she accused, "You told him. That was a secret."

"I said absolutely nothing," Kayn stated, miffed she'd automatically assumed the worst.

Frost teased, "She said nothing. I was watching my brother stare at you like a love-sick puppy dog. You just confirmed my suspicions all by yourself." He took her glass out of her hand again, placed it on the table and whispered, "You're doing this all wrong. You don't want to be a sloppy drunk. You'll make an idiot out of yourself and it will backfire. You need to appear to have moved on. You need to look like his presence doesn't have any effect on you." Extending his hand to Mel, Frost suggested, "Dance with me. Nothing will piss Thorne off faster."

Melody gave her a helpless, comical look as Frost led her to the dance floor. Kayn turned around just in time to see panic cross Thorne's eyes. Frost spun Melody, made eye contact with Kayn and winked. Unable to help herself, she giggled.

Zach leaned in, imitating what he imagined Frost was saying to Melody, "Relax. Go with it. You know what would make my brother certifiably insane? If we slept together, he would be absolutely furious."

"It's for the good of the game," Kayn imitated Frost's smooth conversation.

"I'm sure Kayn would be fine with us hooking up. We have an understanding," Zach chuckled.

He'd added her name to the conversation. The joke fell short of its mark. She laughed anyway. Kayn and Zach were still joking at the table when the empty seat next to her squealed as someone slid up beside her. *It was Thorne.*

With a knowing smile on his face, Thorne sighed, "My younger brother's immaturity level can be astoundingly toddler. He doesn't really think I'm buying this, does he?"

Reading between the lines, Kayn answered honestly, "He's just trying to help her feel better."

Intrigued by her response, Thorne said, "Well, aren't you a breath of fresh air. Not a lie in that whole sentence."

Kayn kept the brutal honesty going, "Why bother making a half assed attempt to lie to you. I bet Frost figured the two of you out five seconds after you saw each other. It was obvious to everyone."

Thorne smiled and admitted nothing. He took two glasses of wine from the tray as it passed by and placed one in front of Kayn. She looked up at him and smiled. Tasting the red wine, it slid between her lips onto her tongue. Her taste buds danced. *She understood what Melody was talking about. She had wanted to taste the wine. She'd been curious. Thorne knew what she wanted without her having to say anything. He would have been a wonderful guy to have as a boyfriend.* They sat in silence with the humming of everyone else's conversations with no need to speak.

Zach piped in, "I'm missing something here."

Might as well. It was out in the open now. "Thorne and Melody had a thing when she was with Trinity," Kayn explained.

Zach looked at Thorne and directed his next question at him, "You were actually together in the biblical sense?"

Thorne watched his brother and Melody dance. He glanced at Kayn and said, "She looks happy. Has she been happy?"

Meeting his eyes, Kayn answered, "She hasn't been with anyone else if that's what you're beating around the bush about."

Thorne didn't reply. He just smiled as he took another sip of wine. Orin was sitting close enough to hear the conversation. He shot Thorne an unmistakable look of disapproval. *Awkward. Thorne slept with Orin's daughter.* The song stopped and Frost scooted into the chair beside his brother.

Thorne scowled as he sarcastically accused, "That was mean spirited. Going after the girl your brother cares about is so unlike you."

Frost chuckled, "Oh, come on. That was my good deed for the day. You needed a push. She went to the bathroom. Go talk to her. You can be alone in there."

"That's the last thing I should do. Troublemaker," Thorne mumbled, watching her walk away.

Slipping into a seat on the other side of the table, Tiberius said, "I was feeling left out of the brotherly bonding moment."

"I was pointing Thorne in the right direction," Frost replied, taking the wine Thorne put down.

The leader of Triad provoked, "Well, isn't that nice of you. You should find me a date while you are offering up your Clan." Tiberius met Lexy's glare from across the table and sighed, "No means no, Lexy. I don't want to date you." Without hesitation, Lexy threw a knife from the table directly at his chest. Tiberius caught it, completely impressed where another would have been traumatised. In absolute awe, he seductively baited, "You really have not one single bit of self-control, do you? That may be my new favourite thing about you."

With unveiled distaste, Lexy scowled. *She was like a machine.*

Tiberius gave her unwanted advice, "Next time, distract me before throwing a knife, you might have taken me by surprise and hit your target."

He threw the knife back. Lexy blocked it with her hand and it went through her palm. Without flinching, she casually yanked out the knife and held up her hand. The wound vanished before it had a chance to bleed. Grey and Orin tried to restrain her, fearing she was going to kick his ass. Kayn was grinning. *It was exactly the opposite. This felt like foreplay between Dragons.* Tiberius gave her a knowing smile. *He had Lexy's number. Tiberius knew how to press her buttons.*

Grey took Lexy's freshly healed hand and suggested, "Let's go get some fresh air."

"Yes, the air smells a little bit off in here," Lexy taunted.

Tiberius pointed at Frost and mouthed, "I think he farted."

Lexy smiled. Grey was grinning as he dragged her away. They almost jogged through the dancing people and out of the hall. Orin looked disappointed as they left.

Zach leaned over and whispered in Kayn's ear, "I don't know what it is tonight but Lexy's looking insanely hot."

Kayn whispered back, "Lexy just tried to stab someone."

"Only Tiberius," he chuckled.

The leader of Triad smiled and shook his head. *He'd heard everything.*

He carried on messing with Frost, "Arrianna's with Markus. Lilarah is a work in progress. Who does that leave? Oh, yes. The tightly wound lion. What was her name again?"

Tiberius was killing two birds with one stone. He was testing her to see if she could disguise her feelings and Kevin to see if he remembered her on a level deeper than he'd admitted to.

"Kayn's not the slightest bit interested," Frost assured.

Meeting Kayn's eyes from across the table, Tiberius taunted, "I know who she's interested in." He raised his voice, "Kevin! Come over here, son! We're all getting to know each other!"

Thorne stood up as Kevin sat down. *She wanted to stand up and leave but she couldn't give him the reaction he was looking for.*

Tiberius prompted, "Don't leave yet brother. You haven't met my grandson. Kevin, meet Uncle Thorne."

Reaching across the table, Kevin shook Thorne's hand, apologising, "Sorry, My grandfather's a bit of an ass."

Smiling, Thorne confessed, "I was really hoping my brother would never have the opportunity to procreate."

"If he was my brother, I'd have hoped for the same inability," Kevin answered as he sat down, humouring his grandfather. *Kayn wanted to avoid being part of the show.* Someone startled her by pulling out her chair. *Why was he always sneaking up on her?*

Cock-headed above her, Tiberius teased, "Let's see what all the fuss is about?" He took the pins out of her hair and it cascaded down her shoulders again.

"Will you cut that out?" Kayn stammered, swatting him away. She attempted to pin it back up.

Tiberius brushed her hand away. Her hair tumbled back down. "A toast to old friends. Drink this," he tempted, handing her another drink.

Glaring at him, Kayn set it back down on the table. *She didn't have to listen to him.*

Tiberius ordered, "Do as you've been told or I will be forced to throw you over my knee and spank you publicly."

Kayn rolled her eyes. Picking up her drink, she sparred, "You can try."

Grinning, Tiberius toyed, "I like her."

Meeting his eyes, she stated, "I don't respond back to men that talk about me and not directly to me."

"You just did," Tiberius teased. Looking at his brother, he whispered, "I don't think she knows I'm really going to spank her."

Frost shook his head, cautioning, "Humour him for the sake of the cease-fire, or he'll become an even bigger pain in the ass. If I have to step in, it'll be a thing."

She was doing her best to avoid looking at him. Kevin was sitting far too close. Tiberius pulled his seat up between the two as his first nice gesture. She stared at her glass and across the table, trying to look anywhere else. Raising the potent purple liquid to her lips, Kayn swallowed, licking a droplet off her lip. She peered up through her eyelashes. *Kevin was staring. He wasn't even attempting to be stealth.*

Tiberius enquired, "Tell me all about yourself, Kayn. Which parent gave you those gorgeous curls?"

Smiling, Frost hinted, "Take a good look."

Tiberius' eyes lit up. He declared, "I'll be damned. Is she Freja's daughter?" He tapped on Kevin's shoulder. Pointing at a blonde man staring at their table, he requested, "Do me favour, kid. Bring Uncle Frey over to meet his niece." Kevin left the table.

Uncle Frey? As witty banter continued between the brothers, Kayn made eye contact with the man. *Why wait?* Curious, she stood up and walked over there. Seeing her approach, Kevin motioned to the man Tiberius called her uncle.

Greeting her with a smile, Frey suggested, "Let's go for a walk to get away from prying eyes."

She followed him across the dancefloor. He opened the fire escape. They strolled out onto a balcony. *He was openly gawking at her.*

"You look so much like her," Uncle Frey commented. "You know what it's like to have a twin. You don't feel like a separate entity sometimes."

"I'm not a separate entity from mine," Kayn countered.

Leaning on the railing, Frey prompted, "I'd imagine you have questions?"

This stranger was a living, breathing member of her immortal bloodline. Kayn responded without looking his way, "Nothing that matters."

Her uncle changed the direction of the conversation, "How have you been finding the transition to immortality?"

"Both good and bad, I guess," she answered honestly.

Her uncle responded, "Isn't everything?" Staring at her, Frey questioned, "Do you mind if I look at something?"

Hesitantly, Kayn granted permission, "I guess?"

Lifting her hair, Uncle Frey checked behind her ears.

He was checking the birthmark to make sure it wasn't on the wrong side. Kayn sighed, "Now that you've checked to make sure the right twin survived Correction, do you know where your sister is?"

"I lost contact with her," he admitted. "There's no ceremony when you're punished and entombed. If her Clan doesn't know where she is, that's usually the reason. If she were anywhere else, Ankh could track her whereabouts. We were in opposing Clans but always kept in contact. Now, as far as the infamous birthmark goes, you can't blame a guy for being curious?"

Gazing into the woods, Kayn asked the question plaguing her thoughts, "What would you have done if the birthmark was on the wrong side?"

He turned to face her, replying with brutal honesty, "I'd snap your neck to take you out of the equation. Third-Tier would entomb you and block your Clan from the Testing."

"That's an overly dramatic response to the position of a birthmark," Kayn countered, sipping her wine.

Her relation chuckled, "You're just like your mother. Don't play dumb with me. I haven't been alive for a thousand years because of my sparkling personality, although it has helped me avoid getting my ass kicked a few times."

She wasn't sure what he'd meant. Kayn stared off into the night. *Her twin sister had a birthmark behind the opposite ear. She'd died and Kayn survived.* She took a deep breath. *Abaddon had done her Correction. She remembered now. If her sister survived, would Ankh have come to her hospital room and killed her in her sleep?* She glanced over at her uncle, asking, "You would have sentenced your niece to entombment without even knowing me, over the placement of a birthmark?"

"I'm glad I don't have to if that helps? Trinity has an Oracle too. So yes, in a heartbeat. I was fairly certain you were fine because of the half dozen times I saw Tiberius playing with your hair discreetly checking," Frey teased, winking.

She took a good look at the immortal. Frey was an attractive guy. He was into men. She'd noticed him checking guys out as they walked past the doorway. Kayn asked, "Your sister wouldn't have been furious at you for killing her daughter?"

Grinning, he explained, "Most of us have been entombed. It's general practice to wipe our memory before releasing us into the wild. She won't remember what she sacrificed to bring you into the world. She won't even recall having a child."

Up till this moment she hadn't concerned herself with thoughts of the woman who'd given her this curse or gift, whatever immortality was. The mother who raised her had also given birth to her. Having a spiritual sire was a strange concept to wrap your mind around. She commented, "Maybe I'll get to meet her one day."

"I'm sure you will," Frey replied.

A waiter with a tray of wine interrupted their chat. They each took a glass as they strolled back inside.

He raised his, saluting, "Good luck in the Testing, kid," and walked away without looking back.

Apparently, family didn't have the same meaning in this life. They didn't need to say goodbye. She was Ankh. Her Uncle Frey was Trinity. When this cease fire was over, they wouldn't be hanging out having bonding chats. He'd only met her out of curiosity. She made her way through the dance floor, white-knuckling a glass of red wine to save herself from wearing it. *She was drunk.* Kayn sat at their table. Peering into her glass, she swished it, saying, "There is something fishy about this wine."

"Mine doesn't taste like fish," Zach remarked, looking into his glass.

Lily choked and almost spit her wine all over the table.

Grey took Lily's hand and coaxed, "Dance with me." He led her onto the crowded dance floor. The space closed between them as music slowed. Lily rested her head on his shoulder.

They were playing nice. That was strange. It felt like she was the only one witnessing the moment until she saw Tiberius intently watching with a hint of jealousy in his eyes. The leader of Triad noticed her and raised his glass in a fake symbolic toast. When the song ended, they smiled at each other and parted company.

Kevin popped into her mind. She glanced over to where he'd been sitting. *He wasn't there anymore.* He was dancing with a girl she didn't recognise, slowly moving to the rhythm of the music with his hand seductively pressed against the small of her back. *Her best friend could dance. She had to stop referring to him as her best friend. He was gone. She was only hurting herself. The ambience was beginning to change. What was wrong with her? Sitting alone watching everyone else dance was like a sad flashback from junior high. She'd always felt like the one girl nobody wanted to dance with.* Taking another glass of wine from the tray as it came by, she fought off the urge to storm over there and scratch the girl's eyes out. *This was not the inner dialogue of a sane person.* The song ended. As Kevin came back to the table, she looked away and took another sip of wine. *She didn't want to acknowledge his presence tonight. Heaven forbid she appear to be the emotionally unhinged, hormone-ridden girly girl he'd accused her of being.*

Sitting down beside her, Lily sweetly questioned, "How are you doing, Hun?"

Kayn quietly replied, "I could have done without seeing that stomach-churning display, but I'm fine." When she looked up, Kevin was making out with someone. *It was like he was scrolling down a list of things he could do to piss her off.*

Lily squeezed her shoulder and assured, "He doesn't know who you are. You're just somebody he used to know. Everything has been erased."

"I guess I just didn't want to believe it was possible to erase everything we were to each other. Maybe it was naive but that's why I couldn't move on. I was certain he'd remember me."

Their conversation abruptly came to a halt to the screeching of Tiberius pulling his chair over, "So Lilarah, you're obviously still enamoured with that meathead Grey."

Flirtatiously placing her hand on his, Lily affirmed, "That's long over."

"What happened? Oh, I remember now," he baited. "You were chasing that mortal again, weren't you?"

That was a sensitive subject.

"His name is Sam, and yes, I lost him again, " Lily answered, apologetically glancing at Kayn.

"You lost him?" Tiberius prodded. "What a shame."

"Why are we even having this conversation? You can't possibly be that interested in my lacklustre love life," Lily teased, steering him away from the topic.

Gazing into Lily's seductive eyes, Tiberius chuckled, "Everybody wants you, even if they don't admit it to themselves. I saw you dancing with Grey. There wasn't a hair on that boy's body that wasn't waving the flag of surrender. Look around this room, my love. Anyone is yours for the taking if you set your gift free. How do you stop yourself from using it when you want someone?"

Removing her hand from his, Lily baited, "Who wants a love that isn't real?"

Tiberius took Lilarah's response like a bucket of ice water in the face.

With impeccable timing, Frost scooted up a chair. Possessively placing his arm around Kayn, he said, "Is my little brother boring you, ladies?"

Intrigued, Kayn sparred, "I wouldn't have pegged you as the older one?"

"We should dance." Frost got up and extended a hand to her.

Kayn shifted her seat back and got up as she enquired, "Do you promise to behave yourself?"

"Define behave," Frost taunted as he swept her into his arms and danced her away from the table as she laughed.

He'd always been good at steering her thoughts away from the past. Frost held her close as their bodies moved to the music like they were a part of the song.

He whispered against her hair, "You're doing better than I thought you'd be. Keep it up. Just act like you don't even see him there."

Snuggling into the crook of his neck, Kayn whispered, "I'll survive."

"I don't doubt that for a second," he teased as they swayed.

As they slowly spun in a rhythmic circle, Kayn accidentally met Kevin's eyes. He was sitting at the table, staring at her. *He looked confused. She knew what each of his expressions meant. For a second, hope surged in her heart, and then she remembered he wasn't her best friend. He looked like him, but it wasn't him.* She met his gaze without looking away until she couldn't keep breaking her own heart. She closed her eyes as they filled with tears.

Frost heard her sniffle. He spun her around to face the other direction and whispered, "Don't let him see you cry." He kissed her hair while mocking Tiberius, "Lions never cry."

Stifling a giggle, she whispered, "How would a lion deal with this situation?"

He laced his fingers through hers and led her away from the dance floor. When they reached the entrance area, he sprawled on the couch.

Kayn sat on the other end. *What was he up to?*

Frost seductively requested, "Give me your feet."

Intriguing? Kayn stretched out her legs. As he undid the straps on her pumps, removed the torture devices and began massaging her feet, she could practically hear a choir of small children singing. *One was cramping!* She tried to squirm away.

Frost chuckled and whispered, "Relax, I'm good at this."

That was the problem. He was good at everything. Succumbing to the pleasure, she closed her eyes. *Kevin was going to walk around the corner and find her getting a foot massage. She remembered* he *wasn't coming to look for her. What was wrong with her? Kevin was just making out with another girl right in front of her and she was worried about being caught having a heavenly foot massage.* Frost smiled and she knew he'd been listening to her thoughts again.

He assured, "You have nothing to feel guilty about. This is an innocent foot massage. I know you hate heels. I also know you needed a speech." Frost began to knead the arch of her foot, Kayn moaned aloud. He chuckled, "Keep doing that, though, and I'm towing you over here by your leg."

Kayn yanked the decorative pillow out from behind her and tossed it at his face.

He laughed, "Seriously, what's with you and throwing pillows at people?" He winked as he kept massaging her feet. "I've been through what you're going through. I know how hopeless it feels. I promise you it'll get better. Unfortunately, there's no way around this part. You're going to have to walk through the shit storm to get to the other side."

With her always entertaining sarcastic wit, she provoked, "Pillows are easy access non-lethal weapons. Would you prefer I throw knives like Lexy?"

He grinned at her and chuckled, "Pillows are fine."

She stared into Frost's eyes and said, "Thank you for not playing the keep away game with me tonight."

He lifted her foot, gently kissed her toes and whispered, "I know I've handled this situation poorly. When you have unreturned feelings for someone, ego tends to get in the way of rational thought. I still want to be your friend, if you'll let me. If you never want more than that, I'll have to learn to be okay with it. If Kevin never remembers what you mean to each other, you have to learn to be okay with that."

Kayn smiled because his little speech made perfect sense.

Frost got up. Picking up her shoes by the straps with one hand, he held out the other, saying, "I think these heels are ready to retire for the evening."

She took his hand and he smiled. They strolled back into the banquet and out to the stacked dance floor, where they danced as he hung onto her shoes. She kissed his cheek when the song was finished and whispered, "Thank you."

Chapter

Kevin's Game

The music was a haunting rendition of an old song turned country as lights dimmed, signalling the end of the night was near. Curious about what the stunning Lily of Ankh was saying to Tiberius, Kevin left his partner on the dance floor. Taking a glass of wine as a waiter passed by with the tray, he sat beside his grandfather. He glanced back at the dance floor. *There was the girl from his dreams in the arms of a complete idiot. At least he had a name for her now… Kayn. She'd been avoiding eye contact with him all night. He didn't blame her. He'd been an asshole. No, he didn't remember her... Not really, but he'd dreamt of her. He knew she'd meant something to him. He'd gone to help her out of instinct when she wiped out on the track the day they arrived. When he helped her up, she whispered his name, and he'd been intrigued, to say the least. Her touch felt like coming home. The track dust on her cheek was incredibly endearing. He'd fought the urge to kiss her wounded knees. When he noticed the symbol of Ankh on her palm, he panicked. That's when Grey showed up. He'd taken her hand and it felt wrong. When she told* off *Tiberius, it felt right. Kayn was a sweaty, dusty, weird girl. That was his first impression, but when he watched Ankh jump off the dock into the freezing water, he had an overwhelming urge to join them. She'd been shoved back into the water as a joke. Patrick helped her out. He'd wanted to be the one to do it, but Stephanie had a chokehold on his arm. She was adorable, standing on the dock with purple lips and chattering teeth. He wanted to dry her hair and wrap her in his arms to make her warm again. He wanted to fix whatever ailed her. She was going to be a serious complication.*

Kevin spent that afternoon talking to Tiberius. *He'd always known his memory had been erased. Once his situation was explained in detail, he understood. Tiberius erased his memory to save him from his memories of her. He needed to forget the weaker version of himself so he could blend into Triad. He had to not only fit in but be able to attach to a new Clan.*

He'd gone back to the track that night on emotional autopilot. He wasn't a sentimental guy, not in the least, but somehow, he'd known she would be there. He'd just planned to tell her Tiberius explained why he'd erased his memory. He wanted to put the strange guilt he felt to rest and start fresh with her. They had to spend an entire week in a campground together while the others went to the Summit. He didn't need any complications like her in his life. Everything he'd planned to say went up in smoke when she ran into his arms. His response scared the crap out of him. Holding her, he smelled her hair and caught himself wanting to tell her anything she needed to hear. His confused heart was racing. He didn't cry. He never cried but his eyes swelled with tears. He blinked them away as the voice in his head said, what in the hell are you doing? He abruptly regained his senses and gave her a much harsher speech than intended.

Tiberius leaned in and whispered, "My brother does look quite smitten with young Kevin's ex. I spoke to her briefly and she made some untrue comments about my genitalia. It wasn't very nice."

Lily almost spit out her wine. She attempted to fix her faux pas by feeding Tiberius information, "Frost was in love with the twin that died. Her name was Chloe."

Tiberius smiled as he commented, "Ah, I see, my brother's attempt at love has been foiled once again by Fate. I'm absolutely heartbroken for the poor boy."

Lily continued to speak freely, "To be blunt, we need her Enlightened. The consensus seems to be that Kevin is the key. He needs to be the one to trigger her abilities."

Thrilled by her suggestion, Tiberius clarified, "Let me get this straight. You want me to get my Kevin to kill your Kayn?"

Listening to the conversation, Kevin was silently sipping his wine while staring at Kayn on the dance floor. He glared at Lily and questioned, "Is this a joke?"

"She's going into the Testing with no abilities. She has to be broken to be built. Our Oracle says, if you kill her in the Testing, she'll become Enlightened. The visions changed. We aren't sure why. In earlier versions, they survive the Testing. Now, the version where you kill her is the only version in which they survive." Lily disclosed, watching his response.

Kevin downed his drink as the knot in the pit of his stomach tightened. He placed the empty glass on the table and suggested, "Can't I just kill him instead." *He wanted to do many things to Kayn. Murdering her had never been on the list.*

Lilarah raised her glass to Kevin and said, "One day I'm sure you'll get the chance to. If any part of you cares about her by the time you go into the Testing, you'll kill her."

Kevin replied, "Did you seriously just say, if I care about her I will kill her? I thought Triad was supposed to be the warped Clan."

Stephanie placed a drink in front of Tiberius, offering, "I'll kill her. No questions asked."

Kevin glared at her. Tiberius chuckled, "My darling, you really need to stop acting like you're planning on boiling rabbits in my grandson's backyard." Standing up, Tiberius held out his hand to Lilarah with a devious smile, suggesting, "Now, with all twisty plots and ill-mannered ex-girlfriends aside. I think we should dance." He led Lily onto the tightly packed dance floor as they began to discuss emotionally devastating plots created for the good of the Clan.

At a loss for words, as they left, Kevin finished his wine. *What would Winnie have to say about this? This was the name of the voice in his head. She'd been guiding him through every action and reaction for a good year. Where was she? Where was she when he was being ordered to do the unthinkable to someone who loved him?* He watched Kayn disappear with Frost. *She couldn't possibly be that stupid. Surely, Frost's reputation preceded him.* Unable to help himself, he got up and made his way through the inebriated dancing crowd. He caught sight of her. She was stretched out on the couch with Frost massaging her feet. *She didn't look like a girl who was desperately in love with a boy from her past. She appeared to be thoroughly enjoying the oldest move in the sleaze bag playbook.*

He heard Patrick's voice say, "You okay, man?" Exhaling, Kevin replied, "Yeah… I'm fine." He followed Patrick back to where they were sitting. *It was a stupid idea to go and check on her. Why did he do that? It didn't make sense.*

Stephanie shuffled into the seat next to him as she apologised, "I've been a bitch. I have a wounded ego. That's all this is."

Smiling at her, Kevin said, "Don't worry about it. I'm all good. Go have fun."

Stephanie grinned and asked, "Do you want me to take that Frost guy out of the equation?"

"Are you offering to be my wingman?" Kevin teased.

Stephanie replied, "I guess so. I'd be curious too. What she was to you. Why you loved her? I personally don't see it, but I'll take one for the team. I can suck it up for a week and allow you to figure it out for yourself. I know you'll be back."

Flirtatiously taking her hand, Kevin seduced, "I always come back to you, don't I?"

Stephanie let go of his hand. Shaking her head, she got up and strutted away.

His booty call had just blown him off. He didn't blame her for that either.

Patrick shoved him and scolded, "I'm not going to defend you anymore if you keep leading her on."

Kevin grinned and said, "How am I leading her on? I'm probably going to sleep with her again."

Patrick chuckled and replied, "Keep talking like that and I may help her gather wood for the fire while she boils rabbits in your backyard. She's certifiable but she's our friend."

"Please get her that T-shirt," Kevin sparred, laughing. He pointed to the other side of the room. Stephanie was already dancing with Zach from Ankh.

"She's going to eat him alive," Patrick sighed.

"She's not going to do anything," Kevin answered. "She's just trying to make me jealous."

Patrick nodded his agreement as he raised his glass of wine towards Kevin in salute and made a toast, "To Stephanie. She's certifiable but our friend."

Kevin clinked glasses with Kevin, repeating, "To Stephanie." *It was time for him to leave. He'd dive into spending time with Kayn tomorrow once his competition for her affection was out of the way. He'd have a week to delve into why this quirky girl was haunting his dreams. That was, if she'd still give him the time of day after the way he'd treated her.*

Chapter 31

A Thorne In Melody's Side

Melody left the dance floor and ducked into the family bathroom, just as Frost suggested. The tears she'd unsuccessfully managed to suppress had caused her mascara to run in streams down her face. She fixed herself up in the mirror. After waiting for a good three-quarters of an hour, she sank down to sit on the bathroom floor. *She'd been waiting for Thorne to come to her as Frost predicted he would. He wasn't going to come. She should just leave. He'd moved on. Why would he leave his lady friend's side to give her closure? She was being ridiculous sitting here waiting for someone as old as he was. He probably got over her in a heartbeat. Maybe she'd read too much into the look that passed between them?* She'd all but given up when she heard a few hollow knocks on the door. Melody stood up. Containing the urge to jump up and down like an idiot, she leaned against the door for a second before unlocking it. She opened the door and their eyes met. Thorne shoved his way in and locked the door. *The most even-tempered man she'd ever met was furious.*

He aggressively walked her back against the wall until she had nowhere left to go, growling, "What in the hell are you trying to do to me?"

"What do you mean?" Melody stammered, frozen in place, breathlessly anticipating what may happen next. He was so close to her, his chest not quite touching hers. *She knew what that look in his eyes meant. He was trying hard to behave.*

Thorne whispered in her ear, "Don't play dumb with me, Mel. You know what you were doing. You were messing around with Frost trying to get a reaction out of me. Well, you got one. Is this what you wanted?"

He was the one playing games with her now. He stepped away, leaving her standing against the wall, aching for this to be another time and place. She whispered, "I tried to get over you. I wanted to be over you... I'm not."

The volatile emotion in Thorne's eyes softened a touch as she confessed her feelings. "I never got over you either, Mel," he admitted as he brushed her hair away from her eyes and disclosed, "I've missed you."

Aching for his touch, she knew he was trying to stay faithful to the girl he'd started something with. *She selfishly wanted to push him a little but knew he'd kiss her back.* It took everything inside of her to place her hand against his chest and say, "I noticed the girl you were sitting by earlier. You have a chance at something more with her, don't you? You can hold her hand in public and be with her every night. I know that's what you want. You deserve to be happy."

He kissed her forehead, holding his lips there for a moment longer than he should. With the length of his body pressed against hers, Thorne whispered, "You come back from Testing. I don't care what you have to do... You come back."

She teased, "I guess you're not going to tell me what it is either?"

He cupped her face with his hands and slowly shook his head, smiling. Thorne leaned forward, kissed her gently on the lips and whispered, "Please, don't ever put me in the position where I have to hurt you. When the Clans are fighting, stay as far away from me as you can."

Melody's heart solidified with his truthful words. *This was where they stood.* Until this moment it had been more theory than truth in her heart. A tear escaped and trickled down her cheek.

Thorne wiped it away and whispered, "I will always miss you."

She knew he meant 'love you.' Mel whispered, "I will always miss you," as he left. With tears streaming down her face, she sunk to the floor, sobbing uncontrollably. Someone knocked on the door.

Grey's voice implored, "I saw Thorne leave. He took off upset. Do you need a friend?"

Wiping the raccoon mascara circles from under her eyes, Mel opened the door to let Grey in. "How did you manage to pull yourself away from that harem that was fawning all over you?" Melody teased as she tried to fix herself up in the mirror.

Grey kissed her head as he suggested, "Come dance with me. I'll keep your mind off you know who and you can keep me from doing something I'll definitely regret."

"Deal," she replied, attempting a smile. *Grey had a way of knowing when not to push.*

He ruffled her hair, pulled her in for a bear hug and whispered, "You look incredible tonight. You are way hotter than Thorne's new girlfriend. Just so you know."

Melody shook her head, smiled and said, "I know."

He chuckled, "There she is, the girl that publicly ridiculed me for the last year." He unrolled some toilet paper and suggested, "You should blow your nose. You sound all nasally."

She snatched the wad of toilet paper from his hand, blew her nose into it and tossed it into the toilet. She flushed it with one of her high-heeled shoes.

"Well, that was sort of sexy," he commented.

She knit her brow and laughed, "What's wrong with you?"

Grey grabbed her handbag off the counter and said, "You look like Rudolph. You're a Healer. How come your body isn't healing that hideously swollen nose of yours?" He opened her handbag and tried to powder her nose without warning.

She swatted him away, choking on the powder floating in the air and complained, "You don't tell a girl that's all broken-hearted that she looks hideous. You moron!"

Grinning, Grey baited, "I said you're hot. Just your nose is hideous." He winked.

He was trying to get her mind off her wounded heart by ticking her off. Melody wiped the excess powder from her face and brushed it off her outfit. *He had it all over him.* Tempted to leave it there, she sighed, "Get over here, you idiot." He stepped closer. She used the paper towel to clean his face and brushed off his dress shirt.

"Why didn't you just tell me?" He questioned.

Melody replied, "About Thorne?"

"Yes, about Thorne," he answered, pretending to be offended.

She answered truthfully, "After what happened in the In-between the day we met, how could I?"

Tucking Melody's hair behind her ears, Grey apologised, "I should've told you I was Ankh. I did what I did for selfish reasons. I don't have any worthy excuses. I had a bit of a broken heart myself and you were there."

Melody cracked an enormous smile and countered, "Ditto."

He chuckled as he replied, "Well, it only took us a whole year to talk that out." Grey hugged her again and they began slow dancing in the bathroom to the music playing outside. He whispered, "It's been fun though…"

Melody answered, "Let's save that conversation for another time."

Grey pulled away from her, sat on the bathroom counter and teased, "I'm going to tell your dad you have serious control issues."

"I haven't even attempted to touch that situation," she sighed.

While perched on the edge of the sink, he replied, "You should. Orin's a great guy. He probably stayed away hoping you'd have a chance at a normal life. If you had no abilities, the Correction would have just passed you by."

Melody said, "One traumatic event at a time, Grey."

Without saying another word, he grabbed her hand and towed her out of the bathroom towards where Frost and Kayn were dancing.

Grey announced, "Frost! We need a bottle of wine stat!"

Frost grinned and followed them back to the table. He took a good look at Melody and said, "I'm not sure one bottle of wine will be enough. I'll be back."

Chapter 32

Bad Ideas

The night had been a mish-mosh of uncomfortable situations, but amidst these moments were quite memorable ones. *She'd met her uncle, kept her shit together in Kevin's presence and waded through the pile of crap that continuously spewed from Tiberius' mouth with a smile on her face. It was mean, but the truth. He was an asshole and a half. She'd been prewarned that this night would be a gong show. They hadn't been wrong.* Grey strolled past with a visibly distraught Melody and made a joke about needing wine stat. They stopped dancing and followed their friends back to the table. *Frost had been doing an excellent job of side tracking her. Maybe she could pay it forward and do the same for Melody?* She gave her distraught friend a hug before finding a seat. *Zach should be here too? She hadn't seen him in a while.* Kayn accepted a glass of water as it passed by her on a tray. *Yes, it was definitely time to dilute the wine.* Grey was sitting beside Mel with his arm around her visibly emotionally demolished buddy. *Either Thorne had come to see her, or he hadn't come at all. It was probably best if she left that whole conversation alone.* Mel was wallowing in her thoughts as Frost disappeared from her side. He wandered up to the bar, reached over it, grabbed a full bottle of golden liquid and made his way back to the table with it.

"That's a horrible idea," Grey sighed, giving Mel a friendly one-armed hug.

Frost grinned as he loudly exclaimed, "Nonsense! It's a brilliant idea!" He took a big swig from the bottle and passed it to Kayn.

She laughed, "Oh, sure… if you want me to puke all over the RV later."

"I promise, I'll hold your hair like a gentleman," Frost teased.

Even though she knew she shouldn't, Kayn took a giant swig of the golden liquid and choked. She teased, "Did the bartender siphon someone's gas tank and pour it into a bottle?" She passed the foul-tasting stuff to Melody, almost feeling guilty as she did.

Her friend looked up with swollen eyes as she took a giant gulp and didn't even flinch. Kayn *was impressed. That took both acting skill and the ability to not care if your throat was on fire.* She peered over at Frost, caught him staring at her and looked away. *The table area had cleared out rather suddenly. Kevin was nowhere in sight.* When the bottle returned to her, she took another baby sip feeling more relaxed in the absence of Kevin. *To see him and have it not actually be him was a level of confusing that didn't mix with well with alcohol. He was gone and she was with her Clan. She was as emotionally safe as she chose to be.* Her eyes travelled back to the hot, dark-featured immortal. *Frost was sitting far too close. She should be drinking water. Only water. Melody was awfully quiet.* When she glanced her way, she realised her friend had passed out cold with her head on the table. Grey was stroking Mel's hair, staring off into the distance. Frost also appeared to be preoccupied with something else. Neither noticed Melody's unconscious state. She followed their gazes and grinned. Tiberius and Lily were getting a little friendly on the dance floor. Watching them felt voyeuristic, she looked away. *Someone was wearing seriously incredible perfume.* Kayn slowly ran her finger around the circumference of her wine glass and giggled. *It tickled her finger.*

"What in the hell is she doing with Tiberius?" Grey whispered, loosening his tie.

Looking concerned, Frost explained, "She's doing exactly what she was ordered to do."

It felt like someone turned the heat up by ten degrees. Sweat glistened on Kayn's brow and the silky material of her blouse was sticking to her. She undid the top button. Through the fog of two am, it clicked… *That heavenly fragrance in the air was caused by Lily's ability. If she was too inebriated to reign it back in, there might be a problem. If she roofied a room full of immortals in opposing Clans, drinking ceremonial wine, it would undoubtedly create some messed-up situations.*

"Oh, lovely. Here we go," Grey stammered.

Kayn could see how this was going to play out. She picked up her friend's hand and it dropped as dead weight to the table. Kayn stated the obvious, "Mel won't be healing anyone this evening."

Frost winked at her and chuckled, "What was your first clue?" He gave Melody's arm a shake, nudged Grey and questioned, "Where's Lexy?"

Grey glanced around the room and replied, "Well, she might not be killing anyone. Tiberius is still here."

Frost looked at Grey and prompted, "Lily's not in control anymore. I can feel it. Go and pull the plug on this."

"Come on man, I can't. You know how long it took me to get over her," Grey pleaded.

"If I go over there and try to stop her in the condition I'm in, she'll set off my ability and shit will hit the fan in an epic way," Frost countered.

Grey downed the rest of the bottle, sighed and declared, "You owe me one!" He got up and strolled over to the couple on the dance floor.

Kayn watched with morbid curiosity as Grey broke up the pair in a well-acted jealous rage. He towed a confused Lily away from Tiberius and the crowded dance floor full of odd pairings of over-affectionate enemies. Kayn gave Frost a peculiar look and said, "Care to elaborate on that statement."

Frost chuckled and whispered, "Why don't I just show you." Without touching her skin, he slowly moved his palm up the length of her arm and hovered it above the pulse point on her neck.

Adrenaline coursed through her, Kayn gasped. Her toes curled as she shivered with pleasure. Her eyes raised to meet Jenna's disapproving glare.

Frost cleared his throat and whispered, "I should go explain. I'll be back in a couple of minutes."

Kayn placed her hand on Melody's back and whispered, "Good idea, stay asleep." Her inhibitions felt like they were holding on by a thread after the mixture of Lily's pheromones, whatever it was that they were drinking and Frost's seductive explanation. She covered her lips with her hand to conceal her expression. *Frost was nothing but trouble.* She smiled as she bit her lip. *He was coming back to the table.* She got up and made her way through the crowd to the bathroom, locking the door behind her. She gazed into the mirror, desperately needing a moment to compose herself. Kayn pressed her hand against her reflection, wishing she could still summon up the image of her twin. Since they'd merged, she'd lost the ability to do this. The images in her mind had become jumbled with Chloe's, it made everything so confusing. Each time she had a sensual moment with Frost, her twin's memories came screaming to the surface. Kayn caressed the place on her neck, where he'd almost touched her. Her pulse raced wildly. She ran the freezing cold water for a minute and splashed the icy liquid on her face as she tried to talk herself down. *He had the ability to make anybody want him without even touching them. All he'd done was show her his gift's reaction to Lily's ability and given her an explanation for asking Grey to stand in front of an oncoming train. Her inner Chloe had to simmer the hell down.* She leaned against the counter and laughed. *She was an emotional, hormonal mess. Kevin was finally here. She'd dreamt of this for so long but the scenario definitely hadn't played out as she'd imagined. He was just some guy who had dreams about her. He looked like Kevin but his mannerisms were not even close to the version of the boy she'd adored since she was five. She was facing a whole week in close confines with her best friend's body double. This promised to be an epically messed-up situation.* When she felt like she could think rationally enough to leave the bathroom, she realised there was no paper towel left. *Fantastic, she'd soaked her face and there was nothing to dry it off with.* She thought about using her shirt but opted out. Instead, she dried off her face with toilet paper. Afterwards, she had to pick the remnants off of her skin. *Oddly, it helped. She felt way less desirable.* Kayn left her sanctuary and ventured out onto the almost empty dance floor. Everyone appeared to be in the process of leaving. Frost was still sitting at the table with Melody. Someone shoved her. She wasn't coordinated enough to stop it, so she braced herself for contact with the floor.

Tiberius, of all people, caught her. He chuckled and taunted, "Why do you Ankh girls keep throwing yourselves at me?"

Kayn scowled as she retaliated, "I'd never throw myself at you." He let go of her. She dropped to the floor with a thud.

Tiberius towered above her and teased, "You were saying?"

He'd actually dropped her on the floor! What a jerk! Kayn racked her mind for a witty comeback but in her pheromone incapacitated state, she didn't have any coherent thoughts left inside of her brain. She decided to call upon one of her own personal rules. When in doubt, just say something confusing. She accused, "That wasn't nice."

Tiberius openly gawked at her and enquired, "Who told you I was nice? You were quite obviously misinformed."

Kayn scrambled to her feet and scolded, "Everybody can make a choice to be nice. Bad manners are just bad manners."

She'd dropped her heels when she fell. He bent over, picked them up and taunted. "I'm assuming these are yours."

She took them from him and said, "Thank you." With both of her hands busy clutching her shoes, Triad's annoying leader released her hair from its restraints. It cascaded as a mess of wild curls down her shoulders but she didn't care this time. *It was the end of the night. She was going to have to pluck them all out eventually.*

Tiberius tucked the pins into one of her shoes, dangling from her hands and warned, "Don't forget those are in there. A bobby pin under a toenail would hurt like hell."

She shook her head at him and baited, "I'm sure you've already figured out which side my birthmark's on."

He sparred, "You're still alive. If it was on the wrong side, your own Clan would have disposed of you." Kayn attempted to move past him and Tiberius blocked her escape by teasing, "Now who's being rude?"

Kayn couldn't help but flash him a genuine grin. She asked, "Is there something you need from me?"

Tiberius answered, "Keep your hair down and quit being so restrained. Allow yourself a little bit of pleasure. It will even out the pain."

She blushed as she glanced back at the tables. Frost was keeping an eye on his brother as she fended off his unwanted advances.

"I wouldn't think one of Frost's girls would blush that easily. Aren't you my brother's flavour of the week?" Tiberius deviously provoked while standing close enough to make his proximity uncomfortable.

The lights turned on as Kayn defended herself, "Frost hasn't touched me. I loved Kevin. You know your grandson. The one you gave a lobotomy to."

"Frost must really like you if he hasn't forced the issue and Kevin hasn't exactly been waiting for you." Tiberius gauged her reaction before continuing, "I know exactly what you need."

Kayn allowed nothing to be read in her unwaveringly calm gaze. She hissed, "Please don't pretend to know who I am or what I need."

"That's where you have it wrong," Tiberius asserted, "I know exactly what you need. I have his memories. They're all stored in my mind. I know about every naughty moment you had together. I know how soft your lips felt when he kissed you. I know everything about you. Your favourite colour is yellow and you snort sometimes when you laugh. I know that you have a strange fascination with bumblebees. I know the agony he felt while you were lying there in a coma for months. I know how much he adored you. You're a unique individual, Miss Brighton."

He had their memories. He remembered every second Kevin had forgotten.

Tiberius enquired, "It's always the same scenario, isn't it? They both loved your sister first. I bet you feel like the consolation prize."

That stung. Kayn questioned, "If you have Kevin's feelings, why are you trying to hurt me?"

The immortal's eyes softened as he replied, "We have more in common than you think. Someday, I'll tell you about it. Perhaps, you won't find me as contemptible then?"

Frost had Melody over his shoulder as he arrived at her side. "Tiberius," he acknowledged his brother's presence.

She could see Tiberius' excitement as her insecurities registered even though she'd tried to conceal them.

"I was just catching up with Miss Brighton," the leader of Triad explained as he gallantly kissed her hand and strolled away.

He'd hit the target he was aiming for.

Frost announced, "I think it's time for us to call it a night. I personally have an excruciatingly long day tomorrow." He placed his hand on the small of Kayn's back as he led her away from the dance floor with Melody as limp as a rag doll dangling over his shoulder.

Tiberius had known just what to say to submerge her heart in ice water. It was true... She was the consolation prize.

Frost whispered, "Ignore my brother. He loves to stir the shit pot. Don't give him the spoon."

She found it ironic that Frost was trying to explain his brother's mind games away. Tiberius had offered validity to the tiny whispers of doubt playing on repeat in her subconscious mind. The tiny whispers she'd managed to stifle. They walked out into the darkness. While deep in thought, she held out her hand. *Was that dew or rain?* Her palm became lightly speckled with warm moisture. *It was rain and it was fitting for this moment. It felt like a goodbye.* She slowed her pace, knowing that once this night ended, everything was going to change. *He was leaving to go to the Summit.*

Frost stopped cold, turned around with a limp Melody on his shoulder and asserted, "We need to move faster. I need to put sleeping beauty to bed. She's dead weight and honestly, she's getting damn heavy." He started walking briskly again.

He was denying himself rest and the opportunity to recharge his ability to make sure they made it back to the RV safely. He was going to the Summit tomorrow. Letting Frost know that she was concerned was the least she could do. Kayn caught up with him and blurted, "Can I ask you a question?" She touched his arm and he stopped walking.

Frost gently placed Melody in the grass. He gazed into Kayn's eyes as he took her hand and whispered, "Whatever my brother said was meant to hurt you or me. You have to just let it go."

He threw her off with his observation and she chickened out. "I was just going to ask you about the Froggy nickname," Kayn asked. *She grabbed a question out of thin air. He'd already basically told her. He just hadn't given her any details.*

Frost gave her the I'm exhausted, uncensored version, "I met you before I met Chloe. You were a little girl looking through a chain link fence with no front teeth and a frog sticker on your cheek. I thought about you over the years. I swear it wasn't a weird creepy thing. I just really wanted to find a way to protect you. I wanted to save you from all of this. When I saw you again, you were all grown up and already in love with someone else."

Kayn smiled. *Now, the nickname was cute.*

He grasped her arm gently as he whispered, "I know what Tiberius said to you. Your thought process is not exactly a quiet one. You were never a consolation prize for me. You were never one for Kevin either."

The nagging insecurity in her mind was silenced as Melody began to stir. Frost quickly picked her up so she wouldn't wake up in the damp grass and cradled her in his arms. "Shhh... I have you," he whispered.

Melody abruptly came to and murmured, "What happened?"

"You got drunk and passed out at the table," he answered.

"Thanks for the lift," Mel mumbled. "I can walk now. I'm all good." Frost placed her upright. She wobbled but got her land legs quickly. Mel whispered, "Thorne didn't see me pass out, did he?"

"No, he was already gone. What happened between the two of you?" Kayn questioned. She watched Melody's expression as she attempted to remember.

The lightbulb sparked up above her head as she answered, "We had the chance to say a few things left unsaid, that's all."

They'd hit the point on the trail where they should split up and go down separate paths. Kayn glanced at Frost. Melody was comically unsteady on her feet, but that wasn't the reason she didn't want him to leave.

He smiled at her and suggested, "You two should just stay in my cabin tonight. You'll be staying there for the next week. I'll feel responsible if Melody stumbles back through the woods in those heels and breaks a limb. Not that it would slow her down for long, but I also have a hangover remedy in the fridge. I'll share it with you."

Kayn watched as Frost anxiously looked at the trails again. *What was that about?*

"Sounds good," Melody mumbled with her heels already off and in her hands.

Visibly exhausted, they both followed Frost down the path. They reached the cabin and climbed the last few creaking steps to the front door. Frost fumbled with the lock before swinging the door open and holding it for them. Melody went directly inside, flopped on the king-size bed and passed out cold. She was dead to the world almost immediately leaving Kayn and Frost sort of alone. Frost grabbed a case of Gatorade and a couple bags of bread from the fridge.

"Ah, you're a brilliant man," Kayn chuckled as he tossed her one. She was amazed she'd caught it as it sailed through the air without taking a plastic bottle to the forehead.

"I'm just old enough to know better," Frost laughed. "Melody, on the other hand, will have to pay for her sins tomorrow."

Kayn grinned at her slumbering friend. She met his gaze and teased, "Thank you, oh mighty drinking master." Frost chucked an entire bag of bread on her lap. She looked at him, confused. *Did he want her to try to eat an entire loaf of bread?*

Frost took a slice out of the bag, ripped the crust off, crushed it into a ball and popped the whole piece in his mouth. After swallowing it, he added casually, "I'll probably be gone before you two get up tomorrow morning."

"I suspected as much," Kayn answered, taking another gulp of her rehydrating drink. She rolled a piece of bread up the same way and ate it. *She learned something new tonight. He just taught her a super-fast way to eat a whole loaf of bread in one sitting. Proof you do learn something new every day.* Kayn closed her eyes, absorbing the soothing sounds of the forest.

"It'll be easier for you to deal with your unresolved feelings, with me gone," Frost noted while staring off into the darkness.

She didn't say anything. *He was right. It would be much easier without him there.*

With understanding eyes, he sincerely said, "I hope you find some closure this next week."

"The last thing I thought I'd ever have to find with Kevin was closure," she confessed as unwanted tears formed in her eyes.

He countered, "Trust me, loving someone you can never be with is an excruciatingly painful endeavour."

"He was my best friend. We have a history. I miss him," Kayn explained. She looked at him through her veil of mascara-clumped eyelashes. Unable to ignore the irritation any longer, even for the sake of deep conversation, she attempted to pick clumps out of her lashes.

Frost leaned over to help rid her lashes of what ailed her and smiled when he got it on his finger. He held it up and showed her as he whispered, "You'll only miss the man you wanted him to be." He blew the eyelash clumped with mascara off his finger.

Kayn chuckled, even though her eyes glistened with tears as she replied, "That might have been the cheesiest thing I've ever seen, and yes, I'm aware that's the title of a country song."

"Do you remember the lyrics? Those lyrics are incredible words of wisdom if you choose to listen," he teased.

She rolled up another piece of bread between her fingertips and said, "I'm sure someone's played it in your honour."

Frost beamed as he sparred, "I'm certain of it." He opened a Gatorade for himself, twisted the lid off another and passed it to her.

Grateful for the opportunity to avoid the hangover everyone else was sure to have, she took it. *How was he being this good about sending her off to sort out her feelings for another guy?*

He answered her thought, "Haven't you ever heard that quote about friendship? It's for a reason, a season, or a lifetime."

Her cheeks were bulging out like a chipmunk because she'd tried to eat three balls of bread at once. *He was looking at her like she was the most magical thing in the world.* She had to swallow it all and take a drink to respond, "Cut to the chase and say what you really want to say. You've been spouting out fortune cookie readings for over half an hour."

His eyes glinted with affection as he admitted, "I'm not allowed to say anything but having this conversation while drunk without telling you everything is surprisingly difficult."

"What can you tell me?" She probed, holding his gaze.

Gazing into her eyes, he replied, "You have what it takes to make it through anything." He stood up, offered her his hand and helped her up.

They stared into each other's eyes without letting go as Kayn admitted, "Tomorrow when you're gone, I know I'll think of a million things I wish I'd said to you. All I can think of right now is... Thank you."

"Thank you?" He questioned.

She wanted to kiss his cheek but didn't as she clarified, "For helping both of us get here safely."

Frost grinned at her, touched her face and picked a tiny rolled up piece of toilet paper off her cheek. He held up his finger and questioned, "Is this toilet paper?"

Kayn sighed, "Yes… Yes, it is." *Is one cool moment really too much to ask for?*

He was grinning as they went inside the cabin. Kayn climbed into bed on one side of Melody with Frost on the other, still wearing clothes. They lay staring at each other in silence until they fell asleep.

Chapter 33

The Land of the Awakened

As Kayn awoke, she heard the muffled chirping of birds. She remained there with her eyes closed, cherishing the moment. It was always a beautiful way to awaken. In the bed next to her, someone dramatically groaned. She opened her eyes and grinned, squinting in the sunlight streaming through the sheer curtains. She heard numerous footsteps walking through the gravel outside with the steady hum of voices. *How many people were out there?* Melody was splayed out on the bed and Frost was gone, just as he said he'd be. *Where did Zach end up last night?* Kayn nudged her hungover companion, prompting, "Come on, Mel. I'm starving and I can't go out there alone. Get up. Have a shower and get dressed. I promise you'll feel better."

Mel moaned, "Please… Shhh. Do not speak. Too painful."

Frost had her back last night. She felt fine this morning. Kayn glanced at the nightstand closest to her. She passed her incoherent friend the bottle of Gatorade Frost left and assured, "Here. This will help you."

After downing an entire bottle, Mel grumbled, "Okay. I'm up." She looked around and mumbled, "How did I get here?"

Kayn stretched while replying, "Frost was a great guy, at the end of the night. You passed out and he carried you, most of the way."

"I noticed you said at the end of the night," Mel teased as she sat up in bed looking like a scraggly-haired cartoon character.

Surprisingly spry, Kayn strolled into the washroom and looked at her hideous reflection. *Had she looked like this at the end of the night?* After having a soothing hot shower, she still had to scrub to remove the blotchy makeup from her face when she got out. Feeling like she was wasting time, Kayn pulled her hair back into a slick, wet ponytail instead of blow drying it. There was a yellow sticky note on the mirror. It read... *Don't worry about behaving yourself.*

I won't be. There was a happy face at the end of the sentence. *This was Frost making sure she understood he was okay with her doing whatever she had to do to put her past with Kevin to rest. Honestly... she wasn't at all sure of how this next week would play out for her, but she knew Frost wasn't likely to behave himself. It wasn't in his nature.*

Mel peered over her shoulder, read the note and laughed, "He's so charming. Why haven't you married this one already?"

They both howled. *Frost wasn't the marrying kind.* Kayn felt a tinge of guilt. *That was how he portrayed himself but not who he'd intended to be. She suspected it was who he'd become due to circumstance.*

Melody tossed her backpack beside her and announced, "Our bags were sitting by the door."

He'd gone back to the RV, grabbed their bags and dropped them off at the cabin before he left. Kayn read his note again. *He was a confusing guy.* She crumpled it up and tossed it in the garbage. *If she planned to sort out her feelings, she couldn't exactly leave it there as a daily reminder.* After putting on her shorts, a tank top and some makeup, she was ready to go. Melody was ready shortly after and they left the dimly lit cabin and stepped out into glaring sunlight.

Mel gasped, shielding her eyes and hissing at the rays like a vampire.

Kayn giggled and teased, "I don't think sunlight is going to be your friend today. Not for a few more hours at least." She draped her arm over Mel's shoulder as they strolled away from the cabin that was their home for the next week. They arrived at the dining hall to find only a few seriously hungover people eating breakfast. *Either everyone had already eaten, or they were all equally hurting this morning.* Even though Kayn followed every step of Frost's hangover cure the night before, her stomach staged a revolt as she lifted the smorgasbord's silver lid and the scent of fried eggs wafted at her.

Melody gagged and mumbled through her fingers, "No eggs. For the love of everything holy, shut the lid."

They opted for toasted bagels. Melody didn't want to risk praying to the porcelain god and if she was forced to hold her hair, she'd be in the stall next to her in seconds, no matter how much hangover remedy she'd consumed. *She'd always been a sympathy up-chucker.* Kayn pocketed a few granola bars, knowing she'd be starving before lunch and they sat across the table from each other, stifling their smiles as more seriously rough teens staggered in. *Suffering through the consequences of partying was the only way to fully understand the hell you had to endure the next day.* Melody wanted to cower in the darkness for a while longer, so they split up after breakfast. With trashy novel in hand, Kayn ventured out in search of the field they'd passed on the way to breakfast, intending to hide there by herself and read. *There it was… her tiny slice of heaven. It was the place she'd gravitated to when they first arrived at the campsite. That's what she needed today. Just a tiny moment to zen herself out and forget all that ailed her.* She manoeuvered through the barbwire fence, found the perfect spot and made herself comfortable in the field of clover and buttercups. After a few hours of delving into her book, Kayn decided she was still hungry. She began trying to open one of the granola bars she'd smuggled out of the banquet hall. *It felt like she was attempting origami while struggling to open the package. Her elevator definitely wasn't going to make it to the top floor today. Talk about adult-proof wrapping.* She gnawed at the indestructible foil with her teeth. *It was a good thing she was completely alone.* She opened it, took a big bite and smiled as she devoured it. *It felt like a random lunchtime at school. She actually missed school.* She stretched out on her back in the grass and squinted in the sunlight. While shielding her eyes with her hands, Kayn tried to make out the clouds above her but it was too bright. She closed her eyes just as a shadow appeared and opened them in the shade caused by the party pooper. *Of course, it was him standing there.*

Concerned, Kevin reprimanded, "I don't mean to be rude but what in the hell are you doing? This field is chock full of bees."

She'd been allergic to bees. Did he remember that? Now, she was curious. Why was he here? "I have plans to spend the day reading and staring at the clouds. By myself," she declared, squinting up at him. She gave him an innocent smile. *She could be the bigger person. She'd be nice to him. They were stuck in this campsite for a whole week together.*

"Okay, I'll bite," he teased. Kevin's look-alike sat down in the grass. He stretched out on his back beside her.

"You didn't use to bite," Kayn rebutted.

He rolled and playfully nipped at her shoulder with his teeth.

She didn't move away or flinch. Her heart flickered with hope. *That was something the old version of Kevin would have done.* Responding as she would have before, Kayn scowled and complained, "Dude, you actually bit me hard. That hurt, rubbing her arm.

"Seriously?" Kevin replied a bit worried.

He thought he'd hurt her. Kayn grinned and giggled, "Well, that still works on you."

"Ha-ha, funny," Kevin sparred as he continued looking at the clouds.

It was easy to make out a few of the puffy white masterpieces in the sky. This had always been one of her favourite pastimes. It had been Chloe's too but she'd never been sure if Kevin had loved it or if he'd come along because it was what they wanted to do. It was a perfect example of her heaven. It was for her, a simple defining act of a peaceful spirit. The ability to lie amidst a field of buzzing, furry bumblebees while trusting they understood she wasn't there to disturb them. For a second, she allowed her heart to believe nothing had changed. It was just the two of them against the world. The air was thick with rapturous scents of impending summer. She inhaled the luxurious mix of the wildflowers and sweet blades of lush grass. "So, that one is quite obviously an eagle," Kayn announced, pointing at the fluffy mass to the left.

"I don't see it," Kevin replied, squinting. "It's too bright. How are you not dying right now?"

He hadn't had Frost's special anti-hangover treatment. He was being a trooper, playing the cloud game hungover. "No… Look," Kayn urged. She reached over and moved his arm, so he could see what she was looking at. "See, there's the beak and those are the wings," she explained.

"Oh, okay. I see it," he declared, grinning.

She glanced over at him and as she did, she saw a vision of him as a child with a messy mass of dark curls. He was about eight years old and they were swinging side by side on the swing set in her backyard. She blinked and the vision was gone.

"Okay, let me do one," Kevin exclaimed as he scanned the sky above. He chuckled, "I know what that looks like but I promised I was going to keep this G-rated."

Who had he promised that to? Maybe she didn't want to know. She started laughing as she clued into what he'd seen in the clouds. *She'd missed him.* Kayn plucked a flower from the grass as she said, "I have a funny story about man parts for you."

"Um, okay," Kevin replied a little shocked but also intrigued enough to hang on her next words waiting for the rest of the story.

"Not from now you moron, from when we were kids. We were both in Mrs. Burnett's class in grade three. We were drawing them in class and showing each other," she explained. "Chloe told on us when she got up to go to the bathroom. We were going to be in so much trouble. The teacher was walking up to our desks. I looked at you and whispered, "Quick! Draw windows." We were scribbling windows on page after page of male genitalia super-fast when she grabbed my paper." Kayn mimicked her teacher's British accent as she continued the story, "Miss Brighton! I am completely disturbed by this! Proper young ladies do not draw naughty bits! You innocently looked up and said, 'But Mrs. Burnett, we're drawing airplanes.' You showed her all your pictures. She got all embarrassed, apologised profusely and Chloe got in trouble for making up stories."

He grinned as he looked up at the sky and whispered, "Tell me something else."

Kayn looked at him as she replied, "Well, this boy was stealing your lunch every day. I pushed him off a bench for you. You were mad at me for weeks."

"Why would you have to push some kid for me?" Kevin asked while grinning.

"Well, you were short, a bit awkward and pretty dorky for a while," she explained. "I was a couple heads taller than you were. You used to get so mad over short jokes. You used to say things like, 'Quit mocking me Amazonian woman.' You were totally hilarious. Well, to me…" Kayn answered, smiling to herself.

"Okay, I was short as a kid. Lots of people are short," he stated. "Is that why your sister never went out with me? I apparently liked her forever. Not you, right?" Kevin asked, gauging her response.

Ouch. Kayn sucked her reaction to the direct hit in and sparred, "We were geeky, zombie loving, Sci Fi Fans. You had acne all over your face for three, maybe four years. There were probably eight million reasons she didn't want you back."

Kevin threw a giant handful of grass at her. He chuckled and said, "Why would I even want to remember this wonderful past of mine? It sounds like I was a giant dork who couldn't get laid to save my life and Chloe, the girl I was desperately in love with, didn't even know I existed."

He couldn't have worded that sentence worse. She sighed, "Why are you here? Why are you laying here acting like you care after the way you treated me at the track?"

Kevin propped himself up on his side and apologised, "I'm sorry about that night. It was a lot to take in. I had just found out that not only were you a real person but you belong to another Clan. I'd spent a lot of time trying to shove my emotions down and you hugged me. I can't even remember being hugged before. If you'll let me, I'd like to spend the next week trying to make you forget about that. I want to know who you are. I'd like to know who I was before all of this crap."

This was a horrible idea but she needed to move past him and there was only one way to do it. She had to wade right through the emotions as they surfaced. Logic prevailed. Kayn replied, "Fair enough. I can do that for you."

"Thank you," he said, breaking the angst-filled moment by grabbing for her book and looking at the steamy cover. He turned it over, read the back and teased, "I'm mortified young lady. Is this Vampire porn?"

She tried to snatch it away as she countered, "It's a frigging romance novel!" They wrestled in the grass until she had him pinned down with her knees on his shoulders.

He started whimpering, "Ouch. Damn it. That hurts. Okay, I give up."

She gazed into his eyes. *It was going to be difficult to remember that he wasn't the Kevin she adored if he kept acting like he was.* Needing to defuse the romantic situation, she dropped a handful of grass on his face.

He blew it away from his mouth. With his hands on her hips, he toyed, "It's going to be difficult to keep this G-rated if you keep pinning me down like this. It's remarkably hot."

Embarrassed, she climbed off him. *Her inner dialogue was always getting her into trouble.* She whispered, "You shouldn't listen to my thoughts." She laid back down beside him in the grass. *This was extremely confusing. Her eyes saw him there. Her heart felt him, but he wasn't really there. She had to get to know this version of him from scratch.* She could tell he sensed her confusion.

"Was I happy with my life?" He asked while gazing at the sky.

She kept staring at the clouds, willing the tears forming in the corners of her eyes to disappear. Another vision of him flashed through her mind. *He was running beside her. When she recalled the past, he was always beside her.* A breeze danced across the surface of her skin. She could almost feel Winnie's gentle touch and hear her sweet voice whispering the words… *Be strong.* After a moment of silence, her bearing on what was real and what was not had been restored. She responded to his question, "We were happy. You were happy. We had each other and that's all that mattered."

"We haven't had each other for the last year. Have you been alright without me?" He probed while looking at her.

The aching in her heart began again. She was treading in dangerous emotional water. Of course, he was going to have questions. It was time to lay out a few ground rules. She answered him honestly before doing so, "At first it was horrible. Once I started to develop my relationships with Zach and Melody, I felt a sense of purpose and that helped."

Kevin was silent for a moment before saying, "Maybe, we should stay away from the deep end of the pool."

She nodded in agreement as she rolled onto her stomach in the grass and began gently playing with the head of a dandelion without plucking it out of the ground or puckering up her lips and blowing the tiny floating seeds into the air. *It was as delicate and weak as her best friend was making her feel.* If he decided to say something cruel or hurtful, it felt like her heart would disintegrate into the wind. *What was she doing laying here with him?*

"So, you obviously had a crush on me first?" Kevin provoked as he playfully tossed another handful of grass at her.

He was attempting to lighten up the conversation in the same way he would have before she'd lost him to Triad. With familiar words and mannerisms, he had reached inside of her heart and made her want to believe. "Oh, good lord no," Kayn laughed as she chucked some back.

He'd diffused the tension with comedy by saying, "Thanks a lot. Are you trying to give me a complex?" He grew quiet.

She sensed he was also trying to figure things out for himself. Kayn admitted, "No, we were best friends. I didn't really think about you as more until after my Correction. Your abilities were also triggered that night. When I came out of the hospital, it felt like it was always meant to happen between us. It was a natural progression." Her words summoned the low, dull ache of his loss to radiate through her being once again. *He was right here beside her. He didn't remember her, not really. Once again, she wondered why she was helping him at the expense of her own heart?*

"So, did we ever... you know… before we were separated?" He enquired, staring at her.

He was wondering if she would tell him the truth. She could see it in his eyes. She answered him honestly, "We wanted to but we didn't get the chance. Everything happened so quickly. We were both with Ankh. You were taken by Triad. We were given the chance to say goodbye and we had one last moment together in the In-between." She paused before adding, "You swore you would never be able to forget me." She stared at the fluffy dandelion again. He leaned over, puckered up his lips and blew the fluffy dandelion's head. Hundreds of tiny white parachutes flew up into the air and travelled away on the wind. She glared at him as he grinned back at her. *His actions had been amusingly ironic. She'd been using that dandelion as a solid representation of her heart.* She searched his eyes for an indication he'd remembered something. *Anything? He was curious, but her Kevin had not miraculously returned.*

"I obviously underestimated my grandfather's ability, didn't I?" He stated. "I saw you with that Frost guy on the couch last night. It doesn't look like you waited for me either."

They were both staring at one lone headless dandelion stem in the sea of grass. Kevin plucked it out of the ground and tossed it aside. It felt like a hostile reaction to seeing her with someone else. She entertained the thought of picking him up and tossing him aside. *Did he know he was sending her crazy mixed messages?* She only had a small amount of patience left for this conversation. She'd give him a few more minutes of the information he was seeking before she took her leave from this mental torture. Kayn replied, "It's not that simple. Chloe's spirit is inside of me. She was in love with Frost. There is something between us. I'm not going to pretend there isn't, but it hasn't been fully acted on."

"We can smell our own Kayn," Kevin taunted as he sat up. He looked straight into her eyes as he grilled, "What do you mean by fully?"

"Why do you care?" Kayn probed. *He was irritated, but why? He didn't remember what they meant to each other.*

"So, you've been intimate with him then?" Kevin pushed.

Crossing her legs in front of her, she covered her face with her hands, laughing, "What do you want me to say? This is all intensely personal information. Why would I tell you?"

Kevin shook his head and apologised, "Listen, I'm sorry. I can't tell you why it's important. I've been asking you questions gut instinct is telling me to ask. It bothered me to see you on the couch with that player last night. I don't know if it was jealousy or just the instinct to look out for you. I'm trying to figure things out. I appreciate your help. I really do. I know you don't have to do this."

She knew how important this conversation would be for her in the future. She needed there to be nothing left unsaid. Kayn confessed, "I always had it in the back of my head that my first time would be with you."

Taken aback by her words, he whispered, "You expect me to believe you waited for me all this time?"

She gave him her emotional confession, "I'm not going to lie to you. I thought I was ready to move on. When it came right down to it, I couldn't. A part of me was always waiting for you."

Overpowered by the raw honesty of her words, it took him a moment to reply, "How's Frost taking us spending a week alone together?"

She could tell once again he was watching for her reaction more than for her actual answer. "He made sure I knew he wouldn't be behaving himself while he was gone," she replied.

Kevin smiled and said, "Right, he probably wanted you to tell him he didn't have anything to worry about so he could put his mind at ease."

"This is Frost we're talking about, I'm actually free to figure out this situation with you," Kayn assured.

"You're assuming I think we have something to figure out," he sparred.

She attempted to get up. *There's the douche version of Kevin. I'd almost forgotten about him.*

He grabbed her wrist and started apologising, "I'm sorry. I didn't mean it the way that it sounded. Forgive me?" Once again, he was staring into her eyes silently pleading for another chance.

Kayn glanced down at his hand. Knowing she should just shake him off and walk away while she still had control over her emotions, she calmly replied, "You were my best friend. That's the only reason I'm still here. Start thinking about what you say before it comes out of your mouth. I'm not going to allow myself to be hurt by you."

Kevin released her wrist and said, "Fair enough." He plucked some grass, glanced at it and tossed it behind him.

There he was. She smiled as she pointed out, "That picking the grass, looking at it and throwing it behind you, thing. You've done that since you were a kid."

He quit doing it as he shifted onto his side and said, "See, it's those things that I want to know. I need to know who I was before I became this person. It feels like it's important. By helping me do that, you'll be dredging up old emotions for yourself. You must have loved me a lot to be willing to do this."

"I need you to stop saying things like that," she whispered as his finger trailed an intimate seductive path down the length of her arm. Her heart swelled in response to his touch as pleasurable goosebumps rose on her skin. She resisted the impulse to pull away. *He wasn't the same person. This version of her best friend knew how to make a girl squirm. It both intrigued her and made her feel sad. He'd grown up without her.*

After a pause, he seductively taunted, "Let me rephrase that. Say we locked the door to one of those cabins for a week and I made you beg me to stop doing things to you that could wreck you for all other men for the rest of your life. We get to live a long time. Kayn. Does that sound like a nice thing for me to do?"

Her eyes widened as her cheeks blushed. She got an eye full of dazzling sunshine. She shielded her eyes, squinting in the brilliance of midday's rays. *She was going to need a moment for a comeback to that.* She whispered her calculated reply, "You clearly have a little more practice talking dirty now, don't you?"

Kevin inched a little closer and flirted, "I'm pretty sure I have a little more experience at lots of things."

She shifted away from his touch. *He was like a different person. Yet somehow, still the same.* Kayn needed him to do something, anything to give her a hint he remembered her. *He was being a flirt. A guy working his game.* Kayn whispered her reply, "If I believed you remembered me, there is nothing I wouldn't do for you."

"I am curious about you," he acknowledged. "We have a week to take a walk down memory lane and maybe it'll be incredible, but at the end of the week, it's not going to matter what I do or don't remember about my past. It's not going to change anything between us."

Kayn replied, "No, it won't. I understand that now." She heard Melody call her name. She stood up and began to shake the grass off.

"Can I kiss you and see if anything comes back to me?" Kevin toyed as he got up and brushed off his clothes.

"You're joking, right?" She provoked as she spun around and marched away.

He chased after her and teased, "That wasn't a no!"

She fought the urge to laugh. *A lot of Tiberius had rubbed off on Kevin and she was pretty sure that was a bad thing.* "You need to earn a kiss from me," she challenged without breaking stride.

Kevin chuckled while trying to keep up with her. He probed, "I've never turned down a dare from you, have I?"

She stopped walking away and allowed him to catch up while giving her reply, "That feeling might be correct."

While thrilled she'd answered him honestly, he baited, "Okay then, I dare you to make me remember you this week."

"Fine, I dare you to remember," Kayn sparred while meeting his intrigued gaze. *What in the hell was she doing?*

"Deal," he answered as he held his hand out to shake on it.

Kayn took his hand and ribbed, "What are we, children?"

"Obviously, attempting to seduce you isn't going to work. Why don't we start over?" He fanned out her fingers and kissed the symbol on the inside of her palm while introducing himself, "My name's Kevin. I'm Clan Triad and I am a Virgo."

He'd done the kissing hand thing from the storybook they loved as children. How could he not remember her if he remembered that? With complete inability for rational thought, Kayn corrected, "You're not a Virgo. You're a Scorpio."

"Well, that certainly explains a lot," he chuckled without letting go of her hand.

"Halloween. That's your birthday," Kayn added as her resolve to stay angry dissipated. He let go of her hand. *Heaven help her. She didn't want him to.* They strolled side by side without touching until they reached the barbwire fence, where he held it up. She cautiously shimmied through. She did the same for him, and in a second, they were walking down the trail. *He was checking her out. It was weird. Kevin never did that. Remember this isn't him.*

As they strolled down the dirt trail through the lush forest towards the cabins, Kevin enquired, "Tell me something about the new and improved Kayn."

She slowed her pace as she shared, "I'm a pretty good karaoke singer. I won a prize once."

"Oh, did you? Are you sure it wasn't a wet t-shirt contest? I for one, can't believe I ever went swimming with you without losing my damn mind, watching you come out of the water. Let's go swimming right now," he flirtatiously teased.

Intrigued by the version of Kevin that openly desired her, she couldn't help but play along. Kayn toyed with him, "I'm already wearing a bathing suit under my clothes. Let's go, right now."

He chuckled while provoking, "You mean I don't get to see you in your sports bra and granny panties again?"

"Those weren't granny panties," she huffed, sensing his eyes on her curves as she sauntered ahead of him. *She was playing with fire. She knew that. That kissing hand thing messed with her mind. It was like he had the information. He just didn't know why it was there.* With the urge to test him, Kayn paused and questioned, "Do you smell that?"

"I have no clue what you're talking about," he teased.

She explained, "You should really make sure this path is safe first. Smell the grass."

Intrigued, he clarified, "Why do I want to smell the grass again?"

"To check for hillbilly urine," Kayn stated while managing to keep a straight face. *She had to see if he'd do it.*

Kevin shook his head and muttered under his breath, "You may very well be the weirdest girl I have ever met."

"I'll take that as a compliment," she countered.

He humoured her as he knelt, yanked out a handful of grass and sniffed it.

Melody strolled over and said, “Hillbilly urine?”

“Is that actually a thing?” Kevin asked.

Looking dead serious, Kayn remarked, “Sure it is... How do you not know about the hillbilly urine thing?”

Kevin shook his head. He glared at the two girls and accused, “You guys are messing with me!”

Zach indifferently wandered up and announced, “You’re the guy that took my place in Triad. I should thank you. I have to be honest, I thought you’d be taller.”

“That’s hilarious,” Kevin replied. “You’re all as weird as she is. Is it contagious in your Clan?”

Zach chuckled as he joined the trek on the dirt path, “I wasn’t weird at all when I was in Triad. I’ve spent a whole year with these people and now I’m as nutty as a damn fruit cake.”

They grinned at each other. Mel quite randomly hip-checked Zach. He almost bit it and fell into a bush but quickly regained his balance. He walked for a few feet before trying to do the same thing to Kayn, but she didn’t go down. Kevin caught her. They had an awkward moment before continuing the casual stroll. Waiting a few minutes so Zach wouldn’t expect it, Kayn hip-checked him into the bush, and he went down. “Score!” She yelled with her hands in the air, obnoxiously dancing.

Kevin appeared to be intrigued by their immaturity. As they reached the dock, he nudged Melody and asked, “Were we friends?”

The lumber sunk into the water as they stepped onto the dock. Melody glanced back at Kevin while responding, “We only met once. The day you left with Triad, I switched back to Ankh. Maybe someday you’ll remember what I did for you. How I bound you together.”

Kevin flirtatiously replied, “Is that supposed to be kinky? It sounds like it is.”

“No! You know that’s not what I meant!” She laughed as she laid her towel out on the dock.

Kayn was thoroughly enjoying the witty banter when the warmth of early summer’s caress on her skin, brought her back to blissful childhood memories. Her family always went camping with Kevin's family. She’d wandered to a wooden dock countless times in her short mortal life. There always seemed to be a patch of sharp rocks to get used to. At the beginning of the summer, her bare feet would always complain because they were unaccustomed to the harsh, rigid pebbles beneath her soles. By the end of the summer, they'd be racing over stones like they weren't even there. She inhaled the familiar scent of the cedar as she felt the coarseness of the wood beneath her feet. *He was staring at her.* She met Kevin's mesmerised gaze as she casually stripped off her clothing and strolled over to where they'd laid the towels. She was intentionally messing with the version of him that found her tempting, knowing the sparse pastel blue material of her bikini barely covered her breasts. She was toned from her running obsession but had always been self-conscious about her larger backside and curvaceous wide set hips.

"You're an evil girl Brighton," Mel observed, giggling as she sprawled in the sun and closed her eyes.

Zach was lounging on his towel, taking in her bikini situation. He chuckled, "He's going to need an intervention from Tiberius to stay away from you after seeing you in that."

Good. Kayn sprawled on the dock, in the warmth of the sun, while avoiding the urge to grin. She made eye contact with Kevin again as he removed his shirt and stretched out beside her. *Touché. His abs were amazing. He was trying to play the same game with her.*

He winked at her as he teased, "Are you guys too hungover to see me? Because you're talking like I'm not lying right beside you."

After a moment of silence, Mel taunted, "Oh no, we know you're there. We just don't care."

Kayn changed the subject, "Zach, where did you end up last night?"

"Wouldn't you like to know?" Zach sparred with a self-satisfied grin.

Instantly interested in their conversation, Mel prodded, "Just tell me what I missed... Spill it."

Kayn glanced at her friend. *Mel was squinting in the sunlight, trying to see Zach's face so she could gauge the truth of his story.* She fought the urge to giggle. *Women are uniquely territorial creatures. Was that a hint of jealousy in her friend's eyes? Mel had been occupied elsewhere. She understood her predicament. She felt that way about Frost. She wasn't one hundred per cent sure she wanted to be with him, but she didn't really want anyone else to be with him either.*

Zach sighed, "I slept with that crazy chick. She may wear me as a skin coat someday, but man was it ever worth it."

Mel smacked him and quietly scolded, "You're such a dog."

After putting two and two together, Kayn winked at Kevin and whispered, "Zach slept with your girlfriend."

Kevin rolled to his stomach, propped himself up on his elbows and assured, "Stephanie can do whatever she wants. She's not my girlfriend."

Intrigued by his denial, Kayn also rolled over. She met his gaze and countered, "Does she know she's not your girlfriend?"

Grinning, Kevin switched topics, "I saw something hot last night involving a few members of your Clan."

Zach chuckled, "Yes, well-timed subject change, my friend. For future reference ladies, men never want to know they've crossed swords."

Acting like he hadn't heard Zach's commentary, Kevin continued his story, "I stumbled across Lily and Grey last night. Literally."

Melody was the first to reply, "Good for them. Grey deserves to be happy. He's a good guy."

Intrigued, Zach sat up and questioned, "I always thought you had a thing for him?"

Squinting in the intense sunlight, Mel replied, "Why would you think that?"

"Well for starters, you never bite when I hit on you," he teased.

"That's because you're a dog, Zach. Case in point, it's possible you slept with Satan last night," she giggled, closing her eyes, pretending to nap.

"I'm only a dog due to lack of bone," he replied. "If I ever thought I had a chance with someone like you I'd never pee on anyone else's tree again."

Kevin chuckled and taunted, "Fidelity, being compared to pissing on a tree. That may be the most romantic thing I've ever heard."

"Anytime you need to use my classy pick-up lines, you feel free," Zach replied.

"I am already working on a few good ones to use on you ladies tonight," Kevin ribbed.

"Please don't," Mel moaned without opening her eyes.

"Alright, just friends then," Kevin teased as he extended his hand towards her.

Melody peered over at him with her hands acting as a sun visor and stated, "Let's just shake on it later."

Kayn dozed off with her face resting on her arms, listening to the comic sparring match. She felt someone touching her hair and looked as Kevin showed her the lint he'd plucked out. *It came from her towel. Lovely.* She puckered her lips and blew it off his finger. The orange bit of fluff landed in the water and floated away. *She'd been certain she knew what each of his expressions meant. She couldn't quite place this one. It wasn't on the list.* She whispered, "What are you thinking?" She grimaced… *She'd just allowed herself to become a female cliché.* She comically thumped her forehead on the dock. *Everything worked out so much better in her mind.* She rubbed the bump, muttering, "That's going to leave a mark."

Oddly impressed, Kevin declared, "Did you really just bang your head on purpose?"

She rubbed her wound, saying, "It was supposed to be funny. Damn it. That really hurt."

Melody sat up and explained, "Oh, Kevin. This is Kayn we're talking about." She laid her hand on Kayn's forehead and healed the giant goose egg.

"Our Kayn is a wee bit accident-prone," Zach explained.

"It was hilarious in my mind," Kayn mumbled to herself. When she peered up, Kevin was sitting beside her with an enormous grin on his face.

He teased, "If you're crazy it's not a deal-breaker... But, I do prefer to know upfront."

Kayn grimaced at the group. *It always felt like she was the butt of everyone's jokes. She did acknowledge that she asked for it most of the time.*

"Everybody's either crazy or boring," Zach ribbed.

A few people they hadn't met from the other Clans began to gather on the dock. They were passing around helpful hangover remedies.

"Here, these might help," an attractive stranger said as he threw sunglasses on the dock in front of Melody.

Mel smiled as she reached out to grab them. "Awe, you're a prince," she replied as she slipped them on. Someone else gave her juice from a cooler and placed Tylenol in the palm of her hand. She took them and sighed, "You're a lifesaver." She paused, knit her brow and questioned, "I wonder why my hangover hasn't healed? It should have healed a long time ago."

The stranger bearing sunglasses and juice said, "I have a feeling that wine was meant to teach us a lesson."

"It definitely taught me one," Melody commented. "How come you're not in pain this morning Kayn?" she asked.

"When we got back to the cabin, I ate a loaf of bread and drank Gatorade." She responded, stretching like a cat lounging in the sun.

Kevin nudged her, enquiring, "You really ate a whole loaf of bread?"

Kayn opened her eyes and motioned with her fingers as she spoke, "You take the crust off and roll it into a ball, it expands in your stomach and absorbs the alcohol."

Kevin snickered, "You guys are a wellspring of strange information, aren't you?"

None of them bothered to deny it. They just beamed.

Kevin passed Melody sunblock as it travelled through the group of strangers. He remarked, "Just because you can heal your burns doesn't mean you should do it on purpose."

Melody lifted her hair, glanced at Zach and asked, "Can you put some lotion on my back?" He smiled while liberally applying it to her back and shoulders. Mel said, "Want me to do you too?"

"If you're offering," Zach flirted. Mel rolled her eyes while massaging the lotion into his skin. "With my permanent tan, I rarely need the stuff," Zach baited. "Enjoyable as it is."

"Famous last words... I don't burn," Mel sparred.

Come on, Mel. You know better. Zach's expression changed. She'd seen this vacant look of emptiness pass across his face before. Kayn gave his shoulder a quick squeeze with a knowing, close-lipped smile. *The past always had a nasty habit of creeping up and stomping out an enjoyable moment.* She knew a few of Melody's secrets but Zach had never told her any. *They'd reminisced about wallpaper once. She knew which conversations to avoid because there were only a few things that set Zach off emotionally. Fire had always been a touchy subject and burn was also a word to avoid using in his presence. It was easy to read between the lines.* He hadn't even looked at her when she squeezed his shoulder. *Melody was aware she'd stuck her foot in her mouth.* Kayn lightened up the situation by saying, "Isn't anyone going to do me?" Zach cracked a smile. Kevin winked at her but didn't offer his services. It was obvious she was trying to get Zach to smile.

Zach smirked and teased, "All right... I guess I can do you both. You have to promise me you won't bang your head on the dock if I don't do a good job though."

"I promise to behave myself," Kayn answered.

Zach gave her a dirty look and mumbled, "You're such a liar."

Kayn arched her back and grinned at Kevin. When he was finished, she laid down, closed her eyes and whispered, "Thanks, Zach."

"Anytime, Candy Kayn," he answered.

He'd used her old nickname. She stealthily observed Kevin's reaction, half expecting the look of confusion as he regained a memory, but he hadn't even flinched. *It was a nickname he'd given her as a child.* She fought the overwhelming urge to jump on his chest and shake him back into her version of reality. *This is just the first day. He has lots of time to remember.*

During their conversation, the dock filled with more scantily clad teens in search of an after-effects refuge. Kayn closed her eyes and tried to nap while listening to the soothing sloshing of the water as it lapped against the dock.

After a relaxing sprawl in the sunshine that was a touch longer than it should have been, they went for a swim. *The lake was insanely cold.* The cloudy appearance of the water beneath the surface had given it the illusion of depth, but she could almost touch the bottom.

They played, splashing each other while doggie paddling in place but their continuous motion really didn't help much. *It was bloody freezing.* Watching Kevin swim for the shore, Kayn let out an inner competitive cheer because she'd outlasted him.

Kevin called out, "Kayn! It's freezing! Get out before you pass out!"

He was already standing on the rocky beach, basking in the sun's rays, and she was freezing half to death. To prove what? An irrational point? She kept paddling in place while trying to convince herself to make a break for the shore. *Was she trying to prove she was stronger than he was, or was she freezing her rump off because he looked incredible standing there in the sunshine? She desperately wanted to disregard her instinct for self-preservation, knowing what kept her in the water. Her heart was trying to build a wall… He isn't Kevin. Get a hold of yourself. You aren't a ridiculous girly girl.* Her skin was aching as she made her way to the shore. She was trembling uncontrollably as she walked out of the water, looking like a soaking wet, blue-lipped water nymph.

Kevin hurried to her side, placed his towel around her, gave her shoulders a rub and pulled her into the warmth of his chest. "You're an icicle," he whispered, holding her shivering, damp body against his.

Kayn wasn't sure if she wanted to snuggle against him or push him away and ask him what in the hell he thought he was doing? He was rubbing her skin to warm her up. She shivered against him, but this time it wasn't because she was freezing. *It was a reaction to the warmth of his chest against hers and the confusion in her heart.*

He whispered in her ear, "I feel like maybe I've lived this exact moment before. Are you sure I didn't have a crush on you? I find it hard to believe I could have ever seen you like this without trying to make a move."

She pulled away and stared into his eyes, with her lips a mere breath away from his. *He was massaging her back in a physically familiar, intimate way. He doesn't remember you.* He inched away while intensely searching her eyes. *He was trying to remember her. She could feel it.* His hand brushed across her chest. Her eyes widened for a second before she realised, he was only wrapping her in the towel. She whispered, "You've seen me a million times, just like this. If you ever saw me as anything more, you never told me."

"I must have been a complete idiot," he acknowledged.

Her lips were still quivering as she spoke, "The cards weren't evenly stacked; it's not your fault. Chloe's gift was like Lily's and Frost's. Everyone wanted her. She was a breathtaking force of nature."

"She's dead then? Did she die with the rest of your family and mine?" Kevin enquired.

She could tell he immediately regretted bringing it up. She replied, "There are things I'm not allowed to discuss with you and that's one of them. I was warned. You'll remember everything when you're ready too."

"There's one thing I already know," he intimately brushed a damp ringlet off her brow while whispering, "I think I could stare at you and count your freckles for the rest of my life and never get bored." He intimately grazed a finger across the pulse point on her neck.

If he wanted to kiss her, he was pushing all the right buttons. She was about to cave when she realised what he was doing. He was playing a game with her. He wanted her to make the first move.

He slowly, seductively brushed his thumb along her bottom lip. She shivered and he grinned. Proud of the physical reaction he'd caused with his not so innocent games, he whispered, "You have a freckle on your bottom lip. I was just making sure it wasn't a grain of sand."

If he wanted her to become so lost in her feelings for him that it wouldn't matter if he wasn't the same person, he was doing a stellar job. Everything about him felt warm and familiar. It would have been so easy to allow him to kiss her. Her feelings for him made her a sitting duck but two could play at that game. He may not remember her but she knew he wanted her. Desiring a girl also made a boy a sitting duck. She casually teased, "Well, as much as I'd love to just lay down naked in a field and allow you to count every last one of my freckles, shouldn't we at least make an attempt to find out what we're supposed to be doing this week?" *She was never this forward.*

It took a minute for him to find an answer. With a pained expression, he said, "I think we're just supposed to hang out here and wait for them to come back."

"Doesn't that seem a little bit strange to you?" She enquired, "We're supposed to be enemies, but this week, we're all friends. Nobody hurt anyone else. Have a great time while we're gone?"

He replied, "Yes, it does, but there's so much dark and twisty crap in my everyday life. I for one am just going to go with the idea of a well-deserved vacation from reality."

They made their way back to the dock to collect their clothes in silence. She bent down in front of him, on purpose as she picked up her clothes and slipped on her tank top over her damp bathing suit. She was enjoying the fact that even though he didn't recall his feelings for her, their attraction was undeniable. She stepped into her shorts, turned around to face him and caught him staring. She picked up their earlier conversation, "There's obviously more to this week off than just a well-deserved vacation. There's always some kind of weird twist."

"Shhh," he placed his finger over her lips and teased, "Don't overthink it. Just relax and enjoy it."

"Right… Relax," she giggled. *There was something about the familiar tone of their conversation.* She leaned in and kissed his cheek. He touched where her lips had been and she saw the recognition in his eyes. She kept it light by teasing, "How can you relax? It's like standing in the middle of a highway ignoring the fact that at any moment, a big rig might come around the corner and squish you like a pancake?"

"Don't hate the big rig. Hate the road. You can stand up and move out of the way whenever you want," Kevin pointed out.

That sentence applied to many things… Mainly her decision to spend time with him. That was the fine print and she could see it quite clearly. One week… You only have one week together. Would she listen? Well, that remained to be seen. They both sat on their towels and as she gazed into the eyes of the boy she'd known since she was five. She smiled and thought, *probably not.* Once they'd warmed up, they ended up taking off their clothes again and stretching out on their towels. Kayn fell asleep to the feeling of Kevin drawing pictures on her back.

When she opened her eyes, he was gone. Everyone was packing up their things. A bell rang. *What was that about?*

Mel answered her thought, "Dinner is being served in the dining hall."

She was hungry. They rushed to drop off their things at the cabin before gathering for dinner. The three Ankh arrived at the hall and took a spot in the lineup for the smorgasbord. *Patrick was in the line behind them but Kevin and Stephanie were nowhere to be seen.* Kayn wanted to question Patrick but decided against it. *She'd allowed herself to be swept away today a little bit more than she'd intended to.* She ate her meal in silence while the others laughed, chatted and joked around.

Zach noticed her silence first and said, "You allowed yourself to get caught up in him today, didn't you?"

Kayn took a sip of water. Over the background noise of clinking plates and conversation, she loudly replied, "Quite obviously." Her eyes kept sneaking peeks at the doorway. *He wasn't coming. He was with Stephanie and she was an idiot.*

"I know you want one of my sweet potato fries," Zach teased.

Kayn laughed as he tossed a fry across the table. It landed on her plate, which was easily the equivalent of a crumpled piece of paper in the trash can goal. Smiling, she popped it into her mouth and glanced at the door again, under the pretence of looking at Patrick. *The super nice Triad was talking to everyone else but purposely avoiding conversation with her. She could read between the lines.*

They finished dinner and the trio made their way back to the cabin, avoiding the topic of Kevin completely. She paused as they started scaling the rickety, worn wooden stairs and glanced at Triad's cabin across the way. The curtains were open. Kevin and Stephanie were snuggled in bed under the blankets together, out cold. *Why was she doing this to herself?*

Placing his arm around her, Zach gave her a brotherly squeeze as he led her up the stairs. He assured, "We sleep like that all of the time and it doesn't mean anything."

"Not naked like them of course, but it could totally be innocent," Mel commented.

She hadn't noticed they were naked. Kayn swung around.

Melody shoved her onto the bed and laughed, "I'm kidding. They probably lost track of time while having a nap."

Zach plugged his cell into the speakers on the end table and began to play some tunes. He cranked it up and Kayn started to laugh as he announced, "They won't be asleep for long!" He laughed as he grabbed Kayn's hands and towed her across the room against her will. He climbed onto the bed and directed, "Get your butt up here, Brighton. If you want to save face, start dancing. You have to act like you didn't even notice he missed dinner."

Soon, all three were jumping from the couch to the bed and twirling to the music in hysterics. They were smoking each other in the face with the pillows and lip-syncing to songs. *She felt better.* Eventually, they exhausted themselves. The music was turned off and it was time for bed. Kayn strolled over to close the curtains. She saw Kevin, wide awake, drinking a coffee sitting on the stairs of his cabin. He made eye contact with her just as she yanked the curtains closed. The three Ankh watched a movie on the laptop and then drifted off to sleep.

Chapter 34

Remember Me

Kayn awoke the next morning to the sun's blinding rays shooting at her corneas like laser beams. *What time is it?* She looked at the cell on the bedside table. *It was only five o'clock in the morning.* She peered over at her sleeping fellow Ankh and decided that neither one would appreciate being woken up to go for a run with her this morning. She got out of bed and toddled into the bathroom. She brushed her teeth, washed her face and pulled her hair back into a ponytail. *This was exactly what she needed.* She needed to hit the open trail. Kayn put on her running shoes, wandered down the steps and sprinted away as soon as she hit the gravel. As the crisp morning dew christened her face, she felt cleansed of the drama from the day before. She ran the trails for a good hour before heading down to the dock. Nobody would even be up yet. *She'd have a moment to zen her mind before the drama of the day began.*

In the bushes before the rocky beach, deer were peacefully grazing on foliage. She tip-toed past them. When she reached the end of the dock, she slipped off her shoes and sat with her legs dangling over the edge and her toes in the water. She stared at the mist as it rose off the surface and closed her eyes to properly embrace the peaceful atmosphere. The tune of the crickets was the harmony and the sound of the water lapping up against the dock, the background music. *It had been a wonderful morning so far.* She'd been so caught up in the moment that she hadn't heard anyone approaching. Someone grabbed her shoulder. They startled her and she fell ungracefully into the lake. She bobbed up, sputtering in the water. *Who in the hell pushed her in?*

Kevin knelt on the edge of the dock with his hand out to help her, laughing, "Oh my God. I'm so sorry. I thought you heard me coming."

Kayn took his helping hand and tugging him into the lake with her. He bobbed to the surface, cursing up a storm. She started to laugh. *Now, it was funny.* They raced for the ladder and wrestled like kids until he let her go first. She offered him her hand.

"Do you think I was born yesterday?" He bickered.

Kayn stepped back and grinned as he climbed out. She planned to shove him in but decided to save it for another time. She sat on the dock with her feet dangling in the water, knowing how easy it would be for him to toss her back in.

Instead, Kevin sat beside her and remarked, "It's not even six in the morning. How are you this hyper?"

Kayn smiled as she replied, "You shoved me in first and I've been running for an hour." With curly hair in a ponytail, she knew she looked the same as she had before her unintended submersion but with bluish-purple lips.

He clarified, "I walked up to you, put my hands on your shoulders and you jumped in."

"I owed you one," she stated.

He questioned, "You owed me one for what?"

"Never mind," she backtracked. *She'd read him all wrong yesterday and didn't want to get into it.*

Kevin kept asking, "What do you owe me for? Are you talking about that first night on the track? I've already apologised."

The water wasn't nearly as cold as it had been yesterday. Kayn glanced at him and said, "It's not important."

"No, I'm curious now. Did I do something?" He prodded, searching her eyes.

"We had a great day together. I thought I'd see you at dinner. You and Stephanie didn't show up? Does any of this ring a bell?" She hinted at meeting his eyes.

"I'm sorry… You lost me," Kevin replied. "You fell asleep on the dock. I went to go have a nap before dinner. I woke up in my cabin alone and you three were jumping around on your bed like a bunch of sugar-amped toddlers. You closed the curtains and went to bed?"

He really didn't appear to know. Should she? Why the hell not? Kayn explained, "You didn't show up for dinner, neither did Stephanie because you were in bed together."

Kevin started laughing, "I see what happened here. So, you're not sleeping in the same bed with Zach then?"

She replied, "Well, yes. Never mind. I see your point. Here's mine. We can't do what we did yesterday. I let myself just fall back into what we were. It's too confusing. This feels too close to what we had."

He began ringing water out of her ponytail while responding, "Let me get this straight. You got spooked yesterday and you want to run away." He sweetly kissed one of the freckles gracing her shoulder.

She shivered. "Kevin," she whispered. He tilted her chin and tenderly kissed her lips. Her heart ached as emotions flooded all sense of reason.

He whispered his response, "I'm not letting you go… Not yet." He kissed her again, seductively darting his tongue against her bottom lip. She instinctually parted hers, allowing the kiss to deepen. *She couldn't help herself. It had been so long since she'd been with him like this.* He momentarily pulled away. Their eyes met. He seductively caressed her cheek and kissed her again with such raw, intense passion they forgot where they were. His hand slipped beneath her soaking wet tank top as frenzied kisses blurred ration. His hand slid down her abdomen to the waistband of her shorts. She gasped and pushed him away, snapping back to reality. *What was she thinking?*

Kevin chuckled as he got up and casually made himself look decent. He teased, "I'm certain that was the hottest kiss of my life. There's no chance of me not wanting to do that again. I'm afraid I'm going to have to decline your request to G-rate this for the next week." He turned around and walked away, leaving her swollen-lipped and utterly speechless. She sat there for a second with her hand over her mouth and then started to giggle. *This was only the second day.* She waited until he was back inside his cabin before venturing up to hers. Kayn opened the door to her bunkmates sitting at the tiny table in front of the picture window. They put their coffee mugs down and began to campy, silent golf clap.

Zach teased, "I thought I was going to have to stomp down there and save you from getting in over your head. I thought we were mad at him? He shoved you in the water and you end up in the steamiest make out session, I've ever seen. How did that even happen?"

Kayn sighed, "I guess you two saw the whole thing?"

Sipping her coffee, Mel asked, "What did he say before he walked away and left you like that? The look on your face was priceless."

Kayn sat down at the table. Zach passed her his coffee. She took a sip and passed it back. She began with, "He scared me and I fell in. I pulled him into the lake when he was trying to help me back out. We both got out. I told him it was too confusing for me to be with him like we were yesterday. I said we had to slow things down. I called him on the Stephanie thing and he asked if Zach was sleeping with me last night. So, maybe it wasn't what it looked like. He kissed me and told me he wasn't ready to let me go."

Grinning, Zach enquired, "We just want to know what he said before strutting away. Judging by the look on your face, it was monumental."

With her cheeks heating up, she replied, "He said, he was pretty sure that was the hottest kiss of his life and he was going to have to decline my offer to go back to the G-rated version of our relationship."

In awe, Zach declared, "That might be the coolest thing I've ever heard."

Kayn swatted him as she went to grab herself a cup of coffee.

"He might be my new hero," Zach chuckled.

Wandering back to the table with her piping hot java, Kayn glared, sparring, "I'm glad you find my painful situation hilarious."

Silent for a second, Mel whispered, "Oh… You're in so much trouble, Brighton."

She definitely was. Kayn responded, "Give me a minute to regain the ability to think straight before we go for breakfast. I've got this." She glanced out the window as she sipped her coffee. Kevin was having a coffee on the steps to his cabin. He'd already changed his clothes. Noticing her watching through the window, he grinned. She smiled back, shaking her head. *She wasn't going to be able to deny she wanted this. That reckless early morning kiss messed with her resolve.*

"He's so much hotter now," Melody sighed.

Raising his cup, Zach teased, "So is, Brighton."

Wandering away smiling, Kayn muttered, "Don't be gross, Zach."

As days passed by, friendships blossomed with opposing Clans. After dinner each night, they sat by a flickering campfire, singing songs, roasting marshmallows, and sharing tales of days gone by. Merely teenagers on a camping trip to boaters.

On a log next to Kevin as she had been every night, it was clear she would have fallen for him this week, even if they'd never met. *His memories were erased, but the connection wasn't.* Patrick and Stephanie from Triad were goofing around, along with Leanne and her boyfriend Caleb from Trinity. *Crap! She was burning her marshmallow.* She waved her stick to extinguish the flames.

The flaming marshmallow flew off and landed on Zach's lap. He shouted, "What in the hell, Brighton?"

This was followed by a chorus of laughter. Stephanie leapt up to save Zach's unmentionables from their fiery demise. *Zach had been spending a lot of time with her.*

Kevin dug through the bag of marshmallows. He placed three on his stick and sat down beside her, dangling his marshmallows in the flames. They were listening to Leanne and Caleb's animated sparring match. *Leanne's British accent was amazing. She was from Whitby, North Yorkshire. Caleb was from Anderson Mill, a small city in Texas, so his was incredible as well. She probably had an accent from growing up on Vancouver Island. You never hear your own accent. Maybe hers was just as majestic to them?*

Kevin shimmied closer, holding up his stick, he offered, "Have mine. I'll make more." When she didn't reach out and take one right away, he tried to take one off for her while saying, "Ow! Ouch! That was still hot!" He held it up to her mouth and fed it to her. He licked the sticky remnants off his fingers and whispered, "You haven't let me kiss you again. I'm going to follow you home tonight if you don't kiss me."

She swallowed her mouthful of marshmallow, leaned in and gave him a sticky marshmallow flavoured peck on the lips. He chuckled as he wiped some ash from the campfire off her lip. *This kind of intimate gesture was almost worse for her heart.* She licked her lips and excused herself, saying she needed to go to the washroom, hoping he'd follow. She walked back to the cabin, quickly scaled the stairs and disappeared inside. Kayn strolled across the room and closed the bathroom door behind her. She checked herself in the mirror before she left. *There were still ashes on her face.* She wiped them off and opened the door, half expecting to see Kevin standing there. *He wasn't.* Disappointed, she walked back to the group. She heard his footsteps and grinned as she turned around.

"You and I are taking a quick detour," Kevin explained as he held out his hand. She laced her fingers with his and he led her to the dock. The path was lit by paper lanterns that created this soft romantic ambiance. *This place looked truly magical at night.* The dock was lit by half a dozen flickering torches. Kevin took off his shirt as he stepped onto the dock and tossed it aside. *Surely, he wasn't expecting her to do the same.* He left his shorts on as he sprinted down the length of the dock and dove into the water with a graceful splash. *He wanted to go for a swim. Each day the water had grown warmer. It wasn't as traumatisingly frigid as when they arrived.* Kayn pulled her top over her head and dropped it at her feet. She slipped off her shorts and stood there waiting for him to surface. She didn't want to land on top of him. He surfaced off to the side and she raced to the end of the dock and dove into the crisp, invigorating water. She emerged from the depths and swam back to him in flickering torchlight.

"I need to say something," Kevin whispered as he pinned her against the ladder. He tenderly caressed her cheek, slowly moved in and seductively kissed her lips.

She loved him. It didn't matter how much she warned herself against it. She was trying to grip the ladder with wet fingertips and slid off. Without missing a beat, he stopped her descent beneath the water's surface. She looped her arms around his muscular shoulders while managing to wedge one of her heels on the slippery wooden steps behind her. She was so caught up in the intoxicating sensation of his kisses that she almost forgot where they were. He didn't push things further than a kiss.

He pulled away. Starring into her eyes, he leaned in, gave her an affectionate kiss on her temple and whispered, "You scare the hell out of me, Brighton."

He'd used the nickname he'd given her. Kayn responded, "Ditto Smith." Kevin looked confused and it occurred to her it might have been the first time he'd heard his mortal last name.

He didn't ask her to elaborate. He whispered, "Why do you have to be Ankh? In a few days, I have to let you go."

He doused out the flame in her heart with his statement regarding their reality. She squirmed out from between Kevin and the dock and climbed up the ladder as quickly as she could. *She had to get away from him.* Kayn scrambled to collect her clothes, strewn in haste on the dock. *What was she doing? What in the hell was she doing? He wanted her and sure liked her a lot, but he didn't understand how much she loved him. How could he?* Kayn tugged her shorts back on over her damp underwear and didn't even bother with her top.

Kevin followed her back down the dock's ramp in silence before attempting to retract his statement, "Kayn. Please. Just stop for a second. Talk to me... That didn't come out right."

She paused without turning around and countered, "No. That's where you're wrong. That came out exactly right. I know you want to remember who you were and you need my help. You don't remember me and I'm still... I'm pretending you still love me. Can't you see what I'm doing? The closer we get, the harder this is going to be for me."

Kevin took her hand, held it to his heart and pleaded, "I need to remember the version of myself that was worthy of being loved by someone like you. For you to love me, I must have been good and kind. I must have been funny and probably just as strange as you are. Do you have any idea how incredible it would be to remember the guy who got to be with you? The more time I spend with you the more I want what's impossible. I want to be the guy, I can never be again. I can't be the nice, funny, sweet, wonderful guy you deserve and survive in Triad. This is my last few days to be anyone you would ever want to spend time with. If you love me, please let me feel loved by you for a few more days. We'll never have this chance again."

Kayn allowed him to tow her into his arms. She hugged him as tightly as she could. *He was afraid. Kevin was afraid of what he was going to become. He didn't have a choice. He had to assimilate or be destroyed. If he didn't allow the darkness in, there would never be the opportunity to walk into the light. She'd forgotten this was about so much more than her wounded ego and broken heart. This was survival of the fittest. She needed him to survive. If he remembered who he was before the Testing, he wouldn't. There's no way he'd mesh with the rest of his Clan psychologically. He'd take his whole Clan down with him. Kevin was asking her for two more days to pretend. She wasn't the only one pretending.* She whispered in his ear, "I understand. We're fine. Let's enjoy this time together while we have it."

Kevin held on tighter, visibly afraid to let her go. He whispered, "I must sound like a complete head case."

Kayn pulled away and repeated his words, "Being crazy isn't a deal-breaker. I do prefer to be warned upfront."

He played along, "Everyone's either crazy or boring."

She leaned in, kissed his cheek and started to walk to her cabin. She called back, "You're definitely not boring!" She heard his laughter coming from behind her as she walked away.

Chapter 35

Strange Sensations

Kayn awoke the next morning invigorated. *It was an unusual feeling. It was like she'd just downed ten cups of coffee. Something was coming.* She glanced around. Melody and Zach were already sitting on the stoop outside drinking coffee. She wandered out into the crisp morning air, asking, "Do you guys feel that?"

Zach looked up at her and said, "That's why we're up."

Kayn went back inside to get dressed. She put her hair in a ponytail, turned on the tap, cupped her hands in the stream and splashed water on her face. She looked up at her reflection. *For a split second, she could have sworn it was Chloe.* Kayn placed her palm against the mirror and smiled. *There was a time when her twin's reflection would have startled her. She was grateful to see her, even though she knew her mind was only playing tricks. Feeling her presence and seeing her thoughts wasn't the same as seeing her face. It wasn't like holding her hand or glancing over at the bed next to her, watching her sister in peaceful slumber. She needed to feel like her twin was still out there in the universe and not just dissolved into nothing like she'd never existed at all. She felt guilty whenever she thought about it. What was going on? Why would she be able to see Chloe this morning when, for so long, it was all she needed to see? Was she seeing her sister today because it was close to the end? Was this a last gift from the universe? Her reflection was once again only her own.* Before removing her hand from the mirror, she whispered, "I miss you Chloe… Every day." Kayn heard Kevin greeting her friends on the stoop and left the bathroom to go see him. Kevin was with Caleb and Leanne from Trinity. They'd all awoken with the same peculiar sense of urgency.

Caleb said what they were all thinking, "Is it the danger of the Testing we're feeling? I think we start as soon as the others come back. Call it a hunch, but it feels like that is what's going to happen. What have you guys been told?"

Kevin spoke up, "It was insinuated to us before they left for the Summit. They said they weren't allowed to give us any details."

As Kayn came down the wooden stairs, she piped in, "Ankh was basically told the same thing. We know the Testing is coming. They just couldn't give us any details."

Leanne interjected, "Trinity was told the same thing."

Kevin locked eyes with Kayn as he suggested, "Maybe, our anxiety over the end of the week together and the Testing is being amplified because we're all in the same place?"

"These feelings mean imminent danger," Melody asserted.

Kayn sat on the stairs, saying, "Maybe they're coming back early? Maybe it's something else entirely but we're sitting ducks with only a few of us Enlightened. We should stay together and wait it out?"

Kevin squeezed onto the stairs beside her and suggested, "If it is the Testing and they're coming back early, we should take the opportunity to tie up loose ends. Maybe we should just enjoy the time we have left together?"

He was giving them a slightly altered version of the speech he'd given her last night. She watched Kevin's mannerisms as he spoke to the group. *He was destined to be a leader. She could see it in him. He had to leave her side to become the man he was meant to be. She didn't feel like she was supposed to be a leader. She felt like she was supposed to be more than she was now but didn't have a clear picture of what her future would look like. She knew one thing for sure. This was another fork in their road.*

Kevin got up, made his way down the stairs and held out his hand. Kayn followed and her hand slid seamlessly into his. *They'd always had an instinctual friendship, but now the pull between them couldn't be denied.* Her heart whispered, *it's almost goodbye.*

Kevin squeezed her hand as he declared, "Whatever is coming for us, is still coming, regardless of whether or not we've eaten breakfast. I for one, would prefer to die with a full stomach."

They silently agreed by wandering in a pack to the dining hall, picking up a few stragglers on the trail. They entered as a unified group of teenagers. They sat together, joking around and laughing, making a valiant attempt to act like everything was normal, even though they knew it wasn't. *It was in the unspoken sentiment behind every smile. Time was up. They would become enemies. It was hard to imagine a shift from this to that.* Kayn was the first one to say the words,

"Why does this have to change? Can't we just refuse to fight each other?"

Caleb placed his hand on top of Kayn's and said, "In a perfect world."

Kevin gave her a look she couldn't quite place. *There was both sadness and resolve in his eyes. She knew what she'd suggested was impossible.* Stephanie touched Kevin's shoulder. He looked into her eyes and nodded. They were having a coded conversation based on what she'd said. *It felt like the couple of feet she sat away from Kevin had become miles.* Kayn turned to look at Zach and Melody. *Her love for Kevin had removed her from their trio. She needed to be closer to them today. It was as though the feelings of urgency had disappeared for everyone but her. They all blew it off and went on with their morning.*

After breakfast, they made their way in a group to the lake. They all stripped off their clothes to jump into the moderately chilly water.

Caleb from Trinity loudly announced, "Wait a second!" He jumped in first. As he surfaced, his eyes became a brilliant hue. He slowly spun in the water, moving his arms back and forth. He grinned as he pulled himself back onto the dock and declared, "Now, jump in!"

They all leapt in, hooting with wild teenage abandon. *The water's temperature had been changed. It was wonderful and much warmer than it had been. If she could have picked a perfect temperature, this would be it.* "Okay, that's a really cool gift. Couldn't you have done it a few days ago," Kayn sputtered as she bobbed to the surface of the lake, that no longer made her skin feel anything but wonderful.

Caleb chuckled, "I did. How do you it think it warmed up so fast? I never understood the purpose until we came here. I honestly felt pretty ripped off in the gift department."

Kayn swam closer to him and said, "I've already frozen in water and died once. I think that's an incredible gift. Our Clan doesn't have anyone who can do that. It definitely would have come in handy."

Kevin swam over, pointing out, "Your Clan has one, Kayn. I bet Caleb can start fires too?"

"No, not yet. Nothing out of the water," Caleb replied. "Maybe, I need to learn how?"

"You can warm up an entire lake," Kayn pointed out as she swam past him. "That is pretty damn cool."

"Well, I showed you mine," Caleb teased, doggie paddling in place.

"I wish I had something to show but I don't have anything yet," Kayn replied, floating on her back. "I can move a mean saltshaker across a table but that's about it. I'm going to get my butt kicked in this Testing. Whatever and whenever it is." She submerged herself under the water, and as she opened her eyes, she saw a boy she recognised as one of the Trinity. He was hovering in front of her. His neck opened into slits resembling gills and he swam away as fluidly as the water, with movements as graceful as a fish. Kayn had gazed into the boy's eyes for only a split second, and it was like he'd mentally convinced her to attempt to breathe. She sputtered to the surface, gagging. Kevin came to her aid, patting her back until she stopped choking. She coughed a last time and sputtered out, "That guy had gills like a fish."

Caleb laughed and explained, "That's David. He can also do a weird mental power of suggestion thing."

Kayn grasped her throat as she declared, "I'd say so." *She was still recovering from his shenanigans.*

Caleb repeated his earlier question, "Well? What can you do Kevin? You are the Prince of Triad. I bet it's something good."

She hadn't realised they referred to Kevin as the Prince of Triad. He was the Prince of Triad, wasn't he? He was the Prince of Triad and she was a foot soldier.

"I see memories," Kevin admitted. "I've been told I may have other abilities, but I haven't figured them out."

He could have just taken whatever he wanted from her. He didn't even need her to play along. Kayn stated the obvious, "Why haven't you tried to look at mine?"

His eyes softened as he answered, "I did try to look at yours. I couldn't see anything."

Kayn smiled. *Granny Winnie had probably done something to block her grandson from seeing more than he was ready too.* Melody was sitting on the dock, dangling her legs in the water. She was listening to their conversation but not participating. People had begun climbing out to sit in the sun.

Swimming to the dock, Caleb held on by Melody, enquiring, "What about you, Mel? What can you do?"

Mel smiled, for she had the most coveted gift of all. She questioned, "Does anyone have a knife?"

They were all swimming in their underwear. Nobody would have a weapon.

Stephanie piped in, "I've got one."

Melody laughed, "Of course you do."

"Where could you possibly be keeping a knife in what you're wearing?" Zach chuckled from his spot beside Mel on the dock.

Stephanie seductively whispered, "Wouldn't you like to know?"

"Oh, I definitely want to know," Zach flirtatiously sparred.

Grinning, Stephanie carefully revealed a tiny dagger hidden in the lining of her bra.

"I'm so copying that idea," Melody declared. "That's absolutely brilliant."

Stephanie handed the tiny dagger to Melody, who stared at it and questioned. "One is the symbol for Triad. I know that, but what does this other one mean? I swear I've seen this somewhere before." Stephanie shrugged, suggesting she had no idea. Mel placed the blade against her thigh and sliced into her flesh. A thin strip of blood seeped from the oozing wound. She reached into the water, rinsed it away and it was healed.

Almost being friendly and personable, Stephanie said, "You're a Healer. Now that is the coolest gift to have."

"What about you?" Melody asked as she handed Stephanie her knife.

"I'm whatever I want to be," Stephanie proclaimed. She leapt into the water and a piece of driftwood bobbed to the surface.

Awestruck, Melody whispered, "That is crazy. I was under the impression that a Shapeshifter could only shift into another living, breathing being?"

The wood stretched and distorted until Stephanie reappeared in its place. The feisty Triad hauled herself back up onto the dock in her human form and smiled as she answered Melody's question, "I think everyone was under that impression. I'm not even sure Shapeshifter is the right name for my ability."

"Does it hurt?" Zach asked, genuinely concerned.

Stephanie answered honestly, "Not anymore."

Zach butt-scooted to the edge of the dock. He dangled his feet into the water, declaring, "I'd like to play along but I have no idea what I am. I haven't been Enlightened yet either."

"It's all good, Zach. Neither have I," Patrick, the gentle eyed Triad, disclosed as he shifted to sit closer. The two boys looked at each other, finding a connection in the unknown.

Kayn swam over to Zach and Patrick, feeling a kinship to those left behind. *They were the underdogs of each Clan. Would there ever be a time in her life or afterlife when she didn't feel like she was less than the others?*

They carried on bonding and goofing off for the entire day until late afternoon. Kevin and Kayn left the others to be alone. *If this was the end and the Testing was upon them, there was nowhere she'd rather be but right here, with Kevin, lying in their field. She now thought of it as their field.* They watched bees and held buttercups to their chins.

Stretching in the grass, Kayn pointed out, "Well, your girlfriend seems to have calmed down a touch."

Rolling over, Kevin gazed into her eyes and whispered, "She's not my girlfriend Kayn."

Shifting onto her side, Kayn whispered back, "You're sleeping with her. She's in your Clan. Isn't that close enough?"

"In retrospect, it wasn't my greatest idea," he whispered while tucking a ringlet behind her ear. There was a moment of silence before he asked, "You actually had feelings for him?"

She knew he was talking about Frost. Kayn answered honestly, "I'm not going to lie to you and say I didn't."

He remarked, "His motives are always so painfully transparent. He can't love you like you deserve to be loved."

"There hasn't ever been a lineup for the job," she sparred.

Kevin replied, "There should have been."

Against her will, her eyes blurred with tears. She didn't want him to see her reaction, so she began plucking grass out of the ground. *He was staring at her.* She tugged a buttercup from the dirt and wistfully plucked off its petals. Knowing he was anticipating eye contact, she purposely looked away. *She had to keep looking away.* She closed her eyes to dispose of her tears and rolled over to look at the clouds. *It was almost over. Time was almost up on their vacation from the real world. She had to start shifting reality back to normal.*

"This week with you is going to stay with me for a long time," he confessed.

She turned from the calming blue sky and their eyes met. *Their fingertips were almost touching.* They inched closer and their fingers intertwined. *She'd lived this moment in a dream.* Their lips met under the warmth of the sun. As they parted, Kayn confessed, "It's going to stay with me too." Her hand rapidly heated. Kevin grabbed his chest. In an instant, they were running to where they'd been summoned. *One of their own was in trouble. That was all they needed to know.* They sprinted into the forest, driven by instinct. With no thought of each other, they kept equal pace. *One of her Ankh was in trouble. Zach or Melody? She couldn't tell.* Her mind was shrieking, *help them! Find them!* Intuition prompted their feet to the fastest route as they left the cleared trail and went directly through the bushes with their arms shielding the stinging branches from their eyes. The unforgiving brush whipped and sliced their flesh as they powered through and burst into a clearing. They saw the rodeo grounds and just knew as they sprinted for it. She heard repetitive footsteps. The crunching of grass and shuffling of gravel and dirt. *They weren't alone. Immortals from all three Clans were coming to the rescue of their fallen. She didn't have to look. She sensed their presence.* They glanced at each other mid-stride as they all raised their hands at the closed gate ahead. With the sheer force of combined energy, it flew open, revealing a sight none anticipated.

Chapter 36

One For All And All For One

They stopped cold to see what they were up against. The grounds were surrounded by empty grandstands. Kayn was vibrating with adrenaline amidst the other Newbie immortals at the gates. On the far side of the open dusty grounds, bound to the furthest wall was one member of each Clan. They'd been beaten to a bloody pulp and suspended. *It was Patrick, Melody and Leanne.* Blocking the path to their wounded were ten people. In the middle was a vaguely familiar man with an ominous presence, wearing jeans and a tight grey t-shirt.

He hollered from where he stood, "So glad you could join us! You've all met so introductions won't be necessary!"

Without fear, they marched towards the strangers who assaulted their people. Standing before Kayn was a boy she hadn't thought of in ages. *Why was he here? How? What was this?* She looked at Kevin with wide, panicked eyes and whispered, "Kevin, we know the guy in the green shirt. His name is Jesse. He's from our school. The girl in the orange is your cousin, Ana. I've seen her in pictures at your house. We all went camping once. What is this?"

Looking at his blood relative with no recognition, Kevin said, "It's a good thing my memory is wiped, isn't it?"

Kayn sensed Zach and glanced to her side. *He'd been stricken to his emotional core.* Concerned, she followed his gaze. *The boy standing before him bore a striking resemblance.*

Zach numbly explained, "My brother is here. He's dead. I saw his body... He's dead."

They all appeared to be having a similar moment. They were probably all looking at someone pivotal from their mortal lives.

A fearless leader by birthright, Kevin marched ahead of the rest, commanding, "Explain yourself. You have five seconds."

With every sense vibrating, Kayn followed. She jumped as the giant gate slammed and locked behind them. *None of the others looked back. She was the only one startled by the noise. Everyone else seemed powerful and fearless.* Kayn reached for Zach's hand, and he took it without hesitation. She shared her epiphany, "Is this is the beginning of the Testing?"

"I have to fight my dead brother," Zach said with cold resolve.

Was she going to fight Jesse? What could the divine purpose of this be? Kayn whispered, "We had a moment before I got together with Kevin. He's just a guy from my school. Mine doesn't make sense." As a united front, the teens marched towards the group of friends and family until they were ten feet away.

Squeezing her hand, Zach whispered, "I have a feeling Mel is safer hanging on the wall than we are fighting whatever they are. She'll be healed before this is over."

The older man's pupils darkened to onyx orbs. He bulked up, gaining fifty pounds of muscle instantly. His shirt ripped apart. He smiled and announced, "We thought it was high time you all had the opportunity to meet our newest Abaddon."

Zach squeezed her hand and whispered, "See, I was right. The Abaddon get teenagers too. They're going to kick our asses to next Tuesday."

"Not mine," Stephanie boldly declared as she marched up to stand beside Kevin. Her shirt bulged and her black stretchy shorts tore at their limit as she bulked up, growing three feet upwards and outwards in a flash.

On the inside, Stephanie was not tiny at all. What was she? She'd shown them she could turn into a log. Was she able to copy this man?

"Well, maybe not her ass," Zach acknowledged.

Her voice deepened as she growled, "Father! Let them go!"

She hadn't seen that plot twist coming.

Stephanie's father threw a knife with professional precision at Patrick's stomach. He cried out in agony as blood sputtered from his mouth. *It was on! Nobody hurts Patrick!* Tri-Clan attacked their Abaddon counterparts. Still confused as to why he'd been selected to fight her, Kayn ran at Jesse. He grabbed her, swung her around and tossed her like she was little more than a rag doll. As her body took flight with a surge of whooshing air, she soared a good twenty feet thinking, *this is going to suck.* She braced herself for impact, hitting the ground on her back with an echoing thud. The wind was knocked from her lungs. *She couldn't breathe. Her chest was on fire.* Stunned, she knew there was only a split second to rise. She heard the echo of Lexy's training in her mind. Her shrill, commanding tone repeated the words, s*tand up, Kayn! Get up!* Her nerve endings rang with intense need to fight, *broken bones be damned.* Writhing in the dirt, Kayn struggled to her knees. While gasping for breath, she took a savage blow to her torso as he booted her in the stomach. She crumpled again, choking on her own blood. She spat it on the dirt in front of her. *Now!* Chloe's voice screeched, *get up, Kayn! Get the hell up! Get off the ground or you're finished!* A fine mist of someone else's blood sprayed her face and speckled the dirt before her. *They were being massacred.* Her ears flooded with the sounds of brutality as she struggled to her knees again. Chloe cheered her on in her mind. *That's right, Kayn! That's good! Stand up! Kick his ass!* Her injuries were serious. Her lungs seared with burning fire each time she endeavoured to breathe. Her attacker allowed her a moment to recover. She managed to make it to her feet. Her twin's voice screamed, *kick him in the head!* Kayn swung around on autopilot. Her kick landed its mark with expert precision.

Jesse staggered backwards before regaining his faculties. He sparred, "Is that the best you can do?"

They were so much stronger. The boy from her past grinned as he came at her. Kayn hauled off and slapped him squarely across the face.

Taken aback, Jesse provoked, "Seriously? I expected more from you. You fight like a little kid."

She switched it up, landing a finger-breaking punch. *He barely reacted.*

He rubbed his jaw, chuckling, "Now, that's more like it."

Her peripheral vision was distracting. Blood was spurting from someone being savagely beaten. A fine red mist filled the air and gushed from another person's throat next to her. Everything was happening so quickly that it was impossible to distinguish friend from foe. All she could see was repetitive red, chunky spray and bodies in flight. Some of her peers were holding their own, but others were in a similar situation. *The last punch she'd taken had done serious damage.* Lightheaded from blood loss, she struggled for a breath. *She couldn't focus on her assailant. There were three of him in front of her. That can't be good.* He swung. She managed to dodge all three blurry fists. *What was different about him? Hair. Jesse had hair now.* He punched her in the stomach. Her legs buckled and she dropped to her knees. *This sucked.* Lost in dust rising around her, she blinked away the irritation. Her eyes teared up to battle the sediment in the air. She focused in on him just as another cloud of dust and blood spatter clouded her vision. Jesse flipped her over and sat on her chest, pinning her shoulders to the ground.

Through the confusion of the rising veil of earth and arterial spray, he justified his actions, "Imagine my surprise when after six months of thinking you were dead, you texted me. You told me you were alive and that you were in trouble. You needed me and I came without question like a damn fool without telling anyone where I was going. I met you in the trails behind what used to be your house. You were alive. I couldn't believe it. I ran to you and we embraced. It took me a second to notice something was off. You stabbed me in the stomach repeatedly until I lost count. I woke up somewhere I could never have imagined in my worst nightmares. I thought I was in hell. I was told I was only halfway there but there was a chance for redemption if I killed you."

Kayn gasped through laboured attempts to breathe, "You know that wasn't me. I'm not evil… Abaddon is."

With cold resolve, Jesse wrapped his hands around her throat, whispering, "If I don't do this, I have to go back. From what I understand, you can't die. It isn't permanent. This is my Testing, not yours." He kissed her lips, disclosing, "I've wanted to do that for years. I have to kill you. I don't have a choice." He tightened his hands around her throat and pushed his knees into her broken ribs.

Brains before brawn. As her vision flickered due to lack of oxygen, Kayn kneed him in the groin. He recoiled and she rolled out from under him. With a well-timed burst of adrenaline, she thrust down, elbowing his throat with the full weight of her body, crushing his larynx. She collapsed on top of him while managing to choke out a few final words, "You always have a choice." She struggled to breathe, but no dice. The world shifted. Her vision flickered and the lights went out.

Chapter 37

If You Lick Toads You Can Time Travel

Kayn could hear the noises of early morning. She embraced the scent of Saturday. *She could smell coffee, bacon and perfume.* She opened her eyes and found herself back in her childhood bedroom. Her heart leapt at the sight of the purple walls. There were crumbled sheets on the bed beside her. She looked at her hands. *They were smaller.* She swung her legs over the side of her bed. They almost touched the floor, but not quite. On the carpet beside her feet were her sheep slippers. She'd been maybe twelve when she'd grown out of those slippers. She smiled as she slipped her feet in. *No, she was younger than eleven. They were too big for her feet. She knew what this meant. This meant they were all still alive.* Kayn left the slippers and wandered past the closet to the bathroom barefoot. *Someone was shuffling around. It was Chloe! She was in there.* Holding her breath, Kayn opened the door. *Please be Chloe. Please, be there.* She startled her twin. Chloe was giving her crap for it, but she didn't care. She just stood there with tears of joy streaming down her face. She dashed into her twin's arms.

"What's wrong with you?" Chloe laughed, "I can't breathe, you crazy dork!"

Kayn held on for dear life, sobbing, "You died! Mom and Dad died! Matty too! You all died!"

Chloe stroked her hair and reassured, "You had a bad dream, that's all. It was just a bad dream."

Kayn clung to her sister, afraid if she let her go, she'd wake up. She whispered, "How old are we?"

Chloe struggled to get away, teasing, "How insane are you this morning? You're choking me. You're ten going on certifiable and you're freaking me out. That must have been one hell of a dream."

Kayn took a chance, allowing her sister to struggle free from her stranglehold of an embrace. She exhaled and Chloe was still with her. She glanced at her reflection. *She was still chubby. This was the age where she started to run. She'd started running because she didn't look exactly like her twin anymore. Someone at school had called her the fat one. She'd never felt equal to her twin after that day. Truth be told, she'd never been her equal. Chloe had abilities.* Kayn stared at their duplicate reflection. *She wasn't fat. She'd always recalled feeling obese. She had ten pounds on her twin, if that. That comment would have never slipped from anyone's lips if she wasn't supposed to be the mirror image of somebody else. She hadn't even told Kevin about being called the fat one. If she was right, it was today that she decided to change it. This was the year they began to grow apart. It was her. She'd taken the first step away from her sister. She'd reversed history in her mind.*

She heard her father's voice, "Hurry up, you two! We're starving! Get your butts down here!"

Chloe ran ahead of her. *She'd always been ahead of her. Only now did Kayn notice that she'd always allowed her to be first.*

Chloe yelled, "We're coming! Kayn's being weird!"

She'd told on her. Kayn loved her sister but she was always tattling about something. Chloe skipped down the hall. Kayn followed her but slowed as she passed by the pictures. *They were exactly as they'd always been. Even the plush rose-hued carpet felt the same under her toes.* Kayn grabbed the wooden railing, sliding her hand along as she walked downstairs until she felt the bump from the knot halfway down. She loosened her grip a touch, allowing it to slide under her palm. The stairs creaked in the right spots as she stepped off the bottom one into the entrance where her mother had died. *Don't think about that right now,* she told herself. *You are going to hug your parents and your brother again.* She followed her sister into the kitchen. The floor beneath her feet changed to a cool, smooth surface. Her parents were standing with their backs to her as she entered the room. Her dad was pouring the coffee, humming a happy tune. *She couldn't quite place it.* Her mom was stirring the hash browns in the frying pan.

Her mom looked at her, smiled as she scooped out a scraper full of hash browns and questioned, "How hungry are you? Are you a tiny bit hungry, medium hungry or as hungry as a Troll under a bridge waiting to gobble up Billy goats?"

"Medium hungry," Kayn replied. Her mom breezed past where she was seated and plopped a pile of hash browns on her plate.

Matty appeared behind her and said, "For the record. We're getting a little old for the serving size Billy goat references. I'm absolutely famished." Her mother stood there waiting for him to say it right. Matt sighed, "I'm as hungry as ten Billy goats."

She smiled and plopped double the serving on his plate. *Matty always had a crazy metabolism. He could eat a damn horse if he wanted to.*

Chloe declared, "I'm medium hungry."

As her mother put Chloe's serving on her plate, Kayn began to tear up. *She couldn't help it. She'd never truly appreciated how weird and wonderful her family was until it was too late.*

Her dad went to walk past her. Sensing her distress, he placed his coffee down, gave her an enormous bear hug and said, "You're having a blue morning. Chin up, love monkey."

Kayn sobbed uncontrollably. *She couldn't stop. Her heart was drowning in grief. Being granted the simplest moment of normalcy was too much for her to take.* Matty touched her leg with his foot under the table instead of kicking her as per usual. She tried to eat, but her chest kept heaving. The tears kept flowing. *She was safe. They'd all been safe. She'd never feel that way again.* Her mom smiled lovingly as she walked around the table to embrace her. Kayn's heart was on overload. *This wasn't her life anymore. People hurt her now. They physically hurt her.*

Chloe whispered the explanation for Kayn's weepy morning, "Kayn had a bad dream. All of us were dead."

Her mom whispered against her hair, "I promise you we're not going anywhere until you're old and grey."

She was dying to scream 'liars!' but her lips knew better. *There was no point. This was only a dream.* She sucked back her tears and gulped down her sobs. *She only had a moment with her family to pretend she was safe and loved.* Obnoxiously loud, rhythmic knocks on the glass patio door snapped her out of her pity party. *There he was in a striped shirt with his mass of wavy dark hair... Kevin.* She smiled, but not a 'glad to see you' smile. It was a 'the sight of you has made this journey back in time complete' smile.

Her father unlocked the door, slid it open and announced, "Mr. Smith, I'm so glad you could find the time to stop by, at seven o'clock in the morning on a Saturday. Did you walk all the way over here by yourself?"

Kevin ditched his shoes, strolled over to the one empty spot at the table and sat down. He declared, "I didn't walk. I rode my bike, Mr. Brighton."

Kayn's mother always left enough for Kevin in the frying pan. She didn't even ask. She just served him, smiling. Kevin began to eat. Kayn watched him in silence. *Every annoying habit he had was magnified, yet still wonderful.* They all sat around the table listening as Kevin filled her father in on why they were all going into the woods today to lick toads.

Her father probed, "Where in the hell would you even get an idea like that, Kevin?"

Kevin replied, "Clay told me he was watching Animal Planet and that if you lick the right toad, you can time travel."

Matt almost spit his breakfast all over as the table erupted in laughter.

Someone else knocked on the patio door. *There stood ten-year-old Jesse. She'd been right. She knew which day she was in now. She'd had a crush on Jesse since kindergarten. Kevin was her best friend and Jesse was her first crush. He'd been nice to her. Come to think of it, he had always been nice to her. That was about to change. Jesse had ended her week of peer-induced hell with a bang.* They excused themselves from the table and put on their shoes with every intention of dashing through the wet grass into the muddy trails on the outskirts of their backyard in search of toads. Kayn hugged both of her parents and told them she loved them before she left. *She had no idea when this dream was going to end. She didn't want anything to be left unsaid.* Kevin and Chloe had already disappeared into the trail when Kayn caught up with Jesse. *He'd waited for her.*

Her father called after them, "Promise me you will not actually lick any toads!"

Kayn yelled, "I won't lick any! I know Chloe won't for sure, but I can't promise Kevin won't!" She heard her father's laughter as he shut the door. Kayn strolled beside Jesse into the woods. It was always extremely cool after it rained. You could hear the echoes of crickets, frogs and toads everywhere. Her shoe got stuck in the mud. When she yanked her foot, it came out of her shoe. After making an awkward attempt at balancing on one foot, she teetered over in the mud with her sock on. It made a disgusting squishing sound. "Oh, that was so gross," she complained.

"Nah, it's not that gross," Jesse chuckled. He squatted in the muck, gallantly yanked her muddy sock off and directed, "Balance on that one. Hold onto me while you take off the other one."

Squeamish as her barefoot sunk into the gooey mud, Kayn took her other sock off and noticed Jesse had done the same.

"I'm not into kissing toads today," Jesse admitted. "This will be way more fun."

Both of Kayn's feet were submerged in the goo, and she was smiling so hard that her cheeks hurt. "I'd forgotten some of the details about this day," she noted aloud.

Jesse laughed, enquiring, "You forgot about this day?"

"Never mind," Kayn replied, grinning as mud squished between her toes.

Her sister's voice scolded, "What are you doing?"

"I lost my shoe in the mud," Kayn explained.

Disgusted, Chloe replied, "So, you took both of your shoes off and just covered yourselves in mud... Sick."

Kevin appeared with a toad in his hands. He shoved it in her face so she would kiss it. Kayn toppled backwards into the mud with a splat. *Now, she was gross.* Kayn sighed, "I better go inside and change. I'll be right back." She stood up and trudged back to the house, knowing what was going to happen next.

Feeling guilty, Kevin followed her, pleading, "Don't tell on me. I'll have to go home."

Just before the door, Kayn stopped to look back at the trails, just as she had on that day so long ago. Her sister's lips were on Jesse's. *It was an innocent kiss. A simple peck on the lips but it was loyalty she appreciated more than anything else. To her, Jesse had just chosen her sister. This week had been a rough one on her young, untainted heart.* She gave Kevin a peck on the cheek and vowed, "I never tell on you."

Chapter 38

Until We Meet Again

A voice called to her. It seemed to be echoing, travelling through her subconscious from the end of a long tunnel. *Wake up Kayn.* She gasped as her senses exploded. As her vision came into focus, she saw Melody's face. She was kneeling above her. *She'd obviously healed her. What happened?* Her mind fought its way out of the foggy haze while hearing echoing, confusing voices in the proximity to where she'd awoken. Her vision sharpened. *There was a pile of dead bodies right next to her.* She recalled the brutal reunion with her childhood friend. *If this was their Immortal Testing, they'd all flunked with flying colours, mostly red. There was a crazy amount of blood soaked into everyone's clothes.*

"You took quite a savage beating," Mel observed.

Kayn's head pounded as she croaked, "You should see the other guy."

As Melody helped her up, she exclaimed, "He's long gone. They all are. At least your boyfriend had the clarity of mind to cut me down before he passed out."

Kayn struggled to her feet. As she teetered backwards, she felt someone steady her and knew who it was without looking. *It was the one person who'd always been there to catch her. The realisation hit her. This was why they'd been separated by fate. He needed to become a leader and she had to learn to stand on her own. Their separation was necessary.*

"Don't feel bad, everyone got their asses handed to them today," Kevin chuckled.

Melody clarified, "Except for these two. They were the only ones still technically alive when I came to. I healed them first and then you. I'm not sure what to do now. We don't have another Healer. This will take me days to do all alone. I'm ready to pass out."

"All you need is energy, right?" Kayn enquired.

Mel began to pace. The dust her footsteps created obscured their vision. She stopped moving as she replied, "Judging by the size of this pile of bodies, I'd say useable energy is in short supply right now."

It was overwhelming as the dust settled, revealing the morbid display. The bodies of their friends had been towed into one area for Mel's healing convenience. Their eyes were glazed over and each one appeared to be staring off into the distance. *They were probably all in the In-between having a slushy Margarita. It clicked, Zach would be alone because he was Ankh and they were both already alive.* Kayn knelt in front of Zach and lovingly closed his eyes with her fingers. *It felt like the respectful thing to do. The already awakened were not the slightest bit concerned. Death was only a temporary situation. They were all Tri-Clan. It was just inconvenient.*

Mel scanned the bodies, "I really am the only Healer, aren't I? If there was another one, they'd be awake by now."

"You're the only one I know of," Kevin acknowledged.

Battling a wicked, 'it sucks that you died,' migraine, Kayn stated, "I thought we had a truce."

Stephanie replied, "With each other. Apparently, there was fine print. There's always fine print."

"Steph, did you call the guy in the grey shirt, Dad?" Kevin questioned.

"You've heard the story. Tiberius won me in a card game," she explained. "Let's just say, he wasn't father of the year."

Stephanie's father was Abaddon. She still didn't understand how everything worked. Kayn had her first moment of empathy for Stephanie. *She didn't know what was worse. To know you were adored and then lose it, or to have never been cherished at all.*

Melody began healing Zach. She was only half done when she began to look like she was struggling.

Kayn offered, "Take the rest of the energy that you need to heal Zach from me."

"That's a brilliant idea," Kevin exclaimed. "What if you took a little bit of energy from each of us, until you've healed everyone? After we've pass out, take a touch of energy back from the ones you heal right after us. Take mine first. There's barely a scratch on me."

Kayn attempted small talk with her Triad nemesis, "How old were you when Tiberius won you?"

Stephanie replied, "I was fifteen. I watched them playing cards for a while before I went to bed. I heard them making bets, but I thought it was a joke. Later that night, Tiberius woke me up. He told me he won me in a card game and that he could save me from Abaddon. I've been with Triad ever since."

He was visibly upset. Kevin had obviously never heard the full story before. This was a confusing situation. He was lying if he said he had no feelings for Stephanie. Kayn felt guilty. *Of course, she'd been acting crazy. She'd walked back into his life and taken him away.* Mel began taking Stephanie's energy. *Out of all of them, the feisty Triad had grown the most this week. She was giving of herself in only one week's time.* They gathered around as they took turns fuelling Mel's healing ability until all three were unconscious.

With a sense of déjà vu, Kayn awoke for the second time that day in darkness instead of sunshine in the middle of the rodeo grounds. She sat up and looked around. The ones who were awake were patiently waiting for others to heal. As they awoke, they helped each other to their feet. *Kevin was still out cold.* Kayn knelt before Kevin and gently caressed his face. *She'd seen him sleeping a million times before. Her mind could easily flashback to endless platonic sleepovers.* She whispered, "I can still see you asleep on my bed in nothing but your Transformer pyjamas."

Kevin cracked a grin before opening his eyes and teased, "That was not even a little bit sexy."

Kayn leaned in to kiss his cheek. He turned his head. Her lips landed on his. She pulled away, for it had been an accident. *She hadn't meant to do that in front of everyone. It jolted her heart just the same.* By the look in his eyes it equally shook his. Kayn whispered, "We have an audience."

"Who cares," he toyed, throwing caution to the wind by pulling her lips to his and kissing her again. Their kiss deepened as he darted his tongue. They were fully making out when they heard applause and abruptly pulled away from each other. She got up first and held her hand out. He appeared confused as he took it. *He hadn't known she meant they had an actual audience capable of mass applause.* He was still weak as she helped him stand. They were no longer separated by Clan as they left the rodeo grounds. They walked back to the campsite as a single herd of partially immortal teens. Kayn looked to either side of her, seeing strength, friendship and unity. *They'd each shared of themselves to save the other.* Kevin was by her side as they pushed their way through the bushes. She revealed, "I had a dream about you."

He poked her and teased, "I hope it was a good one?"

"We were ten. It was you, Chloe and believe it or not, that Jesse guy was there," she disclosed as they burst out into the playground by the swing set. It had been there the whole time in front of the dining hall. Everyone else kept walking into the building as they stayed with the urge to make use of the swings.

"The Jesse guy that murdered you?" Kevin confirmed.

She was grinning as she replied, "It didn't make sense that he was there. I had a childhood crush on him. We were all hanging out one day and he kissed Chloe. After that I just let the idea go. That's not even what I woke up thinking about." Kayn sat on one of the swings.

Kevin gallantly offered, "Allow me." He gave her a giant push and ran underneath her legs, mid-swing. He climbed into the swing next to her and caught up with a few leg pumps.

They were swinging at the same height, in time with one another and she caught herself wishing he could remember the hundreds of times they'd done this.

He asked, "Was that the whole story?"

"No… No, it wasn't," Kayn answered. "You were trying to force me to kiss a toad. I fell in the mud. You thought I would tell on you. I kissed your cheek and told you that I'd never tell on you."

He started to laugh, "I wish I could remember this stuff. From an outside point of view, we sound like really weird kids."

She reminisced before replying, "We were the weirdest kids on the planet but it was amazing."

Zach stuck his head out of the door, looking for them. Kayn leapt off her swing and grabbed a hold of Kevin's to slow him down. She ended up swinging him around in a circle. *He was a lot heavier than he'd been when they'd done this last.* They wandered over to the others, sensing this might be one of their final meals together.

The next day was spent as a group, sitting on the beach, laughing and joking around. *They'd all but forgotten that they were supposed to be enemies. The fight against the Abaddon had unified them.*

In that last week, there had been many moments when Kayn thought perhaps Kevin was beginning to remember his past. *A certain look in his eye. A quick flash of recognition that would only be noticed if one paid attention. It was wishful thinking. She knew this now. She'd become attached to this new version of him by default. She was going to miss the way he made her feel. She loved him anyway. This was what had been determined by her heart.*

On their final night around the bonfire, they stared longingly at each other through the embers that flickered as a wall between them. *It felt like a hint at what was to come.* The veil of flames kept obscuring the details of his face. *Time was up. She could feel it.* Each time the embers popped amidst crackling flames she heard the countdown to goodbye. Kevin kept glancing at her in the middle of conversations with other people, smiling and making goofy faces. *When he did these things, she could clearly see her version of who he'd once been. They'd created some wonderful memories this week. It was ironic that life was most beautiful when the sand from the hourglass was almost empty and time was up. She wasn't the only one at this campfire sensing the sand in the hourglass was almost gone.* Kevin was still making faces at her. *He wasn't helping her persuade herself to stay on this side of the fire.* She grabbed a beer from the cooler and sat down beside him instead.

"Want to go for a walk?" He mouthed silently.

Her heart opened her lips and whispered, "Sure." They strolled side by side, with their fingers intimately laced as they made their way to the dock that had become a special place. The sound of their footsteps shuffling barefoot down the path, magically mixed with a cricket's farewell serenade as brilliant fireflies danced through the night sky above. *These were nature's fireworks. A final farewell.* Music was playing faintly in the background, adding a romantic touch to the moment. Everything had fallen into place to create a beautiful goodbye. The dock was lit by one lone torch flickering in the moonlight. Warm summer rain began sprinkling from above. They stood motionless, staring into each other's eyes barefoot on the weathered wooden dock. Kevin lovingly caressed her cheek. Her heart ached as he trailed his fingers into the spiralling curls framing her face. Both of their minds were chanting in unison, *one final kiss.* He took her in his arms. He pulled away, and as their eyes met, it felt like they were gazing into each other's souls. *Don't leave. Come back to me.* Her heart willed him to hear her silent prayer. His lips edged closer to hers, and as they met in the softest, gentlest, most beautiful submergence of souls, her heart overflowed with joy she'd never known. Her inhibitions loosened as the length of his lean, muscular body melted against hers. Her lips parted as she submitted to his final passionate attempt to know her more intimately by allowing his hands to roam past fabric to silken skin. His experienced hands knew where to touch her. He explored the places that caused soft sighs to escape from her slightly parted lips. She closed her eyes in bliss, and as she opened them, they met his. *He still questioned his instinctual response to her.* As they drew apart, Kayn asked, "You really don't remember how you felt about me? Not anything? Nothing at all?"

Brushing damp curls away from her face, Kevin said, "I would give anything to keep getting to know you. My mind may not remember you, but my heart does. You feel like home."

She allowed him to pull her back into his embrace. Resting her head on his shoulder, she blinked back the tears forming in her eyes. *How was she going to let him go? She knew he was in there. She'd felt it.* He kissed her cheek as salty emotional tears began trickling down. He wiped them away with a stroke of his thumb while attempting to memorise the placement of each freckle on her face, just as he'd done the last time they were forced to say goodbye. He kissed her nose, her cheek and forehead. *She couldn't take it anymore.*

Cupping her face with his hands, he urged, "The next time you see me, you're going to have to kill me. Don't hesitate. Do what you were trained to do."

That had come out of nowhere. Kayn asked, "Could you kill me?"

With agony in his eyes, he replied, "I'll have to if you're caught by Triad. Don't force my hand. Stay away from me."

She couldn't believe what he was saying. They had the rest of the night together. He wasn't even going to wait until they were certain the others were coming back before ending it. He'd already flipped the switch in his head. She was his enemy. It was done. There was nothing left to say. This was where the fantasy ended. Her heart was doused with ice water. "Goodbye Kevin," she stated and turned to face the water, unable to look at him as he walked away.

"Till we meet again," he replied.

She didn't turn around to watch him leave. She listened to his steps echo and fade as he walked from the dock to the sand. They shuffled into the grass and then the sound of him leaving her disappeared. "Till we meet again," she whispered. *She asked for this agony.* Kayn sat on the dock. She shut her eyes and stayed there for a long time, possibly hours, just listening to the sounds of night. The music still played in the distance by the fire. She dangled her feet in the cool water, knowing at one time she would have been afraid to do this. *She would have never allowed her toes to linger beneath the surface of the unknown. She would have imagined sharks, monsters and perhaps a zombie or two waiting beneath the surface, ready to pull her under. She wasn't worried now. Her mortal anxieties now seemed so pointless. Loving someone she could never be with would be pointless.* At least she hadn't allowed herself to fall blindly into the grass by the side of the lake with him. Logic had always stepped in. She'd come into this week wanting to find a way to allow her heart to move on. The first step had been to establish that Kevin, as she'd known him, was no longer there. *This was true, but the instinct to be her friend had not been erased by his grandfather, nor had the desire to covet and protect her.* She stood up to begin her short walk back to the cabin. *Could she kill him? Could he kill her? That remained to be seen. It wasn't going to be a choice. The music had stopped.* She noticed the absence of both her friends and future enemies around the fire. The extinguished blaze was a fitting visual. With the raging flames of the gathering gone, only the smallest trace of smoke still rose into the darkness. *How fast would their friendships be extinguished?* Kayn felt the urge to harness her inner Grey. She listened to the noises of the night once again. The lapping of the water against the wooden dock. There was a toad in the distance, and an owl kept asking her, *Who? Who?* It felt like a humorous metaphor describing her life. *That was the question. Who? Who was she going to become?* Till now, she'd never understood why she needed to force herself to become autonomous. It had been Kevin and Kayn or Chloe and Kayn. When she'd come to Ankh, it had almost been Frost and

Kayn. She'd always been a part of a duo. Her life was beginning anew. She didn't even know who she was without someone else. The idea of them finding each other again and ending up together against all odds had been a fantasy. It had driven her forward through a time when all she needed was a reason to put one foot in front of the other. She pretended to let him go, but her heart had always said, *Wait for him. You must wait for him.* Her mind now warned, *be done waiting. Time is precious. It's over.* She continued to walk as the owl questioned, "Who? Who?" Kayn mumbled, "I know, I know... Just me."

She lay in her bed, tossing and turning that night. Unable to shake the feeling of impending doom from her subconscious. They were all having the same restless sleep. Everyone's covers were tousled. *Something horrible was coming again. She felt it in her bones.* Kayn awoke feeling sick to her stomach. She decided to go for one last walk in the woods in desperate need of fresh air. *None of the wildlife asked her who she was this morning. Today, she knew who she was. She was Kayn of Ankh. One day, she was going to be the Conduit. Whatever that meant? She was going to survive the Testing.* As she thought the word again, she felt queasy. She looped around and was almost back at her cabin when she paused in the trails. *After his whole, 'she had to kill him the next time she saw him' speech, she felt like a stalker. They'd already said their goodbyes.* She froze instead of making her presence known as his door opened and stepped backwards into the cover of the bushes. *Now, she was acting like a stalker.* Kevin walked out onto the deck with a cup of coffee. Stephanie came up behind him and kissed his neck. She took the coffee from his hands and asked him to come back to bed. *Ouch.* She was doused by a giant splash of invisible ice water directly at her chest. She now understood the meaning of the quote, 'Let sleeping dogs lie.' Her heart felt weighted as she continued, passing the cabin where her Clan slept. *She would never mention this moment to anyone.* Her heart made a silent agreement with her mind. *This would be a lesson learned.* She kept walking down the trail, knowing she required a few extra minutes to choke on what she'd just witnessed. She came around the blind curve of the path and saw Frost walking towards her. *She wasn't upset. Nothing happened. She was fine.* Frost smiled at her and she flung herself into his arms. *This personal growth thing was obviously going to take a while.* She continued to embrace him as she said, "I'm glad you guys are back." Then she tried to put him back in the friend zone by giving his back a few sturdy pats before she let him go.

"You are, without a doubt, the strangest girl I've ever met." Frost teased.

Kayn blinked away stray tears and plastered a giant fake smile on her face. She'd mastered the Chloe pageant smile. *Frost wasn't fooled.* He looked concerned but didn't question her. She replied, "I try." They sauntered back to the cabin together to wake the others. She almost tripped on the stairs while sneaking a peek at Triad's cabin.

Grabbing her before her knees hit the steps, Frost whispered, "Chin up, or I'll start quoting country songs."

Smiling at him, Kayn assured, "I'm fine." The others were already awake. She'd never taken her clothes out of her backpack and put them into a drawer, so she was one step ahead of the others. *They were leaving the cabin. It was time to go.* She had time for a quick shower while the others packed. She heard what they were saying while standing under the pleasurable spray. Frost was telling tales of Lexy's insane bravery in the Colosseum. Kayn smiled as she dried her hair, imagining how entertaining Lexy would have been to watch. Ready for the day, Kayn came out of the bathroom to find Grey and Lexy were also there. She embraced them both. *Lexy had a strangely peaceful air about her now.* The others helped them pack their things from the cabin back to the RV. As they approached their sort of home, she realised it had been there the whole time. *They hadn't gone near it.*

Lexy opened the fridge, complaining, "You guys didn't even touch this food. The milk's outdated."

"I know. I didn't come back here. I had everything I needed at the cabin." Zach replied as he sat down at the table.

Melody added, "I'm pretty sure none of us did."

Kayn slid her backpack under the bunks in the narrow hall and sat on her bunk, thinking about how close she'd come to buying into what she wanted to believe.

"You look a little lost?" Frost said as he sat down beside her.

"No," Kayn replied, "I'm not lost... I'm found."

"So, you've worked it all out then?" he asked.

"Not everything," she confessed. She placed her hand on his, confessing, "I think I need to figure out who I am and what I am. That needs to come before anything else."

"Now, that is the most mature thing that's ever come out of your mouth," he taunted.

"Probably the last one too," Kayn admitted.

"I would hate to see you lose your wacky sense of humour," Frost teased.

"My wacky messed-up sense of humour is probably my saving grace," Kayn replied.

"It's definitely mine," Frost chuckled.

He reached over, and it felt like he was going to pull her to him. He plucked a rather large leaf out of her hair and placed it in her open palm. She looked at it, smiling. *She always felt like an unkempt mess. Frost taking large random things out of her mass of curly hair really didn't help. She'd just had a shower. It must have fallen from a tree and landed in her hair on the walk back. She could easily picture Frost continuing to pluck surprising and increasingly humiliating things out of her hair. All she wanted was about five minutes of cool. Five minutes in her entire life. Was that really too much to ask? Five minutes where she didn't have to feel like a big clumsy dork.* She met Frost's eyes, knowing he didn't see her that way. *He always looked at her like he was watching something miraculous.*

"All seriously wacky conversations aside, I'm happy to see you," Frost whispered.

She smiled as she laid her head on his shoulder. *Some things could be replied to without words.*

"Okay, you two. Break it up," Grey jokingly scolded as he pulled back the curtain and found Kayn's head on Frost's shoulder.

"Sorry to disappoint you. It's completely innocent. We're just friends." Kayn teased.

Pretending to be struck in the heart by something, Frost laughed, "I'm joking! Just kidding!"

Grey sat on the other side of her and took Kayn's hand in his, knowing she was upset. *He was intuitive.* Kayn smiled. *She had two of her favourite guys, offering her comfort at the same time.* The curtain pulled back again.

Lexy began to laugh, "I'm not saying a word."

Kayn giggled and sat up straight, still holding Grey's hand. It didn't last for long because Lexy jumped on the bunk, pinned Grey to the mattress and baited, "While we're speaking of bone headed moves born of necessity. You didn't get a chance to tell me about your naughty deeds the night before we left, but I heard it through the grapevine."

"Seriously, Frost? Did you broadcast it?" Grey sighed.

"Not from Frost, you schmuck," Lexy harassed. "You had relations in public. Making a list of who didn't see you would be a lot shorter."

Frost scowled and complained, "Why does everyone always automatically assume it was me?"

"Well, it was bound to happen eventually," Grey confessed, avoiding eye contact with Lexy.

"My friend, I only have one thing to say," she teased. Lexy hugged Grey to her side and whispered in his ear, "Quit hitting yourself."

"Point taken," Grey quietly chuckled, squeezing her back. He winked and probed, "I also heard a rather intriguing rumour about your extracurricular activities involving a certain young Triad."

Rolling her eyes, Lexy countered, "I don't remember the details, but I'm sure it didn't happen for reasons I'm not at liberty to say."

Grey groaned, "Okay, you know what? Every time I use the excuse, 'I don't remember,' you give me shit. What was the speech again? I don't remember doesn't mean it didn't happen."

"Touché, but there are situations where you can be certain there was no interest from the other party involved," Lexy answered.

She knew what Lexy was hinting at. Patrick was sweet, funny and not remotely interested in looking at her in her bikini. Changing the subject, for it was his alone to reveal, Kayn looked at Lexy and enquired, "So, I heard you were chosen to fight for Ankh. You fought everyone all by yourself?" Grey and Frost cleared their throats in unison. *There was obviously a lot more to the story.* Kayn probed, "What was that about?"

Lexy smacked Frost before he had a chance to say anything and warned, "What happens at the Summit, stays at the Summit."

Melody came out of the bathroom, smiled at her and said, "Good job, Lex."

Frost and Grey howled laughing. Lexy glared at the pair as she got up. It looked like she was planning to leave with Melody. Lexy threatened, "You two saw what I did at the Summit. Just try me."

Frost teased, "To be honest, I'm tempted."

Lexy grinned as she dove back on the bunk. In a flash, she had Frost in a chokehold. He tapped out, chuckling as she let him go.

Something epic happened. Kayn asked, "Where's everyone else?"

Lexy's expression darkened as she replied, "They're at the Ankh Crypt, waiting for us."

A twinge of danger curdled in Kayn's stomach. She turned to Frost who met her enquiring eyes. Concern flashed across his face. She glanced back at Lexy, who didn't register anything at all. Grey wouldn't make eye contact with her. *That was always a bad sign. Damn it. Here we go.* Kayn stood up and said, "I'm going to find Melody and Zach."

"Don't be too long. We have to leave soon," Frost said, grasping her arm. He didn't let go as he stared into her eyes. *He was trying to warn her without saying the words. Something bad was about to happen.* Kayn felt sick to her stomach. *This wasn't a surprise. They'd revisited their Sweet Sleeps right before the others left for the Summit. It had been hinted at. She'd been preoccupied. It was the Testing. Whatever it was... It was time.* Kayn left the RV and walked briskly down the path to the water. Her eyes teared up. H*e'd clutched her arm like there was so much more he wanted to say.* Zach and Melody were sitting on the edge of the dock with their legs dangling in the lake. Kayn sat down with them. Zach placed his arm around her as she sighed, "Our Testing is happening today, isn't it?"

Slowly moving his feet beneath the surface, Zach answered, "They only hinted at it eighty times before they left. I had messed-up dreams and woke up feeling like something bad was about to happen. It must be."

Melody's feet splashed around as she sparred, "To miss these signs, you'd have to be in a coma."

Kayn smiled, for she'd been in a coma. *She'd also been so wrapped up in her personal drama that she'd been downplaying the signs. The Testing was always this far-off event. Even though she'd known it was coming soon. It had always felt like a future threat…until five minutes ago. Kevin must have known. That's why he cut everything off abruptly the night before. He was talking about the Testing when he told her she had to kill him the next time she saw him.* Kayn gazed out at the glass calm surface of the lake while declaring, "Lexy took on all of the Clans by herself at the Summit. If she can do it, then we can do it."

Mel chuckled, "Did you seriously just say that, because that girl is like frigging Batman?"

"Nah, she's more like Darth Vader," Zach chuckled.

They all began to laugh. *These were Kayn's jokes. She'd brought them to the nerdy side.* Zach was nervously picking at a sliver of wood on the dock. *Kevin always used to pick at things like that. Could she kill him if she had to?*

"We can do this. We can anything if we are together," Kayn assured. "Brains before brawn, remember?"

"I seriously hope that brains before brawn chant isn't a bunch of bullshit. Only Melody's been Enlightened, and we just had our asses epically kicked," Zach pointed out.

Kayn shrieked and yanked her feet out of the water. She apologised, "Sorry, a fish touched me."

Zach sighed, "We're so dead."

"We can't die. We're too smart and we care about each other. We have a strong connection. This is doable," Melody remarked.

Zach chuckled, "Did you really just say, 'this is doable,' in reference to a blood bath?"

They all laughed uncomfortably again and then there was an awkward period of silence. They sat in the stillness listening to the water lapping against the dock, breathing in air sweeter and warmer than it had been all week. *On some level, it felt like a gift. Calm before the storm.* Kayn dangled her feet back in the water. She shut her eyes and allowed herself to feel the pleasure of the liquid as it flowed between her toes.

Zach made a random observation, "I guess there's no time to bathe in salt?"

"Please... I don't want to think about it. Just one more minute," Mel pleaded.

They were sitting in silence, enjoying their last seconds of peace when they heard Frost say, "It's time to go."

After helping each other up, the trio took a deep breath and followed Frost down the end of the dock and into the woods. As they wandered towards the Ankh Crypt, Kayn kept glancing at Frost, hoping he'd make eye contact with her and give her another hint. *He wouldn't look at her. This was also a bad sign.* She was trying to keep pace with him, but he was walking quickly. *If she picked up her pace anymore, she'd be jogging. Who jogs towards certain death? She didn't have any abilities. She was toast.* Kayn spent the duration of the journey memorising beautiful things along the way, wishing Guru Grey would start spewing out positive thoughts. The light flowed in distinct rays through the trees. *It was quite magical.* The chirping of the birds. The trickling of the stream dancing through the forest. *Where was that damn grizzly? A* toad croaked. A dragonfly whirled past. She ducked out of its path. *There were a million reasons to fight for her survival.* She looked at Frost's behind. He was walking in front of her. *This was always nice.* She giggled. *The best laughter was inappropriately timed.* She raised her eyebrows at Mel and chuckled. *Laughter at this moment was like walking the plank over dozens of sharks while finding your impending horrific demise hilarious.* Frost turned to see what they were laughing about. Zach joined in. He'd deciphered the reason for their laughter.

Frost mumbled, "I think you all might actually be insane."

"That's totally possible," Melody sparred.

The trio burst into a fit of nervous laughter. Lexy and Grey were waiting at the entrance to the Crypt, nestled at the base of the mountain. Grey placed his hand under the lip of the rock and the staircase into the darkness became visible. Grey casually touched the torches as he walked past, and they lit up, revealing the long corridor.

Frost stopped before the wall and announced, "It's time for the three of you to see how we operate the Crypts. This is how we travel to different countries and other realms undetected." He instructed, "Move quickly through each door. They'll close on you and you can be trapped there."

The immortal placed his fingers in the ridges of the stone and pushed the heel of his hand down. The wall slid open. They darted through the opening, finding themselves in another stone room with carvings on the walls. The engraving looked Egyptian. Wall after wall shifted away and allowed them to pass until they found themselves standing in the dark.

"Azariah, bring us light," Frost requested.

The room brightened with glorious shimmering light. It was gold, the walls, the ceiling, absolutely everything. Precious gems were strewn across the ground. The trio gasped in awe at the splendour. Frost and Lily laid their palms flat in handprints on the gleaming wall of gold. Kayn couldn't help but notice their hands fit perfectly in the prints. The wall slid away. They dove through. It slid shut, leaving them feeling exposed in a room of white nothing. There didn't even seem to be a floor. They waited for the stomach-churning sensation of plummeting, but it didn't happen. *They were standing on nothing, surrounded by nothing.*

"Hold hands," Frost commanded as he closed his eyes. Lily also shut hers, but Kayn was curious. The room swirled with colour until it became a vomitus display of stomach-churning excessive information. There was another blinding flash of white light. They found themselves standing on a floating slab of stone that spanned the horizon. The stone beneath their feet shifted ever so slightly and they sensed the life residing within. Frost announced, "We're here! This is the Testing!"

"We're fighting on a floating giant slab of stone?" Zach blurted.

While standing on the stone looking every bit the goddess she was, Lily explained, "No, you three are fighting inside it. Under our feet is a floating Crypt the size of New York City."

"Is there a Colosseum in this?" Zach asked as he tapped his foot a couple of times.

"Third-Tier became bored of that scenario long ago," Lily replied.

"So, it's a giant Crypt like what we just went through?" Melody questioned.

Grey met Mel's eyes as he replied, "Sort of like a mix of that and a maze with walls that move and lead to anything that's ever crossed your mind. There will be randomly available weapons and powers. Remember, this place is magic. There could be anything or anyone in there. There is nothing I can say that's going to prepare you for this. You three can do this… together."

"So, it's like a giant video game?" Zach enquired.

Once again, Kayn thought, *Oh crap. Why did I never embrace the video game thing?*

"I guess," Frost answered, keeping a straight face.

"Keep your wits about you," Lily cautioned. "They want to see how well you've been trained and what you comprehend about who you are now. Every five years the Clans get a chance to acquire the tombs they need. This is how it's done. Only new Clan can play. When you get out, you will have earned a tomb. No matter how many times you're killed, you must stand back up. You won't be fighting on even terms with everyone. Some of you have already been Enlightened. You three are smart and fast. Remember, brains can defeat brawn. When you reach the Amber room, you've made it to the end of the Testing. You'll know it, when you see it. You need to make it there together to be released. One more thing, kill everyone and everything you see. You are no longer friends. They have been told the same."

Lexy clarified, "You're not allowed to enter the game in the same place. Find each other as fast as you can." The crimson-haired Dragon signalled for Zach to come with her as she strolled away. Grey walked away with Melody.

Frost stayed with her as the others left. He tilted her chin with his palm and met her fear filled eyes as he softly whispered, "We only have a second to talk. You can do this. It's going to be hard. Have faith in yourself. The sleep chambers are your only safe place. Use them. The part of your brain that's mortal needs to recharge so even if you don't feel like it. Do it. Watch out for the fountains. Where there's water there are predators, just like in the wild. You can run. You're smart. Use your strengths. You won't stay dead. You have an unlimited amount of lives in the game. Stay focused on finding the Amber room. Stand back up and keep moving. Do whatever you have to do to come back to us. Every time you fall. You stand back up. No matter how impossible it feels, you must find the strength to carry on. That's life's biggest lesson. Stand back up." A shadow of apology crossed Frost's eyes.

He was afraid for her. This was going to be horrible. The stone shifted beneath her feet. She dropped through into the Crypt without any warning, fell ten feet and landed painfully on the stone floor below. She looked up as the stone slab closed above her. Frost's face was full of undisguised apology as he disappeared from sight.

Chapter 39

Lambs To The Slaughter

It took her a second to shake off the sting of the fall. *Use logic. The others dropped through where they were standing. They weren't that far away.* After surveying her surroundings, Kayn leapt to her feet. *She couldn't die, but that didn't mean that the premise of excruciating pain didn't terrify her. What did she know? The Crypts had moving walls. Everything was grey, dismal and plain. It felt like she was missing something. Things are never as they appear.* Afraid to move, she paused to contemplate her options. *Had she turned around as she fell? She'd been startled… She wasn't sure.* A wall slid open, revealing a narrow passageway. She'd yet to move, but this was an obvious direction to walk in. *Would it be a trap? She couldn't stand here forever.* She moved quickly through the first open wall. It immediately shut behind her. The walls appeared to be shifting by themselves. *She would have to be careful where she decided to pause.* Kayn managed to control the urge to call out, knowing she'd also be disclosing her location to everything else. Her stomach tightened. A wave of nausea washed through her. *This was never a good sign.* Her skin rippled with adrenaline. Goosebumps rose on her bare arms. She felt the familiar urge to void the contents of her stomach. *She knew what this was… This was the impending doom warning system she'd been gifted with on that first day as she walked away from the track into her new life with Ankh.* Her mind prodded, m*ove Kayn. Steady forward motion. It was game on. Kevin was down here.* As hope surged within her heart, logic slapped it down. *He'd been told to kill her if she'd been told to kill him. If she managed to avoid him, perhaps neither one would have to find out how far they'd be willing to go for their Clans.* She started to run. The walls seemed to be running on sensors. The second she ran through, they closed behind her, leaving no way to change direction. *Brains before brawn.* S*he had to figure this place out. Would they open again once she'd gone through?* Kayn stopped cold and spun around to see if she could go back through the door she'd just passed. She might be forced to change direction. *The wall didn't budge. Not even an inch. Problem solving skills.* She searched for grooves on the surface. *There was nothing. Well, this was inconvenient.* Her stomach churned with impending doom. *She had to find the others.* The wall beside her opened by itself. T*his was going to be a lesson in trial and error. That much she was sure of.* Kayn sprinted through the opening into another narrow, dimly lit corridor. She stroked the Ankh symbol on her palm. *It hadn't gone off. Bet they were wandering around aimlessly, just like she was.* Three options opened where she'd paused for a breath. She decided to trust instinct. She took off, allowing her mind to pick an option at a moment's notice. *It felt like she was moving in a circle.* She spoke to herself aloud, "Think Kayn... Think."

Multiple voices began whispering, "Think Kayn… Think."

The walls were mocking her distress. "This can't be good," she commented.

The walls creepily echoed her words, "This can't be good… This can't be good."

She dove out of the way as a wall slid down directly above her. Her only warning had been the crackling of stone. *She needed to run. She'd stood in one spot for too long. It was forcing her to move, corralling her like partially immortal livestock.* Dodging through ever-shifting walls, she reached a dead end. Kayn glanced above her and to each side. *There was a small crawl space above her to her left.* Her heart pounded a steady rhythm. *Brains before brawn. Would that crawl space close before she made it through? She had to find a way to test it.* While understanding she only had a limited time in each spot, she dug through the pockets of her jeans. Thankful she was still wearing her street clothes, she removed a penny from her pocket. *Logic, use logic, Kayn.* She tossed the penny into the crawl space and it closed in seconds. *There was no way to move through it fast enough. She'd be crushed. The obvious exit had been a trap for the weak-minded.* Kayn searched the walls for grooves and ridges, anything to suggest a way out. She glanced around the cube-like room. It resembled a jail cell. She looked up while crossing her fingers and hoping the ceiling would stay put long enough for her to figure out an exit strategy. A sword materialised. It was suspended from a rope attached to the ceiling, roughly ten feet above her. *She needed to find a way to get that sword.* Something crazy popped into her mind. *Kevin made her watch this guy on YouTube. Parkour… Why not?* Kayn raced at the wall, leapt halfway up and launched her body in the other direction, jumping high enough to reach it. Now, she was hanging on to the rope above the sword in the centre of the room. *This was not how the situation played out in her mind. In her mind's plan, the sword just came off and dropped to the floor.* Kayn swung back and forth, hoping to loosen it. *At least she made it high enough to grab the rope. It could have been worse. She could be hanging from a blade.* The grinding of stone on stone indicated the wall in front of her was about to open. *Was it friend or foe?* She swung back and kicked off the wall just as a few Trinity dashed through the opening. With perfect timing, she sailed past them, letting go of the rope as she soared through the open wall. She heard the sword ting as it hit the ground in the chamber. *She'd given her enemy the weapon she'd worked for, but they weren't fast enough. One of them raced for the sword as the wall ground shut.* Knowing she only had seconds to flee, she raced through each wall as it opened trying to put distance between her and the Trinity she'd left behind. *She needed to be able to defend herself.* She quickly scanned each room for weapons as she passed through. She heard the walls opening and closing ahead of her. *Someone was coming.* It sounded like more than one person setting off the sensors as the repetitive rhythm of grinding stone mixed into an intimidatingly ominous echoing rumble. *She didn't have a weapon. She had to run!* Kayn sprinted down a long stone corridor that curved at the end. She kept running until she saw an out, as the wall opened with precision timing to her forward motion. Just as she leapt through the opening, it slid shut behind her. *Was she stuck in a giant maze like a rat?* She raced down another stone corridor and paused. *Wait. Why am I wasting energy running? She needed to think. She had to find her Clan. What if she'd just run away and left them there fighting in her confusion?* From the corner of her eye, she saw something impossible. *Nothing good is ever seen out of the corner of your eye.* It was a shadow in the distance, a lingering figure in her mind, nothing more than a mirage based on her worst fears. *It couldn't be?* She shuddered with revulsion. *It's impossible. This must be a trick. Salt... She needed a bag of salt. She'd just dealt with this demon. This wasn't real.* The shadow against the wall moved, triggering a vision of the ominous figure in the hallway on the night her mortality ceased.

Her body used instincts built in her darkest hour. With a life of their own, her legs spun her around and ran. She heard her twin's voice reaching out from beyond the grave, imploring her to run for her life, as she had on the night of her Correction. Adrenaline coursed through her being as her mind travelled backwards in time. The scent of metal accosted her nostrils as she sprinted down the stone corridor. *His footsteps were keeping time with hers. He was behind her!* Kayn dove through each wall as the next slid open. *She could get away! She could lose him in here!* The stone opened and slammed, narrowly missing her. *Her perspiring, foul-scented assailant was closing in on her. It's not real! It can't be real!* She leapt through the last opening just as it closed. *It felt like she'd escaped.*

After a deep breath, she laughed nervously. Her surroundings shifted and her blood ran cold. *She was standing in the trails behind her house.* "It's not real," she stated aloud, as if speaking the words could make it true. *This is a Crypt. We are floating in the sky. It's like the In-between. I can't die here.* Her stomach clenched and she didn't need to look behind her because she felt his dark presence just as she had on that night. She started to run again. Every detail was the same. This was the woods behind the house she'd grown up in. As her bare feet hit the wooden bridge, she told herself it wasn't real but couldn't will her body to stop running away from the pain her pursuer would cause. *It's not real. There are no trails here. It's part of the test.* About to burst through the bushes into the neighbour's yard, Kayn braced herself for the excruciating sensation of the knife. *No man was smoking on the porch. She was heading towards the bridge again.* After a couple of laps through the forest that abruptly ended a breath before her assailant's first stab, she realised she was caught in a loop. She came to the same bridge and felt her feet thudding on the rough wood again. She raced through the bushes, never reaching the end, and then, she was on the bridge again. *She sensed that by trying to run away, she was only postponing the inevitable. She didn't hear the repetitive echo of his footsteps behind her anymore.* She stopped to take a breath as her nostrils filled with the foul, tinny stench of blood. *The scent had been seared into her soul on that night. Whenever her mind recalled that night, the scent of her blood as it evacuated her body haunted her. She felt the sensation of the warm, sticky fluid. Her mind was playing tricks on her.* She ran her hands over her back, and of course, nothing was there. *This had all been in her mind.* She exhaled, laughing. *Her attacker was just a messed-up, warped hallucination created from somebody's ultra-sick sense of humour.* Shivers crawled up her spine. Her mind whispered, *look behind you. She didn't want to... Shit.* Her expression shifted with the knowledge of what was about to happen. *She'd lived this moment on repeat. In her dreams at night and even in her thoughts during the daylight hours. Lived, was not the word to be used.* Like a mountain lion, he'd crept up on her in silence. His hand covered her mouth, giving her only a split second of preparation before his blade seared a scalding path of agony through her torso. It happened, over and over, until her mind began to flicker. *She knew there was no help coming.* She clawed at his hand, but with her lack of nails it accomplished nothing. Sickened by his excited panting mixed with the vile scent of his skin, she relived her worst nightmare. After being repeatedly violated by his blade and bashed across the face with a large stone. The lights went out.

When she awoke naked in the woods, the brutal defilement of her fragile mortal encasement continued until she couldn't will her shocked mind to fight back, knowing there was no escape. *There was only acceptance. This was happening but not happening. He was there but not there. It was the essence of him. He was a ghoul, a demon… a spectre of depravity. He was a nightmare to be experienced.* She felt his blade carving her flesh. Her soul screamed from within her tortured mind. His face came into hazy focus. Their eyes met in recognition. He vanished. She no longer had the visual, but his knife kept sinking into her flesh until it felt like her soul was on fire. *She was burning!* The forest flickered and the grey of reality filtered in for a second. The greenery came back, along with the sensation of rain on her skin. She saw the branches waving in the wind above where she lay as grinding walls prompted her to remember where she was. The forest flickered again to a flash of a familiar face against a backdrop of stone. The trees appeared above her for only a flash. She felt the tiny particles of something on her skin. The forest was gone in a breath and so was her saviour as her world went black.

The world became bright. Kayn scrambled to her knees. Her stomach tightened and released. She managed to control the urge to vomit. Kayn felt her torso. Expecting to be gutted and covered in blood, relief washed over her. *She was physically fine.* She heard the steady clashing of swords through the walls. *Stand back up. The fighting was close by.* Her mind taunted, *you're missing an eye.* She panicked as she felt her face. Her senses were reeling from the torture but her body was unscathed. *There were no wounds, at least none that could be seen with the naked eye. Stand back up.* Kayn took a breath to calm her hysterical nerves. *Her mind was a mess. She couldn't think. There was no way she could fight.* She sat in the corner, hugging her knees to her chest. *Shut it off. You've got to find a way to shut it off. This is not the location for a mental breakdown.* She was brought back to reality by echoing screams of agony. They grew closer by the second. By the sounds of things, everyone had found a sword or a weapon. *Maybe this was the right time for a mental breakdown.* The wall behind her ground open. She spun her head around. *It was Zach. Oh, thank God.* She was still huddled in the corner. Zach grinned as he threw her a knife. For a split second, she thought he was throwing it at her and ducked out of its way. It hit the stone beside her head with a tinny clank.

Her concerned Clan member suggested, "I'd grab that if I were you." When she didn't move a muscle, Zach asserted, "Get your mind straight! Get up! Get ready to fight!"

She couldn't convince herself to move. She heard Winnie's voice in her head. S*tand back up.* The wall ground open. *It was Kevin.* He attacked Zach, throwing him against the wall. Kayn's heart caught in her throat. *Kevin was smiling. He seemed to be enjoying every second of this. Could he really switch it off this fast?* Kayn clung to the wall as she struggled to stand.

"Run Kayn! You're not with it yet! There's too many!" Zach hollered. More Triad appeared through a quickly sliding wall. The wall crushed one before he made it through and sliced the other in half, spraying her with blood from his torso. On the teen's face was an expression of shock as the top part of his corpse slid down the wall and fell stunned to the stone.

Kevin froze as he saw her. Their eyes met. Recognition with a touch of panic flashed across his expression. *It's not Kevin. He's not Kevin.* Knowing Zach stood no chance if she left him here alone, Kayn raced at the Triad and booted him back through the wall. It slid shut. Zach seemed evenly matched with Kevin as he swung back and sliced Kevin's chest with his sword. He barely flinched. Kevin grinned and attacked Zach. *He was having fun.* The wall opened and her own fight began. Kayn skilfully dodged each thrust of the Triad's weapon. With her blade clutched in her hand, she jumped against the wall and launched herself at her attacker, knocking him to the ground. She didn't wait for him to stand. *This wasn't the time for civility.* She leapt on his chest and slammed his head against the stone floor, knocking him out cold. She looked behind her. Kevin and Zach had disappeared behind the swiftly opening and closing walls. The half Triad corpse had also disappeared from the floor, leaving behind an ominous pool of blood. Feeling like a badass, Kayn strolled through an open wall. *Behind you.* She spun around. *The Triad was coming after her. She'd only knocked him out momentarily. She should have finished him off. Double tap. Just like a Zombie movie. Lesson learned.* Kayn darted through each opening with no sense of direction. Just when she was almost certain she'd lost him, the cold metal of a sword slid through her chest and stole her breath in an excruciating explosion of pain. She sunk to her knees. The world wavered around her as Kayn looked up to see the face of the person who killed her.

Patrick was kneeling before her, distraught, "I'm sorry. I didn't know it was you."

Well, if it had to be someone. Kayn's vision blurred as she slipped into oblivion.

Her head was pounding. She opened her eyes, took a deep breath and scrambled to stand on seriously wobbly legs. Her vision was foggy for a second before it clarified her surroundings. She saw a black felt bag in the corner of the room. She attempted to shove it into her bra and noticed she didn't have one on. *She wasn't wearing street clothes anymore. Everyone else had been wearing white.* Guess *she had to die a few times to get comfy.* Moving through walls as they opened, Kayn began collecting felt bags as they magically appeared in every room she entered. *It was like a video game, but she'd been rewarded for dying instead of living.* She wandered from room to room, shoving bags into her sarong with no semblance of time. There was no way to know if it had been three hours or three days as she continued running through the maze, avoiding confrontation and collecting bags. She hadn't found any weapons besides the one Zach had thrown. It was on the floor beside her when she awakened. Mentally and physically exhausted, she walked through a sliding wall and came across a large area with a marble fountain and flowing water. *Watch out for the fountains,* she heard Frost's warning in her mind. *It was odd that she'd come across this place the moment she felt like she needed it. She hadn't let herself think about how thirsty she was.* She knelt beside the fountain. Cupping her hands to fill them with refreshing liquid, she drank from her palms until her thirst was quenched. At the bottom of the fountain, a glimmering flash of gold caught her eye. *It was a sword.* She fished it out of the water. *It was beautiful. Weapons had never impressed her, but this was exquisite, with intricate carvings on the handle. It had the symbol of Ankh. Someone knew she was coming.* She gapped out, entranced by the beauty of the blade. *She should get out of here. There could be predators at the fountain.* She felt stinging pain as something hit the back of her head. Stunned, Kayn staggered backwards. While attempting to wield her sword in her defence, she was shoved down and pinned to the floor. Kayn opened her eyes. Face to face with Kevin.

Out of breath, he scowled. Covering her mouth so she couldn't scream, Kevin hissed, "Damn it, Brighton. Just stay the hell down." He took off.

Hidden by the fountain, listening to whooshing arrows and clashing swords, Kayn was maybe eight feet from the opening to a doorway. Stealthily, she glanced around. *There were at least ten Clan actively fighting around her. Could she make it?* Kayn launched her body up from the floor and through the open doorway. It closed behind her. Kayn looked around the room. There were cushions on the ground like in the underground Ankh Crypt. *This must be a sleep chamber. She felt safe.* Kayn removed the bags from her sarong. She opened one and dumped the contents in her hand. *No rose quartz, but there was salt and various spiritual privacy stones.* She placed the stones around the room even though she sensed she didn't need to. One of the bags contained dried figs and a bunch of small round things. She licked one to see if they were edible. *It tasted like candy.* Kayn ate a couple and saved the rest for Zach and Melody. *If she ever found them again.*

Chapter 40

Love Me Or Let Me Go

She wandered over to the wall she'd entered through. *Kevin had knocked her down to protect her.* She sensed him on the other side of the door. Against her better judgment, Kayn pressed her palms against the stone. *It didn't open as she'd expected.* She noticed the ridges and indents, and while operating on nothing but instinct, she placed her fingers in the grooves and pressed the heel of her hand down. The door slid open. They stared at each other for a second, just breathing. *Everyone else appeared to be gone.* A wall on the far side of the room opened. Kevin was forced to jump inside with her. The wall slid shut behind him.

"Why in the hell did you let me in? You know you're not supposed to let me in here," he reprimanded, pacing back and forth, avoiding eye contact.

He couldn't leave now. Someone would see him. He was stuck with her. Kayn tried to articulate what she wanted to say. *She'd watched him hurt Zach.* A part of her wanted to walk over there and beat him senseless but ego wanted to call his bluff. *He wasn't going to be able to kill her. When faced with the opportunity, he'd saved her.*

He turned to face her and scolded, "We are supposed to be enemies. They could be watching us."

Kayn pointed out the obvious stones she'd situated around the room. She didn't remember the words but gave it a shot, "Let there be silence inside of the circle." Kevin let out an exasperated sigh. *She suspected she'd said it wrong.* She tried again, "Let there be silence outside of this circle?" *She honestly couldn't remember which one was correct. She didn't know the words in Greek.* Kevin wasn't moving. *He looked guilty.* "How's Stephanie?" Kayn stated coldly.

Kevin took an aggravated step closer as he said, "Are you joking? This is our Testing. This is serious shit. I've always been your enemy. You have always been mine. We took a vacation from reality. You can't keep dramatically pausing in the middle of a fight to stare at me."

She slowly shook her head. *He was lying to himself. His actions didn't match his words.*

He callously clarified things, "We have nothing left. We're done. Stay away from me. Run away and hide if you see me. I don't want to have to hurt you. I don't want that on my conscience."

He'd stomped on her ego by telling her to run away and hide. He wouldn't have to hurt her? Was he serious? With her back up, Kayn stammered, "You know what! You followed me in here! Where do you get off saying I'm being friggin dramatic? You were looking at me too."

"Listen, I was told to entertain you," he explained. "I was ordered to get to know you. You're a nice person. I like you and I'm not a complete ass. Regardless of what you might think. That is the only reason I came in here. I'm here to warn you, just this once. I have to kill you the next time you're standing in my way when my Clan is around."

Stepping towards him, she questioned, "Could you kill me? Could you sink that knife into my chest without dying inside yourself?"

Turning his expression to stone, Kevin took out his blade, backed her against the wall and said, "Last week was nothing more than a lapse in judgment on your behalf. I knew you would let me in. Maybe, I came in here to kill you?"

With trust in her eyes, she grabbed his blade, raised it to her heart, placed the tip against her skin, and whispered, "Then just kill me and quit acting. That's what you have been doing all week right? If you have no feelings for me, it should be easy." Willing himself to do it, Kevin shook his head, tearing up. Kayn caressed his cheek. He closed his eyes as she touched him. Shifting the wispy material of her dress to reveal her scar, he traced the ridge with his thumb. *He was trying to remember her. She could feel it.*

He gently kissed the nape of her neck with his blade pressed against her chest, nuzzled her and buried his face in her hair. "Damn it, Kayn," he whispered. He dropped the knife, and it tinged to the floor.

She snuggled into him. They clung to each other. Their eyes moist with unshed tears. *She couldn't be his enemy. Their connection was too strong.*

He whispered against her hair, "You need to kill me the next time you see me. Make it look real. I want you to. I need you to be the one to do it. We have to look like enemies."

Kayn squeezed him tighter as she whispered through her tears, "I knew you'd come back to me."

With agony in his eyes, he asserted, "I'm not back. We can never go back to who we were. Don't you get it? You have to stop loving me." He abruptly turned and walked away.

"You love me too," Kayn whispered. "I know you do."

Placing his fingers and hand in the grooves on the door, it slid open. He bluntly stated, "Loving you would be pointless."

The wall ground shut and he was gone. His words replayed in her mind. *Loving you would be pointless.* She understood why he'd walked away, but it didn't stop her from feeling like he'd just kicked her in the chest. *He'd been intentionally cruel.* The version of Kevin that she'd grown up with didn't have a vicious bone in his body. Kayn stood there motionless for a minute. *He'd been brutal to her. Presumably, so he could work up the ability to kill her. There was a wellspring of crazy information dancing around in her head. He was right. She would be forced to kill him at some point. She was just a mortal girl trying to outrun a mob of immortals. At this moment, she felt like a normal, heartbroken teenage girl. She wasn't allowed to feel this way. She didn't have the time to feel this way. She had to be stronger than that.* Kayn slid down against the wall and sat there hugging her knees to her chest. *She would have to avoid Kevin for as long as she could. Whenever she thought about him, her mind still wanted to sugarcoat the situation. There was no possible way to sugarcoat this insanity.* She rocked herself ever so slowly and closed her eyes. *She needed a hug from a real person. She needed a hug from her mother.*

In her mind, she travelled back to the sensation of her mother's embrace. Her heart ached, knowing she'd never experience that feeling of all-encompassing adoration and security again. *Maybe it was searching for that feeling that drew her towards a Kevin that was no longer? In his arms, it felt like home. This was why she couldn't draw that line in the sand and why she hadn't been able to force herself to let go of that last irrational shred of hope. This was not a fairytale. This was a nightmare. A nightmare with no foreseeable end.* Kayn got up and stared at the wall separating her from the madness. *She was only postponing the inevitable by hiding in this room. That much she understood. She needed to find the rest of her Clan.* If she stayed away from him, neither of them would be forced to do the unthinkable. *Brains before brawn, she could do this. She was strong enough to face her fears head-on. Angry... she had to be fierce. She'd have to be consumed by rage if he expected her to kill him. Who was she kidding? She wasn't going to be able to hurt him either.* She rested her ear against the stone entrance, pointless as it was. *She couldn't hear anything outside. What new sick and twisted torture awaited beyond the security of her temporary sanctuary?* Kayn placed her fingers in the grooves, inconspicuously etched into the stone. The wall slid open. *She appeared to be alone.* She left the safety of the room and sprinted past the fountain, darting through the first wall that opened. She kept running through each wall as it slid away. It was as though each obstruction had a will of its own. Each wall could decide to allow her through. Kayn was beginning to find it strange that she hadn't bumped into anyone since she left the sanctuary of the sleep chambers. *Where was everyone?* A wall opened as she ran but it closed before she made it there. *It felt like that was the way she should go. Maybe she should wait for it to reopen?* A different wall slid open. Even though she felt apprehensive, she raced through it. Her stomach lurched as she began to freefall into nothingness. She braced herself for the inevitable impact with an unseen ground as she plummeted into the unknown. *It felt like she was descending at a rapid rate.* After a few minutes of the same feeling, she suspected she was stationary. *She was floating with the sensation of falling.* She started to make a swimming motion, hoping she could manoeuvre through the nothing and bump into something. Each time she shifted her weight, she began to spin, with the sensation of endless space around her. *If she set off her symbol, she'd be able to get a look at her situation.* As she floated through an ominous icy patch of air, it triggered her memory, and she decided against shedding light on the situation. *During the redo of her Sweet Sleep, she'd come to a place just like this. She knew what hovered in the never-ending darkness. Don't think about it.* Kayn drifted through more icy patches of air. *She had been set adrift in a sea of wicked things.* It felt like she'd been falling for hours when the wall slid open. Unaccustomed to the light, it momentarily blinded her. She saw a familiar face. I*t was Zach. She also saw everything better left unseen.*

Zach hollered, "Try and move closer to me! The wall is going to shut in a second! When I open it again, try to reach for my hand."

"Don't leave me in here!" Kayn shouted. Hundreds of hollow-eyed, haunted beings turned her way as the wall closed. *This is why you don't yell out for help in the darkness.*

"You will never leave this place," the dark entities' wicked words echoed in the void.

The icy currents of air swirling around her arms and legs felt like they were trying to keep her there. She tuned out the intimidating whispers of fallen souls and focused every ounce of her energy on trying to make it to the wall without spinning and losing her sense of direction.

"You will be lost here, as we are… Forever. You were sacrificed by your Clan. There was never a way out." The haunted voices taunted.

She had an idea. She used the same motion as swinging on a swing set and somersaulted forward instead of spinning. She slammed into a hard surface, bounced off and tried to catch her breath but the wind had been knocked out of her. The wall opened. Kayn reached for Zach's hand before it closed but wasn't close enough. It started to open again. She flung herself at the wall right as it started grinding and soared out, skidding on her stomach across the stone slab floor.

Standing above her, Zach chuckled, "You're lucky I came along. I was stuck in one of those for a while."

Kayn struggled to get up but her balance had been severely altered. Her arms were incapable of holding the weight of her body. She took a deep breath and tried again. Zach came to her aid and tried to help her regain her balance. She collapsed in his arms.

He held her close. While stroking her hair, he affirmed, "I've got you."

Closing her eyes, Kayn rested her head on Zach's shoulder and whispered, "I just need a second." They were quiet for a moment before she commented, "Did you just say there was more than one of those rooms?" She snapped out of it and got up.

"That room was nothing," Zach replied, summoning her to follow with a wave of his hand. "I found a room like yours and then wandered into another pitch-black room where I was viciously attacked by those hovering demons. Did you know they had claws? Well, they do, and let me tell you, that was a most unpleasant experience. I'm starting to think there's a lot more to this test than finding some Amber room at the end."

"Aren't you the fortunate one to have found them both, though," Kayn chuckled, following him through each sliding wall.

Zach enquired, "Have you been stuck in that room for a long time? We couldn't find you anywhere."

She told him a version of the truth, "I had a run in with a sword. A few fights. I was in one of those safe rooms for about half an hour. I was running and then falling."

He nodded, taking her answer at face value. Zach exclaimed, "We spotted a place to rest. We just couldn't relax until we located you. I was worried you were stuck in one of the rooms and I was right."

They entered an open area with a fountain, *like the last. There appeared to be no other Clan around.* Zach walked to the wall, laid his palm against it and it opened.

Melody beamed as she stood up and waved them over to a platter of fruit, rolls and figs. She addressed Zach, "Was she stuck in one of those rooms?"

"Yes, I was." Kayn answered for herself. Relieved to be in the same place as her friends, she strolled over and greeted Melody with a hug. She whispered over Mel's shoulder mid-embrace, "I'm famished. Where did this food come from?"

"It appeared after Zach went looking for you," Melody replied. "I thought I'd wait for you guys to get back."

They sat on the colourful large pillows to enjoy their mini feast. As she grabbed a handful of figs, Kayn recalled the bags she'd found. She reached into her sarong and removed her private stash of salt, figs and sugar-coated candy, surprised they were still there after her endless free fall. She placed the bags in front of her friends as she interjected, "When I second guessed myself, I got shut in that room. I think we're supposed be following our instincts. They'll guide us where we need to be."

"That might be the deepest thing you've said all week," Zach provoked as he dumped out the contents of one of her little black bags.

Kayn sparred, “You know what? Under ‘deep’ in the dictionary there happens to be a smiling picture of me.”

“Really? Your picture is under ‘deep’ in the dictionary too?” Zach teased.

Melody started to choke. Zach humorously patted her on the back. “Keep your mouth shut when you’re eating. I said I wanted to date you, not be covered in dates by you,” he playfully bantered. Zach tossed a date into the air and caught it in his mouth.

He’d probably taught himself to do that to impress his younger siblings. It was something her brother Matt had done to entertain her. “Be careful what you wish for,” Kayn remarked. After chuckling at her witty comeback and stewing on Zach’s somewhat romantic confession, she nudged him, asking, "Why don’t you want to date me?”

Zach winked at her and teased, “Honestly, I’m not sure I could wear a Darth Vader costume to turn you on without creeping myself out.”

“Touché,” Kayn replied without an attempt at denial.
She tried to copy his trick by tossing a date in the air and opening her mouth to catch it. It bounced off her nose. They laughed.

Melody tore off a piece of the large roll, saying, “I haven’t seen any other Clan for a while.”

“They could be stuck in those rooms?” Zach responded while taking a sip from his goblet. “Triad definitely doesn’t do the brains before brawn thing. I’m fairly certain Triad’s mantra is just the opposite.” Mel covered her mouth as she laughed so she wouldn’t spit out her mouthful of bun. Zach chuckled, “Seriously, keep it in your mouth.”

They all raced to say, “That’s what he said.”

Kayn shifted on the pillow and grinned as she launched a surprise date at Zach’s face.

He caught it in his teeth, chewed it up and swallowed it. He grinned and teased, “Don’t mess with the master.”

They giggled until confusion simultaneously passed across each of their faces. *Throwing dates in Zach’s mouth wasn’t that funny. Even the act of breathing was hysterically hilarious.* The room wavered. *Oh, oh.*

“I think someone drugged our food,” Mel snickered.

Zach chuckled, “I do feel excessively happy. It's like I just sucked back laughing gas.” He waved his hand in front of his face.

In awe of what he was seeing, he whispered, "Oh… Wow. Will you look at that?"

Kayn got up. *None of them had seen this plot twist coming. They had to eat. Didn't they? There was a meal provided for them. Why wouldn't they assume they were supposed to eat it? Wait... Maybe it wasn't the food? The air smelled funny.* She lifted her hand and noticed a thickness in the air. Kayn declared, "We're being gassed. It's not the food. There is something in the air. Don't you guys see it?" Kayn waved her hand in front of her. You could see the haze. Zach jumped up and made an uncoordinated effort to get to the door. He pressed his hand into the grooves. As it ground open, fumes billowed out of their sleep chambers into the open area. Kayn staggered behind the other two. A hazy cloud was travelling in from other areas.

"The whole place is being gassed," Zach stammered. "We can try to outrun it. Maybe it's not everywhere?"

Sensing the urgency of the situation, the Newbie immortals staggered away from the fountain through the first open door. They were cautious to stay together, knowing if they separated, they could get stuck in one of the rooms. They entered each door that opened two at a time while one waited a millisecond longer to follow. As they staggered down a third corridor, the outline of the walls wavered, and they realised there was no way to outrun the toxic fumes.

Out of breath, Melody asserted, "We should have stayed in that room. We were safe in there."

With his hands out to his sides for balance, Zach said, "I hope you remember the way back? If my phone number was written on the back of my hand, I couldn't read it right now."

Kayn couldn't stop giggling while in pursuit of the duo. She was wobbling around on Jell-O legs like she'd downed a case of peach cider. Her comic timing kicked in, "I'm pretty sure there's no cell service in hell... Just a guess." *She meant to say no cell service in here. It still worked.*

Chuckling, Zach staggered into the next room and tripped over bodies, slurring, "Poor little fellas."

The bodies were sprawled out next to an unconscious mix of a boar and a lizard. As Kayn stumbled by, she looked at their faces. *It was Patrick and a Trinity she hadn't known.* She fought the urge to drag the gentle Triad away from the creature. *She wasn't supposed to be his friend anymore.* She wasn't paying attention as the others went through the next wall. *He was a nice person.* She still thought of him that way, even though he'd accidentally stabbed her. *The mortified expression on his face had been apology enough.* Her eyelids felt heavy so she started rubbing them. *Was she ever dizzy*? When she looked up, a wall opened in front of her and she assumed that was where Zach and Melody went. She wasn't capable of running anymore as she wandered through the open wall into a room full of drugged sleeping demons. *Well, this is both lucky and unlucky.* She tip-toed to each side of the room and stood by the wall, hoping it would open. When nothing happened, Kayn's heart dropped. *She was stuck. The walls weren't going to open by themselves.* She leaned against one of the walls as she realised she'd left her sword in the room. *Shit.* Kayn pulled the tiny dagger out from under her sarong. *Why was she still awake if demons triple her size were out cold?* She watched them sleeping peacefully. *The moment had finally arrived. She was about to experience Grey's worst nightmare.* Kayn walked over to one with her dagger clutched in her hand. *She could kill them? No… She'd better let sleeping demons lie.* She sat down against the wall. Feeling something bulky, a flickering lightbulb lit up above her fume-intoxicated head. *There were still pouches tied on her belt. She had salt. She could cover herself in salt. She had no water. The salt would just slide right off her skin. If she licked her skin, salt would stick to it.* She licked her arms. *There wasn't going to be enough for her entire body.* She would have to hold onto one of the pouches and throw it at them when they awoke. *It might buy her all of one second. Damn it. Melody and Zach, where are you?* Either it was the fact that she was drugged or an act of sheer brilliance, but she wondered for a moment if the walls were alive. *They opened and shut like they knew she was coming. Not now, though. Right now, they weren't listening to her at all.* Kayn stroked the wall she was sitting against, quietly imploring, "I need your help. I know you're listening to me. Please, I don't want to be eaten alive. Help me." The wall slid open on the far side of the room. She leapt up and almost made it there before it closed. She stood directly in front of the wall, silently willing it to give her another chance. The demons began to stir. *Come on. Please help me. Please. They're waking up.* She whispered, "Please, please. Open up for me again." The same wall slid open in response to her plea. She dashed through into the next room. *Interesting. The walls will open if you ask them to. She couldn't wait to tell her friends. This was a game-changer.* She went through the next wall into a room full of fumes. Holding her breath, she staggered through the next open wall into another room in a similar state. *She had to breathe it in. She had no choice.* She practically levitated through the next open door. S*he should have passed out a long time ago.* She stumbled and dropped to the floor.

As Kayn awoke on the unforgiving stone, she remembered to listen before opening her eyes. *Anything could be waiting for her to awaken.* When she felt certain she was alone. Kayn scrambled to her feet. Standing in a seemingly endless dark hallway, she cautiously made her way down it. There was no point in running with no obvious exit in sight. "What have I gotten myself into now?" She whispered as she scanned the smooth corridor for grooves on the wall. She paused, sensing something was coming. Once again, her pulse raced. Her stomach clenched as instinct warned her. She spoke aloud, "Can you help me out here? I seem to be in another one of those trick rooms." *Nothing happened.* Kayn started to grasp the situation. *What are my options? I can run down the hall that never ends like a complete moron, or I can embrace the whole brains before brawn thing and think my way out of this?* She began scanning the walls again for the telltale finger holes and grooves. She slowly walked down the hall while inspecting the stone from the floor to the ceiling. *There had to be a trick here. There was a way out. She just had to find it.* Kayn felt a vibration. Rushing water began flooding in from dozens of vents on the ceiling. Her pulse raced as panic tightened her chest. *What the hell was this shit?* She sloshed down the hall in ankle-deep water in search of an exit while desperately pleading her case to the walls, "Open up! Please! Open up!" The walls weren't listening to her as the water rose. She looked up at the vent she was closest to. *She could try to escape through one of those vents, but she wouldn't be able to reach it until the chamber filled. It might be possible.* She glanced down at her hips and up at the size of the vents. *A tiny built person would fit through with no problem. She might not make it. There was a chance her curves were going to be the death of her.* The vents appeared to be the only way out, and she was already knee-deep in water. *There wasn't going to be a lot of time to plan her escape. She'd have to wedge her dagger in the vent to keep it from closing. Escape routes always closed fast in here. She wasn't certain of many things, but by this point, she knew the Testing wasn't going to make it easy. Still, an impossible plan was better than no plan at all.* The steady rushing of water reminded her of something, but she couldn't pinpoint the memory.

The tunnel was filling up quickly. Adrenaline pulsed through Kayn as her feet rose off the stone. She was going to have to tread water. *Brains before brawn. Brains before brawn. She had to conserve energy. She'd float for a while and then tread water. Drowning was probably not the worst way to go.* She was furiously treading water when she was able to touch the ceiling of the Crypt. With only moments to do what she'd planned, she wedged her knife into the vent. *It was going to work! She might fit!* Hope rose within as she curved her fingers over the top and began pulling herself out. There was the briefest moment of salvation as her face burst through. She made eye contact with the person who would seal her drowning experience.

Stephanie smirked and chuckled, "I don't think so," as she pushed her back under the water.

Kayn fought with everything she had. She would have torn her frenemy's flesh to shreds if she'd had nails. She struggled until her head began to pound. Watching Stephanie's satisfied smile through the swirling curtain of liquid above, she attempted to fight back once more as her headache subsided. Her mind began to soothe her fighting spirit. *Sleep Kayn. Just go to sleep.* Kayn's mind made a plea for her sister, *Chloe… Where are you? Chloe, help us.* No answer came from her twin dwelling beneath the surface of her skin.

A voice whispered, "*You want to go to sleep. It's time to sleep. Close your eyes. Everything will be okay.*" Sedating warmth wrapped her in its calming embrace and held her close. "*Sleep,*" the voice whispered. "*It's time for you to sleep.*"

Her struggle ended as her fingers loosened their grasp on Stephanie's flesh, sliding down silky skin into the liquefied weapon of her demise. Her arms floated freely as an angel's wings, having been released from the mortal chains that bound her to this reality. She'd been set free. Her empty vessel floated down the liquid corridor. Even though her eyes remained open, they could no longer see. The strands of her golden hair danced through her liquid nightmare to an unheard song. She was gone…

With a breath and a gasp, Kayn awoke in the Testing, soaked to the bone in the same corridor but it was void of the water she'd submitted to. Breathing foreign oxygen into her lungs, her chest burned. She sat up, clutching her deprived brain. *Her head felt like it was on fire.* She heard a scraping sound. Her eyes followed the noise to the ceiling. The vents opened as the hallway began to flood again. "Seriously," she sighed. *She'd made the wrong decision. The vent above her wasn't the way out.* She stood up and ran down the hall while she still could. Stephanie couldn't possibly be at every vent. *It wouldn't matter. She didn't have her knife anymore. She had nothing to wedge in the vent to keep it open.* Her feet were compelled to leave the ground by the rushing force of the water as the corridor flooded. She began treading water. The tomb had filled much faster the second time around. *Less time for pleasantries but also less time for panicking.* The water got to the level where she could attempt to pull herself through the opening, and, of course, it shut. *This is bullshit!* She allowed herself to succumb to her watery grave. After the exploding headache came a Sweet Sleep. Once again, she floated down the corridor.

She awoke, and this time, she was on board with what was about to happen. She took an extra moment before she opened her eyes, suspecting this was what set off the Crypt's internal countdown to her next demise. She was soaking wet and shivering. Her body lay limp and exhausted on the damp stone. *She needed time to think.* Kayn knew there would be no time granted once she opened her eyes. *Where did the water go? If she could find out where it drained, maybe she could find the way out.* It began again before she even had a chance to sit up. *The Crypt had figured her out.* As the water filled, she wasn't looking up. She was looking down to see where it went. *There was not even a ridge on the floor. It had to go somewhere?* As the water filled, she wondered how many times she was going to be forced to drown before she figured out the secret of the corridor. *She would have to wait for it to fill.* She took a deep breath and didn't even bother to reach for the opening.

Without attempting to get out of the water, it didn't close. She sunk beneath the surface and scoured the stone floor with her eyes. She swam to the vent, stole a single breath and slipped back under the surface. She could see where it was beginning to empty under the water. It swirled, funnelling beneath her. Kayn swam up, took another quick breath and then allowed herself to be sucked into the opening as it drained. She was spat out into another room below alive. Kayn got up and staggered down the hall as the new room began to fill with water. "Oh, you've got to be frigging kidding me," she sighed. About halfway up the wall, she noticed finger grooves. As the water level grew higher, she swam to the wall, placed her fingers in the grooves and laid the heel of her hand against it. It opened slowly. She used her last bit of strength to pull herself through into an adjoining room. The wall slid shut rather abruptly.

She sat there for a second to catch her breath. *Oh, thank god that's done.* Above her, something grunted. Kayn looked up, and all she had time to say was, "Shit!" The hideous, inbred-looking demon's teeth sunk into her legs. She struggled as it dragged her away. With both of her legs in its salivating jaws, it swung her entire body back and flung her against the wall.

Kayn woke up again on her back, staring at the ceiling. The room was morbidly drenched in blood. *She imagined it was hers.* With her mind still reeling from her last brutal demise, she lay there. *At least it was a quick one.* She tried counting the deaths on her fingers, but her math skills were non-existent. "I've died four or five times already. What in the hell is this place?" She whispered aloud. Kayn got up. It took a second to regain her balance. *The demon may still be here.* She nervously glanced around before taking a deep breath. *She was demon-free for the moment.* Kayn felt down her torso. *She was all in one piece. She didn't remember much, so she must have been killed instantly.*

Chapter 41

Anything You Fear Will Be Used Against You

Fear: a distressing emotion aroused by impending danger, evil, pain. The threat is real or imagined. The feeling or condition of being afraid.

Kayn spoke to the wall furthest from where she'd climbed in, "Please open," and it did. She darted through the opening, noticed a knife on the floor and grabbed it, clasping the unusually cold metal in her hands. *Why was it so chilly?* She cautiously commenced walking down the narrow corridor before her. As she travelled into the shadows, she paused. *The end of the corridor was too dark. She couldn't tell what she was walking into.* She stopped moving as a familiar sense of foreboding crept into her subconscious mind, urging her to be wary of what awaited her in the darkness. Before she could take another step, she heard the rumbling of a chainsaw and exclaimed, "Hell no! That's not going to happen!" She spun around and sprinted in the opposite direction, scanning the walls for a way out. She didn't need to look behind her. The vibrating humming echo of the chainsaw was growing louder by the second. Without knowing anything about what pursued her but the fact that it was carrying a chainsaw, Kayn began frantically banging her fist against the wall, pleading, "Please! Open! I'm not into playing chainsaw games today!" The wall slid open slightly faster than usual in response to her urgent plea for salvation. She darted through onto a flight of stairs. The wall slid shut. *Would this route be better or worse?* The stairs descended into darkness. *There was no choice but to proceed down with caution, especially if the option back there had a chainsaw.* After taking a moment to listen to her instincts, she made her way down the stairs with one hand securely against the wall to keep her steady. She was still shaking and didn't want to trip and fall. She had no idea how far the staircase descended. She couldn't see twenty feet in front of her. Something was scurrying around on the stairs. She took a few more steps down. There was a large rat directly in her path. *She wasn't afraid of rodents, so it wasn't a big deal.* She took a step towards the kitten-sized rodent. Kayn whispered, "I'm just going to sneak right past you. I'm not going to hurt you. I promise there is no need to be afraid of me." The rodent looked up at her and cocked its head. *It was kind of cute. She was almost tempted to pet it.* The rat bulked up to twice its size. Kayn took a few steps back up the stairs as she said, "Well, you're not a normal rat, are you? It's okay. I'm not a normal girl. I am cool with you, even at double the size. It's all good. I just need to get past you little buddy." The rat bulked up again. Now, it was blocking the width of the stairs. It smiled at her. Those long square teeth were more intimidating on a rat the size of a large dog. *This wasn't that bad. She was still okay with the creature. She just needed to go past it to go down the stairs. This wasn't a big deal.* Kayn scanned the walls on either side of her for grooves or ridges. *There had to be another way out. What was she thinking? Stairs usually had a way out at the top and at the bottom. At the top, there was a chainsaw. At the bottom was a rat. Granted, it was an enormous rat, but it was still just a rodent. She'd go downstairs versus the alternative.* Kayn quietly bargained, "Hey, little buddy. I just need to sneak by. Not going to hurt you. It's all good."

Its body bulged and shifted. Out of its torso, eight long hairy legs unfolded. *This went from passable to utterly terrifying in five seconds. Nope.* On either side of its square teeth, long razor-sharp fangs grew. *Hard no.* Kayn stepped backwards up the stairs, whispering, "It's fine. I've changed my mind. I don't need to get past you. I'm going to go now. You can just carry on with your giant spider rat transformation thing." Clutching her knife, Kayn gingerly moved backwards up the stairs, knowing she'd have a heart attack long before the creature touched her. Thankful the spider rat hadn't chased her up the stairs, Kayn made the conscious choice to brave the chainsaw versus the messed-up creature.

When she reached the top, she laid her hands against the wall and said, "I've changed my mind. The chainsaw's not that bad. I'm alright with it now. Open up." Something jolted beneath her feet. *Oh, no.* The stairs turned into a slide. Kayn's feet came out from under her. She landed flat on her back and shot down the staircase at lightning speed. She was going so fast that she caught up with the spider rat. *She couldn't help herself. It was like the high-pitched squealing was coming from somebody else. She'd been absolutely terrified many times in this new life, but she was flying down a slide riding on a giant hairy spider rat.* She scrambled away, kicking and flailing. The spider rat appeared equally terrified of her screaming, but it was hard to tell the difference between terror and excitement as you shot down a slide. She ended up on top of the creature as they shot across the floor at the bottom.

Kayn managed to pull herself together. She raised the blade above her head. *They were bumping into hairy things as they sped by. Don't think about it. Just deal with this one first, and then worry about the rest. Just breathe.* She stabbed the monstrosity. *Her mind continued to shoot through scenarios she might be facing.* She couldn't see in the dark but heard the echoes of scurrying legs across the stone. *She imagined that hundreds of rat spiders would be able to see just fine.* She gripped the knife, prepared to fight until her last breath. *She was grateful she couldn't see anything. She couldn't handle the visual.* Kayn felt a searing pain in her leg. *Something was biting her!* She reached down and yanked it off. *She knew what it was as she tossed it across the room. Oh… Crap!* She heard countless scurrying legs. *No! No! No!* She whirled around in the darkness, launching away each abomination that sunk its teeth into her flesh. Her hand pulsed a few times in the darkness. The meagre amount of light revealed that she was surrounded by an enormous swarm of furry beings. *She'd faced this challenge before. She had been in this situation.* Kayn stood her ground, gathering strength from somewhere deep inside. She hissed, "You want a piece of me! Come and get it!" Her leg had begun to burn. Her hand began to pulse, allowing for brief flashes of vision in the darkness. It was a slow, radiating burn. She glanced down at her leg. It was swollen to double its size. She was covered in hives. *Oh, wonderful. I'm allergic to bees and spider rats. Good to know.* She stood, slowly rotating in a circle to keep watch on the swarm of creatures that appeared to be just watching her in each strobe of light. *They were waiting for something. After watching countless low-budget horror movies, she'd given her imagination plenty of ammunition.* The swarm of spider rats parted to allow something large passage. With her blade poised before her, Kayn's mind set on one thing and one thing only. *She would stab this mutant son of a bitch at least once before she went down.*

Suddenly, it felt like she was breathing through a tiny juice pack straw. *Deprived of oxygen, her mind flashed back to the embarrassing fanny pack she'd worn through elementary school, containing her EpiPen. It wouldn't do a damn thing now.* By the light of her flashing Ankh symbol, she saw an enormous creature moving slowly through the middle of the swarm with an ominous rattling. Her ability to inhale air ceased. In her last seconds of consciousness, she saw the monstrosity approaching her. *It had a rat spider's body and a mesmerising rattlesnake's tail. Pass out! She needed to pass out!* It opened its jaws and sprayed something at her. She felt her body spinning in circles. *Why was she still conscious? What in the hell?* She was methodically encased in white as her headache ceased and her mind turned off.

Kayn opened her eyes. *Of course, she was still encased in white. She could breathe. This was good... or was it? Sensing she wasn't alone, she was afraid to move. Breathe in and breathe out. Don't move the web. She had to figure out how to put one foot in front of the other.* Those were Lily's words of wisdom. *She had the urge to try, but she knew how spiders operated. She shouldn't move.* She recalled Frost's words. K*eep your eyes closed and pretend to be asleep for as long as you can. They want to see your pain. You can buy time by pretending to be unconscious.* She thought of Grey's words of wisdom. S*urvey your surroundings.*

Kayn could see faint outlines of something moving outside of the veil of sticky silk she was encased in. *Spiders save their food and drink their insides. Oh, crap. This was going to suck.* She grinned. *She hadn't intended to joke about her impending death. She'd prematurely died of an allergic reaction. That wasn't how this scenario was meant to play out. Others would have simply been encased in silk to be savoured later. The longer she went without attempting movement, the more time she'd have to figure out her escape. Sensing the predators were gone, she decided it was now or never.* She heard muffled moaning. *She wasn't the only snack being stored here.* Kayn whispered, "You have to be quiet. I'm going to get us out." *She must have been gripping her knife when she died. It was still in her hand. They were suspended on a web. If she moved too much, she'd signal the spiders to come back.* She had thrown many a small bug on a spider's web as a child. This was divine karma.

Somewhere in the universe a reincarnated fly was snickering, "I got you, Kayn Brighton."

She shifted the blade in her hand without being able to see which direction it faced and felt it slice into her skin. *That was obviously the wrong way.* She hoped she wasn't bleeding too much. *That would probably signal them back just as fast as the movement on the web would.* She sliced into the silk, knowing she'd have to do this quickly. *She couldn't do that without movement.* She swung and sliced her way out and fell through layers of web. She bounced and toppled downwards until she hit the stone floor. Above her, she saw the cocooned Tri-Clan in need of help. She ran to one corner of the room and sliced the supporting web. The cocoon tumbled down and came to rest beside her. She sliced the webbing with her blade. It was Leanne from Trinity. She'd gotten to know Leanne well during their week together. *They'd been given the opportunity to get to know each other and understand that, in the end, they were all the same.*

"You're not going to kill me now, are you?" Leanne asked, wide-eyed.

Kayn stated the obvious, "Why would I go through all of the trouble of helping you to kill you? We should get out of here before those spider rat things come back."

"Thank you," Leanne replied as Kayn helped her up.

Kayn smiled as she said, "Not a problem." As the girls turned around, they saw three doorways. Leanne was standing in front of her with an ominous circular bulge on the side of her neck. *She should mention it.*

"I'll take this one," the girl from Trinity prompted. "You take the other. We probably shouldn't be seen together."

Kayn agreed, "You're right, but first, I should mention that there's something on your neck."

Leanne reached up, felt the giant hard blister and said, "I think I'm okay. It's a bite. Thanks again. If I get the chance, I'll return the favour."

Kayn watched the girl she thought of as a friend as she took off down the dark passageway. *Maybe they could just choose to be friends?* Kayn began running down the passage next to the one

Leanne had chosen. She was about thirty feet in when she heard her friend's high-pitched screaming. She raced back to help. Kayn found her on the ground, either dead or unconscious with thousands of tiny spiders rushing out of the bulge on her neck. There were shivers up her spine as she tried to brush them off, but they just kept coming like there was an endless supply. This took bravery on Kayn's part. *No matter how many times she dealt with spiders and no matter what the size, they made her skin crawl.* Kayn heard people coming and recognised the voices. *It was Trinity. Leanne would be fine now. She wasn't separated from her Clan anymore. They'd take care of her.* Kayn turned and sprinted back down the tunnel and dove into the one she'd originally come from. She ran without thinking of the consequences down the tunnel until she reached the open space at the base of the stairs. *At the top of the stairs, there was someone with a chainsaw. At the bottom, Trinity was going to appear.* She raced up the stairs, taking notice of the rim on the edge of the stone staircase, planning to jump on it and brace herself with one foot on either side of the stairs if they turned to a slide when she touched the wall. She could hear Trinity. They were already coming up the stairs. She placed her hand on the wall at the top. The stairs shifted to a slide just as she'd suspected it would. She leapt on the edge with a foot positioned on either side, then jumped through the opening to the echoes of the Trinity sliding down the stairs.

Knowing what was coming for her next, Kayn bent over and took a moment to breathe with her knife clutched in her hand. *Not losing the knife was a miracle.* She scanned her body for bumps. *The last thing she needed was a million surprise spiders. She didn't find anything. It was time to harness her inner badass.* She straightened her posture and hollered at the darkness, "Well, come on then! Let's do this!" A chainsaw rumbled. Instead of running in the other direction, she gripped her blade, grimaced and sprinted straight towards the sound. A hooded being with a rumbling chainsaw ran at her. She kept going against the urge to stop and ran right through him. *It was a hologram.* She skidded down the end of the hallway and hit the wall, hard enough to smart. The ground slid away and she fell directly onto a startled Kevin. He scrambled to his feet, ready to rumble with a silver dagger in his hand. *He wasn't alone. He was afraid. She understood what they were going to have to do. They would have to fight and it had to look real.* Kayn faced him, with the knife she'd acquired firmly in her grasp. There was the briefest moment of standoff, before he shoved her against the wall and they began to struggle. The next wall slid open and they fell through it. She landed on top of him with her knife poised above his stomach. He nodded, letting her know he was alright with what she had to do. She stared into the eyes of the boy she'd adored since she was five and tried to find the will to do what she knew she was supposed to do. *No… This isn't right.* "I can't do it," Kayn whispered.

He quietly asserted, "It will make me feel a whole lot better if you stab me first." Hearing grinding walls, they scrambled to their feet. He grabbed hold of her arm and towed her through the next few sliding walls. When they paused to catch their breath, he said, "If you're not going to kill me, you have to get out of here. If I get caught helping you, it will just make things worse for me. I can only get out of this place with my Clan. I can't afford to have them all pissed off. Go find your Clan, Kayn."

She shoved him and accused, "You were the one that yanked me through the last couple of walls! You could have just left me there!" The walls began to shift again. Kayn sprinted away from him, down the next corridor. He followed her. Ahead of her there was a large part of the floor missing. She ran directly at it, leaping over the missing chunk of corridor. She'd attempted the feat to prove a point but only managed to prove one to herself. *She was trying to show off. She wanted to show him that she wasn't afraid anymore.* Kayn was left dangling over the edge with the tips of her fingers as her only salvation. Kevin made the jump. He hung over the side and grabbed a hold of her wrists, just as she lost her grip. *She could hear rushing water beneath her.*

Struggling to hold on to her, he hollered, "I can't keep doing this! We can't keep doing this!"

Staring into his eyes, she replied, "Then let me go!" She slipped down a bit. He grasped a hold of her tighter.

As the wall opened behind them, he said, "Hold your breath."

She dropped into the water. She'd thought he'd let her go but as she bobbed to the surface of the swiftly moving current, she saw him. *He'd jumped into the rapids after her.* There were roots and foliage, just out of arms reach, as the force of the rapids took them downstream. There was jungle in this part of the Crypt. Kayn swam for the side as she rushed through the current, half expecting the vines to be a hologram but they felt real. She successfully grabbed a hold of one and stretched out her legs into the current attempting to either slow him down or give him something to grab hold of. The vine tore loose and she was sucked under. The water swirled around her. She swam for the bubbles above her, inhaling a giant breath of air while noticing the waterfall up ahead. *There was no time to plot strategy.* "Kevin!" she called out his name trying to warn him as she went over the edge. She dropped at least fifty feet before hitting the water at the bottom as though it were made of concrete.

She heard the rushing of the falls. Kayn opened her eyes and realised she was behind the waterfall. The water from the falls was a haunting liquid veil with jungle visible through it. She felt his presence and turned around. Kevin was sitting against the stone, waiting for her to come to.

He teased, "You're not supposed to attempt to do a belly flop from that height. I thought everyone knew that little rule of life."

"Do I hear birds? I swear can hear birds," she exclaimed.

Kevin was cutting up a piece of what appeared to be some kind of fruit with his knife. He handed her a piece. "We're in the jungle," he explained. "I have no idea how that's even possible but we're here. I took a good look around and there doesn't appear to be any obvious way out. We could be trapped together for a while."

As Kayn took a bite of the fruit, it gushed down her chin and she laughed.

Kevin scooted closer to her, wiped off her chin with his hand and returned her smile. Their eyes met and she bit her lip in anticipation. His lips parted and he quickly retreated to where he'd been sitting before, appearing to be conflicted. He got up and offered her his hand with the mystical soundtrack of the waterfall playing in the background. He helped her up and she squeezed his hand lovingly before letting go.

His eyes softened as he clarified, "We're making this more difficult than it needs to be. We need to find our Clans. We can't get out of the Testing together. What if we lose our chance to get out of this place while we're wasting time messing with Fate?"

He was going to walk away and she couldn't allow him to do that… Not again. Kayn grabbed his wrist and stopped him. *The look on his face said everything she needed to know. He was fighting against his feelings for her.* She urged him closer with a gentle tug.

With raw emotion in his eyes, he cautioned, "Don't."

She pushed him just a touch further, "Kiss me goodbye."

Kevin moved in as he gently caressed her cheek. Visibly in awe of her, he confessed, "I'm always fighting off the urge to count your freckles. Why is that? I can't even force myself to hurt you. I can't let go of your hand without jumping in after you. We're never getting out of here if we don't stay away from each other. It's not that I don't want you. It's that I can't." He took her hand and placed it on his Triad symbol branded on the flesh above his heart.

Kayn traced her finger seductively along the ridges of the mark that would always keep them apart. *She missed the boy she'd grown up watching clouds with, almost as much as she missed the way they loved each other. The way he could still love her now… If he allowed himself.* She gently kissed him and pulled away, needing to see his reaction.

Emotion caught in his throat, "Is this what you want?" He walked her backwards until he had her pressed against the stone. The tension between them rose to a tumultuous peak. He was a breath away from his lips touching hers when he paused.

"I know you want me too," she provoked as she ran her fingers through his hair and drew his lips the rest of the way to hers. They melted together in an exquisitely seductive dance of tortured souls as he caressed her silken skin in pleasurable places, triggering reckless abandon she'd never experienced. She whispered her love for him against his damp hair. He pulled away from her like she'd thrown a bucket of ice water on him. Aching from the absence of his touch, she reached out for him.

He blocked her hand and cautioned, "If you keep trying to seduce me Kayn. I'm going to give you exactly what you're asking me for. I don't have the strength to keep turning you down."

"I know you care about me," Kayn whispered.

Placing his hand against her chest to keep her from coming closer, he said, "Of course I do but the guy you're in love with is gone. That's not who I am. I could never be him and survive in Triad. I have to become colder and stronger to be a leader. The person I need to be, to survive is the opposite of what you want."

Kayn knew his words were the truth, but it didn't matter. She couldn't will herself to stop forcing the issue even though she knew it was stubborn and reckless to keep pressing his buttons like this. She implored, "I hear what you're saying. I know you're right but can't we pretend for a little while longer?"

Kevin groaned, "That's just it. It's time to stop pretending everything hasn't changed between us. It's only postponing the inevitable."

She whispered, "We get to choose our path. We can choose to keep our friendship alive. We can choose to always care about each other." Kayn kissed his cheek. Kevin stared at her for a second before gently kissing her lips in response. She slipped her fingers into his hair and pulled him closer. She parted her lips, deepening the seduction until every nerve ending in her body was pleading with her to make him keep going.

He feathered seductive kisses on her neck, down her shoulder to her collar bone. She gasped as he breathlessly whispered against her skin, "Do you want me to take you? I can keep going. It won't make me remember you and it won't make me love you back."

He was right. She placed her hand firmly against his chest to signal that he'd made his point. He stepped away from her and it felt like the emotional version of taking the plug out of a bathtub full of water as any hope that lingered began to funnel down the drain. *Why couldn't she manage to grasp the reality of this? He'd given her the same speech repeatedly. She couldn't force him to love her back. She couldn't kiss him into magically remembering what they'd once meant to each other. She was selfishly trying to find shelter from the storm. He was right. Her version of him could never withstand the trials of Triad. That version of Kevin could no longer exist. If she truly had loved him, why would she continue to force him to hurt himself? If she truly loved him, she had to let him go. She'd never understood this quote. It made perfect sense now.*

"I don't want to hurt you," he explained. "I have to count on the other Triad to get out of here and they have to feel like they can trust me. I can't be seen helping the enemy. Stephanie's already going to go postal on me for jumping in after you back there. I left my own Clan to make sure you were safe. I jumped off a cliff with you. I followed you into rapids. I left Patrick and Stephanie standing there wondering, what in the hell I was doing? They need to get out of here. They're stuck in hell and I ditched them for one more second with you. We need to stay away from each other. In this new life, we can only bring each other pain."

Kayn said, "You realise that in one breath you say you don't feel the same way, and in the next, you act like your feelings for me can't be controlled with anything but my complete and total absence from your life?" He touched her arm. Kayn turned to look at him, shook her head and whispered, "Don't."

They walked out from under the falls in silence. *It was time to step out of the past. It was time to take care of the situation at hand. She needed to find a way out of this place. She needed distance from him.* They were in a mystical jungle with a cave spouting out a waterfall. Kayn wondered if they'd be forced to go back out the way they'd come into this wonderland. *It was a truly miraculous place.* After all that grey her senses were practically sparkling while standing in the lush, fragrant vibrantly coloured jungle. *She had to do something to quiet the part of her that wanted them to be stuck in here together. Eventually, he would remember her. Someday, he'd give in to the feelings building between them. They could be happy. Those were childish fantasies. She wasn't a child anymore. Being happy at the expense of someone else would come with repercussions. They would trap both of their Clans in this place forever. They would destroy the people they were meant to stand beside and protect.* As Kayn glanced down at the mark on her hand, she knew they weren't meant to stand beside each other anymore. *As much as those words hurt, it was the truth.* Every time she was close to Kevin, she wanted to ignore the signs and jump in with both feet. *Maybe this was part of her test?* She strolled beside him without words. *What do you say to somebody you care for beyond the point of reason? How do you pacify your own ego after someone has given you the same kiss-off speech twenty times? She knew he was only trying to make her understand that what they were, was impossible. Not because he wanted it to be that way, but because it had to be. All hail to the new reigning king of mixed messages.* Kevin wandered off in search of the way out. Kayn sat in the grass in front of a group of beautiful purple orchids. A bumblebee buzzed and tiptoed across the top of one, his legs covered in yellow pollen as he moved on to the next orchid. She reached over to touch the sticky part of the exquisitely beautiful purple flower. *Everyone has a sticky centre and he was stuck in hers.* She allowed her inner Chloe to pick the orchid and smell it. She smiled as she tossed it into the water and watched it drift away. She heard a rustling noise and glanced up.

Kevin sat down beside her and said, "I don't want to keep hurting you."

"I know you don't," Kayn replied. "I should have listened the first dozen times you gave me that speech."

He tugged another flower out of the ground and passed it to her. *It was a fitting gesture. He'd given her a purple flower the day they met and he was giving her one now. This was really goodbye.*

She hesitated before taking it, so he tucked it behind her ear as he questioned, "What would we do in these fantasies of yours? See each other once or twice a year and be forced to fight? Maybe, we'd sneak away from our Clans and steal a kiss or have sex in a closet? It wouldn't be romantic. It would be torture. You would spend every single day aching to be with me. I'm a guy. If I slept with you it would make things easier for me. Question answered and territory conquered. It's not going to be about anything more than that for me because I'm not the same person."

Kayn couldn't help herself. Starting to laugh, she teased, "Don't sugar coat it or anything."

Kevin grinned and retaliated, "I can see how we would have been best friends though. Everything about you is appealing. You are so weird. You have a warped sense of humour. Your hair always looks messy and I swear, I've never seen you without dirt on your face. I don't even know how you do it. We just got out of the water."

Suddenly concerned, Kayn questioned, "Is there actually dirt on my face right now?"

Kevin reached over and wiped the streak of dirt off her cheek with his thumb. Determined to be strong, Kayn closed her eyes as he touched her and opened them without a tear. *It was time to let go. He was right. The all-humiliation Kayn channel was once again stuck on the same damn episode. Kevin Dumps Kayn. It's a good show. She'd seen it countless times now and she just kept pressing play, didn't she?* She felt ridiculous as she glanced back at him and he winked at her. She removed the flower from her hair and methodically plucked every second petal off. *He'd hung out with her and flirted with her because he wanted to get her into bed. He hadn't gone through with it because he still had a glimmer of instinct to protect her. That was all it had been. She could have sworn he had real feelings for her. She had read so much between the lines and only allowed herself to hear what she wanted to hear. This time, she heard him loud and clear. She had to get back to her Clan. She had to find Melody and Zach.* Kayn stood up and tossed the flower into the water. It drifted beside the other one for a second before the current pulled them apart. She shut her eyes and thought, *be strong. Be brave. You've battled spiders and won. You are a badass.* She spun around and declared, "Let's get out of here."

Kevin grinned and agreed with her, "Sounds like a plan."

Kayn recalled something from her watery grave. *What if the answer was simple?* She glanced at the base of the waterfall right where it funnelled under the surface. *They'd have to swim underwater for the way out. She could feel it. Would she be showing him where Ankh's secret Crypts were hidden in the real world by telling him about swimming under the waterfall?* Kayn said, "There's an entrance above the falls. What if the exit is below the falls?"

"You mean underwater?" Kevin clarified.

"It would be the most inconvenient place for one to be." Kayn stated, "That is kind of how this place works."

A toucan flew past them and Kayn smiled, "You brought the Fruit Loops toucan on your rescue attempt, how adorable."

Kevin smiled while probing, "Fruit Loops toucan? What are you talking about?"

"From the cereal box," she explained. "We ate a lot of it, when we were kids." She stopped cold and said, "Never mind. It's not important."

"When we all get out of this place, I'll try some and think of you." He assured as he walked into the water.

She replied, "I hope both of our Clans make it out of here so you can."

"I hope your Clan makes it out too," Kevin replied.

They waded out to the ledge of the drop off and swam out to the falls. The closer they came to the falls, the less they could see with the mist on the surface. Taking one last look at him before diving under, Kayn swam into the current at the base of the falls. It sucked her in.

She bobbed up inside a pool in the cave without him. Kayn swam to the rock and pulled herself up on the ledge. She sat there for a minute, waiting for him. *What was she waiting for? It was time to part ways.* Kayn stood up and walked towards the rock face. It appeared to be easy to climb. She grabbed the stone, gripping it with her fingers, she hoisted herself up. Kayn didn't look back until she reached the opening of another dark cavern at the top. She glanced back. *He still wasn't there.* She stepped into the cave. Beneath her feet was soft silky sand instead of hard cold stone. She drew herself a symbolic line and stepped over it.

Chapter 42

The Lion

She began her journey down the sandy hallway into the isolation of the darkness and suddenly, there was light. *The flickering torches had lit themselves. It felt like magic.* The sand was warm underfoot as she strolled down the hallway with an unusual unwavering sense of calm. *Surely there had to be more to this Testing, a deeper meaning. There was something that she was missing.* She turned down a long corridor but felt no danger or urgency in the presence of the tranquil dancing flames. It occurred to her that she'd been walking for a little too long and that even though she felt safe, logic prodded her to open her eyes and acknowledge that she wasn't. Shivers travelled up her spine as her instincts whispered, *you're not alone.* She whipped around. *There was nobody there.* Goosebumps peaked on her skin as she spun around again, certain someone was there, having that creepy indefinable feeling of being watched. As she made her way to the end of the lighted hall, she saw a female figure. She cautiously took a few more steps and it was her mother, standing in the flickering light with her arms open to receive her in her maternal embrace. There was no wind, yet her mother's hair and white gown shifted as though it were moving in a delicate summer's breeze. *She could smell her mother's perfume in the air.* The heart-wrenchingly familiar fragrance invaded her senses, confusing her. Kayn whispered, "Mom, is that you?" Logic prodded her brain. *This is a trap. It's not your mother. It can't be... Proceed with caution.* "Mom? Is that you?" She whispered as she came closer. *Since when had she listened to logic?* Kayn stopped about ten feet away with her senses screaming, *brains before brawn, dumb ass!* Kayn bent down, grabbed a handful of sand and tossed it at her mother. *It was a hologram. Her mother wasn't real. A scented hologram was evil genius. What was she being distracted from seeing? That was the question.* A shiver travelled up her spine. The kind you get when someone's standing right behind you. Kayn sighed, "What now?" *She didn't want to turn around because she knew somebody was there.* A blade pressed against her throat.

Kevin's voice whispered in her ear, "I have to."

His blade slid across her neck. In shock, she staggered forward, clutching her throat, choking on her blood as it spurted into the sand. *No! She loved him! He couldn't!* The bare feet of the Triad ran past her. She raised her teary eyes, with her hands desperately clutching her neck as her essence strained through her fingers. Triad disappeared down the sandy corridor. *He did it...*She sunk to her knees in the sand as her soul shattered into millions of unsalvageable pieces. *He did it.* She released her throat and allowed death to take her, feeling nothing but the devastation of his betrayal.

Kayn awoke, twitching her fingers in the... *wet sand?* The memory of her death flooded her being with all-encompassing fury. *He'd killed her. Her best friend had slit her throat. She hadn't been capable of killing him when faced with the same moment. She was a frigging fool.* Enraged, she scrambled to her feet. *She was going to kill every one of them.* Her chest tightened then moved to the pit of her stomach. She felt something twisting inside of her, demanding to be set free. Kayn lost her footing, teetering over she reached for the wall, and it shocked her, launching her violently through the air. Her body hit the opposite wall with bone-splintering force. An incapacitating surge of energy caused her muscles to spasm. Her limbs twisted and contorted until her body became limp in the sand. *One of her hands was still stinging.* Unable to move, she forced her eyes to look at it. *It was almost touching the wall.* It took everything she had to shift it an inch. She tried to grasp the sandy floor with her fingertips, knowing she needed to pull her body out of range. *What in the hell was that? She needed to get out of here. She was so hot. Did she have a fever? She was sweating profusely. She was so thirsty, so hungry. She was starving to death. She needed to eat something. She had to find sustenance. She had to find it right now.* She struggled to get up. Using her arms for balance, she noticed her veins were brilliant blue. *What was happening to her? Instinct prodded her to search for her Clan.* Her heart constricted again with such brutal force that she dropped to her knees in the sand, shrieking in agony. When the pain finally ceased, all she could think about was the hunger in her soul. *She was starving.* Fighting off the urge to touch the wall again, she distracted herself by looking down at the blood-soaked sand. *That was her blood.* She placed her hands in the gory wet mush as her mind replayed his knife slitting her throat. Her heart clenched again. She forced herself to stand. Every cell in her body was screaming about the severity of his betrayal as she staggered away, disorientated by the sweltering heat. She was gifted with a jolt of adrenaline so powerful she began to sprint through the sandy maze as though it were possible to outrun emotions. The walls began to open for her as she approached. It was as though they were getting out of her way. Her senses raged with a primal, savage need for vengeance. *She never wanted to feel weak again. That was not who she was meant to be.* She heard Tiberius' voice whispering the words, *'You were meant to be a lion, not a mouse.'* She stopped cold as the sand beneath her feet turned to stone. Sweat was streaming down her forehead, her hair damp with salty perspiration. *She'd been attempting to hang on to the girl she'd once been. It was time to let her go. It was time to become something more.* Standing up straight, she took a deep breath as an intense surge of adrenaline washed over her. A blaze within her smouldered in the pit of her stomach as her blood coursed through clearly visible veins. She scanned the walls for grooves and ridges as she prowled down the long stone corridor, a lioness hunting for prey in a concrete jungle. She entered a circular room with a floor of sand. In the far corner towered an enormous man facing the wall. There were human bones piled at his feet and scattered throughout the room. *She wasn't afraid. The energy surging through her made her feel indestructible.* Kayn strolled into the middle of the room and announced, "Well, let's do this!"

The man turned slowly, revealing one enormous onyx bee-like eye in the centre of his forehead. Neither had a weapon. He growled and cocked his head at her, opening a hundred tiny eyes where she'd thought there was only one. *He was a hologram. He had to be.* He shrieked in an ear-piercing pitch as he came at her with his bulging muscles and rock-solid torso, appearing to be an impenetrable force. Kayn planted her feet in the sand and stood her ground. Something poked the arch of her foot. *It was a blade.* She kicked it in the direction she was headed as she dove out of the way. As Kayn hit the sand, it spewed up around her. Fate had her back as she reached for the blade, leapt up and sprinted at the being, sticking him once before he ripped her off him and tossed her against the ceiling. She hit the roof with brutal force and then dropped to the sand, landing at the feet of the beast with the knife still firmly gripped in her hand. Gifted with no pain and yet another insane surge of adrenaline, she rolled out of the way as it attempted to stomp her face. She slashed its ankle. The stunned beast dropped to the sand before her. She leapt on top of the abomination and stabbed him through the centre of his hundred eyes. *Double tap. She didn't need this one getting back up and coming after her.* Kayn yanked out the blade and knifed the creature's chest. Blood sprayed from its wound in thick, beating spurts, soaking her skin and sarong crimson red. Kayn's hand still gripped the weapon that impaled the creature's chest as its hundred eyes, minus the ones she'd stabbed, rolled back. A shock rippled up her arms into her chest and she was thrown across the room. Kayn lay squirming on her back, writhing in agony, shrieking as her blood boiled beneath her skin. She clawed at the sand, trying to escape herself, as her head pounded its revolt against the agonising process of her Enlightenment.

With an overwhelming hunger, she scrambled to her knees in the sand as the embodiment of the lion she was meant to become. A hunter by nature, need rippled through her being. She leapt to her feet with inhuman agility, suddenly aware of the clashing swords and tortured screams of agony. *It was close by. It was happening on the other side of the circular wall... but who was it?* Kayn hovered her hand above the stone and commanded, "Show me!" The wall opened, granting her access to Triad fighting Trinity. Kayn met Kevin's eyes from across the room and felt no longing, no love, absolutely nothing but the overwhelming need for revenge. He looked shocked to see her. She raced head-on through the violent madness with a shock or a burn each time someone wounded her. Kayn savagely thrust her blade, taking out everyone that stood between her and the boy she now despised as she ferociously battled her way across the room, tossing Clan around like the warrior she was meant to be. When she reached Kevin, he didn't attempt to stop her as she launched him against the wall. It registered that she'd been fatally wounded. If she only had time for one act before this death, it would be to have her vengeance. She gazed into his solemn eyes like he was nothing as she dragged her blade across his throat. As the warmth of his blood began trickling through her fingers, her heart released a wail of anguish. For a millisecond, her soul allowed the buried emotions to surface. *He hadn't been sure she had it in her. She knew this by the look in his eyes. He hadn't even attempted to fight back. He'd allowed her to kill him.* She collapsed against him, smelling the scent of his skin as she succumbed to her own final reckoning. Her heart ached as they crumpled to the ground together.

Kayn twitched her fingers. She was no longer lying in sand. She was lying on stone. Wherever she was, she knew he was gone. *She was alone.* She thought of his expression as she killed him and tears began streaming down her face. She curled up in the fetal position on the cold stone, sobbing. *She'd done something that would forever alter her soul. She knew this.* Kayn caught sight of her veins. *They were even darker than before.* She knelt with her hands clasped together. "I'm sorry," she sobbed. "This isn't who I wanted to be." She pressed her hands to her lips, then as realisation hit, her eyes widened. She covered her mouth with one of her hands. *What had she done?*

She heard Leanne's voice behind her, "Get out of here! Run! Triad and Trinity have temporarily joined forces. They're looking for you!"

Leanne had done as she'd promised. She'd returned the favour. Kayn gathered her bearings as she stood up and said, "Thank you." She sprinted away from Trinity, down the long corridor, continuing to follow it as it curved and came to a dead-end. The wall shifted aside. She darted through the opening, moving through each wall as it opened. She ran as far and as fast as her exhausted limbs would carry her. *She was so tired. She could barely keep her eyes open. How long had she gone without sleep? How long had she been separated from her Clan?* She manoeuvred through the next shifting wall and dropped into a giant ball pit. *This was weird?* Primary coloured softball-sized balls filled the room. *She'd always loved ball pits.* A see-through lid slid shut above her, and she felt like a lizard in a terrarium. *That can't be good.* Each time she moved, she sunk further into the plethora of balls. Struggling to climb out, she slipped deeper into her childhood fantasy. *Soon, it was all she could see. If someone was watching her, judging each decision she made, this would be seriously entertaining.* Music began to play. She recognised the tune. *When she was little, she'd had a jewellery box with a ballerina that spun on the top as this song played. What was the name of this song?* She remained still, needing to see if the balls shifted without her movement. *She appeared to be alone.* Each time she tried to climb out, the balls shifted around her. *She was so tired. This was way too much cheery stimulation for her mind. Brains before brawn. Did it really matter which wall she busted out of? Probably not.* She forced her way through the balls at the bottom of the pit until she hit a transparent barrier. *It appeared to be plastic.* She wanted to knock on it but knew it was a horrible idea to make excessive noise before scoping out your surroundings. *They used to play sharks in the ball pit. That would suck. She'd better not even think it. She needed to be thinking of puppies, kittens and fuzzy baby chicks. There was always a way out. She had choices. If she tried to break through it, the noise might add something to the situation. She needed to see the landscape outside of the wall in each direction.* Kayn shoved her way through the bottom of the ball pit to the next wall. It appeared to be dangling off the edge of a cliff, with no floor for the last few feet of her encasement. She carefully backed up and shifted her way to the next wall. There was a fully lit corridor. She felt the wall for an exit in this direction. *It seemed like the best option so far.* She was hungry, exhausted and covered in feather-light brightly coloured balls. *It was overstimulating as hell. She was so sleepy.* She made her way back to the centre as the name of the song her jewellery box played popped into her mind. *Why are there so many songs about rainbows? She was so sleepy. Yes, she needed to close her eyes for a second.* It occurred to her as she closed her eyes that there was a disturbing lack of fresh air. *She was too tired. She went to sleep.*

Kayn awoke face down in an empty plastic box. She opened her eyes as she wearily raised her head. *The balls were gone. They had been a brilliant distraction. Without the balls, the plastic encasement reminded her of a superhero jail from the movies. There appeared to be no way out.* She walked to the wall she hadn't made it to. *Yes, it was sealed airtight.* She glanced at her feet. *She was standing on sand. She hadn't been before. She needed to harness her problem-solving skills.* Kayn knelt as she dug through the sand in search of answers because the sand beneath her feet was the only difference in the scenario. She grimaced as her knuckles hit plastic. *It was only a thin layer, maybe a foot in depth. There had to be more to this. It felt like a clue.* Kayn cleared away a patch of sand. She raked her hands through it and the area surrounding it. She kept repeating this action in the sand until she felt something ominous. She brushed the sand away. It was a giant red button that had the word 'easy' written on it. She grinned. *This was an absolutely hilarious thing to do to a human being.* Kayn sighed and said, "Is this a good thing or a bad thing? Do I just push the giant red button?" *She was talking to herself because she was tired again. The box was running low on oxygen.* With a deep breath, she embraced the humorous cliché by pushing the button.

The bottom of the pit dropped out from under her, and Kayn plummeted into the darkness. She saw the shining ripple of water approaching with enormous, translucent circles floating everywhere. *Jellyfish… Oh, Shit. A belly flop onto a sea of jellyfish would be an epically bad idea.* She straightened her body to enter feet first. *Physical pain versus emotional might be a refreshing change.* She plunged into the water, past the jellyfish, feeling the searing agony of their stings. Kayn came close to hitting bottom. *The jellyfish slowed her down.* She saw an underwater passage and swam for it, managing to hit the flow of the current. She shot through into another room. Kayn pulled herself up on stone as the world hummed around her. Her vision flickered as she succumbed to the poison.

It felt like she'd been in a sound sleep for days. She awoke refreshed. Kayn glanced at her arms. The sketchy veins vanished. *She was back to normal. Whatever that was? How many days had they been in the Testing? She hadn't seen Zach or Melody in a long time. It had been too long. Her priorities weren't messed up anymore. She had to make finding them her goal.* Once again, she had a rock face to scale. It was easy, just as the last one had been. Foot and hand to stone, she gripped and climbed her way to the top with energy to burn this time. Kayn stared at the two caves before her. *Should she go left or right? Which route should she choose?* She stood up, squeezed her eyes shut and spun around, choosing her direction as a child would have. She was pointed at one of the openings and went that way. *Well, bring on the next messed-up scenario.*

Kayn wandered corridors of stone for a long time, with no drama or anxiety. As she reached the final flaming torches, no walls opened as her stroll led her into darkness. *It was becoming uncomfortably hot. She felt nervous.* T*hat was never a good sign.* Her instincts whispered, *danger ahead.* At this point in the game, dying was expected but not nearly as upsetting as the idea of the intense pain preceding death. Something growled at the end of the corridor. She froze in place as shivers cascaded down her arms. *How many times would she have to die before her body's instinct for self-preservation ceased?* Through the darkness large red eyes glowed. Kayn glanced back at the empty corridor behind her. *Should she run away? Would it make a difference in the end? She was changing. Yes, she still had the instinct for self-preservation, but she also understood death was an unavoidable fact in this place.* Out of the shadows jumped a scaly tiger-like creature with a hard shell-ridged tail. Kayn froze, contemplating her next move. *She had salt on her. The temperature had left a slick film of perspiration on her skin. The moisture would help the salt stick. If the creature was a demon it might deter it.* She pulled the bag out and untied the top while quite laughably trying to maintain dominant eye contact with the salivating, jagged-fanged beast. Scared shitless, she dumped salt in her hand. *The lion within her had picked an inconvenient time to vanish. This left her at a disadvantage. In that state, she would have taken on this beast without batting an eye.* The glowing embers of hope were instantly extinguished as she saw the enormous stinger on its tail. *This was definitely her nightmare and that meant there was no way out.* She cautiously stepped backwards. She'd always identified with the scorpions in pet stores. She'd stare in the glass tanks and think, *why do I find you so intriguing? I could never even hold you. A scorpion's sting was the strength of ten bee stings. She was allergic to bees and knew she was fascinated with them because they were a representation of her mortality. A scorpion was an epic icon of her mortality. She understood. There was no escape from an abomination born of her worst nightmares, but perhaps she could buy herself enough time to get her shit together so she could die with some dignity.* In a high tone reserved for small children and animals, she cooed, "Aren't you an exquisite creature. Nice kitty, scorpion, or whatever you are." Kayn backed up as it strode confidently towards her with majestic agility. She sensed playfulness in its devilishly animated eyes. *Cats like to play with their prey before consuming them. This was going to be unpleasant.* She continued backing away, calmly whispering, "Nice kitty. Let's just pretend you're just a giant kitty." The creature smiled at her with its grill full of gnarly jagged teeth. *Awe, shit. It has a sense of humour.* She noticed a small knife in the sand and grabbed for it as she slowly backed away. It wasn't long before she found herself backed up against the wall with nowhere to go. *Just wonderful.*

"Come on… Please, open up," Kayn pled her case. It didn't budge, of course. T*hat would have been far too convenient.* Her eyes were scanning for ridges as the large cat-like creature crouched and started making chirping noises like a house cat excited about a bird too close to the window. The wall opened behind her. Someone snagged her arm and yanked her through just as a hail of fire and lava came spraying out of the creature's jaws. For the briefest moment, she believed she'd been saved. It took a second to register the horror. Watching flaming lava engulf her arms, flesh melted from her bones. She sunk to her knees as crippling indescribable torture encompassed her being. Her soul screamed from within as she burst into ash and disintegrated into the stale air of the Crypt.

Chapter 43

Weapons Of Mass Destruction

Kayn gasped as her soul awakened, with her mind still reeling from the excruciating pain of her last death. *Something was boiling beneath her skin.* It was visible as she stared in awe at her arms. Red welts bubbled on the surface. She'd just exploded into ash and was concerned she was about to relive that excruciating demise. Her veins were putrid green instead of brilliant blue but visible to the naked eye. *It didn't hurt.* She clicked. *This was another part of her Enlightening. It was starting again. How long did it take? As* Kayn looked at her hands, her bubbling skin abruptly stopped. *It was like she'd calmed it down by understanding what was happening.* That one thing had ceased, but blood was still rushing through her veins, competing with the whooshing echo of her heart. *Did she have to calm down or push it further to get it to stop? It felt like if she didn't do something to release the energy, she was going to explode.* With a blood-curdling scream, Kayn released the pent-up rage consuming her. *It sounded like she'd stepped outside of her body, and it was coming from someone else.* Kayn shrieked again and again as her heartbeat sped up to the intensity of her pitch. Adrenaline rippled its way through her body with an intensity she'd never experienced. *Damn it. That felt amazing.* Every battle ceased as her screams echoed through the city-sized endless tunnels. Enlightened Tri-Clan had a moment of silence in admiration for the power that must have flowed through someone to make them purge it with such exquisitely pitched anguish. Her screaming seemed to move along the walls. It echoed and grew louder, taking on a life of its own as it travelled through the endless corridors of the Crypt.

Spent, Kayn lay motionless on the cold, unforgiving stone. Her mind was empty of all mortal turmoil as her eyes came into focus. She got up and steadied her jelly-like legs by placing a hand against the wall, still humming with her anguish. This time, the contact caused warm, exhilarating energy to travel up her arm. Any normal person would have yanked their hand away fearing what came next, but for Kayn, fear was in short supply these days. She was intrigued by the sensation. It hit her chest as glorious euphoria. Power surged through her being. *Addictive didn't fully describe it. She felt dangerously explosive and volatile. She didn't want to let go of the wall but her fingers were burning.* She staggered backwards and stared at her Ankh symbol as it glimmered with a pale yellow light. *Her symbol had only flickered a few times since the spider rat incident, no matter how horrific her demise.* The torches lighting up the Crypt flickered and went out.

It felt like she was forgetting something important while standing in the isolating darkness. Logic stepped in, prodding her to move. *Her screaming would have given away her location. They were already looking for her. She hadn't exactly spent her time in the Testing making friends.*

Using instinct to guide her in the absence of light, she sprinted through the Crypt. Doing surprisingly well, running blind, Kayn came to a dead-end. Slamming into the wall, her pulse raced as she experienced another soul-altering surge of energy. The wall slid open into a lighted corridor. *She could see!* Her fingertips were crackling with static electricity. *What was this?* Her knife grew too hot to hold. She dropped it as it sizzled her skin. Kayn clasped her hands together and blew in the centre. *That hurt!* There was hazy blue energy surrounding her fingers, crackling and hissing in the space between them. With morbid fascination, she put her fingers together, touching all ten in the middle and slowly pulled them apart. An orb of blue energy expanded between her palms. *What in the hell is this shit?* She moved her hands around the energy in awe of her newfound ability. Each time she took a deep breath, it felt like she was drawing energy from the room. *She wanted more… She needed more.* With the orb in one hand, she touched the wall with the other. Expecting pleasure, she was basted by a massive electrical surge. Thrown through the air, she landed with an unforgiving thud face down on the unforgiving stone. *Everything hurt.* Her brain seared with tortuous agony as her chest squeezed making it impossible to breathe. It was excruciating until it rather abruptly vanished. Kayn got up and brushed herself off with power circulating through her. *She didn't need to run now. She felt capable of levelling the Crypt. She wanted more.* As she reached for the wall, it began grinding open behind her. She lowered her hand and peered down, preoccupied with the static energy tickling her fingertips.

"Oh! Thank God, it's you! We've been looking for you for so long. Where in the hell have you been?" Mel stammered, frazzled with worry.

Unconcerned by Melody's presence, Kayn had slipped into a trance, playing with what she'd formed between her fingertips.

"What is that?" Mel questioned. "Are you okay?"

"Now, I am." Kayn blankly responded, mesmerised by the steadily expanding orb in the palms of her hands.

"Kayn," Melody urged cautiously, "We should get out of here. If I heard you, so did everybody else. I don't know what you've been up to but the other Clans are out for blood."

Casually glancing up, Kayn stated, "Let them come." The unique grinding of stone on stone signalled the appearance of a Triad. She peered up. *It was Stephanie. Wasn't this convenient? The girl Kevin was with for all of those months while they were apart. The girl he still cared about. The girl who pretended to be her friend then coldly drowned her.*

Stopping cold when she saw her, Stephanie provoked, "I wish you could have seen the look on your face when Kevin slit your throat."

"Oh, Steph. Do you ever have bad timing," Mel sighed with intuition in high gear.

Kayn wanted her dead. She wanted to strangle her with her bare hands. In her mind, Chloe whispered, *let's kill her.* Stephanie drew her sword, smirking as she cockily strode over. Kayn smirked as she held up the orb of energy she'd been building.

Stephanie froze, enquiring, "What in the hell is that?"

With not a touch of emotion, Kayn coolly replied, "You know, I'm not entirely sure what it is… Catch." She tossed the ball of blue energy directly at Stephanie. It blew her into a million bloody pieces of red pulp. Experiencing a disturbing amount of pleasure as she released it from her hands into the air, Kayn snapped out of her trance to the horror of what she'd done. Shards of Kevin's booty call had flown everywhere. Bloody, slimy chunks of meat and oozing brain matter covered poor Melody from head to toe. *Whoops.*

"What did you just do? What in the hell? What did you do?" Mel stammered.

An explosion of energy was a Healer's Enlightening. Kayn had condensed energy into something more and manipulated it. She'd channelled it into a form and used it as a weapon. She couldn't say that. "I have no idea. I was upset. I could see my veins," Kayn explained with room temp emotion. "I wasn't myself while I was holding the energy, but as soon as I let it go, I felt amazing and then normal."

Aghast at the gory chunks of flesh wallpapering the corridor, resembling a sick scenario from a slasher film, her friend slowly spun around. "Remind me to stay on your good side," Mel mumbled. "Are you okay? You don't feel the urge to blow anyone else up, do you?"

Dizzy and exhausted, Kayn murmured, "I don't think so." She was in shock. *She hadn't really meant to blow the girl up. Had she?* Chloe's voice sinisterly whispered in her mind, *Yes, we did.*

Mel urged, "Come on! We have to get back to Zach!"

Side by side, they sprinted through the Crypt. Mel seemed to know her way through the sliding passageways. Once they'd covered enough ground and were far away from where Kayn was screaming, they slowed their pace to a stroll.

Mel enquired, "Do you want to talk about it?"

She knew her friend was asking about Stephanie's revelation, Kevin had slit her throat, but she had to tuck that down deep inside of her for the time being. *Thoughts of his betrayal brought up violation and confusion over what she'd done in response. It wasn't clear in her mind. She knew she'd killed a room full of Clan in a rage, but the details were sketchy. There were flashes of impossible images leading to the big picture. She knew one thing for sure. She'd lost a part of herself during her vengeance. There was a hollow space where her love for him used to be.* Kayn responded, "It's better if I don't. I have something for you though." She dug around in her top.

Melody winked and teased, "Oh Hun. I'm not sure I'm ready to pitch for the other team."

She chucked the bag of figs at her friend and countered, "Ha, ha. You're hilarious." *She knew Melody loved figs. She loved them more than candy. She'd enjoyed them at a time when she hadn't been forced to.* This was her symbolic fig leaf for covering her in pieces of Stephanie.

Eating one, Mel teased, "For the record, if it's ever a choice between you blowing me up and me deciding to bat for the other side. I'd totally be into trying something new."

Kayn laughed. *She needed her Clan. She needed them to shut off the torture and to remind her that even if he no longer loved her, there were people who did. Ankh needed her. Now that she finally had her Testing priorities in check, they had to make their way back to Zach and find their way out of this place.*

Amped up, Mel prompted, "Can you do that orb again? Do you think you could figure out how to make those on command?"

"That was the first time. I've never done it before. I honestly don't have any idea," Kayn replied as they strolled down the long hall.

Mel asked, "Is that what sent everyone over the deep end or did you do something else?"

"Something else. I'm not sure how I did it, though," Kayn explained. "My emotions shut off when I killed everyone I that room. It was easy. I didn't register the pain of my injuries. I didn't care about anything but killing him. I killed Kevin the same way he killed me. I don't want to know if I can do that on command. That's not what I want to become."

With understanding in her eyes, Mel reworded it, "I can't imagine you doing something like that but when the other Clans catch us, they're going to go fifty shades of slasher film. This is the place to embrace that part of you. If you can turn off your emotions, it might save us in the end."

She had no clear memory of how she'd killed everyone in that room, just flashes of throwing people with strength she'd never experienced. Her hands were burning. She recalled that much. There had been a surge of anger, and she'd released it.

"You've wounded over a dozen partially insane hormonally imbalanced egos. Saying, I'm sorry, I don't know how I kicked all of your asses at once isn't going to stop the testosterone and estrogen-fuelled redemption fest they have planned," Mel sparred while wandering down the stone passageway.

Touch the wall. Hesitantly, Kayn placed her hands against the Crypt. She felt warmth as energy moved from within the wall, up her arms into her chest. It felt amazing until it burned, and she was blasted away. Struggling to breathe, Kayn regained her balance, clutching her chest. *That knocked the wind out of her.*

"You're doing it again," Melody whispered in awe.

Her glowing fingertips silenced turmoil. Touching her palms together, Kayn pulled them apart, making a ball of energy. Entranced, she stared at the destructive orb. *She could feel her sister with her again.* Chloe's voice whispered in her mind, *'Show Melody what it does... Throw it at her. Kill her. She'll stop asking questions.' Semi-aware that her dead twin shouldn't be in her mind giving murder pep talks, concern tingled, but she barely cared. Not enough to beckon drama. This was a dangerous game. She was playing with a gift she hadn't yet learned to control. An ability that wanted to hurt everyone, regardless of Clan status.*

Not seeing a downside, Mel urged, "You could easily dispose of everyone. We could make it all the way to the end."

"Yes, I will dispose of everyone," Kayn whispered, distracted by the glowing circle in her palm. She made it larger and then smaller. Moulding it into the perfect weapon, she confessed, "I'm not coming out of here as me if I keep doing this. I'm slipping away."

"What do you mean by that?" Melody asked.

Kayn gave her unpolished honesty, "I can't explain the euphoria. How it felt to take energy from that wall. It feels both right and wrong. I want to experience what I felt when I released it." Melody was standing there with her lips slightly parted. She was reminded of what she used to say whenever Kevin had that expression. *He was catching flies.* Memories of humanity yanked on the other end of the emotional rope and towed her back. Kevin had killed her, and she'd killed him, severing the last attachment to her mortal life. *All of those beautiful memories they'd created during that week together, and now, she felt nothing but regret. It was something though. She felt something. Perhaps it happened for a reason.*

"I've been there myself," Mel explained as they walked. "Our abilities present themselves with the urgency of addiction. If you're afraid you can't control it, that's a good thing. That feeling shows you have control. You're aware of the danger. Don't worry about it. We can find a way out of here without using it. We need to find Zach. Last time I saw him he was fighting Kevin."

Kayn commented, "I killed Kevin and all of his friends. Then I blew up his ex-girlfriend. It would be a good idea to avoid bumping into him while on emotion-dulled autopilot. Was that my Enlightening?"

Walking ahead, Mel replied, "That my friend, was only the beginning. Your Enlightening can take anywhere from six months to a year. It's an immortal growth spurt. Except this growth spurt is in your brain. Your partially mortal brain is striving to activate dormant areas. It sucks and on occasion, it's excruciatingly painful. There's no point in sugar coating it."

Yes, this was definitely the situation to rip the bandage off. She'd already been primed for disillusion and trauma. She'd been attacked by rat spiders and chainsaw-wielding hooded creeps. Someday, perhaps this madness would feel like a normal Saturday night.

They sprinted beside each other into another open space with a fountain and surveyed the area before running for water. They splashed it on their faces and drank liquid heaven from their palms. In a hazy mist, Zach materialised out of nowhere. He was frozen, staring at his hands. He patted down his chest. Zach covered his mouth, silencing himself. Mel hugged him. *His last demise must have been brutal.*

The trio chose a sleep chamber for rest and a place to talk openly. Up till this point, it had been running, fighting and dying with no game plan. *It was time to change that.* Kayn placed her fingers in the holes and palm down on the wall. It slid away to reveal their saferoom. They all jumped inside as it ground shut behind them. They slid down against the cement walls onto the pillows, mentally exhausted. They told their horror stories, giving accounts of the hideous situations they'd found themselves in since falling through the ceiling into hell. *They'd each landed on the stone and began to play a role in various versions of their own personal nightmares.* Melody told her of rooms they'd found, both together and separately. They were tortured by Triad. Stephanie was the ringleader. Zach's fling from before being dumped into hell dismembered them while she took off with Kevin. *She wasn't even sure she could explain why she left for so long. She was firing emotionless blanks now.* Kayn disclosed, "I didn't believe he'd be able to do it. When Kevin killed me, something happened. I changed, I lost myself. I hunted him down and the others were nothing but white noise. They were collateral damage to my rage."

Zach's eyes softened as he admitted, "I had a hard time buying what they were saying knowing who you were but evolving is part of this immortality deal." He scooted up beside Kayn and held her.

She laid her head on his shoulder and closed her eyes. *Showing trust was all she had to give.*

He kissed her head and said, "I'm glad you're here and just so you know, this was part of the job description. The torture and the agony, we all agreed to it. We made a choice to live this way for the opportunity to survive. I'd be tortured every day to keep either of you safe and I would know it was worth it. I'm alright Kayn."

Melody added, "Ditto."

"How come we couldn't find you? Where were you all that time?" Zach questioned.

She opted to just unfiltered spill her guts. Kayn explained, "Well, you guys know I was attacked by the demon from my Sweet Sleep. Patrick accidentally killed me. Zach found me in that room. We were drugged and I lost you two. I was drowned three times and then wrapped in a cocoon by an enormous rat spider. I fell into rapids with Kevin. We went over a waterfall and ended up in the jungle, where he dumped me for the eightieth time. We split up and I saw my mother, it turned out to be a distraction. Kevin killed me. I hunted him down, killed him and everyone else. A bunch of messed-up things happened and then a giant scorpion tiger spit lava at me. I was burned alive and turned to ash. That wasn't even the high light of my day. I learned how to make blue balls of energy. Melody and I found each other and then I blew up Kevin's girlfriend."

Grinning, Zach declared, "Now, that's a creative way to solidify a breakup." He tussled her hair, hugged her to his chin and kissed the top of her head.

He wasn't angry. Neither of them were.

"I bet the lava experience was unpleasant," Zach whispered.

"There are no words," Kayn replied.

"I haven't yet had the joy of finding the drowning rooms," he added.

Kayn continued to rest her head on his chest, listening to his heartbeat was incredibly soothing. Emotionally drained, she felt like closing her eyes. Kayn whispered, "It's actually not that bad compared to the other ways to die...The drowning room."

As he stroked her hair, he whispered, "Close your eyes if you need to. I've been told my shoulder's a great pillow."

She didn't need him to say anything else. She shut her eyes, still listening to the conversation while giving her senses a rest. She felt Zach shift her head to his lap. He continued to stroke her hair.

Mel commented, "She looks remarkably peaceful for someone recently drowned, eaten, dumped and attacked by a lava-spitting tiger lizard."

"She's almost asleep," he whispered while stroking her hair lovingly.

She heard Zach offer Mel his shoulder or lower down on his legs. She didn't open her eyes. She heard Melody give Zach a kiss on the cheek.

Zach whispered, "What was that for?"

Melody whispered back, "You're a great guy. We should be telling you that more often."

He teased, "Trust me, I'm not that great."

Kayn spoke from his lap, "I've noticed a lot of people call themselves down because they're not up to their own version of perfect. Sometimes, all someone is really looking for is a soft, safe shoulder to lay their head on."

While stroking her hair, Zach chuckled, "For someone with absolutely no dating experience whatsoever, there was a lot of wisdom in that statement."

Grinning, Kayn whispered, "Every once in a while, brilliant things just pop in my head." She heard them laughing quietly as she drifted off to dream.

Chapter 44

Punch Drunk

Kayn dreamt of many things both good and bad, that night or day. With no moon or sun in the sky, time seemed unimportant. They were sleeping because they were tired. The events she'd experienced replayed in her mind as it attempted to make sense of it all. A tunnel appeared and she ventured down it. Frost was at the end with his arms outstretched. Gazing into his eyes, she came to him without a second thought.

He intertwined his fingers with hers, kissed her hand and whispered, "I can't help you."

She agreed, "No, you can't. I have to help myself."

"You're not alone. Look beside you," Frost's voice urged.

As his image floated away in the mist, his words echoed in her mind. Kayn opened her eyes and saw Melody. She looked up and saw Zach slumped against the wall, sound asleep. *Filled with the renewed knowledge that she owed these two everything, she felt guilty for selfishly serving her own needs. She understood what her subconscious was saying. They would always be there. They were bound together forever in a spiritually platonic marriage of souls. She'd been focused in the wrong direction. She was too strong to think that a broken heart would destroy her world. It wasn't going to destroy it, but it would forever alter her perspective.* She struggled to her feet with numb legs from the awkward position she'd slept in. There was food in the corner of the room. It hadn't been there when they'd fallen asleep. She looked at the other two. Zach was curled up in the most uncomfortable position. Melody was sprawled across his legs. *His legs would be asleep when he tried to stand. They'd been tortured. They were mentally exhausted. She suspected that version of her death was yet to come. She'd died many times physically, but emotionally, she'd died a thousand deaths.* Kayn felt harder on the inside now. *If only someone could wipe her memory. She didn't see the downside to a clean slated mind.* The others began to stir. Once they were fully awake, Kayn pointed out the food in the corner of the room. There was a giant tray of fruit and a loaf of plain bread. She walked over and found a reasonably comfortable cushion to sit on. The pillow poked her in the butt. She noticed something pointy sticking out of it. *What is it?* She pulled it through the material. *It was a long, brilliant red feather.* She held it up to the others and asked, "What do you think this is from?"

Zach replied, "With our luck it's from a giant man-eating parrot."

Melody glared at him and hissed, "Seriously Zach? Shut your mouth!"

Kayn groped the rest of the pillow. *It was full of tiny feathers?* She tore it open to look inside. *The rest of the feathers were tiny, delicate and brown.* The hamster wheel between her ears started to spin. *What if there were more of these giant feathers hidden in the other pillows? What were they for? Everything unusual that she'd come across had a purpose in this place.* Kayn ripped another pillow with too much gusto and thousands of tiny brown feathers exploded into the air. They began to descend slowly, magically, all around her.

Zach said, "Are you done tearing the place up yet? You're like a kid searching for a seagull feather on the beach. Yes, it's a giant red feather. Yes, I'm certain there's a messed-up future situation where it will come in handy but I'm sure the next group unlucky enough to be stuck in the place would appreciate the use of at least one pillow." Zach wandered towards her. He blew a path through the feathers with pursed lips. They separated, allowing him a feather-free walk. They drifted eerily to the ground on either side of him.

Kayn passed Zach the red feather and said, "You keep it. I still owe you for the torture."

Zach didn't take it from her hand. He left her hanging and chuckled, "We already had this conversation. You don't owe me anything. I expected my little fling with Stephanie to end with something epically messed-up. I boarded that crazy train all by myself. You had nothing to do with it."

Kayn took the red feather and playfully tickled Zach's arm with it. She teased, "But was she worth it?"

Mel wandered over, glared at Zach and wisecracked, "Don't you dare say it was worth it." He started to laugh and didn't reply for a second. Mel socked his arm.

"She wasn't," Zach laughed. "You were both so nice to me before we took a nap. I guess love Zach fest is over?"

Kayn determined it was wine in the goblets by the scent. She passed Zach one as a peace offering. *These immortals consumed red wine with everything.* She would have preferred a goblet of orange juice at this point but felt obligated to drink the enormous, heavy goblet of wine. *It was obviously some sort of reward or gift. They were supposed to be safe in the sleep chambers. Hopefully this time, that was the truth.* Kayn recalled the gas. *They'd left the sleep chambers though. Had they stayed there, they might have been just fine. They would have had a nice sleep and woken up refreshed. That is where they'd split up the last time.* Kayn had learned a few lessons during their separation. She learned to value what she already had. She also was finally able to let go of that last piece of her past that was pulling her under. She'd been weakened by her feelings for the enemy. Kevin was now and would always be her enemy. Her childish fantasies had been snuffed out as quickly as he'd snuffed her out with the sharp end of his blade.

She gulped down the bread and fruit, half-starved. They raised their glasses of wine.

Zach gave a toast, "To learning to accept the inevitable."

Kayn and Melody both raised their goblets and repeated the words, "To accepting the inevitable."

With no concept of time, she had no idea how long she'd gone without food or water. Nothing made sense, except each other. It was a new state of being for her. For the first time, she saw herself as only one of three parts. Only the three of them together, made a whole. Her guilt for not fully understanding this earlier began to dissipate. *She was having the best time. She almost forgot where they were.* As they ate the food, it reappeared. As fast as they consumed the wine, the glasses were magically full again. *Were they drinking too much wine?* Kayn attempted to stand and toppled over, howling laughing as she landed on all fours. Blood trickled down her flesh. She showed Melody her skinned knees. Running on instinct, she laid her hand on Melody's thigh. Her hand warmed and became uncomfortably hot. Her knees began to tingle.

Mel moved away from her as she accused, "Your hand just burned me? You just healed yourself with my gift, didn't you? How'd you do that, Brighton?"

Kayn followed Melody's eyes to her knees. She wiped off the blood to reveal freshly healed, scratch-free skin. She attempted to give her an explanation, "I don't really know? I felt like I should touch you. It wasn't a planned thing."

Mel whispered, "You didn't take my gift from me, did you?" She took her knife, sliced her palm and healed instantly. "I healed faster than normal. I think you did something to amplify my ability."

Kayn shrugged as she stared at her hand and whispered, "I guess you learn something new every day?" *They looked concerned.* As she gazed down, she understood. *It was happening again. Her veins were clearly visible.*

"That's a little bit creepy," Zach commented.

Kayn shrugged again and sighed, "Brain growing pains?" *Had she amped up Melody's ability to heal?* She got the shivers. *What did this mean? She had an ominous feeling about sharing the knowledge that she could do that.*

Zach looked at Kayn and requested, "Can you give me some of whatever you gave Mel? I haven't been Enlightened yet. I still have a target on my back."

Kayn shimmied her behind closer to Zach and said, "I can try." She left her uncomfortable cushion, crawled over to Zach with no coordination whatsoever and touched his chest with both hands. She glanced at Melody and asked, "What do I do?"

"I can't really explain it." Melody laughed. "I want it to happen and then it just does."

Kayn touched him repeatedly… *Nothing happened.* Frustrated, she sighed, "Well, that's obviously not going to work." *Maybe she needed more energy?* Kayn fumbled her way over to the wall. Looking at her friends, she said, "Promise to bring me back if lose my marbles again?"

"Do you really have to ask?" Zach teased.

Kayn placed her hands against the wall and was blasted clear across the room. *That sucked.* With her nerves jangling, she sat up, shook her head and announced, "Shit. That hurt!" She'd once again landed on her knees.

Mel laughed, "You can't keep stealing my healing energy so you can spend all day healing the same injury."

Kayn groaned as she wiped away the blood with her hand. *She was already healed. What in the hell? She was healing, just like a Healer.*

"Creepy, did you just heal yourself again?" Zach questioned.

Wandering over to Zach, Kayn whispered, "I wonder how long I get to keep the ability for?" She touched his arm.

He leapt away from her, accusing, "You shocked me!" Zach opened his hand. Playing along, Kayn handed him her knife. He grimaced while slicing his palm. Nothing happened. He sighed, "Are you going to help me out or just want to watch me bleed, Mel?"

Melody suggested, "Kayn... Why don't you try?"

"Why not?" Kayn answered.

"You're not going to electrocute me again, are you?" He teased.

Kayn answered, "I honestly have no idea." Zach hesitantly allowed her to take his hand. Nothing happened. He just continued to bleed. Then, something miraculous occurred. Her hand grew warmer. Her heart raced as her hand became scalding hot. Zach tried to squirm away. She released his hand from her grasp. He wiped off the blood. *His palm was healed. She'd healed him.*

Staring at freshly healed skin, Zach mumbled, "So, you're a Healer now?"

Kayn's pulse raced as veins rose on her arms, legs and chest in reaction to the energy coursing through her being. *She wasn't a Healer. She was something else. She'd been told but couldn't recall the name.* As she struggled to catch her breath, her mind kept prodding, *you're starving. You need energy. Find more. You're hungry.* Ripples of excruciatingly painful fire surged through her. She collapsed, squirming on the stone. Her mind kept whispering, *you need to eat something. You need energy.* She rolled over. Gasping for breath, she crawled towards the Tomb's wall.

Knowing what she was experiencing, Mel blocked her path, asserting, "No. Not yet. You can't do it while your mind is screaming. Wait until you're calm. Just a minute or two longer. I promise the pain will stop."

Animalistic fury surged through Kayn's being as she writhed on the floor. She fought against her, gasping, "I'm starving! I need it!"

Aggressively pinning her down, Mel assured, "It will pass. Let it pass."

Her brain kept telling her she was starving to death. The hunger was too strong. Fighting the urge to feed on Mel's energy, Kayn thrashed, shouting, "Get away from me! I'm going to hurt you! I need it!" Mel held her ground as she struggled. *She was slipping away again.* With her emotions funnelling the drain, Kayn met Melody's eyes, pleading, "Don't make me hurt you." Panic ceased as sentiment shut off. An autonomous being once more, Kayn's expression darkened as she ominously stated, "Fine. I'll eat you."

Mel panicked, "Shit!" Rolling off her, she hollered, "Zach! Jump on her! She'll get too much energy from me! If she makes it to that wall in this state, we won't be able to stop her!"

Zach tackled Kayn as she lurched for the wall. With his full weight on top of her, he whispered, "You don't want to hurt me. I love you. Fight it." Melody put her weight on top of Zach, avoiding direct contact with Kayn's skin to keep her there.

Kayn growled, "Get off me! Let me go!" She struggled beneath them.

Holding her down, Zach said, "I can't let you go. I promised I wouldn't let you get lost."

His words triggered something in her memory. Kayn felt the rage and hunger subside. He spoke soothingly until her tortured soul unravelled, and she went limp beneath him.

When she awoke, her friends were lounging on pillows, comically intoxicated. Zach was caressing her arm with the red feather.

"That tickles," Kayn whispered.

The laughing ceased. Zach's eyes filled with happy tears as he began apologising, "I'm sorry I asked you to try to give me some of your ability. When you asked me to bring you back if you got lost, I didn't understand what that meant."

That didn't sound ominous at all? "What happened?" Kayn enquired while trying to recall what she'd done. *It started to come back to her. She'd healed herself and then she'd healed Zach. She was hungry. She was going to hurt Melody.* Feeling guilty, she looked at Melody. *What should she say? Sorry I tried to eat you?*

Handing her a goblet of wine, Mel assured, "You have nothing to apologise for. You need to learn to control it. You can't be blamed for what you do while under the influence of magic. Take this wine and try to catch up. We took a vote while you were recovering. It was unanimous. We've decided we're long overdue for a mental break. We're safe in this room and we've been stuck in this damn Testing for lord knows how long. It's time to give our brains a well-deserved vacation. The second we leave this room the shit will hit the fan again. We will continue to die in increasingly inventive ways until we find the way out. Right now, I say we list the reasons we want out of this shit hole. Let's think of the things we still want to do. Let's all embrace our inner Grey."

Kayn took a drink of her wine and remarked, "I'd like to see Grey again."

In unison they raised their glasses and cheered, "To Grey." The laughter began because they all knew Grey would be impressed by that toast.

Zach raised his glass and praised, "To jumping off docks into freezing cold water." They all repeated what he said while raising their glasses.

Kayn saluted, "To the pink flamingo glasses in the RV. They are a hell of a lot lighter than these ones. I feel like I'm lifting weights."

They carried on with the comical toasts until Mel declared, "To us."

They all solemnly finished the rest of what was in their glasses in silence.

Zach randomly changed the subject, "Admit it Kayn, blowing Stephanie up had to feel just a little bit awesome." He took a sip of his magically refilled wine as he winked at her.

Melody started laughing and choked. Once she managed to calm the coughing, she added, "You should have seen Stephanie's face. She did not see that coming."

Kayn replied, "I had no idea that would happen. It was like boom! Surprise brains everywhere." She dramatically spread out her arms, showing how far Stephanie's brains had flown.

"Where's a giant herd of zombies when you need one," Zach sparred, shaking his head.

"I think zombies are a real thing," Mel threw into the peculiar conversation.

"Those demons from the Legion of Abaddon, with the hollow faces remind me of zombies." Kayn far too casually noted.

Zach giggled as he teased, "Go home, Brighton! You're drunk! Zombies are decomposing reanimated dead people!"

Melody shoved Kayn over and climbed on top of her moaning, "Brains… Brains! Whoops, wrong person!"

Kayn was pissing herself laughing when she caught the well-timed dig and said, "Hey." The trio kept drinking the wine as fast as their goblets magically refilled. "You know what? We're all drunk!" Kayn announced. Her serious tone caused titters of laughter.

"Quite obviously," Mel replied.

"Yes, I believe we are tuned up quite nicely," Zach added while swigging back more.

While lost in la-la land and thoroughly enjoying the break from their harsh reality, a thought popped into Kayn's mind. She shared it, "Oh, crap! What if the wine's not a reward? What if it's meant to sidetrack us from leaving the sleep chambers?" *How were they going to fight anyone or even manage to stay together while hammered?*

Melody slurred, "How is your hamster wheel still spinning?" They were all silent for a second as the hamsters between their ears tried to catch up. Mel groaned, "It's entirely possible that we're the stupidest people alive on the planet. Didn't we get drugged the last time we had something to eat?"

Kayn flopped back on the pillow and sighed, "No, don't you remember? We thought we were drugged but we were gassed."

Zach raised his goblet as he toasted, "Are we actually still alive or even on the planet? Now that is the question, we must ask ourselves."

"Know what? I have no idea?" Mel slurred.

Kayn began to roll up the bread into balls and eat it as Frost had taught her to do. *Maybe they were all equally stupid?* A horrible thought flashed through her mind. *What if we are the only ones who got wine?*

"I heard that thought and it'd be hilarious," Zach replied to her unspoken words. He attempted to get up but wasn't coordinated enough to get past being on all fours. He flopped on his belly and drunkenly suggested, "Let's just stay right here till we sober up."

Kayn sprawled out on her back, stared up at the grey ceiling and commented with her inner voice, *this place is all about distractions. The wine, the food. It's all an elaborate, albeit fun… distraction.*

Mel clapped her hands to rally the drunken troops. She sat up and declared, "We need water. There's none in here. We're going to get chased down and killed while hungover. That will epically suck. The water we need is out there."

"I'll go get it." Kayn volunteered. "Maybe if I let a few of them smack me around, I can quench their need for water and revenge at the same time. If they're in the same state as us, they won't be coordinated enough to do any real damage." Kayn managed to stand up. She grabbed her sword and swung it, narrowly missing the other two as they ducked out of the way.

Melody struggled to get up, saying, "If what they did to us is a hint of what's in store, you can't be the one to go out there. They'll slaughter you."

Zack hiccupped. Covering his mouth with his hand, he said, "I think the tables have turned on that scenario. I pity the fool that pisses Kayn off."

Mel tossed a handful of feathers at him, saying, "You can't let her go Zach. You're the man."

Zach sparred, "Listen. You can't use that, 'you're the man speech' only when it applies to something completely suicidal. Kayn's the strongest and I have to be the one to reel her back in. You can't do it, Mel. She might be right about offering them a chance at her, while they're incapacitated. Maybe, everyone's too drunk to be focused on retribution or wounded egos? Act too drunk to torture."

Right… Too drunk to torture. Kayn dumped the contents of the wine glasses on the floor. *I'm so dead.* She cradled all three glasses in one of her arms as she placed her opposite hand against the wall in the telltale grooves. It slid open. The walls to the other sleep chambers opened at the same time. *What are the chances of that? There was a bright side. They all appeared to be equally stupid.* They stared each other down from their spots at their sleep chamber doors. *Who was going to go first?* Kayn decided it would be her. She darted from the safety of her chamber. The second her feet left the security of the chamber, they all raced for the fountain. Kayn waited for the inevitable smackdown. Nobody fought, they were all morons barely able to stand. They watched each other cautiously while drinking the water from their hands. *Someone would be sober enough to remember who she was and what she'd done.*

"Isn't that the girl we were looking for earlier?" One slurred as he gestured in her direction.

Cue drama. Kayn didn't react to his comment. She continued to drink from the fountain. Somebody swung a sword at her. Kayn caught the blade mid-swing with perfect hand-eye coordination. Clutching metal in her palm, she smirked as she yanked it out of a Triad's hand. *She was supposed to be pretending to be too drunk to torture.* She dropped it. The deep slice across her palm healed instantly. *She still had Melody's ability.* She hid her hand against her stomach. *They were on to her now. She'd been recognised.*

One of the Triad slurred, "Don't think we're afraid of you."

It sounded like, *'Don't think we're afraid of shoes.'* Kayn turned to face the Triad and asked, "Why are you afraid of shoes?" *It was too hilarious to pass up.* The Triad smacked the glasses out of her free hand and they plopped into the fountain. Her instinct was to jump on the Triad and drown him. *With every breath she felt herself changing.* Kayn took a calming one and thought of the bigger picture. *She had to keep pretending she was drunk and allow them to get their licks in.* As she bent over to fish the goblets out of the fountain, she felt the all too familiar sensation of a blade plunging into her back. Adrenaline commenced racing through her system. *Calm down. She had to calm down. This was not the time. They all needed to be able to come out of the room. They would need more water.* Her assailant shoved her into the fountain and staggered away. Kayn sat in the water for a moment, regaining her bearings. *The water wasn't turning red. Her back felt warm. She'd already healed. That was too fast. She had to act drunk and get back to the room.* Kayn gripped the edge of the fountain for support and scrambled out, having discovered a little secret. *Being submerged in the fountain water sobered her up and calmed her temper.*

"So, you're a Healer now? That's an interesting development. I guess you're not the almighty Conduit that everyone thought you were destined to become," Stephanie announced to onlookers.

Kayn noticed Stephanie inching towards her. *She was trying to make it look casual but knew how she operated.* Her Triad nemesis swung and backhanded her into the fountain. Kayn allowed Stephanie to win this small battle. *After all, she'd blown her up and murdered her friends. Ankh now had the upper hand. Brains before brawn, she had to keep acting drunk. They got in a few good shots. Perhaps they'd feel less of an urge to torture her later?* "I have a sword," Kayn slurred dramatically as she scrambled out of the fountain, wielding an imaginary weapon.

"Stephanie laughed. "No, you don't! You've gone crazy. You are going to die in here. Your wimpy little Clan doesn't stand a hope in hell. You're just a Healer. You have two Healers and a nothing. You were supposed to be a big deal. I bet that's disappointing."

Kayn kept her mouth shut, listening to Stephanie's drunken rant. *She'd left her weapon behind in lieu of goblets. She was losing her patience with this bitch.* Steph's smug expression was making behaving herself extremely difficult. Every bone in her body wanted to smack that look off her face. *A chair to hit her over the head with would be lovely right now. Her Clan needed to be able to come out here and submerse themselves in the fountain without anyone else discovering what they were up to. This was the method to her docile madness. She'd just allowed that bitch to hit her to stay on the high road, but the high road now felt overrated. She wasn't programmed for tolerance anymore.* Kayn threatened in a breathy whisper, "The first time I blew you up, it was an accident. Do you need a refresher course on the reasons why I don't need my sword?"

Stephanie's eyes widened. She rolled them and huffed, "I'm over it." She wandered back to the safety of the other Triad.

Out of the corner of her eye she noticed Kevin standing by the opening to Triad's safe room. He'd been watching their drunken sparring match. Kayn met his eyes and for the first time since killing him. *She felt nothing.* Her heart was a solid mass in her chest. It was an impenetrable fortress. There was no lingering anger and no agony. Kayn didn't bother maintaining eye contact. *It was time for the other Clans to be inconsequential.* She pretended to wobble back to Ankh's sleep chambers and opened it. She presented her Clan with their water by throwing it on them.

"What the hell was that for?" Zach hissed.

Kayn stated the facts to the rest of the trio, "The fountain itself, sobers you up. Let's go accidentally bump each other into the fountain. You need to be submersed in it. Keep acting like we're drunk until we're back in here, we don't let anyone else in on the secret. If anything goes wrong, I've been sober for a while. I've got it covered." *She was emotionally void. She neglected to mention that tidbit of information. It was more important that they all managed to sober up. She'd find a way to keep it under control.* They noisily staggered out of their sleep chambers. Nobody had come back out. They all jumped into the fountain, drank water and submerged themselves in it. The doors opened. *The others were watching. They had to make it look good.*

Zach obnoxiously slurred, "You clumsy bitch! That's not funny!"

"Actually, you prissy little man child. It's friggin hilarious," Melody sparred.

Kayn pretended to topple into the fountain, no longer able to find the ability to laugh. Her veins were visible on her arms again. She fought with the urge to grab hold of Melody and feed. She pretended to struggle to get out. They all staggered back to their safe place in a performance worthy of a comedy award. The door slid shut. Zach and Mel high-fived, and she left them hanging.

"What do we do now?" Zach whispered.

Kayn mechanically stated, "Now, we get the hell out of here, with a head start."

Zach noticed the change in her personality, "Are you sure you're okay?"

"I need to stay like this for a while," Kayn blankly replied. "You'll know when I'm not okay."

He nodded, understanding her need to be emotionally vacant. Kayn had to be able to think logically without the inconvenience of emotional conflict. She walked over to where the food was and shoved bread into her sarong. Mel followed suit. Zach had nowhere to store anything. She grabbed the feather she'd found in the pillow and passed it to Zach.

He grinned as he took it from her and chuckled, "Where am I supposed to put that?"

With an inability to joke around, Kayn took it out of his hand and placed it behind his ear.

Mel teased, “Oh, look. It’s Peter Pan in white. That’s a lovely look for you. I hope Wendy likes it.”

He tossed the feather onto the floor and said, “Is it necessary to kick me in the junk every time you speak?”

Picking up the symbolic gesture he’d completely missed, Kayn tucked it into the tie at her waist. She passively listened to their argument, as she planned their escape. *The obvious exit was through the centre of the rooms by the fountain. This place was built by magic. Perhaps treating it as such was in order.*

Chapter 45

Unavoidable Demises

Kayn addressed a seemingly solid wall in the sleep chamber, opposite the direction to the fountain, "Door open." It opened at a turtle's pace, revealing a large room full of ice.

"I don't really want to freeze to death," Melody whispered.

"So, out the front door it is," Zach declared.

Kayn robotically stepped away from the wall and it slid shut. She said, "Let me try something." She whispered, "Open," to the side wall in the room. It ground open, revealing a winding hallway. They quickly walked through the best option. The trio wandered down the twisting stone corridor until they came upon another noticeable door. Kayn instructed, "Please open." Once again, the door opened to the frozen room they'd attempted to avoid earlier.

"Maybe this isn't a choice? "Zach stated.

"Can't we walk just a little further, to be sure," Melody pleaded with a hint of desperation.

She recalled words of wisdom. *There is no easy road to acceptance.* Kayn glanced up, noticing the next obvious ridges on the opposite side of the hall. She placed her fingers and the heel of her hand in it. It slid open to yet another room full of ice. This one resembled an enormous restaurant freezer. *There'd be no final visions of beauty for her sentimental friends in this version of their icy demise.* Kayn acknowledged the painfully obvious, "The question isn't, what's next? It is only, what version of this death do you prefer? Do you want to freeze where it looks like winter on a picturesque mountainside, or do you want to get locked in a restaurant's icebox? We must choose one."

Zach replied, "I'd prefer the natural version. At least there will be beautiful scenery as we go."

Mel explained her hesitation, "There's always some kind of messed-up twist. What if the natural version comes with an abominable snowman or two that plan to eat us?"

"Then the restaurant icebox it is," Kayn replied. She turned back towards that opening.

Mel grabbed her arm, stopped Kayn from opening the door and insisted, "Let's keep walking. Just for a bit, humour me."

She didn't want to start dying again. This was understandable. Kayn felt the urge to smile. *Her emotions were coming back.* She suspected this would be inconvenient timing for that to happen. As the three strolled down the oddly peaceful hallway, the contents of Kayn's stomach began to curdle. With one glance, she knew they were all on the same page. Behind her the corridor began making fizzing, crackling sounds. *Their reprieve was over.* They sprinted away. Kayn looked back out of curiosity as balls of lava began spitting from the walls. *Fear! She felt terror! She was back!* Kayn gasped, "Run! It's lava!" *She'd experienced this demise once before. Saying it was unpleasant was an extreme understatement.* They ran just a breath ahead of each ball of liquid torment. Each time it hit the opposite side of the hallway, it splashed back. A droplet of lava scalded Zach's skin. He cried out in agony. Kayn grabbed his hand, yanking him forward. There wasn't a second for shock. The lava corralled them all in one direction without choice. A room opened up. They dove inside, escaping the spitting lava. Each one with a sense they'd only postponed the inevitable as the Crypt's door ground shut. They stood there for a second, surveying their surroundings for danger. *The coast appeared to be clear. There was no obvious form of a frozen demise in this room.* Kayn announced, "We're doing this wrong. I can feel it. We have to stop running away from things."

Zach was visibly in excruciating pain from the melted skin on his back. He managed to find his sense of humour through his agony as he teased, "You can feel it? That's good to hear. I thought we were going to be forced to stage an exorcism."

Kayn replied, "The next version of death we come across I'll prove my theory to you." She strolled over to one of the walls, hovered her palm and opted out, "Not this way." She walked to the other side wall. Her stomach winced. As her skin began to crawl, she announced, "There's something bad in this direction. We need to accept whatever fate lies on the other side of this wall."

She didn't give them an opportunity to respond as she requested, "Door, please open."

The wall on the other side opened graciously, and they stepped through the threshold without hesitation. The wall ominously slid closed behind them. Their path was blocked by a majestic grey creature. It appeared to be part lizard and part lion. The lion's mane had every hair perfectly in place, giving the appearance of being carved out of stone.

Zach looked at Kayn and exclaimed, "I hope you're right about this."

"I thought you said it was a scorpion tiger?" Melody whispered as she gingerly backed away from the beast.

"The last one was a scorpion tiger... This is new," Kayn replied. She could see the excitement in the salivating creature's eyes. She glanced back and whispered, "Don't act like you're afraid."

"You're backing up too," Zach fired back.

Kayn assured, "Not for the same reasons as you are. We need to stay together. It can't be just me that dies. We all must make this sacrifice. We're only postponing the inevitable. It will take longer to get out if one of us misses a version of death."

"What if you're wrong? What if you're supposed to use your gift and blow the frigging abomination up?" Melody stammered, grasping at straws. Zach and Melody kept gingerly backing away. Kayn had to stay with them. They continued to back up until all three were flush against the wall.

"I think I understand what's going on in here. If it freezes us, I'm right," Kayn whispered. *She'd figured out the concept of the Testing. She just had to get the others to play along.* "It'll be a quick death," she added.

Zach quietly replied, "You're far too comfortable with that idea Brighton." He questioned, "What if it's planning on eating us?"

"I've already been eaten today. Nice kitty," Mel musically preened. Unable to move an inch further, she closed her eyes, mentally preparing for the horror that was about to unfold. Mel desperately pled, "Door open. Please, just open up and let us out!" She opened her eyes and met Kayn's with a brave smile, saying, "It's not going to let us out, is it?"

Kayn sparred, "We could have chosen one of the easier ways to be frozen and didn't, now did we, Mel? You've already been eaten today. If I'm right, it won't eat you."

The creature's eyes glinted as it cocked its head and smiled like it understood their conversation.

"Maybe, you shouldn't have said it out loud," Zach whispered.

Stepping forward, Kayn boldly announced, "I don't think it matters what we say."

Mel grabbed for her, stammering, "What in the hell are you doing? You don't need to ask for it."

"That's where you're wrong. I think this Testing is about facing your fears and making it to the other side. If it must carry through with whatever it's here to do, why not speed things up a little?" Kayn bravely suggested. *It wasn't that she wasn't terrified.* She inched closer to the creature. *She'd just come to understand that each outcome was inevitable.*

Melody stepped away from the wall. She grabbed the cloth on the back of Kayn's sarong and clung to it as she forced herself to follow her lead. Mel repeated Kayn's earlier words, "It's only going to freeze us?"

Zach hesitantly edged closer to the beast, whispering, "Freezing doesn't sound that bad. I almost wish we hadn't taken a breather. It feels like we're starting over."

Melody hissed, "Bite your tongue!"

With brilliant comic timing, the lion hissed like a snake, and a long slick black forked tongue protruded, swaying from between its powerful jaws. Kayn shivered as hair prickled up on every inch of exposed skin. The creature began to choke. It appeared to have something lodged in its throat. It hacked and coughed until a large round ball of something travelled up and out of its throat into its mouth. The creature bit down with its fangs and sprayed a fine mist of white fluid at the trio. The reaction moved rapidly up Kayn's arms, crackling a tortuous, icy path to her shoulders, then her torso. Her chest squeezed as it began to solidify. *Her heart was being constricted. It was agonisingly painful.* It echoed in her ears as her heartbeat slowed and finally ceased with her eyes still open and her mind aware. They stood together as three frozen statues of bravery, joined by their hands and hearts. Kayn stood in front, with Melody positioned slightly behind her, still grasping her sarong. Zach had his hand on Melody's arm. He'd been frozen solid while attempting to pull them out of the way. It happened so quickly. They were all alert under the agonisingly painful, slowly constricting ice they'd been encased in. The monster approached Kayn. It stared into her eyes. She wouldn't have flinched, even if she'd been able to. Her spirit didn't waver. *I'm not afraid.* There was something in the beast's eyes that made her sure it heard her thoughts. *She had the sense that the beast was proud of her. It was a strange sensation to feel a moment before something finished you off.* It roared inches from her face. She saw the hairs on its mane waver for the first time. It smiled with its eyes and smacked her with a powerful claw. In soul-jarring agony, Kayn exploded into tiny pieces, disintegrating into the air of the Crypt.

Kayn awoke on the floor of the room she'd been killed in. Melody was usually the first one awake, but not this time. Kayn's brain was pounding as she forced herself to sit up. Clutching her head, she noticed both Mel and Zach were still. *It felt strange being the first to wake. It was an isolating feeling. This must be how Mel felt each time she had to wait for them to rise.* Kayn noticed the bread missing from inside her sarong and the crimson feather was absent from her waist. *Well, taking those things had been pointless.*

Mel mumbled from face down on the stone floor, "That sucked."

Remembering her epiphany, Kayn surmised, "I think once each of us has died in every way, we can get out."

Smiling weakly as she sat up, Mel commented, "That means Zach and I have to drown. We've all just completed freezing." The two girls rose to stand as Zach began to stir. They gave him a moment before urging him to get up. Once Zach regained his balance, they left.

As they darted through a sliding wall, Kayn disclosed, "I've fallen. I think I've been eaten. I was out cold at the time. I hope that counted. We've all been stabbed. I haven't been tortured yet, so I'd imagine that's still on my anti-bucket list." They turned down a corridor with sand on the floor and torches lighting up the length of it. Kayn removed a torch from the wall and prompted,

"Grab one, the torches can be used as a weapon. I didn't think of that last time."

Mel removed one from the wall as she whispered, "There are thousands of ways to die. What if we add things to the list by thinking about them?"

Kayn's stomach clenched again. She suspected their reprieve from violence was over. She could tell by their expressions they'd felt the same thing. Kayn sighed, "What comes next?"

"Enough, I get it," Zach complained. "We're supposed to embrace the insanity, but we don't have to go out of our way to create messed-up situations. Don't let anything else cross your mind. We don't even know what's going to happen. This Testing could be no big deal. It could be easy." There was confusion in Zach's eyes.

Mel froze. She clarified, "What did you just say?"

Kayn felt waves of nausea wash over her. *It wasn't because something was coming. He was going. They were close to losing Zach. He needed to be Enlightened. He was losing his mind.*

He answered cautiously, "I don't even know what you guys are talking about. I dropped through the ceiling five minutes ago."

"Is that the last thing you remember?" Mel asked.

Zach responded, "We had an amazing week. The others came back. We fell through a giant hovering slab of stone?"

Kayn recalled what her doctor told her after she'd awakened from her coma, *'The human mind can only take so much before it begins to shut down. It shuts down to protect itself.'* Lexy said something similar during their training in the In-between. She spoke, "Zach, we've been in here for a long time. Do you remember when we were forced to keep jumping off that cliff together in the In-between? We were being trained by Lexy. Your brain is shutting down."

He knew to trust her. He responded, "How did I die last? Maybe, if you tell me it will jog something?"

"We were just spit on and freeze-dried by a lion lizard," Kayn answered honestly.

"Sorry I asked," Zach mumbled as he began checking his body for injuries.

He really didn't remember anything. He had to. They needed him.

With a blank expression, Zach questioned, "How long have we been in here?"

Mel's eyes teared up as she admitted, "We don't know. We've lost track of time."

"Heal his mind. You have to at least try," Kayn calmly urged.

Mel faced her as she answered, "If I were capable of healing Zach's mind, I would have healed yours."

The gravity of the situation began to sink in. *They couldn't leave unless they were together. Once they'd all emotionally checked out, they'd become trapped in this place. This is how it starts.* Kayn cupped Zach's face with her hands and gave it to him straight, "We can't leave without you. You can't check out. You're the only one that can bring me back. We can't do this without you. We'll be trapped in here."

He sweetly touched Kayn's hands as he declared, "In my mind we just got here. I feel fine. Maybe it's a good thing? Have I been Enlightened yet?"

They had to find a way to get him back. What if he had to redo everything because he didn't remember? Kayn met Mel's eyes in a panic.

Mel nodded at Kayn as she tapped Zach on the shoulder. He spun around and she planted a seductive kiss on his lips that continued for a minute longer than it should if it was only for experimental purposes. Mel pulled away, leaving Zach stunned.

As he regained his faculties, he teased, "Wow, Mel. Now, I'm going to be on you like a fungus."

Melody smacked him, scolding, "I'm serious, Zach! Don't you even consider checking out on us! We need you! If I have to follow you to hell and beat the shit out of you for leaving me, I will!"

They embraced as he chuckled, "Mel, that was a little hostile but sort of beautiful." He cupped her face gently in his hands and whispered, "We're all getting out of here together. I'm not going anywhere. I promise."

Sort of paying attention to their exchange while gazing at the flickering flame at the end of the torch she was holding, Kayn pulled her eyes away from the entrancing fire, concluding, "We have to accept each version of death by staying together as we die."

"You realise how insane that sounds?" Zach teased.

Melody's eyes met his as she pointed out, "You said it first. Embrace the insanity."

Balancing the torch between her legs, Kayn placed her fingers in the wall's grooves, announcing, "Ready to die?" The door slid open, revealing another empty corridor. As they began walking down it, vents opened on the ceiling and water began streaming in. "I've done this one already. More than once," Kayn sighed as the water level rose. "Just be calm and submit to it. It's almost painless and fast. Don't fight it or you'll have to do it again." The room filled much faster than it had when she'd been alone. *There was no point in holding onto the torch. It was a pointless prop.* She dipped it into the water and listened to it hiss. It wasn't long before they were treading water together. *Why in the hell did she have to do this one again?* Something large brushed by. She felt it again. *Shit.* That was all she had time to think before it sunk its teeth into her leg and yanked her under. Unable to help it, she looked at the shark-like reptilian beast flinging her around by her legs. *Hurry up and drown. It's going to eat you. She wasn't afraid.* Inhaling water to speed up the process, she understood it needed to happen to move on as a group. *They had to drown and she had to be eaten.* She repeatedly screamed into the water, releasing nothing but bubbles, purging her soul-altering agony as the savage jaws tore into her abdomen. Her mind began whispering, *shut it down. Don't fight it. Let go.* Her ability to feel pain turned off as her torso was torn to shreds and ingested. *Don't fight it or this will happen again.*

When Kayn was pulled under, the others panicked, believing they were next on the menu as a cloud of brilliant red exploded beneath them. They fought the drowning instead of surrendering to it and tried to climb out of the vents that predictably closed to block their escape. They awoke on the floor, soaking wet and gasping for breath.

"Well, that was extremely unpleasant," Kayn croaked. The vents opened and the corridor began to fill. She cursed, "You are enormous assholes! It doesn't even hurt. You couldn't just die frigging peacefully? I'm going to be so pissed if I get eaten again!" The cool water was up to her knees already. Kayn looked at her legs and grimaced, knowing how this was going to go down.

Zach stammered, "Okay, in all fairness, you got eaten right in front of us. Tell me you wouldn't freak out if I got eaten in front of you?"

Their feet left the ground and they were treading water again. Something brushed up against Kayn's leg. *No! Come on! Shit!* T*his was going to suck!* "You assholes!" She swore as the creature sunk its razor-sharp teeth into her flesh and yanked her under. Teeth tore into her flesh, scraping her bones and every nerve ending was torched with blinding agony as a red cloud of blood exploded around her. The trauma ceased as the pain shut down. One of her limbs floated past her line of vision. She squeezed her eyes shut. Inhaling metallic-tasting crimson water, she let go.

They awoke gasping for air, with their skin and hair dry.

"I'm so sorry," Mel apologised as they shook off the trauma and got up.

Racking fingers through her wild, curly mane with a lion-like, predatory glare, Kayn winked and teased, "That's what karma's for." Neither bothered to defend their actions. *What could be said in the moments after something ate you? There was nothing that could make it better, especially after you'd been eaten two times in a row. It was an experience with no comparison.* As Mel hugged her, Kayn reused her words, "You can't be held responsible for anything you do while under the influence of magic."

Zach sweetly enquired, "Can I get in on this?" As he joined the embrace, he whispered, "I wonder what's going to happen next?" Kayn shot him a deranged look.

Chapter 46

Demons And Monarch Butterflies

They continued walking down endless hallways of stone until their minds were numbed by the monotony of it all. *Were the other Clans still stuck in the sleep chambers? Surely, they would be free by now?* A monarch butterfly flitted its way through the Crypt. They followed it, drawn to the magnetic pull of its delicate beauty. A touch of wonder in a land of exile made of stone. A wall slid away, revealing something miraculous. *A sight Kayn's mind had been longing for.* They followed the brilliant orange and black monarch into a plush grassy field. *It was exquisitely beautiful. It felt like a trap.* The three stood, knowing they should turn around and leave. It was difficult to convince their minds of that with the glorious scent of spring in the air. Kayn's heart whispered, *No. Don't go yet.* The monarch landed on the back of her hand. They gathered around to watch it wander across her skin. Kayn's stomach began to turn. She made eye contact with her friends.

Melody whispered, "We need to leave."

Zach said, "I second that motion."

They turned to go, but there was no sign of the stone they'd entered through and nothing but wondrous meadow in every direction as far as the eye could see.

This time it was Zach who pointed out their dilemma as he said, "We can't leave. We made the choice to come in here. It has to play out."

Kayn noticed the bees underfoot. She was busy staring at the bumblebees when something pinched her hand. The monarch flew away. *She was bleeding. That was weird?* A small bead of blood expanded in size on the back of her hand. Confused, Kayn remarked, "Butterflies don't bite," Thousands of monarchs took off out of the field of green. It looked like they were going to flit off in the opposite direction. They turned and headed straight for Ankh.

Zach sighed, "Really? Now it's death by monarch butterfly?"

A wall appeared and slid open behind them. Melody dove through it giving the others no choice but to follow. *They had to stay together.* The door slid shut, leaving one lone butterfly in the Crypt. It vanished before they could squish it. Kayn imagined the monarch was off to lure the next group of suckers into the field.

Dazed, Zach complained, "Thanks Mel, now that monarch is going to come flitting back with a million friends to pick our bones clean while we're standing in a stone corridor instead of a beautiful field."

Before Mel had a chance to respond, the stone shifted beneath their feet and slid away. Both girls grabbed for the edge. Zach fell through. As they dangled above the heated glow, Kayn urged, "Let go! We have to stay together!" Kayn released her grip and plummeted into the glowing sweltering heat. She kept her eyes on Melody as Zach began shrieking. Bravely, Mel released her grip. Kayn didn't look down. A second later, her mind exploded.

Kayn awoke flat on her back on the stone. *She hadn't allowed herself to view this last demise. She'd kept her eyes trained on Mel until her brain shut itself down.*

This time it was Zach waiting for the others to awaken. He announced, "Now, we've all done lava."

Kayn squeezed her eyes shut as she sighed, "I've done lava twice." A voice was whispering from the walls, *you want to go to sleep. Lie down, close your eyes and go to sleep.* Kayn lay sprawled on the stone, staring at the ceiling as she whispered, "Do you guys hear that voice too?

"What voice?" Melody quizzed.

Zach nodded and disclosed, "I've been hearing it for a while. It's telling me I need to go to sleep."

Kayn stared into his eyes with the knowledge that they were in danger. *Real danger. She wanted to succumb to it with every inch of her being. She needed to close her eyes and go to sleep. It was difficult to ignore. The tone was so soothing.* T*he voices were chipping away at her subconscious need for this madness to be over.* As voices from the walls told her to sleep, Kayn fought the urge to drift off to the soothing words.

Harshly shaking her, Mel ordered, "Get up! Neither of you can check out on me! I'm not going to let you go!"

Kayn scrambled to her feet and explained, "It's surprisingly difficult to ignore. It's like the voice is trying to hypnotise us into going to sleep."

"Maybe this never ends if you succumb to that voice," Mel countered. "Don't you want to get back to the others? At least there are good times to look forward to amidst the bad."

Zach was struggling to get up. Clever plot twist. Kayn helped him steady himself.

"If there was a way to tune out the voices, it would help," he groaned.

Mel squeezed his shoulder and said, "Baby chicks."

Knowing what Mel was trying to do, Kayn grinned as she thought of what made her happy. She reminisced, "Floating dust in a ray of sunshine." She glanced at Zach and urged, "Your turn."

"Kissing Mel," he baited.

Melody grinned and vowed, "I'll kiss you every day for a full month if you don't check out on me."

He smiled and taunted, "I'm holding you to that."

"What do I get for not checking out?" Kayn asked.

Mel provoked, "I can't imagine a kiss from Frost would be anything less than remarkable."

Her emotions for Frost were more volatile than loving now. He would have known about the plot to have Kevin kill her during the Testing. Kayn glanced at Mel as she disclosed, "My situation has changed. I'm sure it would have been remarkable before he was involved in a plot to kill me." *Having the love of your life murder you puts things in perspective.* Her stone heart twitched. *She'd spoken the words aloud. He'd slit her throat.* No tears came. *The time for tears was long gone.* They wandered in silence with no shifting walls. *Nothing happened. They were granted peace to have their epiphanies.* Kayn announced, "I think my future goals need to be about experiencing life and honing my skills. Love needs to be on the back burner."

Zach teased, "That's all part of experiencing life, Brighton. When we get out of here, maybe you need to be young and stupid for a while? Start living in the now."

Spinning around, Kayn sparred, "The here and now isn't all that appealing."

"You know that's not what I meant," he laughed. "I meant strip off your clothes to dance in a field naked. Kiss a stranger."

"I second that dare," Mel declared, sauntering down the hall.

Those were appealing dares. Kayn taunted, "Which one?"

Putting his arm around her, Zach provoked, "It doesn't matter which one as long as you step out of your safe box."

Safe boxes were a thing of the past. "By the time we get out of this place, none of us will fit the box we came in," Kayn whispered as her heart twitched.

They noticed the extended break in the violence. The lack of clashing swords. It had been a while since they'd stumbled upon any depraved chambers. There was only the sound of their footsteps on the stone.

Mel picked up a small black bag. She looked inside of it and announced, "It's empty." They remained there for a minute. No walls moved. Melody enquired, "You guys aren't hearing those voices anymore, are you?"

"Mine are gone," Zach replied.

"Mine are gone too," Kayn answered, understanding why they'd gulped that wine back, repercussions be damned. *They'd needed a break. What she wouldn't give for a sleep chamber and a goblet of wine right now. How long had it been since she slept?* Kayn opened the next room by asking it politely. Zach and Melody walked in. A barrier kept Kayn from following. She bounced off the entrance, blocked by an invisible force. Trying to get to her, Zach couldn't. Zach tried to get to Melody. They were also divided by a transparent barrier. *Oh, Lovely. What now?* Kayn made another attempt to get in. She pressed her hands against the see-through barrier. A charge ran up both of her arms and set fire to her chest. Adrenaline pulsed through her. The need for energy was humming in her brain with an undeniable urgency to feed her ability. She watched Zach soundlessly squirming and crying out through the impenetrable transparent barrier. *She couldn't help him. He couldn't save her from herself if she gave in to this urge to stretch her boundaries. They were both reliving something horrible.* A goblet of wine appeared in front of her. *It was a hologram, a distraction.* Kayn stared at the enormous glass. Tempted, she went to pick it up. *It was real. She could turn off her mind with this wine.* She felt a subtle surge of energy from simply grasping the goblet. Raising it to her lips, Kayn paused and threw its contents against the invisible barrier. Purple liquid dribbled down the force field. *What in the hell was wrong with her? What was happening in her mind? Since when was it more important to turn off her own pain? This wasn't like her. She was losing it a bit.* She placed the goblet on the ground and shook her head. *They would have found a way to help her by now.* She looked at the goblet. It was magically refilled so she kicked it over. *She needed salt. It looked like they were experiencing what she'd gone through moments after they'd arrived.* She was going to have to leave to look for it and endeavour to find her way back. Glancing back at her friends, she sprinted down the corridor. Darting in as each room opened, she scanned the area and moved on. She raced down a winding cobblestone path and turned the corner into a swarm of monarch butterflies. Kayn stammered, "Shit! Shit!" She swung her arms around, swatting them out of her path and kept running even though she'd been bitten numerous times.

Encountering sacks of salt, she made her way back to her Clan led by instinct. She bolted through the swarm of ravenous monarchs without a second thought. With her skin covered in bleeding welts, she sprinted through the maze of sliding walls to rescue her fellow Ankh. Kayn took a handful of salt and tossed it at the first barrier. *She could hear Melody now.*

Melody was sobbing, "He's just a baby. No, please don't hurt him. He's only a little boy." She began screaming, "No! Please! Don't! Stop! Please! Hurt me! Take me! You can do whatever you want to me! He's a baby! You're hurting him! You're hurting him!" She began to shriek and tear at her face with her fingernails.

She needed to be smarter than the Testing confining her. She didn't have a lot. Kayn threw salt. Baptised by tiny particles of demonic forgiveness, Mel gasped as she opened her eyes and lunged forward to vomit. Stroking her back as she heaved, Kayn consoled, "It wasn't real. That wasn't real."

Wrapping her arms around her chest, Mel repeated, "It wasn't real."

Sombrely, Kayn echoed, "It wasn't real."

Confused, Melody touched her face. She stared at her bloody hand, then showed Kayn.

"Honey, you were scratching at your own face. That's your blood. You've healed yourself," Kayn whispered. "I think Zach is being Enlightened. Throwing salt at him didn't stop anything. I'm afraid to touch him. I don't know what to do. I think we just have to wait it out." She helped Melody sit up to show her Zach's situation. There was a sound. Kayn was grabbed from behind and yanked through the wall with a hand over her mouth, stifling her squeals of protest. Her captor tightened his grip around her throat. She stopped struggling.

Kevin's voice scolded, "Why couldn't you just embrace what you're meant to become? Why do you keep fighting it?"

Her heart felt like a lump of stone within her ribcage. *It wasn't fluttering because of her love for him anymore. It ceased to ache because of what they'd done to each other. It was the dull hum of nothing.* Kayn struggled to reach the wall. Her hand made contact. *It wasn't working. Why wasn't it working?*

"Your abilities won't work in here, stop trying." He whispered against her hair, "You forced me to do this." He tossed her into another room as the wall slid away.

Kayn landed on all fours. The wall slid shut before she could glance back. She was encircled by undisguised Abaddon in their darkest form. She tried to crawl away. Two grabbed her arms as the third knelt above her, whispering words in a language she couldn't place. Under normal circumstances she might have made more of an effort to get away. Kevin had thrown her to Abaddon. He'd slit her throat and she'd killed him in return. She couldn't process the idea of self-preservation. She'd shut down emotionally to the point where she was looking forward to the pain. She gasped as her captor slid a serrated blade into her abdomen. As the faceless being began to slice upwards, blood drained from her body as though it were spilling sand from a broken hourglass. She succumbed to the pain and rode waves of agony as her essence pooled behind her on the stone until she lay in a bed of liquid warmth. This was the only peaceful sensation at the end of her will. She allowed her mind to find a disturbing version of peace in the rhythm of the blade that tortured her.

A raspy voice whispered, "Yes… Ride the pain until it becomes a part of you. It will stay with you long after the ride is over. It will be a lingering voice in the back of your mind, an ache in your soul. You'll remember me always. I will become a part of who you are. I will be the nightmare you see when you close your eyes. I'll be the voice in your head that whispers, never again."

The pain all but disappeared as blood loss numbed her mind. Kevin had delivered her to the Abaddon to experience a tortuous version of death. *Breathe in... Breathe out.* She choked, sputtering out blood. The being laid its hands on her head. Her mind began to hum. The excruciating pain returned instantly. Blinding waves of agony plunged against the shore of her mind. *How lovely… He was going to make her feel every second.*

The raspy male voice whispered, "I have something to show you Conduit."

The dark being reached into her exposed stomach contents. She felt a tugging, burning sensation as he yanked out the length of her intestines. Sliding them slowly through the arch where his palm met his thumb, it presented them to her. He grinned with mangled, jagged teeth. *This isn't real.* The other vacant-eyed fiends swarmed her body in a panting frenzy. *This isn't happening.* She watched in horror as beings feasted on her intestines, yanking and tearing her apart with their razor-sharp teeth. Her heart began to palpitate. Even after being told her ability wouldn't work, she commanded her emotions to cease. *Turn it off. Shut it down.* She felt a tugging sensation as her body was savagely ripped apart. Through her numbed mind, she saw one gnawing on the meaty end of one of her legs. It was no longer attached to her torso. In that instant, Kayn stepped outside of herself and screamed until she lost consciousness.

She awoke on the ground with a gasp. The room was drenched in her blood. *She'd been killed in so many ways she'd lost count. This was the death of her emotional self. The demise of a large portion of her humanity. She'd been tortured, disembowelled and shown her own insides. She remembered every horrifying second. Kevin had been the one who delivered her to this horrendous version of death.* She lay in the still and the silence without attempting to move a muscle. *There are some things you can't come back from.*

The wall opened, and she was dragged through it by a familiar face. Patrick stammered, "I don't have time to explain but things are not as they appear to be."

Patrick left her emotionally vacant on the ground, staring at the stone above. She didn't try to stand up, nor did she attempt to seek vengeance. *She was one with the floor. She would close her eyes and become a part of it now.* She heard someone coming. *They were Triad.* They looked down at her and kept walking. She heard one of them say, "She's almost gone, don't bother."

She lay motionless on hard stone with her eyes wide open, without even the will to blink. *They were right. She was almost gone.*

The walls around her began whispering, *you're finished. Go to sleep. You can't take anymore. It's over... Let go.*

She heard her sister's voice pleading, "Get the hell up, Kayn! You have to stand back up! You need to get up now! We have to go find the others!"

Kayn mouthed the words, "I can't." She closed her eyes and decided it was best if she slipped away into a dream. Someone started poking her. Kayn opened her eyes. Her twin sister was leaning over her. *She was clearly hallucinating.*

Her sister's voice hissed, "You get your ass up! This is not just about you! The others need you! They can't leave here without you! I can't leave here without you! You have no right to give up! Get the hell up!" Chloe hauled her to her feet and dragged her limp body into the first room she came across.

Kayn tried to focus. She clutched her sister's arm, "You can't be here. This isn't real."

Her twin's voice vowed, *I'm here with you. Now and always, but if you don't get your ass in gear, I'm going to take over. Do you want me to do that, Kayn?*

"Sometimes," Kayn whispered. "Sometimes, I do want you to do that." Her twin was staring at her, perplexed at what she was talking about.

Chloe crouched before her, urging, "You have to keep going, Kayn. There are so many things that still need to happen."

"What has to happen?" Kayn groggily asked.

Chapter 47

The Other Ankh

The girl in front of her changed. *This was not her sister. It was a friendly female stranger.*

A girl at least six feet tall, with a pixie cut, grinned and said, "You see me now... Don't you? My name's Astrid and I've been in this place for a long damn time."

Kayn repeated her name, "Astrid?" *She had a fancy British accent.*

"My parents were hilarious," she explained. "Family name. Long story."

Taking in her mannerisms, Kayn clarified, "Long time?"

Astrid clarified, "I'm Ankh."

Kayn abruptly regained her mojo. *This girl had been in here for at least five years. How was that even possible?*

Showing her the Ankh brand on her palm, Astrid explained, "I know you're thinking there's no way she's been in here that long without losing her shit. My ability generates a euphoric state. I can exist in my mind. I even managed to keep the other girl I came in here with somewhat mentally hinged. The rules are simple. You can't leave this place unless you possess everyone you came in with. There's something they don't tell you. Once two Clans have found their way out, the third can't leave. They're stuck in here. Haley and I were the last Clan out during our Testing. We were denied departure. We kept each other sane, waiting for the next group of Ankh to come through Testing. We're just praying we can get out with you three on a technicality. Haley went to find the rest of your Clan."

In awe of the girl sitting before her, Kayn let it sink in. *How long had she been in here?*

Astrid smiled as she responded to her thoughts, "We've been waiting a long time for you guys."

Kayn's heart thawed. *It was quite apparent the unstoppable girl named Astrid possessed enough faith for all of them.*

Astrid took her hands and gently squeezed them, urging, "Look at me. Try to smile. You'll start to feel better. We know the way out. It's time to gather that last breath of courage. It's almost over. I promise you, Kayn. It is almost over."

Intrigued, Kayn asked, "How do you know my name?"

"Haley's an intuitionist," the girl answered. "That is sort of like an Oracle who doesn't see, she feels it. The walls in this place have been buzzing about you. You, my girl, have been foretold to be a big deal."

Kayn attempted to smile. If this girl who'd been stuck in here for lord knows how long was still capable of smiling, she'd better suck it up and return it.

Astrid burst into a giant grin as she declared, "Welcome back to the land of the living."

As Kayn rose to her feet, she could have sworn she heard Winnie cheering in her mind. *Wishful thinking.* She asked, "You really know the way out of this hell hole?"

Astrid replied, "I know where the Amber room is but we need to find the rest of the Clan first."

Sufficiently convinced, she began following Astrid through the labyrinth of gliding walls. Kayn understood the rules of this place. *Whatever her darkest thoughts conjured up would pale in comparison to the Testing's interpretation of her fears. With an imagination as strong as hers, it was difficult to stop her thoughts before they surfaced, providing ammunition for this depraved game of phobias.* She pictured them all stuck in actual amber as though they were nothing but ants preserved in tree sap. She immediately shut the image down. A shiver of adrenaline coursed through her veins as her mind reeled through visions of what she'd already gone through. Astrid opened the wall by asking it politely to move. She stepped into a long corridor. As Kayn followed her blindly, it occurred to her that she could be following a demon or a hallucination. The path began to snake around the corners. *If she had to believe in something to bring her soul back from the edge of despair, why not this girl?* Kayn took a breath and pursued her beacon of renewed hope.

Astrid closed her eyes and murmured, "Come on. Where are you guys?" She glanced down at the symbol on her hand, raised it to her lips and kissed it while saying, "Be forewarned, if we get to the Amber room and I find out we're the last Clan through again, I will lose my shit and it will be epic."

Kayn looked down at her palm. Her heart warmed a touch further. *Zach and Melody were close by. She could feel it in her soul.* Kayn's bond to them began responding to the magnetic pull. She led Astrid down countless twists and turns until they reached a dead-end. *They were on the other side of this wall. She was certain.* She felt an instinctual pull prompting her actions, much like when she needed to touch the carvings on the wall of the Ankh Crypt back in the land of the living. *Could she resist the urge to touch the wall and use her ability?* She lifted it and hovered it a foot from the wall. She opted out of saying the words aloud and thought them, *Open for us... Please. Help us find the others.* The wall stood solidly defiant against her internal pleas. Finding her temper difficult to restrain, Kayn loudly demanded, "Open for us! Help us find the others!"

Astrid kindly repeated Kayn's words while laying her palm on the wall, "Open for us. Please."

It stood solidly in their path, denying their request with silence. They both leaned against it, slid down and sat on the floor. With her back touching the wall without intention, nothing magical happened. Kayn glanced at Astrid and said, "Are you real? Just tell me you're real. I think I may be beginning to lose my mind."

Astrid pinched Kayn's arm and teased, "Do I feel real to you?"

Kayn smiled and rebutted, "It is pretty convincing." They sat there semi-defeated. Kayn insisted, "I can feel them. They're right there on the other side of this wall." *Her mind wasn't playing along with her survival plans anymore. She knew there was something she should do, but couldn't remember what it was. She just needed to close her eyes and relax for a while.* Her eyelids grew heavy. She felt her nerves begin to calm as her pulse slowed to a gentle whooshing in the isolating quiet. Her mind was too exhausted to keep operating.

Astrid elbowed her. She opened her eyes as the tall blonde stranger ordered, "No sleeping, Kayn. I know this is all too much and you don't understand how your gift operates yet, but I heard your Enlightening. Haley was able to find you, emotionally attach and track you because of it. A Conduit can absorb and transport magical energy. It sounds like a cool ability to have. You should be able to take energy from all that is magic. Take it if you need some."

Kayn struggled to her feet. *That actually made sense. Leave it to a stranger to explain what she was with absolute clarity.* She looked at Astrid and tried to explain her predicament, "I'm afraid to. I did some messed-up stuff after my Enlightening. I blew someone up. There was a huge mess. It was traumatising, to say the least."

"New abilities are always scary," Astrid replied.

Kayn reworded it, "It wasn't my ability that scared me. It was the feeling. I enjoyed it too much. Every time I try to use it, I lose myself in it."

Astrid grinned and whispered, "It takes both the dark and the light."

Swallowing the fear of losing what was left of her, Kayn rubbed her hands together and placed her palms flush against the wall. She felt her hands heating. The essence of the wall travelled up her arms and settled in her chest. She shivered as she tugged her hands away. *This time she had more control.* She clasped her palms, and as she parted her hands, a brilliant ball of energy formed between her fingertips.

Astrid's eyes widened as she whispered, "Shit."

Void of emotion, Kayn commanded, "Open up or I'll blow this whole place back to hell where it belongs!"

The wall obediently ground open, revealing their trapped Ankh. Zach lay unresponsive on the floor. Melody leapt up and raced at Kayn. She froze when she saw the orb balanced in the palm of her hand. It was then that Melody noticed the tall girl with short hair. Mel grabbed her weapon and held it menacingly towards Astrid. Without thinking, Kayn shifted the orb to one hand and touched Melody's shoulder to let her know that Astrid was a friend. Mel crumpled into a ball on the floor. *Whoops.* She crouched beside her fallen Ankh. As Mel opened her eyes, Kayn assured, "She's not our enemy."

Mel groaned while attempting to push her body up from the ground. Managing to get herself halfway, she stammered, "What did you just do to me? Who in the hell is she?"

Kayn felt her grasp on reality wavering again, "She's a friend and I don't have any idea what I did to you."

Astrid stepped in and held out her hand, offering to help Melody up. When she didn't accept it, the unbreakable girl said, "My name's Astrid. To make a long story short, I'm Ankh. I've been stuck in here with my friend Haley for a long time. We haven't gone completely insane because I have a happy place. We know how to get out of here." Astrid held up her palm to show her symbol.

Taking Astrid's hand, Mel answered, "A happy place sounds incredible right about now."

"I guess you haven't run into a girl with pink shoulder-length hair?" Astrid enquired.

Grinning, Mel replied, "Not yet, but I can't wait to meet her."

Astrid crouched by Zach, commenting, "He's hot." He began to moan and flail around. Astrid teased, "Quite obviously mentally disturbed, but pretty damn sexy."

Mel sparred, "Aren't all of the best ones?"

Astrid sighed, "Sad, but true. This may look a little gross but trust me." She licked her fingers and placed them on Zach's head. He stopped flailing. She grinned and assured, "Sexy Zach is now having a wonderful dream. Leave him for a few minutes before you try to wake him. I need to find Haley. If you keep heading in this direction, you'll come across sleep chambers. Wait for us there. Please, don't leave without us. I promise we won't be long."

They watched Astrid run away in the opposite direction.

As Kayn stood watching Zach, her hands began shaking.

Noticing her volatile state, Mel said, "You have to release the energy you take. I can take it from you."

"What if someone comes before Zach wakes up?" She replied.

"You're visibly shaking," Mel pointed out.

"I can last a while longer," Kayn responded over the humming of her amped mind. She thought of what Astrid told her about the Conduit ability. *Had Frost known that Kevin had been ordered to kill her during the Testing? Was he a part of this twisted plan?* She thought of Patrick's words when he pulled her from that room. *Nothing is what it appears to be. What did he mean? Why did he help her?* She felt the need to explode subside. *She was overthinking everything.*

Mel whispered, "You disappeared. Where did you go?"

Kayn concentrated on breathing as she replied, "Talking about it won't help me calm down. Let's talk about Zach."

"He hasn't been conscious for any length of time since we parted," Mel explained. "I've been towing him around and playing dead whenever we bumped into anyone else. Nothing bothers you if you're already down. I'm not talking about just the other Clans. Even the creatures walk away from you if you play dead."

Actively ignoring the wall's endless chatter, Kayn whispered, "One of the other Clans must be dwindling in numbers." *Maybe it was them?* "Do you really not hear the voices?"

Mel looked at Kayn and confessed, "It's been getting harder to open my eyes, and yes, I can hear the voices now. It's more than that, an empath ability has been triggered. I feel everything. I hear them crying in the walls. My new gift is on overdrive. The emotions are weakening me. A lot of the voices have succumbed to darkness and rage. Some are rooting for us. Others are so sad and lonely, it's heartbreaking. Can you imagine what that would be like to be living, breathing beings trapped in stone? Some just want to make our transition easier. Those are the ones who keep telling us to sleep. It's not because they're evil, it's because they're forgotten tragic souls who have lost all hope. They understand where we are in the game and what our odds are with only three. I don't know how much more of this I can take. I'm afraid the next time I die, I won't come back again, and I'll just disappear into these walls."

Meeting her solemn expression, Kayn confessed, "That last room was more than my spirit could handle. I was done when Astrid found me. It was the strangest thing. I thought Astrid was Chloe."

Mel reached for Kayn's hand and vowed, "When Zach wakes up, we'll find the others and follow them out."

Staring into her eyes, Kayn whispered, "I hope that's true."

"Maybe taking some of my empath ability will help you stay with us?" Mel suggested, enticing her by offering her hand.

Her hand started heating while thinking about it. Foreboding urged her to decline. *She was hanging on by a thin thread.* Kayn calmly replied, "I won't be able to stop myself. It would be counterproductive. I need to continue evolving into what I'm meant to become." They sat in silence. *Anguish, despair and violation were key ingredients in the evolution of a warrior. She didn't want to think about it. She knew what she was becoming.* She felt the solid mass of strength and resolve swallow what remained of her heart.

The deep conversation was interrupted as Zach groaned, "Well, that epically sucked." Both were instantly at his side as he struggled to stand. He placed his hand over his heart, complaining, "It's like someone lit my chest on fire."

Kayn's heart flickered with the urge to join as Mel and Zach embraced. *Would she attempt to take his energy? She couldn't trust herself. Hurting him was the last thing she wanted to do, after all he'd suffered through during his Enlightening.* She changed the subject, "We have cool news to share with you."

Zach smiled and said, "I could use some cool news."

"We found two more Ankh girls in here. They've been in here for a long time and they know the way out," Kayn explained.

"Hallucinations," he teased. "There's no possible way to stay alive in here for any length of time."

Excited, Mel replied, "They're real. One of the girls has a happy place as a gift." There was a brief pause in conversation as she assured, "I realise it sounds insane, but it's true. Isn't it Kayn?"

Kayn smiled. *Zach wasn't buying it.* She confirmed, "They're real."

He patted Mel's shoulder, teasing, "I understand you believe they're real, so I can't wait to meet our new imaginary friends."

The walls shifted position. Confused, Kayn looked around as she exclaimed, "We're supposed to meet at the sleep chambers." Mel seemed equally perplexed. *Apparently, neither had been paying attention. This was going to complicate things.*

"Let's go. Why wait? Which way to the sleep chambers?" Zach questioned.

Scrutinising her surroundings, Kayn slowly spun in a circle, admitting, "The walls changed position while we were waiting for you to wake up. I'm not sure."

He joked, "Seriously walls, this isn't helpful. I thought you were supposed to be on our side?"

"Do not mock the walls," Kayn scolded.

"Yes. Never mock the walls," Mel reprimanded while wandering around, trying to use her new ability.

"Pick a direction and I'll go," he declared. "We should get going. People are coming to kill us."

Trying to trigger her intuition by feeling each wall, Mel replied, "I think we're over trying to kill each other. We're all just trying to get the hell out of here now." Looking directly at Kayn, she admitted, "I can't tell. I don't have any idea."

Without touching the walls, Kayn paced back and forth. *Come on. Give us a hint.*

Mel squeezed Zach's shoulder and announced, "You were Enlightened. Do you feel different?"

Zach shrugged as he looked at his hands and stated, "I don't feel like giving up anymore."

"Good to hear," Mel replied.

Kayn randomly piped in, "I guess we'll have to wait until you get pissed off to see what you can do."

They all looked at each other and began to laugh. *They were so tired. Even if they had the urge to keep fighting, they were beginning to lose their marbles.* Kayn asserted, "Let's just think for a minute. Remember, brains before brawn. I say we find out which direction the walls want us to go."

Zach walked to each wall and asked politely to be allowed out. Only one direction opened. He shrugged as he started to walk through the opening.

Kayn grabbed him, warning, "That's not the way." She strolled over to the opposite wall and just knew, "Walls shifted and moved to prevent us from finding the sleep chambers. Why would they point us in the right direction?"

Zach came at his logic from another angle, "What if they knew you were smart enough to figure that out and gave us the way out, knowing we would make the choice to go in the opposite direction?"

Second-guessing herself, Kayn paused. *He had a point.* Recalling Winnie's words, she asserted, "If you follow your instincts, you always end up in the right direction. That hint was courtesy of Winnie. My instincts say they're trying to trick us."

Mel walked over, stood beside Kayn and declared, "That's a good enough reason for me."

Kayn ordered, "Open!" The wall ignored their requests, for this was not the path the Crypt wanted them to take. Each of the others tried asking, but nothing happened. *Politeness wasn't going to get them anywhere at this point in the game.* "I guess we have to get out, the same way I got in," she explained. *This was a horrible idea, but somehow, instinct knew it must be done.* Glancing back at her friends, Kayn cautioned, "I'd stay away from me for a while after I do this." She laid her hands flat on the surface and took a deep breath as she felt the energy travelling from the wall through her fingertips into the palm of her hand. *It hurt. It was burning.* She fought against the urge to pull away. The veins in her arms were visible as the fire travelled at an excruciatingly slow pace up her arms into her torso. It gathered in her mid-section, setting it aflame. Internal conflict silenced as she forcibly broke her connection to the Crypt and began deliberately moving her palms apart, moulding an eerie orb of energy, entranced by it.

Mel whispered, "Are you still with us, Brighton?"

She wanted more. She needed more. Emotionally vacant, Kayn replied, "What if I destroyed this place?" *She could make sure no Second-Tier ever had to go into the Testing again. She'd be willing to sacrifice herself for that cause.*

"This isn't who you are. Stay focused," Zach whispered.

She heard him through her savagely intense need for more power. *He'd gotten through to her.* She began chanting in her mind, *you are only opening the wall, nothing more.* Zach reached for her but she was coherent enough to move out of the way.

Melody stepped between the two and cautioned, "I was blown halfway across the room the last time I touched her when she was like this."

Staring at the wall, Kayn declared, "I'm only asking nicely once, open!"

When the wall didn't comply, Kayn thrust her palms surging with power against it, screaming, "Open!" Her command echoed throughout the Crypt. The wall opened. Standing on the other side were two stunned girls from Ankh.

The taller one with short hair said, "The walls switched around on you, didn't they? I hate it when that happens."

"You two are real. I can't believe it," Zach chuckled.

The girl with shoulder-length pink hair saucily replied, "Last time I checked." They held up their palms so he could see their Ankh symbols. His face crinkled into a joyous smile.

Haley, with the fluorescent pink hair, requested, "Can we please get out of here?"

They were going to leave. They all grinned. *Expelling that energy made her feel way less murdery.* "I hope someone can carry me," Kayn said with Jell-O legs.

Haley glanced at Mel, assuring, "It's safe to touch her now. You can give her energy."

Trusting her, Mel took Kayn's hand, giving her a warm surge of healing energy. *She felt better.*

"Okay ladies. Show us the way out," Zach announced.

Astrid pointed at the stone ceiling and proclaimed, "We climb up and out."

Kayn repeated Astrid's words, "We climb up and out?" They all looked up.

Gawking at the ceiling, Melody clarified, "I thought you guys knew a way through this maze to the Amber room?"

Kayn saw the genius in the simplicity of Astrid's idea, "Can we do that? How many levels is out?"

"This place is magic," Zach rationalised. "How do we get up there?"

"Together," Haley replied. "We'll have to go together."

It seemed far too easy. There had to be a catch. Kayn asked, "Are we allowed to just climb out?"

Astrid answered, "Nobody clarified how we had to get to the end."

They began their journey up and out of the Crypt. The ceiling above opened without complications and stayed open long enough to make it into the room above. *The immortals stuck within these walls probably appreciated the irony.* They helped each other up and through the ceiling again. Kayn repeated an unanswered question from earlier, "How many levels are in this place?"

"It has infinite levels," Astrid replied. "This Crypt is the size of a city, created by magic. There are several stages of this game. The first is accepting death. Once you've grasped the concept of immortality, you must understand death is inevitable, and last, but not least, you have to prove yourself worthy."

Haley delved deeper, "The walls keep shifting and changing, so the route to the Amber room inside of the Crypt will never be in the same place for long. It isn't found with skill. It's just blind luck and perseverance. The tricky part is staying sane long enough to find it. We've made it to the outside before. That route is obvious. Once you get out, you can see the Amber room in the distance."

The ceiling above opened once more for Ankh. They pulled each other through. Exhausted from climbing, they all sat and took a breather. *Up and out was a physically exhausting route.* Kayn leaned against the wall accidentally. She felt it shift. Only it wasn't shifting open. It shifted towards her. She scrambled away, announcing, "We have a problem!" Kayn spun around. *The walls were closing in on them.*

Mel stammered, "We have to find an exit! Kayn! Make it stop!"

"She can't." Haley sighed, "You three haven't been squished yet, have you?"

With defeat in his eyes, Zach countered, "I haven't had the displeasure."

Kayn hadn't. She slowly shook her head. Mel did the same. The walls paused. *They stopped. That was close.*

Astrid looked at Haley and asked, "It's not done, is it?"

Haley shook her head and closed her eyes in preparation. The walls slammed together at lightning speed, stomping them out like ants on a sidewalk.

Melody was already awake when she came to. Kayn opened her eyes and groaned, "Tell me that was a onetime deal?"

Astrid struggled to her feet by the early risers as the others began to stir.

Haley opened her eyes and answered, "Unfortunately, there are no guarantees. Let's just get out of here and chat when we make it to the next level." She helped Zach up.

Kayn laced her fingers and gave Haley a boost. The ceiling opened allowing the five passage with no issues. One by one, they pulled each other up to the next floor. *This was exhausting.* Haley looked around, made eye contact with her and ominously shook her head. *Here we go.* Kayn's stomach was twisting and churning. Her pulse was racing as she inhaled the oddly humid air. Beads of perspiration formed on her face and chest. She wiped the sweat off her brow with the back of her hand. *What fresh hell was this?*

"You know what they say? If you're going through hell, keep going," Zach quoted as he laced his fingers to boost someone up. Nobody moved a muscle.

Haley glanced his way, reprimanding, "I know you feel it too." His panicked expression gave him away. Their new pink-haired friend instructed, "We must sacrifice ourselves without giving it a second thought. Those are the rules of the game. It's instinct to fight for survival but I'm certain you figured this much out before we found you. Ankh's numbers have changed, not the plight. Has anyone died this way?"

"Died from the heat? Does lava count?" Kayn responded as the temperature continued climbing. Slick with sweat, her throat so dry, she kept trying to swallow to create moisture. *It felt like they'd been lost in the desert for days. She knew better than to allow messed-up things to cross her mind.* White light blinded the group, and when it ceased, they were all barefoot in the sweltering desert.

Zach groaned, "Which one of you gave us the visual?"

Kayn owned it, "My bad. It crossed my mind." The temperature continued to rise. They all began jumping around to avoid the scorching sand underfoot. *Science.* Kayn dug a hole. *The sand was much cooler. Desert survival skills courtesy of Lexy.* The others followed suit, but Haley didn't opt for an easier route. She continued dancing around in agony on broiling sand. *She had a stubborn streak. She appreciated that attribute in someone.*

Zach dug her a hole and bitched, "Oh, for heaven's sake, Haley! Quit being stubborn and get in a hole. Dying from heat exposure takes a while. It's not going to kill you much faster burning your tootsies."

He made her smile. *Tootsies?* Kayn dug a deeper one so it was cooler and sat in her hole. There was nothing but blue sky above. A buzzard flew by. *She'd never seen one in real life. She'd seen buzzards on shows and cartoons. They were creepy birds. Buzzards were scavengers. They were waiting for someone to die. This hallucination was rather realistic.* Her mouth was so dry swallowing was impossible. Her tongue kept sticking to the roof of her mouth whenever she attempted that simple operational act. *Inborn reflex wanted to swallow continually now that she couldn't. Under normal circumstances, if you didn't swallow, you'd drool.* She glanced at the others. They were all sitting in holes. *This was her first slow demise.* With her throat void of lubricant saliva, it began to constrict her airway. Her lips were cracked and oozing. Blinking was becoming difficult. Her eyelids kept sticking to her eyeballs. *Why hadn't she thought of a hot tropical rainforest instead of a desert?* She slightly altered the position of her lips, and her bottom lip split in half, right down the centre. She couldn't close her eyes anymore. Her eyes were sizzling. Her flesh was bubbling and charred as the temperature rose. Through her charbroiled eyes, the scenery now had a white film. It was like peering through a sheer curtain that gradually became thicker until everything was white. *This was an extremely long, drawn-out, unpleasant way to die.* She was no longer feeling her head pounding. Now, she was listening to the beating of a drum in her brain. The rhythm slowed. Whispers in her mind tranquilly urged her towards the final step. *Go to sleep. Just go to sleep. Everything will be alright.* Her head wobbled. Her neck couldn't hold it upright any longer. It slumped to one shoulder. *Go to sleep.* She couldn't hear anything but the voice whispering inside of her head. Her brain ceased to pulse. *Go to sleep.* Kayn's pruned body crumpled into the molten heat of the desert sand.

Gasping in that first breath of oxygen, Kayn was relieved when cool air hit her lungs. She opened her eyes. *Oh, that sucked so bad.* She ran her fingers through the cool sand. *Why am I still in the sand? No, no. What is going on now?* She was on her feet in an instant. *The others were nowhere to be seen.* She spun around. *Where are they? What do I do? Should I stay here? What if they just haven't been healed yet? Was she hallucinating? Was she lying there almost dead and delirious? She was still standing in the desert, but it wasn't hot. Could this be the In-between? Maybe they miraculously found their way out of the Testing? What if that was the last test?* Kayn inhaled the perfect air. *It sure felt like the In-between. She had to find the others.* There was a small hill in the distance. *They could be on the other side of that hill. Had she wandered off disoriented and blind before she died?* Kayn walked to the rounded slope of sand. She started to run up it and sand shifted underfoot. Losing her footing, she tumbled like an empty barrel all the way to the bottom. When her body came to rest, she was horrifically dizzy. *What in the hell?* She opened her eyes to look. The hill was much higher. *She'd go around it.* Kayn rolled over and forced her wobbly legs to stand upright. *There was no way around it.* Now, she was standing in a ten-foot-wide valley surrounded by sand. Still disoriented from her spinning descent, she had no idea what side she'd tumbled down. *Awesome. Apparently, the Testing was now conspiring to separate them.* She thought of something she'd seen Astrid doing. She kissed her Ankh symbol. *Come on. Where are you guys?* Kayn placed the hand bearing her symbol on her heart and slowly turned with her eyes closed. She felt a flicker of warmth and a tickle in her heart and opened her eyes. *This was where she'd climb up.* It was a surprisingly difficult feat, with a heavy-footed sensation like walking in snow. She scaled the slope and made it to the peak, overlooking a lush green area with a cabin and a lake.

She had the sensation of descending, yet her feet hadn't moved. She wasn't on the top of a mountain anymore. She was on a patch of sand by a meadow. She looked back, and the desert was gone. There was a thick forest in its place. *Either she was in the In-between or this was one wild mirage.* As Kayn stepped off the patch of sand, a gust of wind passed through her. She whirled around and watched the sand she'd been standing on vanish with the breeze. *It's a good thing her mind didn't require a rational explanation for anything anymore.* She walked towards the log cabin and made her way around to the front door. *She knew where she was. This was Kevin's family's cabin. She must have found her way to the In-between. They must be free. The Testing must be over. Maybe they didn't really need to find the Amber room?* Anticipation flickered in her heart as she opened the door and went in. *It was empty. Nobody was there. Who had she expected to see? It was so realistic.* She walked over to the door in the kitchen with grooves dug into the wooden frame. This was a makeshift growth chart for Kevin and Clay when they were children. She ran her finger across Kevin's name to the carved number seven. *He was this tall when he was seven. They were enemies now. Eventually, she'd forget about this cabin. Her memories of this beautiful place would fade away.*

She wandered over to the picture window with a view of the lake. A few fish jumped. The teenage version of Kevin would be freaking out right now, towing her out to the dock with a fishing rod in his hand and a container of raw bacon. They'd sit on the dock for hours. S*he could see them all there now. Her family and his would* *have been together.* She took a step back. *What was she doing to herself? This life was gone. She must be close to acceptance; it didn't hurt as much anymore. Her Kevin had died the day he went with Triad.* She exhaled as peaceful resolve enveloped her. *She'd died that day too.* She closed her eyes and willed herself to leave this place. Nothing happened, so she wandered to the bed and laid with her head on one of the scratchy feather pillows. *This was just a dream. They'd destroyed these pillows during a pillow fight in the In-between. That version of this place wasn't reality either. Kayn* rolled over and bounced off the bed with the pillow clutched in her hands. *What was reality? Everything was magic. It didn't matter what she did. Nothing was real.* She saw a vision of Kevin and her on the bed, tickling each other until they kissed. She recalled the safety in his arms. *Safety had become a foreign concept.* The reel from her internal home movie continued as they hit each other with the pillows until the air was a cloud of gossamer feathers. Her mind flashed to his arms around her throat, telling her she'd forced him to do this. *He'd delivered her gift wrapped in her own despair, straight into the bowels of hell.* Clutching either side of the pillow, she ripped it in half, tore it to pieces and raged out, hitting the bed. *It felt amazing.* She screeched as she grabbed the other pillow off the bed and tore it in half. Goose down filled the air. Slamming the pillow into the bed until she exhausted herself, she laughed. Sensing someone watching, Kayn looked behind her. The rest of her Clan was on the other side of the picture window looking in. She dropped what was left of the pillow, strolled over to the door and opened it.

Zach commented, "That was a remarkable Lexy impersonation you just did there. Only it was a pillow instead of a severed arm."

Kayn responded, "I had a few things to work out."

"There's a tiny feather stuck to your top lip," Zach pointed out.

She puffed up her cheeks and blew it off with a tiny burst of air. It floated out the open door. *Just one perfect feather set adrift on the breeze.* She quietly watched it until it landed on the surface of the water. *A fish ate it. Fish don't eat feathers.* She giggled.

Mel cracked an enormous grin and said, "It's good to hear you laughing. It's been a while."

Kayn embraced her, closing her eyes. *It was surprising what a hug from a friend can do in a dark moment.* She allowed Melody to lead her back into the light.

Astrid scolded, "It took us a while to find you. Why did you wander off?"

"Nobody was there when I woke up. I wasn't sure what was real," Kayn explained.

Astrid placed an arm around her as they began walking back to the woods and whispered in her ear, "I can relate."

They strolled into the cover of trees with the distinct scent of cedar. Kayn's emotions twitched. *She'd always loved that smell.*

"How are we going to find our way back?" Zach asked.

Astrid taunted, "Theoretically, there is no way back."

He knit his brow and said, "I'd rather be killed in the desert. The forest has bears and cougars."

The scenery flashed brilliant white and they found themselves back in the desert.

Seriously? Kayn sighed, "Thanks for putting that out there."

Zach chuckled, "No problem."

The sand wasn't hot. The sun was not stifling. It was just like when she'd woken up all alone. Kayn deduced this wasn't a good thing. *What if they ended up going in a circle? Dying from exposure had taken a long time. They'd already done that version of death. What was next? She no longer feared the premise of death. That fear had ceased. She didn't dread the idea of pain. She'd accepted that as a part of her existence. She'd fully grasped the concept that everything was temporary. She didn't need to vent anymore. She felt spiritually cleansed. That was a rather large epiphany for her to have. It felt remarkable to shriek like a psycho and tear up pillows in a frenzy of fury*. Dust rose from the desert floor in the distance. There was a hill obscuring her vision. *Something was coming. It was gigantic.* Ankh stood bravely without attempting to flee.

Zach comically announced, "And the contestant who gets to kill us next is?"

Kayn chuckled as she caught sight of the enormous scorpion running towards them, hypnotically swaying its body. *Whatever. Bring it on.* The sand began sliding from under her feet. She sank into it. Kayn gagged and choked as she attempted to find a pocket of air, but the grains of sand kept slipping to fill in the gaps. She couldn't move her hands to cover her face. She was inhaling it. *Guess this is what we're doing now.* Her brain throbbed and pounded, pleading for oxygen. Once again, she heard the voice whispering. *Go to sleep Kayn. Just go to sleep.* The lights went out.

She resurrected, landing with a stunned thud on unforgiving stone, feeling like she had sand in every orifice with no way to rid herself of the irritation. *It was all in her mind. It's all in your mind.* Zach materialised, hyperventilating, frantically brushing imaginary sand from his mouth and eyes. She crawled to his side. Massaging his back, Kayn whispered, "The sand's gone. It's all gone. It was only a hallucination. It wasn't real, Zach. Breathe in… Breathe out." She was concentrating on him as everyone else regenerated back into the game.

Grateful for her intervention, he started to explain, "During my Correction, I..." Astrid muffled his lips with her hand. He got the hint.

It was surprisingly hard to avoid thinking up creative ways to die while dying creatively.

Astrid glared at Kayn and sighed, "Keep a muzzle on that imagination of yours. Do not think up crazy shit. Please, don't do it. We'll never get out this place if you two keep adding versions of death to the list."

Her mind wanted to be creative. She was losing grasp of her sanity. Happy things, she repeated to herself. She began to make a list of things that couldn't be messed up to keep her inner dialogue occupied.

Astrid chuckled, "That's right. Keep thinking about puppies, kittens, Shetland ponies and gummy bears."

"I can hear water running. I bet there is another fountain close by. I'm so thirsty," Melody pointed out.

"Okay, we'll stop for a quick break," Astrid conceded. "We can't be too long. Trust me, there's no worse feeling than getting to the end and discovering two Clans made it out and you were left behind."

They walked through the next opening towards an exquisitely crafted Jade fountain. *Nobody was around.* They hadn't seen any other Clans since the two girls had joined their search for the Amber room. The Crypt was dead silent except for the trickling water. There were no clashing swords, muffled voices or screams of Enlightenment echoing through the walls. They knelt before the fountain. Submerging cupped hands, they drank as much as they could. The water was surprisingly refreshing. Kayn sat on the edge of the Jade oasis, looked at Astrid and spoke the words, they'd all been thinking, "What if they don't let you come with us?"

Astrid had an honest response, "We need to believe it's possible."

Zach assured, "Nothing is impossible in here. That means there's a good chance it is possible."

"Well, I can tell you one thing that isn't," Haley wittily bantered.

Zach grinned and teased, "I'll bite. What isn't possible?"

Haley sparred, "Finding a hairdresser to get rid of neon pink hair. It's been like wearing a flashing dinner is served sign. I totally didn't think this style choice through prior to being chased around this place for countless years."

As they got up and walked away from the fountain, a loud click, click, clicking echoed through the grandiose archway, and in scurried an enormous scorpion. They dashed for a sleep room. The door slid closed a heartbeat before the scorpion made it there. As though they were of one mind, they all looked up and saw finger grooves. Zach gave Haley a boost. It wouldn't budge. *Useless finger grooves. The room was taunting them with the possibility of opting out of dealing with the creature clicking loudly outside the door.*

Zach smiled and exclaimed, "It did seem far too easy."

They'd opted out of dealing with the scorpion in the desert. Kayn confidently declared, "We are getting out of here, even if we have to die a thousand more deaths. We can't walk away from any version, even if each one is more horrifying than the last. Those are the rules. We are getting out of this hell hole today!"

"I certainly hope that wasn't supposed to be a motivational speech," Zach taunted.

Kayn smacked his arm and teased, "At least I'm still attempting to give them out."

Chapter 48

Clowns And Confessionals

She didn't care how her motivational speech came across. She was in a volatile place mentally. At this point she didn't give a damn if she was killed eighty more times today. She really wanted to blow something up. It was aching in the pit of her stomach. *It felt like everyone could see her violent urges. She couldn't look anyone in the eye.* Kayn placed her palms against the safe room door. She glanced back at Haley and Astrid. *Even after all their experience with death and the many 'you can't avoid it' speeches, they didn't want to deal with this being. It was only a giant scorpion. It wasn't even mixed with something else. She'd always felt a kinship with the creatures, even if it was twenty feet long. She kind of wanted to see it again.* She looked at everyone else and decided to just open the ceiling. *There wasn't a person in this room who wanted to see that scorpion again.* Kayn looked at Zach and prompted, "Give me a boost. I'm going to use my powers of motivational speaking mixed with the threat of blowing this whole place sky high."

Zach linked his fingers and gave her a boost as he teased, "Theoretically, we are hovering in the sky."

Kayn's hands had almost touched the ceiling when Haley shoved Zach. He dropped her. Kayn landed with a hollow thud on the hard floor and accused, "You dropped me!"

"She shoved me," Zach responded, pointing at Haley.

Kayn directed her eyes at their new intuitionist and questioned, "Is there a problem?" *Had Haley seen right through her?*

Haley smiled as she replied, "Only if being dismembered is a problem."

"Yikes, I personally find being dismembered a problem," Mel remarked.

They all stared at the ceiling. *They could opt to be dismembered by a giant scorpion or whatever was behind door number two. It was going to happen. It was an inevitable fact. There was no way around each version of death. They had to go through it. They'd used enough free passes. This next level was going to be painful.* Kayn glanced at their nervous faces and fought the urge to smile. *Was she going crazy? She was excited. If dismemberment was the death on the table, her opponent would undoubtedly be something evil and far worse than the giant scorpion scratching at the door. It might even be something she could justify blowing up.*

Zach moaned, "I've been dismembered far too many times. I'm not sure my mind can cruise through it again."

"This is where I come in," Astrid assured. "We have time to preplan this. Let me show you how we've managed to survive in the Testing."

"What exactly are you planning to do to us?" Mel probed.

Grinning, Astrid said, "My gift is a fast-acting hallucinogenic virus. I'm going to put us all in my happy place. It will trick your minds into seeing a more pleasant version of what is really happening."

"Can you put us all in there?" Melody grilled. "Are you strong enough to do that?"

Haley explained, "It has nothing to do with strength. Her gift is more like a transmittable virus capable of creating a mass hallucination. The main perk being you can't feel any pain."

Astrid clarified her intentions, "I'll have to kiss you, to infect you with a virus. Melody, you're a Healer. The virus may not stay in your system that long. I might not be able to do that much to protect you. Try and stay in the middle of everyone else. We need to make a conscious effort to keep the Healer protected and stay together."

Kayn was far too excited and not the least bit afraid. She was now a danger-seeking energy junkie. She had to stop herself from smiling.

Astrid instructed, "Kayn, you'll have to open the ceiling using your ability."

Haley touched her shoulder, gave her a light squeeze and instructed, "After you've opened the roof, you'll need to keep it reined in, long enough for Astrid to infect you. Once she does, there's a good chance you'll lose control. Please try to avoid blowing up your friends. Blow up clowns. There are usually a large amount of clowns in Astrid's happy place."

Kayn smiled. *Haley was on to her. She'd read her mind.* Kayn nodded, opting out of a verbal reply. She'd thought only Melody could understand this intense, addictive, overwhelming need.

Zach whispered in Melody's ear, "Well, this doesn't promise to be disturbing at all."

Kayn was boosted up, and before she placed her hand against the roof, Zach's commentary made her chuckle. Kayn mock complained, "You guys really have to stop talking. I can't be intimidating if I'm laughing." He made the motion of zipping his lips. Kayn pressed her palms against the ceiling. She felt the euphoric bliss of the energy as it coursed up the length of her arms. *She didn't want to stop.* She gasped as the visions of those lost to the Testing began shuffling through her mind. *So much brutality and death. There was too much information. She heard someone calling her name. It was a hollow echo that she felt detached from, as though it were coming from the end of a long tunnel.* Her heart began to wildly palpitate. *It felt incredible.* Her nerve endings hummed with intense pleasure that blurred all sense of reason.

Someone hollered, "You have to stop!"

D*rowning in bliss as the Crypt's energy coursed through the connection of her arms into her soul,* she felt herself gaining strength with each passing second. *She wanted to keep going.*

Zach's familiar voice was shouting, "Kayn! Please! Listen to me! You have to stop!"

She snapped back to reality and severed the connection with the ceiling. Her hands were humming with energy. *It tickled.* She gaped out, mesmerised by the all-encompassing euphoria of the power coursing through her. *She wanted more.* She pressed her fingertips together, and as she slowly drew them apart, her pulse raced with pleasure.

Zach's voice was saying, "Kayn, are you still with me?"

She had no reply to that question. She heard other voices, but they'd ceased to be of any importance.

Zach yelled, "Do you need Mel's help?"

Snapping out of the trance-like state, everything around her came into focus as she responded, "No, I'm good." Even though she continued to be amused by the crackling sensation of the ball of energy she was manipulating between her fingers, she was with them now. Kayn's expression darkened as she looked up at the ceiling and commanded, "Open!" The ceiling opened without hesitation. Astrid kissed Haley on the lips. She laughed as the others gave her a boost through the roof. She wedged her dagger into the grooves, just in case their escape hatch into the insanity tried to close before they all made it through. Astrid kissed everyone, and with teamwork, they were quickly helped through the opening before the toxin was in full effect. Kayn had managed to calm down enough to rid her palms of the visible energy, but it was still there, fighting against her as she slowly inhaled and exhaled.

Astrid looked at her and said, "Be honest with me. Are you in control?"

The struggle was in her eyes as Kayn honestly replied, "I'm trying."

"That is all I needed to know," Astrid responded.

Kayn had never kissed a stranger and couldn't help but grin as Zach's dare crossed her mind. *It was a girl and a stranger. That had to be bonus points on her unbucket list.* She felt her cheeks redden as Astrid kissed her softly on the lips and quickly boosted her through the opening. The others yanked her into the next room. Kayn's last rational thought before the virus took hold of her mind was, *that was nice.*

Kayn was standing in a glorious lush field with a brilliant blue sky above her. *It was miraculous. Her happy place appeared to be the In-between.* Even in her moderately unhinged state, she recognised the In-between as her home. It wasn't the RV they travelled in. That was only a temporary place to rest her head. It gave her warmth and security to recognise she still had a place to call home. Bubbles were floating all around her. *This was incredible.* She felt like a child full of wonderment and awe as she caught one in the palm of her hand and stared at it. *There was a rainbow.* She sighed. *Astrid had a beautiful imagination.* She heard music from an ice cream truck. A couple dozen clowns danced through bubbles towards the Ankh, holding brightly coloured balloons. *This sight created joy in childhood but made her feel a little anxious as an adult.* She stepped backwards and tripped. As her hands touched the grass, it shocked her. Her mind whispered, *it's not really grass.* The vision flickered with a disturbing sound bite of what was really happening. *Chainsaws.*

She'd avoided the chainsaws once before. She shivered with adrenaline as a voice in her mind whispered, *you can kill the clowns. Don't kill your friends.* Energy surged through her and she rose to her feet with her fingers sparking. *This was going to be fun!* She manipulated the orb until she'd created a giant blue bubble of destruction between her fingertips. Childlike clowns were twirling and prancing through the field, towing vibrant balloons. Chuckling, Kayn pitched the orb, blowing the clowns into a million shards of clown meat and colourful material. The bubbles stopped floating around her. *The virus was beginning to dissipate. How was she still healing herself? She'd assumed the gift she'd borrowed from Melody was temporary.* In the distance, another herd of clowns sprinted at her. *These clowns weren't carrying balloons. They had chainsaws. She was about to be attacked by a dozen assailants wielding chainsaws wearing maniacal clown masks. She'd have to take more energy if she wanted to have fun with it.* As she knelt, more of the façade was revealed. The grass was now the stone floor of the Crypt. The uplifting ice cream truck music changed to the raucous rumbling of chainsaws. Someone grabbed her arm and pulled her up. *It was Astrid.*

Astrid abruptly kissed her lips and said, "I gave you the opportunity to let your freak flag fly and blow up a few dozen clowns, but you have to allow this version to happen, or they will just keep coming. Just go with it."

The toxin took hold. Kayn was instantly super chill with the ice cream truck music playing again. *Just go with it.* The clowns were holding balloons, twirling towards her. They released the balloons. It was beautiful against the magnificent backdrop of azure sky. She watched them fly away as the clowns began tickling her. She laughed and laughed until the lights went out.

The group awoke in a room covered in blood and chunks of clown. Kayn flung a red foam nose off her chest. *That was ten stages of messed-up.*

Zach chuckled as he pointed out, "Your version of a happy place is slightly different than mine."

Astrid countered, "After being stuck in here for this long, we should all feel lucky my happy place isn't further off the deep end."

"My version of what we just experienced was strange but pain free, and that my friend, is all that matters," Mel chuckled.

Astrid exclaimed, "Well, you'll all be travelling down the rabbit hole with me until we find the exit."

They continued their trek into madness, wandering darkened corridors with whispering walls until they came across white, smooth marble stairs that appeared to spiral upwards forever.

"Does this feel too obvious to anyone else?" Zach questioned.

Haley grinned, announcing, "Nope, this is the right direction."

The first stair had something written on it. *It was in another language.* Kayn said, "Does anyone know what it says?"

Haley quietly mumbled, "I know what it says but reading anything aloud in here always backfires on me."

"Does it warn us to beware of something?" Mel asked. "I don't care about anything else."

She wasn't sure how, but Kayn knew what was engraved on the stone. *She opted out of mentioning it. She'd freaked everyone out enough.*

Haley explained, "We are supposed to tell each other about our past as we climb up the stairs. It's nothing overtly ominous."

Kayn fought the urge to crouch down and run her fingers over the engraved poem. It was almost poetry. It read, 'To pass the test, you must have told stories new and old.' She smiled and stepped onto the first stair. They began to climb the staircase as a group.

Haley casually asked, "How's Greydon doing?"

Kayn gave her a funny look before she clicked. She cooed, "Greydon? Awe, that's such an adorable name." They scaled the first flights of white marble stairs.

Shaking his head, Zach chuckled, "I bet that reaction is exactly why he gets everyone to call him Grey now."

Astrid teased, "You'd know, Zach. Is your real name Zachary or Zachariah?"

Zach sighed as he trudged up the stairs and said, "Just Zach is fine."

Kayn scaled the seemingly endless staircase. *How many flights of spiral stairs had they gone up? There appeared to be no end in sight.* They were all panting and exhausted.

Astrid sat down first on the stairs and signalled Zach to sit beside her. The rest of them followed suit. Astrid chuckled, "Zach, you're a good-looking dude. I bet you walk past girls and they signal you in like a plane."

Haley gave him a once over, "You do have a sexy 'Legends of the Fall' thing going on."

Kayn took a good look at Zach. *He was hotter. His hair was longer and wavy. When did that happen?*

Astrid checked Zach out and ribbed, "We'd have to soak him down with water and get him to run across the room before I can be certain."

He teased, "Is that the polite way of saying I need a haircut?"

"Don't you dare!" Astrid sparred.

Kayn smiled and kept quiet, watching the cute, flirtatious exchange. *She was confused by the changes in Zach. How did she miss that?*

"So, tell us about the drama. When we left, Grey was with Arrianna, but not seriously. Frost was well... Frost. Jenna and Orin had just broken up. I bet that didn't last long. The Clan was searching for Freja. Did Frost end up with her? I always thought there was something more between those two. Lexy was a ticking time bomb and Lily was insanely beautiful."

They were all dumbfounded. *Uh, oh… That timeline was a touch off five years.*

Mel enquired, "What year was it when you guys came in here?"

Haley cautiously answered, "1994. I guess it's almost the year 2000. That is going to be so much fun. We could be out of here for New Year's 2000."

Zach looked at Melody and then back at the others. He clarified, "You guys came in here to do your Testing in 1994?"

Haley repeated, "Yes, in 1994."

"Do one of you guys want to tell them?" Zach passed the buck. "I'm a guy alone with four girls. I'm afraid you will all turn on me."

When nobody volunteered, Kayn decided it should be her. *Why not?* She met Astrid's eyes as she disclosed, "The year is 2014."

Astrid shook her head and laughed, assuming it was a joke. She sparred, "Funny, but there's no possible way we've been stuck in here for twenty years."

Kayn knew how to clarify the timeline, "I'm Freja's daughter and Mel is Orin's daughter. We're both over eighteen. Arrianna is with Markus." *Kayn had been told she looked just like Freja. If they had known Freja, then they would know her explanation of her lineage to be the truth. Melody looked nothing like Orin but looked just like Jenna. They'd assume Jenna was her mother.* Haley and Astrid were shocked. Neither one spoke for a minute or two. Everyone sat on the stairs in awkward silence.

Astrid stood up and began to walk up the stairs without speaking. The rest followed her obediently. Kayn tried to avoid eye contact. *What could you say? Sorry you lost twenty years of your life in an immortal version of hell? Sorry our Clan left you here for twenty years?* Kayn honestly had no idea how long they'd even been in this place. *Time was irrelevant while you were being repeatedly slaughtered.*

Haley was the first to speak, "I guess it's safe to assume the world is different. How much has it changed?"

Smiling at her, Zach said, "We have phones that we carry in our pockets. That's pretty cool. We take pictures with them instead of cameras. There are still cameras but you don't have to get film developed. The internet turned out to be a big deal. We have social media sites where we tell each other about our day and bitch about things. Tell jokes and stuff like that. We have flat screen TV We don't all drive spaceships. We still have cars. Things haven't changed so drastically that you'll appear different."

Astrid shrugged and commented, "I'm a little disappointed about the no personal spaceships thing. Is Star Wars still cool?"

Climbing the marble staircase, Kayn chuckled, "Star Wars will always be cool. You and I are obviously going to be friends."

Astrid grinned as she enquired, "So, who are you in love with? Do you have a boyfriend or a girlfriend?"

They didn't know about her past. Kayn replied, "It's complicated. That's the biggest cliché ever, but the truth."

Confused, Astrid paused on the staircase as she enquired, "Why is 'it's complicated' a cliché?"

Kayn started to laugh. *This was going to be strange to explain.* She answered, "On social media you can put 'it's complicated' as your relationship status. It's a joke for people who break up a lot."

Astrid knit her brow and toyed, "You're serious?"

Kayn chuckled. *It sounded crazy. They had been climbing this staircase for a long time. How long were they going to keep doing this?*

"I need to sit down," Zach said. "It's possible we may be climbing these stairs forever."

Kayn sat down next to him. She looked him over. *How had she not even noticed the changes in him?*

Staring at her with a giant smile, Zach teased, "Is there something wrong?" He reached over and tucked a stray ringlet from her crazy mane of hair behind her ear.

Was he flirting? Kayn shifted away from him and stood up. She started to climb the stairs without saying a word to the rest. *She felt so disoriented. How had she not even noticed that Zach's bloody hair had changed? He'd bulked up. He was way more muscular than when he'd come into this place. It occurred to her that she might have changed.* She paused and looked down at her body. She lifted the bottom of her thigh-high sarong. *She was damn toned. She'd always been.* She felt her butt and wondered, *Was it smaller?*

Astrid cleared her throat, asking, "What in the hell are you doing?"

Awkward. *She'd flashed a staircase full of people while wondering if her butt shrunk during her time in the Crypt.* Kayn mumbled, "I was just wondering… And then… Oh, it's nothing. I wasn't thinking."

Grinning, Zach provoked, "Explanations are never necessary where you're concerned, my friend. Our Kayn has embarrassing accidents all the time. Once you get to know her, you won't even flinch."

Kayn shook her head. As she scaled the stairs, she changed the topic, "Don't we have to share our stories?"

Astrid declared, "You're first, Kayn. I want to hear the reasons behind your 'it's complicated' status joke."

Mel attempted to hint that it was a sensitive subject. Kayn glanced back and responded, "It's okay. They've been stuck in here for the last twenty years. I can share my pathetic tale of teenage angst."

Haley stared up the middle of the staircase and exclaimed, "If we ever want to see the end of this staircase, you'd better get started."

Kayn grinned. She kept climbing as she said, "I'll start us off. Hello, my name is Kayn, my family was slaughtered including my identical twin. I was chased through the bushes and stabbed a dozen times. I was in a coma for seven months. I fell in love with my best friend, Kevin. Frost showed up to give me the, 'you are partially immortal' speech. In a twist of fate my best friend slash boyfriend Kevin had psychic lineage, so he was also claimed by Ankh. Chloe loved Frost. I had to absorb my twin's spirit because we share a soul. Tiberius turned out to be Kevin's Grandfather. Triad stole Kevin and erased his memory. They killed my brother Matt and Jenkins. In the year after that I was ignored by Frost while dealing with twin merge glitches. He caught onto me having Chloe's memories. I started to fall for him but wasn't over Kevin. I spent a week with an altered version of Kevin before Testing. We became close again. It was both incredible and heartbreaking. He was ordered by Triad to kill me during the Testing. Apparently, Ankh set it up to trigger my Enlightening. We made out and he dumped me for the thousandth time. He slit my throat. I killed him and a room full of Tri-Clan in a homicidal rage and blew up his psychotic girlfriend. After dying countless times in extremely messed-up albeit creative ways, Kevin kidnapped me and fed me to a pack of demons who gutted and ate me. I was done when you found me, Astrid." There was an awkward silence after Kayn's story.

Astrid paused on the stairs and declared, "That's awful. I'm sorry I asked. I didn't see that coming."

They all stopped on the stairs. Kayn was the first to sit down.

Sitting, Zach placed his arm around her and said, "You realise the next time I see Kevin, I'm going to kick his ass." He gave her a brotherly one-armed hug. He was furious, but she felt nothing, having quite successfully tucked her emotions away.

"We have to keep going," Mel prompted, helping her up. They continued their journey up the never-ending spiral staircase.

Astrid spoke next, "Well, my name is Astrid and I've been in here for decades. It blends together. I was here but not here. You know what I mean. I had an idyllic mortal life with my mother, father and five siblings. Everybody died, as is always the story. I don't remember what happened that day. I guess I became Enlightened during my Correction and disappeared into my happy place. I was in a sanitarium, in a catatonic state for years. When I was released, Frost was waiting outside, he told me to get into the car. I didn't have anywhere else to go so I got in. I was with Ankh for a few years before we came here for our Testing."

Kayn huffed, trudging up the stairs. *She was in amazing shape but this was physically impossible.* Blindly scaling stairs to nowhere with no end in sight, Kayn questioned, "I wonder how many gifted people with incredible imaginations are stuck in a sanitarium?"

Astrid laughed and answered, "It's a scary thing to think about, isn't it?"

"It definitely is," Kayn replied, beginning to feel dizzy. She looked at the others. *Who was going to go next? It had helped her on some level to talk about it. She'd needed to say the words aloud. The weight was removed from her chest.*

Noticing everyone staring, Zach chuckled, "Am I supposed to go next?"

"I know I want to hear about your life before all of this," Kayn responded.

He winked, teasing, "You may regret asking about it. It wasn't a good one." After a moment or two of silence, he began to speak. "I had a bunch of siblings, six to be exact. I was a dorky teenager. My father was an abusive drunk douche bag who beat the crap out of my mother. I wasn't biologically his, so he beat the crap out of me almost every day until we ran. We spent years on the run, but he always found us. The last time he beat me and buried me alive in a cornfield. My older brother must have tried to stop him because he was with me. He burned down our farm with the rest of my family, including my grandparents inside. Tiberius was there when I dug myself out of the dirt. I was with Triad for a year. I was taken by Ankh, after Triad left me behind and they became my family. I guess my brother wasn't dead, because he was with the Abaddon, we fought at the rodeo grounds. Testing has sucked in a morbid rather epic way. I became Enlightened but still have no idea what I can do. I met you guys and we're walking up an endless flight of stairs for no reason. Soon, I'm going to pass out and you ladies are going to have to carry me."

They took his last comment as a signal to stop and sit on the stairs. Kayn noticed Melody couldn't stop looking at Zach. *That's why he'd panicked after being buried alive in the sand. Hopefully, they wouldn't have to be buried alive again. She wasn't sure he could take it.* Kayn instantly regretted allowing it to cross her mind. *They had never gone into detail about their past.* They'd mentioned a shade of a carpet or a familiar pattern of wallpaper but only referred to their mortal lives. It felt like they were climbing the stairs towards salvation, ridding themselves of their battle scars through confession.

Haley began to speak, "I was hit by a car. I woke up in the hospital with no memory. I was a Jane Doe. I don't remember anything from my life before. I used to see posters in grocery stores and wonder why nobody was looking for me. I was staring at one of those posters when I met Lexy. She said she liked my hair and told me I was supposed to come with her. I named myself. I was with them for almost three years before my Testing. Ankh is the only family I remember. I'm grateful for Astrid's gift. It kept us alive in here for decades. I had no idea we'd been in here that long. I'm not sure how I feel about it. I met you guys and things started happening. It's hard to explain but we've been in a fantasy for so long. It's what's saved us but it's like living in limbo. I'm praying with everything inside of me that we can get out with you guys. I don't know what I'll do if we can't."

Kayn couldn't help but feel sad for Haley. She had no memories of her childhood and she'd spent most of her existence in a dream state. *Maybe her family was still alive somewhere? Haley was just a lost teenage girl with funky pink hair that wanted to find out who she was.*

Melody nudged Astrid and whispered, "While we're speaking of living in limbo, how long are we going to go up the stairs that quite obviously have no end?"

Astrid looked at Haley as she replied, "She's the one I'm following. Haley's always right."

Haley confirmed, "I know this is what we're supposed to be doing. I never get to know why but the reason is always clear later."

"That's good enough for me," Zach declared. "I have my steam back. We should keep moving." He held his hand out to Haley and helped her up. They continued to scale the endless staircase.

As they climbed, Mel volunteered, "I had two little brothers, a mom and dad. I was crazy in love with the most incredible guy. One night my mom came to pick me up from his house. My little brothers were in the car. We went for ice cream. My mom told me she was pregnant while we were there. On the way home, she passed out behind the wheel. I took off my seatbelt off to reach the brakes. I was thrown out the window and down an embankment, but I could still see the car. My baby brother was still alive. He was crying and begging me to help him. His tiny hand was pressed against the window but I couldn't move. I tried so hard but couldn't. A big rig hit the car as it came around the corner. I heard grinding metal and an explosion. I woke up a few days later in the grass by the side of the road, completely healed. They thought I was in the car with the others. I climbed up the hill and wandered down the road until I came across a memorial for my family. My dad found me and I got to go home again. I healed my ex-boyfriend and my horse. My current boyfriend saw me heal the horse. My Correction happened but I'd already been Enlightened. They killed everyone. I was filled with so much rage that I blew up my house. I walked out of the fire untouched by the flames and Lily was waiting there. It was that whole, 'get in the car if you want to live' thing. My first stint with Ankh was short-lived. Trinity ran us off the road, chased us down and stole me from Ankh. I was with Trinity until a couple days before my eighteenth birthday. I was with them long enough to fall in love with Thorne and then I was stolen back by Ankh."

Impressed, Haley clarified, "Superhero voice Thorne? Otherwise known as the hot leader of Trinity?"

With an enormous grin, Mel replied, "That'd be the one."

They'd been walking upstairs for an illogical amount of time when Haley abruptly stopped and directed, "Stop right here." She placed her hands on the stone wall. A hologram appeared about an inch off the surface of the stone in English. It was the word 'Confess.' Haley announced, "I think we can get out through this wall. We must have to confess something."

"Isn't that what we all just did?" Kayn asked.

Haley grinned and replied, "It wasn't good enough. A piece of the puzzle must be missing. One by one, let's walk up, place our hands against the wall and confess everything you can think of. No matter how big or small."

Mel shrugged as she volunteered to go first by walking up, placing her hands on the wall and saying, "I was a cheerleader. I teased a few people in school. I broke my first love's heart when I fell for someone else. He never saw it coming. I tried to atone for that by healing him when he got hurt during a game. I tried to heal my horse. I blew up the farm." The wall didn't budge. The word 'Confess' still hovered there.

Haley asserted, "You have to confess something bigger. Don't worry about what we think. We all have to do this."

Melody continued to confess, "I did a lot of things with Trinity I wasn't proud of. I tried to kill myself more times than I can count after my father and boyfriend died. I know it was wrong. I just felt so guilty for being the only one who survived. I had this amazing friendship with Thorne. He was always so wonderful. He was so patient with me. He didn't judge me even though I must have been an enormous pain in his ass. I couldn't see past my own pain. The last night I was with Trinity, I was going to jump off this cliff. I knew I wouldn't die but I felt like I deserved to be in pain. He stopped me and we ended up sleeping together. I loved him but knew I wasn't supposed to be with Trinity. I broke his heart when I went with Ankh. He may have thought I was stolen, but I willingly went with Ankh. I did it on purpose. When I attached Kayn and Kevin's souls so they could say goodbye, I understood I was making a conscious choice to change Clans. I knew I would never have the energy to get back out myself." The wall still didn't move. The word 'Confess' still hovered there.

Haley winked and urged, "There must be more?"

Mel looked into Haley's eyes as she admitted, "In the In-between, I was on a self-destructive kick. I was with Grey before I knew he was in my Clan." The wall didn't budge. Mel grimaced. She looked directly at Kayn and Zach, confessing, "We hooked up after that and kept it a secret."

The wall became transparent. Melody was allowed to pass through, but it solidified before anyone else could. Zach and Haley were both granted passage as they confessed their sins to the wall.

Astrid looked at Kayn, pleading, "I need to go last. I promise I won't ever repeat anything you're forced to say, but I have to confess alone."

Suspecting there were things Astrid wasn't ready to put out there, Kayn placed her hand on the wall. The word 'Confess' hovered above it. She started with, "I used to feel guilty for being the twin who survived. It felt like I had caused the death of everyone I loved. I felt guilty for allowing people to die, even if it was for the greater good. I had real feelings for two people at the same time. I loved Kevin. He was my best friend. When I'm with him there's an indefinable sense of coming home. I wanted everything in that week to be real. He killed me. I didn't think he'd be able to do it. He unleashed a terrifying version of me." The wall didn't allow her to pass. Kayn knew she would be forced to say the words she'd been afraid to say. *The things she'd felt but was afraid to admit.* She looked at Astrid and silently hoped she could trust her as she continued, "There was a rush when I killed those two Clans to get to Kevin. I don't know how I did it but it felt amazing. Kevin killed me first but there was this burst of agony when I killed him and then it was like somebody turned off a switch inside of me. I enjoyed killing Stephanie. There was no confusion there. Just power, I want to experience again." She paused before admitting to the secret in the back of her mind, "My crescent birthmark is on the right side behind my ear. My twin's birthmark was on the left. I know what that means. Chloe's a part of me now. Her darkness is too. Before Kevin killed me, I didn't feel it, but now, I know what I am. I'm not a lion anymore. I'm a Dragon." The wall opened. *She'd said the words aloud. She'd known it for a while. She was becoming a Dragon.* Kayn glanced back at Astrid as she walked through into the other room. There was no judgement in her eyes, only understanding.

Chapter 49

The Escape Clause

In the room Kayn entered, the others were waiting patiently for them to confess their way through. Five large black gargoyles paced back and forth on the far side of the room. Kayn looked up at the ceiling, perhaps for divine intervention. A tornado dropped from the ceiling into the centre of the room.

Kayn stared at it in awe as she said, "What is that?"

"That's our way out of here," Haley replied. "We all have to jump in together. It seems to only come down one time for each of us. That means as soon as Astrid comes through that wall and looks at the ceiling, it will come down. We're all going to hold hands and jump into that tornado. There isn't going to be a second to think."

Kayn watched it disappear into the stone above her. *Would Astrid jump into an indoor tornado blindly because Haley told her to? Now, that was the million-dollar question?* Kayn glanced back at the wall. *It had been a while. Astrid must have a lot to confess.* They laced their fingers together, leaving Haley as the last link on the chain.

As Astrid appeared through the wall, Haley held out her hand and declared, "Just take my hand and jump." Astrid took it without question as her funnel descended from the ceiling. They all leapt into it. It sucked them up, and they spun in the wrath of nature's harshest brutality. Against insurmountable odds, they fought to hold onto each other's hands. There would be no option of freedom from these walls if they were minus even one. Kayn knew she had less than a minute of spinning motion left in her before she either passed out or painted the funnel with vomit. Her skin rippled with her mouth wide open from the sheer force of the wind as if in a permanent scream. *She was going to be squished against the walls or the incoming end of the funnel's cement passageway.* Her mind pleaded, *open! Please! You must open!* As they flew towards impact, it did, and she shot into the sky. A burst of fresh air came as a welcome explosion to her senses.

It was difficult to wrap her mind around the moment of glorious freedom, impossible to think about anything except her stomach-churning upwards motion into the clouds. There was a briefest pause as she stopped moving up and began her rapid descent towards the grey stone surface of the enormous and from this vantage point, extremely intimidating Crypt. *Stop yourself!* She continued falling. *Stop yourself!* Her mind screamed. She clicked into the reality of the red splat she was about to create on the Crypt's surface. She managed to stop, hovering a foot from impact. Everyone stopped themselves except for Zach. They scrambled to their feet. Zach's head lay there with eyes gazing forward into nothing. *Where was the rest of him?*

Astrid approached, holding Zach's dripping severed arm. She explained, "The Crypt must have closed on him."

They stood there frozen. *What in the hell were they supposed to do now?* Astrid was about to panic. *They'd finally made it out. The two lost Ankh's escape plan had been twenty years in the making.* Kayn's mind felt numb. *They would have to go back in and find the rest of him. They'd never have the strength to get back out again. They could spend years searching for the rest of his body. There was no option. They wouldn't leave him behind. They couldn't.* Kayn wasn't sure she had it in her to last another day. She sunk down beside Zach's severed head and stared into his wide, glassy eyes. Kayn looked up at Haley and said, "Well, what in the hell do we do now?" Haley squatted beside her and stroked Zach's hair. *They were staring impending doom in the face and she was grinning at the sight of Haley petting Zach's severed head.*

Astrid noticed her grinning and exclaimed, "You really are a little sick in the head, aren't you Kayn? You were probably certifiable far before any of this went down, weren't you?"

Kayn couldn't wipe the grin off her face. *It was even more funny now that somebody who was certifiably insane had called her on her lack of sanity. Could nobody else see Haley stroking the hair of a severed head? How was this not hilarious?*

"Her messed-up sense of humour is a coping mechanism," Melody explained. "She always tries to make the situation funny. It helps everyone else. I know it helps me."

Kayn comically urged, "Oh, come on. Just think about it for a minute. We have to go back in there, because we only have a few pieces of Zach and Haley is stroking his severed head. In what world is this not an absolutely hilarious situation?"

Haley looked like a lightbulb just turned on between her ears. She announced, "We are still out of the tomb. We should be sucked back in already. It must still be possible. We'll just bring the parts of him with us. We need to get to the Amber room. We have his head. We have the hand and it's even the one with the Ankh symbol on it. This feels possible. It must be."

Kayn couldn't stop laughing. *It was quite possible the, 'let's just bring his body parts with us' motivational speech finished her sanity off.* The amber-tinted bubble could be seen vaguely in the distance. Haley gazed down at Zach's severed head and grabbed his brain matter-oozing mass of hair and goo. Astrid held his severed arm and they sprinted towards the Amber chamber in the horizon. It was far enough away for them to grasp that if they'd continued their journey in the interior with distractions, it would have taken weeks to find it. They didn't know if this insane idea would work with only pieces of their third member and two extra Ankh they hadn't come into the Testing with. This competition was rigged for failure. Had they not run into the others, their minds wouldn't have been capable of living through many more hours, let alone days. The four girls and hunks of Zach raced across the top of the Crypt. Nothing was as it appeared. They ran and ran without feeling like they were getting much closer to the Amber room. It stood out in the distance, its rounded glossy tower beckoning them from afar. They finally reached its smooth amber surface with their teammate in hand. *Quite literally.* Breathless and absolutely soaked in perspiration, the four girls collapsed on top of it. *How were they going to get inside?* They were momentarily blinded by an intense white light. The four girls opened their eyes to find themselves standing in the centre of an actual Colosseum. The kind Zach had imagined the Testing would be held in. All four were still huffing and puffing, unable to catch their breath. *She was going to snap if a two-headed monster appeared. She was going to lose her shit!*

Her twisted sense of humour could only take her so far. Kayn sighed, "Oh, shit. Please… No more." *She felt like she'd forgotten something crucial. What was it? Her brain was a puddle of mushy goo.* Kayn spun her head around and stammered, "Where's Zach! Where is he? We have to go back!"

The crowd roared as Zach appeared out of thin air. He was standing there in one piece right beside her. Kayn had to stop herself from jumping into her friend's arms. *They were whole again. The three of them had made it out of the Testing. Whoops, there were five now. It crossed her mind that they might still get in trouble for smuggling out the other two. At this point, she was so far past caring it was ridiculous.* She received her second wind. *Bring it on.*

A booming voice echoed through the Colosseum, "Walk forward, Clan Ankh."

Kayn looked around. *It's a circle. Which way is forward?* At least twenty pink stones appeared in the dirt about ten feet from her. The group walked towards the stones and stood before them.

The gravelly male voice chuckled, "What clever young Second-Tier you are climbing out through the top like that with two from a prior Testing. This has never happened before… Impressive."

The crowd cheered. *They looked like normal people of various shapes and sizes dressed in togas.* Kayn glanced behind her at the Crypt that hovered in the sky, spanning the horizon. *We made it out.* Kayn smiled and looked at the others. *They were going to let them all go home.*

The voice commanded, "Choose your stone."

Kayn instinctively gravitated to one. She knelt to pick it up and felt her life force bind to the stone. The symbol of Ankh appeared on the rose quartz in her palm like it was carved by magic. She glanced at her equally amazed Clan.

The voice spoke again, "You are now bound to your Clan. You are no longer contained beneath mortal skin. You will be now and forever more Ankh."

An incredibly tall woman with her face hidden by a veil strolled through an archway into the centre of the Colosseum. She stopped, raised both hands into the air and let out a high-pitched sound. They were blinded by light as the crowd cheered again.

Cowering from the overwhelming glare, Kayn opened her eyes to find herself standing in the soft, silken sand of the In-between. No diamonds were present this time, only the forms of their Clan walking towards them in the distance against the backdrop of a breathtaking sunset. It was beautiful to witness the expressions on everyone's faces as they realised five Ankh had come home. Kayn stood back and watched as they laughed and embraced. Zach noticed her absence. He grabbed her hand and towed her over to the rest of her Clan. Kayn went with Zach even though she felt like being by herself for a little while longer.

Jenna hugged them at the same time. She whispered, "Dragons need a Handler. Zach, you are now Kayn's Handler." Jenna walked away and embraced Haley without an explanation.

Kayn released a burst of laughter at Zach and said, "I don't think so."

Zach hollered at Jenna, "She's not going to listen to me! This is a bad idea!" He shook his head and grimaced at Kayn. "I know you're not going to listen to me."

Grinning, Kayn shook her head as she responded, "Probably not." Zach took off to try to get Jenna to listen to reason. Watching him chasing their Oracle around, she chuckled. *He can't even handle himself! What was Jenna thinking? If the aim of that conversation had been to make her laugh and cheer her up, it worked.* She met Frost's stare. He smiled and winked at her as Astrid hugged him.

Lexy came over to Kayn, embraced her and said, "I'm glad you made it."

They strolled away together towards the flaming orange backdrop of the sunset. *She had a new position in the Clan. There would be expectations. It made her nervous. Dragons probably weren't supposed to feel nervous. She was supposed to be a hurricane, a plague, an apocalypse. She was a method of destruction. It was an intimidating job description.*

Lexy whispered as they walked away, "From one Dragon to another, you don't have to listen to anyone. They won't expect you to."

Kayn had come to the end of this part of her journey. She'd had to lose one version of herself to find another. Tiberius had been wrong. She wasn't a lion or a lamb. She was destined to become a Dragon. Kayn never anticipated this plot twist in the story of her life.

Two Dragons walked off into the flaming sunset until they disappeared together in the magical land of the In-between.

The Beginning

Biography

Kim Cormack is the author of the dark fantasy series, "The Children of Ankh." She worked for over 16 years as an Early Childhood educator in preschool, daycare and as an aid. She has M.S and has lived most of her life on Vancouver Island in beautiful British Columbia, Canada. She currently lives in the gorgeous little town of Port Alberni. She's a single mom with two awesome kids. If you see her back away slowly and toss packages of hot sauce at her until you escape.

Happy Reading XO
Kim Cormack

Warning

The information contained within this book is not intended for mortals. Reading this may inadvertently trigger your Correction. If you show great bravery during your demise, you may be given a second chance at life by one of the Guardians of the In-between. For your soul's protection, you must join one of three Clans of immortals on Earth. *You are totally still reading this, aren't you? You've got this.* **Welcome to the Children Of Ankh Series Universe.**

Please take a moment to share your love via review and subscribe to the universe website. Read Let There Be Dragons Next!

Fresh out of Science Fiction majesty of the Immortal Testing, our Paranormal Fantasy antiheroes are deeply traumatized after being killed thousands of times in increasingly ghoulish ways, to prove themselves capable of being Immortal. Kayn has become a Dragon, capable of shutting her emotions off, and Zach has been made her Handler. *What could go wrong?*

www.ingramcontent.com/pod-product-compliance
Lightning Source LLC
LaVergne TN
LVHW020648110826
845149LV00012B/1945

* 9 7 8 0 9 9 5 2 3 0 5 4 5 *